HISTORY

OF THE

GREAT CIVIL WAR

VOL. II

HISTORY

OF THE

GREAT CIVIL WAR

1642–1649

BY

SAMUEL R. GARDINER, D.C.L., LL.D.

LATE FELLOW OF MERTON COLLEGE OXFORD

ETC.

IN FOUR VOLUMES

VOLUME II.—1644–1645

THE

WINDRUSH

PRESS

LONDON

History of the Great Civil War
was first published by
Longmans, Green and Co.

This edition first published by
The Windrush Press
50 Edithna Street
London SW9 9JP
in 1987

ISBN 0 900075 15 5 (cased)
ISBN 0 900075 05 8 (paperback)

British Library Cataloguing in Publication Data

Gardiner, Samuel Rawson
History of the Great Civil War.
Vol. 2: 1644–1645
1. Great Britain—History—Charles I,
1625–1649   2. Great Britain—History
—Commonwealth and protectorate, 1649–
1660
I. Title
942.06'2   DA405

ISBN 0 900075 15 5
ISBN 0 900075 05 8 Pbk

Printed and bound in Great Britain by
Biddles Ltd, Guildford and King's Lynn

CONTENTS

OF

THE SECOND VOLUME.

———◆◆◆———

CHAPTER XIX.

THE SURRENDER AT LOSTWITHIEL.

CHAPTER XX.

THE ARMY OF THE EASTERN ASSOCIATION.

CHAPTER XXI.

THE SECOND BATTLE OF NEWBURY, AND THE RELIEF OF DONNINGTON CASTLE.

CHAPTER XXII.

PRYNNE, MILTON, AND CROMWELL.

CHAPTER XXIII.

THE FIRST SELF-DENYING ORDINANCE.

CHAPTER XXIV.

THE EXECUTION OF ARCHBISHOP LAUD.

CHAPTER XXV.

THE NEW MODEL ORDINANCE AND THE TREATY OF UXBRIDGE.

CHAPTER XXVI.

TIPPERMUIR, ABERDEEN, AND INVERLOCHY.

CHAPTER XXVII.

THE PROJECTS OF THE EARL OF GLAMORGAN.

CHAPTER XXVIII.

THE SECOND SELF-DENYING ORDINANCE, AND THE

NEW MODEL ARMY.

CHAPTER XXIX.

THE NEW MODEL ARMY IN THE FIELD.

CHAPTER XXX.

DUNDEE, AULDEARN, AND LEICESTER.

CHAPTER XXXI.

NASEBY.

CHAPTER XXXII.

LANGPORT AND BRIDGWATER

CHAPTER XXXIII.

ALFORD AND KILSYTH.

CHAPTER XXXIV.

SHERBORNE, HEREFORD, AND BRISTOL.

CHAPTER XXXV.

CURRENTS OF OPINION.

CHAPTER XXXVI.

ROWTON HEATH AND PHILIPHAUGH.

CHAPTER XXXVII.

BASING HOUSE AND SHERBURN.

NOTES.

MAPS.

THE GREAT CIVIL WAR.

CHAPTER XIX.

THE SURRENDER AT LOSTWITHIEL.

IN the defeated army personal jealousies had led to a grave military disaster. In the victorious army grave political differences led to personal jealousies. For the moment, indeed,

1644. July. Rupert's opinion of Cromwell. Cromwell's splendid services bore down all opposition. Rupert, with soldierlike instinct, gave to him the name of 'Ironside,' by which his Puritan followers soon learned to distinguish him.[1] When the army of

Cromwell and David Leslie. the Eastern Association first joined the Scots, Cromwell had urged that David Leslie should take the command of the united cavalry. Leslie had turned a deaf ear to the proposal, and had preferred to serve under Cromwell.[2] Nothing had since occurred to change the gallant Scotsman's appreciation of him who was from this time to be his rival. "Europe," he generously said of the horse and foot of Manchester's army, "hath no better soldiers."[3]

With less generosity Cromwell threw a veil over the hearty

Cromwell's letter to Valentine Walton. co-operation of Leslie. "Truly," he wrote to his brother-in-law, Valentine Walton, whose son had been killed early in the fight, "England and the Church of God hath had a great favour from the Lord in this great

---

[1] "Monday we had intelligence that Lieut.-General Cromwell, *alias* Ironside, for that title was given him by Prince Rupert after his defeat near York," &c. *Merc. Civ.* Sept. 16–26. E. 10, 11.

[2] *The Parl. Scout.* E. 50, 16. [3] Watson's *Relation.* E. 2, 14.

victory given unto us, such as the like never was since this war began. It had all the evidences of an absolute victory obtained by the Lord's blessing upon the godly party principally. We never charged but we routed the enemy. The left wing, which I commanded, being our own horse, saving a few Scots in our rear,[1] beat all the Prince's horse. God made them as stubble to our swords. We charged their regiments of foot with our horse, and routed all we charged. . . . Give glory—all the glory—to God." Then, turning to the subject which would be next to the father's heart, after glancing at his 'own trials this way,' in the loss of that son who had died in the spring at Newport Pagnell, Cromwell proceeded to tell of young Walton's death. " He was a gallant young man, exceedingly gracious. God give you His comfort. Before his death he was so full of comfort that to Frank Russell and myself he could not express it. 'It was so great above his pain.' This he said to us. Indeed it was admirable. A little after he said, ' One thing lay upon his spirit.' I asked him what it was. He told me it was ' That God had not suffered him to be any more the executioner of His enemies.' "[2]

The thought that the godly were the executioners of God's vengeance upon His enemies was ever uppermost in the mind of Cromwell. It led him at one time, in opposition to Crawford, to fling open the doors of promotion to all who, with a single mind, would devote themselves to the task. It led him at another time to exclude from all charitable construction the deeds of those who aimed at making peace with the enemy instead of executing vengeance upon him. Since Vane's controversy with the three Generals we may well believe that Cromwell had lost all patience with the Scots and with those who sympathised with the Scots in refusing to strike directly at the King. It was no part of Cromwell's character to make allowances for men who were, as he understood the matter, not merely his enemies, but the enemies

Cromwell in opposition to the Scots.

---

[1] Leslie had three regiments, that is to say, about twenty-two troops out of the seventy troops of which the whole cavalry under Cromwell was composed.

[2] Cromwell to Walton, July 5,   *Carlyle*, Letter xxi.

of God. In his mind the seeds of tolerance and intolerance were planted very closely together.

Cromwell's ill-will towards the Scots could not but embrace his own General, the Earl of Manchester. In the Scots the

Cromwell and Manchester.

desire to make peace was combined with a desire to enforce the Presbyterian discipline in the teeth of the men whom Cromwell regarded as the most zealous executioners of the enemies of God. Hitherto Manchester had not taken much interest in the dispute between Presbyterians and Independents, and he had listened to Cromwell as to a trusted favourite. His affable and irresolute nature had been startled by Vane's proposals. To strike at the King, he

July 18. The three Generals declare for Presbyterianism,

thought, was to strike at the nobility. On the 18th, two days after the surrender of York, he joined Leven and Fairfax in addressing a letter to the Committee of Both Kingdoms, in which the three Generals, after declaring their resolution to decline no danger in defence of their solemn covenant, expressed a hope that the Houses would take 'the building of the House of God and

and for peace, if possible.

settlement of church-government into their chiefest thoughts.' They added a recommendation that attention should be given to the making of peace, though they acknowledged that it was no time to lessen their efforts to carry on the war, 'that being the best way to procure peace.'[1]

To establish a Presbyterian government and to make peace with the King was the incoherent advice of the three Generals

Incoherence of their proposals.

commanding the one victorious army in England. If all the commanders of that army had been united in opinion, they could hardly have failed to give the law to the nation, at least till their scheme had time to break down from its own inherent rottenness. Notoriously, however, the army was not unanimous. The letter of the three Generals was practically a declaration of war against Lieutenant-General Cromwell.

After this it was perhaps as well that Cromwell and the Scottish army should not remain together. Nor did the work

[1] Leven, Manchester, and Fairfax to the Com. of B. K., July 18. *Com. Letter Book.*

in the North any longer call for a combination of the three armies. Clavering, who had been joined by some of the fugi-

Royalist
movements. tives from Marston Moor, was at the head of a Royalist force of about 3,000 men in Cumberland and Westmoreland, and Rupert with about 5,000, most of them cavalry, had made his way into Lancashire. Rupert, however, was in need of ammunition, and was not likely to take the field soon unless supplies reached him from Ireland. Accord-

July 30.
The three
Genera s
agree to
separate. ingly, when, on July 30, the three Parliamentary Generals met at Ferrybridge to discuss their plans for the future, they resolved to act apart. Leven, with the Scots, was to take in hand the siege of New-

castle. The Fairfaxes, with the Yorkshire levies, were to devote themselves to the reduction of Scarborough, of Pontefract and Helmsley, and of the other fortified posts of less importance which held out for the King in their own county. Manchester and Cromwell were to return to Lincolnshire, to devote themselves to the service of the Eastern Association. As yet there was little ground for supposing that their services would be required in the South to repair the consequences of a disaster beside which the check inflicted on Waller would appear to be of little moment.

So far from decisive had the affair at Cropredy Bridge appeared to Charles himself, that on July 1 he thought it best,

July 1.
Charles's
movements
after Cro-
predy
Bridge. on hearing that Waller was about to effect a junction with Browne, to slip back to his old quarters at Evesham. Yet the very speed with which Charles was able to carry out his purpose told Waller where the superiority of the Royalists really lay. Charles's army, in

Composition
of the two
armies. fact, was more easily handled than that of the Parliamentary commander, partly because it was better horsed, but still more because the infantry regiments

were composed of men who had, from poverty or other causes, taken service with the intention of devoting themselves to a soldier's life, whilst the bulk of Waller's force consisted of trained bands or local levies, sent out for the most part without any great heart in the matter. "I am of opinion," wrote Waller, as the difficulties of his position rose before him, "before this business be done we shall be the longest-winded army in England. I hope we shall never be weary of well-doing, let the way be never so long and rugged, God sustaining us, in whom alone is our trust." [1]

Waller was soon to learn that he had to command men who were weary of well-doing. London trained bands, as he

The City Brigade.

ought to have known by this time, were not to be relied on for permanent service. "In these two days' march," he had already been compelled to write, "I was extreme plagued with the mutinies of the City Brigade, who are grown to that height of disorder that I have no hope to retain them, being come to their old song of 'Home ! Home !'" Browne's little army was in the same confusion. The men from Essex were already talking of leaving him. The Hertfordshire soldiers murmured at 'a night or two's ill quartering.'

Waller recommends a military change.

"My Lords," concluded Waller, "I write these particulars to let you know that an army compounded of these men will never go through with your service, and till you have an army merely your own, that you may command, it is in a manner impossible to do anything of importance." [2]

It was from Waller, not from Cromwell, that this first suggestion of the New Model came. Waller knew that citizen

First suggestion of the New Model.

soldiers, whose hearts were in their shops or their cornfields, could not make an efficient army ; but he knew, too, that the root of the mischief lay deeper, in the inefficiency of local committees, always certain to slacken in their efforts as soon as danger was removed from their own borders. A standing army would bring with it many dangers, but the King was already less dependent on local organisations than the Parliament was, and unless Parliament could secure its mastery over the local associations, it must be content to succumb in the struggle which it had invited.

Yet though Waller had suggested a true remedy for the disease, he had not suggested a complete one. The improvement of a faulty organisation counts for much, but it does not

[1] Waller to the Com. of B. K., July 3. *Com. Letter Book.*
[2] *Ibid.*, July 2. *Com. Letter Book.*

count for everything. From the beginning Parliament had mainly relied on Puritan enthusiasm, and the coolness of the *Decline of* Essex regiment was a sure token that, even in the *enthusiasm.* most Puritan counties, Puritan enthusiasm was limited in quantity. It looked as if, in their extreme need of soldiers, the Parliamentary leaders had been driven to seek support in strata of society in which little zeal for religion was to be found.

Whatever might be the cause of the mischief, Waller was at his wits' end. His junction with Browne, so far from strength-*July 8.* ening his army, had gone far to ruin it. "My Lon-*Waller's* don regiments," he wrote on July 8, "immediately *further* *complaints.* looked on his forces as sent to relieve them, and, without expectation of further orders, are most of them gone away. Yesterday no less than 400 out of one regiment quitted their colours. On the other side, Major-General Browne's men, being most of them trained-band men of Essex and Hertfordshire, are so mutinous and uncommandable that there is no hope of their stay. They are likewise upon their march home again. Yesterday they were like to have killed their Major-General, and they have hurt him in the face. Such men are only fit for a gallows here and a hell hereafter. . . . I am confident that above 2,000 Londoners ran away from their colours."[1]

The Houses could not fail to be impressed by Waller's counsel when it was accompanied by such news as this. On *July 12.* July 12 an ordinance was passed, directing the for-*A new army* mation of a new force of 10,000 foot and 3,050 horse, *voted.* to be levied in the eastern and southern counties for permanent service, in place of the trained bands which had proved so untrustworthy. This auxiliary army was to be ready to march on July 20.[2]

It was evidently impossible that within the short space of eight days the expectations of Parliament could be fulfilled. In the meanwhile it was only to the absence of the King that Waller owed his safety. On the 12th, indeed, Browne

[1] Waller to the Com. of B. K., July 8. *Com. Letter Book.*
[2] *L.J.* vi. 629.

succeeded in reducing Greenland House, near Henley, where a Royalist garrison had for some time been of the greatest

July 12. Capture of Greenland House.

annoyance to the country round. Its capture was, however, likely to be the limit of his success. On the following day he was compelled to dismiss the

July 13. Browne at Reading.

Essex men, and was obliged to content himself with occupying Reading with his remaining force, where he laboured at the restoration of the fortifications which had been destroyed by the Royalists when they abandoned the

July 20. Waller at Abingdon.

place. On the 20th Waller threw himself into Abingdon, having with him a bare 2,500 horse and 1,500 foot. Most of them were, moreover, only anxious to leave him, and the Londoners especially refused to stir 'one foot further, except it be home.' [1]

The march of Essex towards the West, always hazardous, had thus, by the collapse of Waller's army, degenerated into a

July 7. Charles resolves to pursue Essex.

foolhardy adventure. On the 7th a council of war, assembled at Evesham, recommended Charles to seize the opportunity of crushing Essex before help could reach him. It was characteristic of Charles that he finally decided upon accepting the advice, not because it was strategically the best, but because it would bring him into the neighbourhood of the Queen. [2]

At that moment Henrietta Maria was still at Exeter. On June 16 she had given birth to her youngest child, the Princess

June 16. Birth of the Princess Henrietta.

Henrietta, the future negotiator of the treaty of Dover. Suffering before, the Queen suffered still more after her delivery, and she pleaded with Essex for a safe-conduct, which would allow her to benefit by the

Essex refuses a safe-conduct to the Queen.

healing waters of Bath. To Essex Henrietta Maria was merely a mischievous politician, endowed with unusual capacity of doing harm, and he bluntly answered that she should have no safe-conduct from him. If she would go to London he would himself conduct her there, where the best medical advice was to be had. As her impeachment had

[1] Com. of B. K. to Essex, July 16. Waller to the Com. of B. K., July 20. *Com. Letter Book.*

[2] Walker's *Hist. Discourses*, 37.

been voted, and as there were prisons in London as well as physicians, she naturally declined the offer.

Sick and wretched as she was, Henrietta Maria preferred to trust herself to rough roads and the perils of the sea rather than to the mercy of the Puritans. Making her way, in pain

July 14.
The Queen
sails for
France,

and weakness, to Falmouth, she embarked on July 14 for France. A Parliamentary commander pursued her, and fired at the vessel in which she was.

July 16.
and lands at
Brest.

Escaping unharmed, she landed at Brest on July 16. She at once betook herself to the baths of Bourbon, to seek that help from the mineral waters of France which had been denied her in England.[1]

Two days before the Queen left England Charles set out from Evesham. As he passed through Somerset he made an

July 12.
Charles
pursues
Essex.

ineffectual attempt to enlist the population in his favour. The country people crowded to gaze at the unwonted spectacle, but not a man, with the exception of a few who had previously offered their services, could

Want of
popular en-
thusiasm.

be persuaded to join the army. Popular enthusiasm could no more be aroused by Charles in the West than it had been aroused by Waller in the East. A settled indifference to both parties was manifesting itself in every quarter.[2]

On July 26 Charles reached Exeter. On the 27th he rode out to Crediton to review the army of Prince Maurice, a rein-

July 26.
Charles at
Exeter.

forcement 4,600 strong.[3] Essex was not ignorant of the danger with which he was threatened. On

Essex at
Tavistock.

the 26th, the day on which Charles entered Exeter, the Parliamentary General took up his quarters at Tavistock. Thence he despatched Stapleton to represent the condition of his troops to the Houses. Hitherto,

Aug. 2.
Stapleton's
report.

said Stapleton, when he reached Westminster, the march of the Lord General had been a triumphal progress. Plymouth was no longer threatened.[4] Yet a great

---

[1] *Rushw.* v. 684. *Letters of Henrietta Maria,* 250.

[2] Walker's *Hist. Discourses,* 45.   [3] *Ib.* 42, 48.

[4] Whitacre's Diary. *Add. MSS.* 31,116, fol. 135.

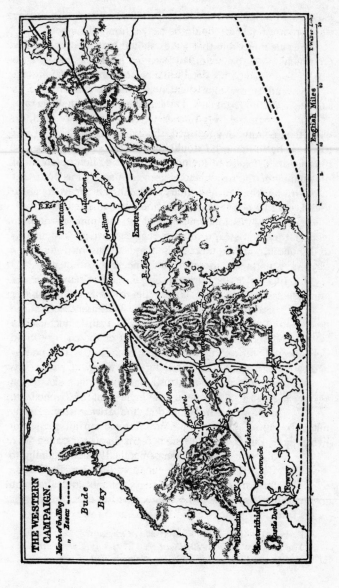

danger had now arisen in his rear, and unless men and money were promptly sent he would be cut off from all support.

It seems incredible that Essex should have chosen the day on which he despatched Stapleton with such a message to announce his determination to throw himself into an adventure more hazardous than any that he had as yet undertaken. He had been advised, he wrote, 'to march yet further westward into Cornwall, to clear that county and to settle the same in peace.'[1] It was true that by so doing he would forsake the neighbourhood of the friendly defences of Plymouth, where he might safely await the coming of the necessary reinforcements. It was true that in Cornwall the Parliamentary cause had scarcely a single friend. Lord Robartes, however, and some of Lord Robartes's officers had estates in Cornwall, and were naturally anxious to recover them. Essex, firm as a rock against all temptations to dishonour, was like wax in the hands of his own comrades when they attempted merely to influence his movements.

July 26.
Essex re-
solves to
march into
Cornwall.

On July 27 Essex, driving Sir Richard Grenvile before him, crossed the Tamar. When he reached Bodmin bitter disappointment awaited him. The assurances of the 'Western men' that he 'should want no victuals' in Cornwall, and that a great part of the country stood well affected, proved to be an utter delusion. The county had almost unanimously risen for the King. Charles was already in pursuit, and had entered Liskeard on August 2. Orders had been sent to Grenvile to occupy Grampound, that the Parliamentary army might be cut off between the two forces from all chance of living upon the country. Essex, fearing to be assailed at a distance from the sea, marched from Bodmin to Lostwithiel, where he called lustily upon Parliament for provisions for his hungry soldiers, and above all insisted that Waller should be despatched to effect a diversion in his favour by attacking the King's army in the rear.[2]

July 27.
Essex enters
Cornwall.

Aug. 2.
The King at
Liskeard.

Aug. 3.
Essex at
Lostwithiel.

---

[1] Essex to the Com. of B. K., July 26. *Com. Letter Book.*

[2] *The Kingdom's Weekly Intelligencer.* E. 4, 20. Essex to the Com. of B. K., Aug. 4. *Com. Letter Book.* Walker's *Hist. Discourses,* 51.

How little Waller was in a position to succour Essex was well known in the Royalist army. Charles thought the occa-

Aug. 6.
Charles's
overtures to
Essex.

sion fitting to make an overture to Essex, inviting him to join him in the. enforcement of a reasonable peace, in order to prevent the conquest of the kingdom by the Scots. As usual, Charles, anxious as he was for peace, had failed to understand the character of the man with whom he was dealing. Essex returned the reply which he had always given, that without the authority of Parliament he would enter upon no negotiations.[1]

The overture thus made was probably not entirely owing to Charles's ignorant goodwill. In his own camp there were loud

Desire for
peace in
Charles's
army.

murmurs at the interminable war. The gentlemen who served him so well in the field were all but ruined by their exertions, and were as anxious as the trained bands of Essex and Hertfordshire to be back amongst their cornfields and their woods. To Rupert and the military chieftains they were bitterly hostile.

Of this ill-will Wilmot, the Lieutenant-General of the horse, gay and dissolute as he was, had made himself the spokesman.

Wilmot's
intrigues.

He, too, unless the King was grievously misinformed, had been talking, probably in his cups, of deposing Charles and of setting up in his stead the Prince of Wales, as having had no share in the divisions of his country. When Charles's message was sent to Essex, Wilmot accompanied it with a private message of his own, which, perhaps with no very good reason, was thought by Charles to be the cause of Essex's refusal to accept the hand held out by himself.[2]

Charles was desirous of peace, but it must be a peace of his own making. In his distress he had thought of raising

Rupert to
succeed
Brentford.

Rupert to the supreme command in the place of Brentford. That Brentford was a good soldier and knew his business in the field was allowed even by his enemies. But he was old and deaf, a hard drinker, and slow of speech at the council table. It was not possible for

---

[1] The King to Essex, Aug. 6. Instructions to Harding. Walker's *Hist. Discourses,* 53.

[2] *The accusation given by his Majesty.* E. **7,** 27.

an old Scottish veteran to wield such authority over the English gentlemen of Charles's army as had been wielded by Leven over the Scottish nobility at Dunse Law.

As yet Rupert was unable to leave the North, but he sent to Charles's help the man who, of all others, was least fitted to restore order in a mutinous army. On August 7 Goring, who had thrown away his chance of victory at Marston Moor, arrived at Liskeard. A double traitor, he was as drunken and dissolute as Wilmot, and he was less ready than Wilmot to subordinate his indulgences to his duty as a soldier. On the day after his arrival Charles stripped Wilmot of his command of the cavalry and appointed Goring in his place. Wilmot was put under arrest, and subsequently sent into confinement at Exeter. He was ultimately allowed to leave the country, and retired to France. At the same time Lord Percy, his friend and ally, having been permitted to resign his post as Master of the Ordnance, also retired to the Continent.

Aug. 7.
Goring's arrival.

Aug. 8.
He is placed in command of the horse.

Wilmot's arrest.

Not merely was Goring's appointment obnoxious to men who, like Hyde and Culpepper, had no share in Wilmot's intrigues, but it was resented by the officers of the cavalry, many of whom had sympathised, if not with Wilmot, at least with his aims. It was perhaps to soothe their jealousy that Hopton, who was as desirous of peace as any of themselves, was appointed Percy's successor. Yet it was not easy to satisfy them. They had called on Charles to lay before them his reasons for dismissing Wilmot, and had prepared a petition, in which they suggested that Brentford and Essex might meet, each attended by six other persons, to 'consider of all means possible to reconcile the unhappy difference and misunderstandings that have so long afflicted the kingdom.' Charles let them send their proposal to Essex, and received from him in return the same answer as before, that he had no power to treat without the consent of Parliament.[1]

Percy succeeded by Hopton.

---

[1] *Clarendon,* viii. 404. *Walker,* 59. Digby to Rupert, Aug. 15. Goring to Rupert, Aug. 15 (*Warburton,* iii. 9, 16), where the date of Goring's letter is omitted.

These futile negotiations were utterly without influence upon the progress of the war. Their importance lies in the fact that men on both sides—men as distant from one another in intellect and character as Vane and Wilmot—were beginning more or less vaguely to recognise that Charles's personality was the main obstacle to peace.

All that could be done to render Essex's position at Lostwithiel untenable was done by Charles, or more probably by

Essex outman-œuvred.

Brentford. Skilfully the toils were drawn around that inactive commander. Charles had now some 16,000 horse and foot, whilst Essex could not count on much more than 10,000. On the 4th Boconnock, Lord

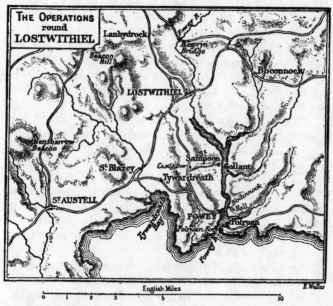

Mohun's house, to the east of Essex's headquarters, was seized by a Royalist detachment. On the 12th Grenvile, finding Respryn Bridge, over the Fowey river, unoccupied, seized it, together with Lord Robartes's house at Lanhydrock. There was now free communication for the Royalists across the

Fowey river from east to west. Having thus blocked Essex up on the land side, the Royalist commanders resolved to cut him off from the sea. Essex indeed had taken care to possess himself of Fowey, on the western side of the entrance to the harbour, but he had neglected to secure any single point on the eastern shore, and on the 14th Sir Jacob Astley secured for the King the posts which the Parliamentary commander had supinely left without a guard.

Hall,[1] Lord Mohun's house on the top of the steep hill which rises on the eastern side of Bodinnock Ferry, was the first to be occupied, and from that point the Royalists were able to make themselves masters of Polruan Fort, opposite Fowey, at the very mouth of the harbour, so as to make it difficult, if not impossible, for vessels with supplies to enter. Essex was therefore obliged to content himself with such provisions for his men as had been already landed, and to support his horses for a time on the scanty forage which was still to be found in the fields round the head of Tywardreath Bay, with the addition of a few boatloads of necessaries which might be landed on the open beach.

No wonder Essex showed signs of distress. "Braver men than are here," he wrote to the Committee two days after his last mishap, "I never knew, this army being environed by four armies,[2] in great want of victuals." "If any forces," he complained a few days later, "had followed the King, as we expected when we came into these parts, by human reason this war would have had a quick end, but since we are left to the providence of God, I cannot despair of His mercy, having found so much of it in our greatest straits."

Aug. 16.
Essex gives
an account
of his con-
dition,

Since the days of Nicias no general at the same time so devoted, so incompetent, and so self-satisfied, had been placed at the head of an army. In the eyes of Essex everything that

---

[1] "Sir Jacob Astley and General Goring," says Walker (p. 63), "went to view Hall." Clarendon, being ignorant of the locality, imagined 'view' to be a proper name, and calls the place 'View Hall' (viii. 109). Hall is now known as Hall Farm.

[2] *I.e.* the King's, Maurice's, Hopton's, and Grenvile's.

went wrong was solely the fault of others. "I marched into
these parts," he wrote again on the 23rd, "by the
advice and at the desire of some in this army that
are of this country, and also of Plymouth, and for
no ends of my own ; and had there been forces awaiting on
the King, I should not have doubted of giving a good account
of the war, had they been but 4,000 horse and dragoons."[1]

Aug. 23.
and calls for
aid.

To find a body of 4,000 men was beyond the power of the
Committee of Both Kingdoms. Middleton, indeed, with a
party of 2,000 of Waller's horse and dragoons, was
hurried off into Dorset and Somerset to hang about
the King's rear and to hinder supplies from reaching
him, but what could so small a force avail in the emergency ?
The new army which was to have taken the field on July 20
was not yet in existence. Browne, who was now at
Abingdon with an unpaid and mutinous force, threw
the blame upon Waller, and Waller, who had fallen back on
Farnham, retaliated upon Browne. Waller cried aloud for
soldiers, but except with the aid of the local committees no
soldiers were to be had. Kent did its duty, but
Sussex held back. On September 2 Waller wrote
that he had but 1,400 men with him, and that
though they had 'brought their mouths with them,' he had
but three weeks' pay to enable him to supply them. On the
6th he reiterated his complaints. All things possible
he was ready to do, but he hoped that no more than
was possible would be required of him.[2]

Impossi-
bility of
sending it.

Browne's
men unpaid.

Sept. 2.
Waller's
distress.

Sept. 6.

To relieve Essex was, when these words were written, no
longer possible. On August 26 St. Blazey was occupied by
Goring, and from henceforth Essex's horse would
have to depend for their forage on a little patch of
land three miles in width, which was already almost
exhausted by the calls made upon it. The biscuit and cheese
which had been tardily despatched from London by sea had

Aug. 26.
Goring occu-
pies St.
Blazey.

---

[1] Essex to the Com. of B. K., Aug. 16, 23. *Com. Letter Book.*

[2] See the letters of the months of August and September in the *Com.
Letter Book.* No traces are to be found of Waller's reluctance to support
Essex.

not yet arrived, and Essex, outnumbered and outgeneralled,

Aug. 30.
Essex prepares to withdraw

was in no condition to hold out long. On the evening of the 30th two deserters brought to Charles the news that the Parliamentary cavalry meant to break through on that night, whilst the infantry was to fall back on Fowey, to await the arrival of the expected transports.

Charles at once despatched orders to his troops to stand to arms during the night to keep the cavalry from escaping.[1]

Charles's dispositions.

Yet, strangely enough, he took no special precaution to guard in force the road from Lostwithiel to Plymouth, by which an escape would be most easily effected, contenting himself with throwing fifty musketeers into a cottage by the roadside, and directing the Earl of Cleveland to watch the passage with the horse at his disposal.

The King's army was not only scattered over a wide circuit, but the greater part of it was dispersed in search of provisions, which were by this time hard to be found. Cleveland, for instance, could rally round no more than 250 men to carry out the orders he had received.[2] When, therefore, about

Aug. 31.
The escape of the Parliamentary cavalry.

three in the morning of the 31st, the enemy's horse (about 2,000 strong) broke out from Lostwithiel under the command of Sir William Balfour, no serious attempt was made to stop them. The men in the cottage did not fire a shot, and Cleveland with his handful of men did not venture to charge. Balfour rode through the Royalist lines unmolested, and though Cleveland, whose numbers were later in the day augmented to 500, followed him closely and took some prisoners, the fugitives made their way without serious loss to Plymouth.[3]

[1] Walker's *Hist. Discourses*, 70.

[2] This is the number given in Cleveland's own report in Walker (p. 71). Symonds in his *Diary* (p. 62) says there were only 100.

[3] According to *Walker* (p. 75), Goring was sent to follow Balfour when he arrived at 4 P.M. on the 31st. According to *Symonds* (p. 65), he was not sent till the morning of the 1st. In any case, he found that Balfour had gone too far to be caught. In Bulstrode's *Memoirs* (p. 109), is a letter purporting to be from the King to Goring ordering him to follow. It cannot be genuine, as it speaks of Balfour's horse as having nearly surprised Sir Edward Waldegrave's brigade in their passage, whereas Walde-

With the deserted foot soldiers it fared far otherwise. The 31st was wet and stormy, and the army on its retreat to Fowey was forced to abandon four guns which had hope-

lessly sunk in the deep mud. The country was, however, intersected by thick hedges, which threw obstacles in the way of the Royalist horse now gathering round the King. Fighting bravely, the Parliamentary army gave way step by step. It was not till four in the afternoon that Goring, who had been summoned to join the King when the flight of the Parliamentary horse was known, but had not received the despatch till ten in the morning, appeared upon the scene. By this time Essex had drawn up his train with his baggage and his remaining guns within the earthworks of an old British camp, locally known as Castle Dor, which lay on the high ground on the western side of the river, and had thrown out two regiments to his right to guard the passage between Castle Dor and the river. Just before nightfall one of these two regiments broke and fled in disorder, and the other, left without support, fell back on the main body. The Royalists poured in through the gap, and, swinging round to their right, so threatened the road to Fowey—which place was still two miles and a half distant—as to render it impracticable to a retreating army.

To Essex the night which followed must have been one of bitter looking forward to an uncertain future. He could no

longer conceal from himself that there was little prospect that a surrender could be averted. Death in the battle-field he was now, as always, ready to face ; but the gibes and taunts of Charles's courtiers were more than he could bear to think of. When morning arrived Skippon

brought him word that the demoralised soldiers could not be trusted to move from the spot which they occupied without taking to flight. Upon this Essex took his course. Leaving orders to Skippon to make the best terms

grave, as we learn from Walker, and by implication from Cleveland's report, was with his regiment at Saltash, which was not reached by Balfour till late in the day. Mr. Firth, in his life of Goring in the *Dictionary of National Biography*, has disposed of Clarendon's story that Goring was delayed by being drunk.

possible with the King, he slipped away in company with Lord
Robartes and Sir John Meyrick to the river-side, and, putting
off in a small vessel, escaped to Plymouth ; 'it being,' as he
wrote, 'a greater terror to me to be a slave to their contempts
than a thousand deaths.'[1]

No doubt the lot which would befall Essex as a prisoner in
the Royalist camp might well appal even a heart as stout as
his. Yet there have been men who, having led their soldiers
into so evil a plight, would drain the cup of humiliation to the
dregs rather than separate their lot from that of those unfor-
tunates. For once the Court newspaper, the *Mercurius Aulicus*,
enlivened its career of dull jocularity with a flash of wit when
it asked 'why the rebels voted to live and die with the Earl of
Essex, since the Earl of Essex hath declared that he will not
live and die with them.'[2]

Skippon had no course left but to obtain the best terms he
could. Those which were offered him were far better than he
had any reason to expect. On the morning of the
2nd the Parliamentary infantry laid down its arms,
on the understanding that the men should not fight
against the King till they had reached Southampton or Portsmouth. Charles, on his part, was to supply them with a guard
to conduct them safely through the Western counties. It was
not in his power to protect them at the outset of their march.
The men and women of Lostwithiel, where many a grudge
had been stored up against them during their occupation of
the town, seeing, or pretending to see, that some of the soldiers
were carrying away their arms contrary to the agreement, fell
upon them, and subjected them to much contumely and ill-
treatment. As soon, however, as the train was clear of the
neighbourhood of Lostwithiel all went well. The guard
assigned to them protected them from all further harm, and
did not leave them till they were safe under the care of
Middleton's Horse, which had by this time advanced into
Somerset.[3]

Sept. 2.
Skippon's
surrender.

---

[1] Essex to Stapleton, Sept. 3. *Rushw.* v. 701. Walker's *Hist. Discourses,* 70. *Clarendon,* viii. 115.

[2] *Merc. Aulicus.* E. 10, 19.   [3] *Walker,* 79.

That Charles did not insist upon the complete surrender of his enemies as prisoners of war has always been a matter of surprise. His explanation was that his own army could not long have held out, apparently in consequence of the scantiness of his stock of provisions.[1] Yet it is hard to believe that he was so ill supplied as to be unable to block up a dispirited force of less than half his own numbers for twenty-four hours, and it can scarcely be doubted that Skippon would have been compelled to surrender at discretion before twenty-four hours were over.

Charles's motives for leniency.

In London attempts were made to minimise the defeat, and to dwell rather on the preservation of the soldiers than upon the loss of the munitions of war and the failure of the campaign. " By that miscarriage," wrote one of the newspapers, more candid than most of its contemporaries, "we are brought a whole summer's travel back." It was not, in truth, merely the loss of a certain number of muskets and of a certain number of barrels of powder which had to be set off against the victory of Marston Moor. Whatever might be the immediate cause of the failure of Essex, the really serious side of the disaster was the discord between the commanders and the entire failure of Parliament to reinforce or support the army in Cornwall. The whole organisation of Southern England had broken down. Would the forces of the North and the East be able to redress the balance?

Results of the surrender.

---

[1] " God's protection of a just cause was never more apparent than at this time, for had our success been either deferred, or of another kind, nothing but a direct miracle could have saved us." The King to Rupert, Sept. 3. *Fortescue Papers*, 218.

CHAPTER XX.

THE ARMY OF THE EASTERN ASSOCIATION.

THE effect of the success of Charles in Cornwall was the greater because it was now known that even the army of the Eastern Association—the one English army capable of forming a nucleus round which the scattered forces of Essex and Waller might rally—was torn asunder by internal distractions. Of that army Cromwell was the soul. Gathering round him men like-minded with himself, such as Ireton and Desborough, Fleetwood and Pickering, his one thought was to carry on the war relentlessly till the King had been crushed beyond possibility of recovery. With this object he had filled every office under his control with men who would make no terms with Charles's politics or Charles's religion, but who for that very reason were abundantly tolerant of the most extreme diversity of opinion within the bounds of Puritanism.

1644. Aug. State of Manchester's army.

Cromwell's following and aims.

Between Cromwell and Manchester there was little in common. Especially since the day on which Vane, backed doubtless by Cromwell, had advocated the actual or virtual dethronement of the King,[1] the General of the army of the Association regarded his Lieutenant-General with grave suspicion. Whilst Cromwell, with his firm grasp upon existing facts, looked upon peace as only attainable by victory, Manchester hoped for it as the result of mutual concessions. He rightly judged that no solid political edifice could be raised on a merely military foundation, especially if the army was to be composed of enthusiasts alone. Yet his

Cromwell distrusts Manchester.

[1] See vol. i. p. 368.

view of the situation was merely instinctive without intellectual clearness, and was deeply tinged by his dislike of men who endangered the position of the peerage in the English world. He could indeed blame some isolated actions of the Parliament—its reiterated demand, for instance, that the King's supporters should be excepted from the general pardon, or its sweeping confiscation of the lands of the Irish rebels[1]—but he could not go to the root of the matter by proposing a religious settlement capable of satisfying reasonable men on both sides. " I could contentedly," he said to his chaplain, " part with half my estate upon condition the discipline of Christ was established and a good ministry settled in every congregation of the kingdom ; yea, with those conditions, how gladly would I betake myself unto a country life, and leave all other contentments in the world ! "[2]

Manchester's views.

Peace, in short, and a Puritan establishment under Charles was the object at which Manchester aimed. Never able to understand why this apparently simple object was unattainable, he was like a ship without a helm upon the sea of politics. He could not urge peace as matters stood, because to urge peace would be to secure the triumph of the enemies of Puritanism. He could not conduct war with vigour, because to conduct war with vigour would be to secure the triumph of the enemies of peace. Amiable and garrulous, he chattered to all who would listen to him about the blunders of the fanatics, and fell easily into the temper which sees a mountain in every molehill, and which prefers to do nothing rather than to risk defeat.

On the way from York to Lincoln Manchester reduced the Marquis of Newcastle's house at Welbeck, whilst Crawford mastered the resistance of Sheffield. Yet his reluctance to undertake any more hazardous operation was extreme. He

[1] Watson's deposition. *S. P. Dom.* diii. 56, xiv. The series of depositions to which this one belongs were added to the collection of State Papers after the publication of the *Quarrel of Manchester and Cromwell*, edited by Prof. Masson for the Camden Society. They are invaluable for a true appreciation of the events before and after the second battle of Newbury.

[2] Ash's *True Relation.* E. 22, 10.

forbade Lilburne, who was now a colonel in his army, to send
a summons to Tickhill Castle, and when Lilburne, impatient

Manchester's reluctance to engage in hazardous operations. of restraint, not only summoned the castle but took
it, threatened to hang him for disobeying orders.[1]
Many of his officers urged him to block up Newark,
the chief Royalist fortress in the Eastern Midlands,
and so to give protection to Lincolnshire from the rapine to
which it was subjected without other possibility of relief.
Their urgent entreaties were received coldly, and when Manchester at last reached Lincoln he remained there without
doing anything, and apparently without the intention of doing
anything.[2]

No doubt there were difficulties in Manchester's way,
difficulties far greater than Cromwell was willing to acknow-

Manchester's difficulties. ledge. Victorious as the army had been, it had
been worn away by the fatigues of the campaign till
its numbers were reduced to 6,000, and of these
many were, for the present, disabled by sickness. Reinforcements were sadly needed ; and, even in the Eastern Association,
committees were not very much more vigorous than committees
elsewhere, and of the money due to the army for the year
ending on the last Lady Day no less than 30,000*l.* was in
arrear, whilst of that which was due for the succeeding four
months not a single penny had been paid.[3] As for sending
recruits, the Committee declared it to be absolutely impossible
as long as they were expected to furnish men for the new army
which had been ordered by Parliament.[4] Fortunately for
Manchester, the Committee of Both Kingdoms came to his
help in the matter of recruits, by ordering that 1,800 men who
were to have been sent to the new army were to be despatched
to him.[5] Yet the temper which had been shown by the
Association did not bode well for the success of an attempt

---

[1] Lilburne's deposition. *S. P. Dom.* diii. 56, iv.

[2] Cromwell's narrative. *Quarrel of Manchester and Cromwell,* 78.

[3] Manchester to the Com. of B. K., Aug. 1. *Quarrel of Manchester and Cromwell,* 4. [4] See p. 6.

[5] Manchester to the Com. of B. K., Aug. 1, 10. The Com. of B. K. to Manchester, Aug. 7. *Quarrel of Manchester and Cromwell,* 2, 7, 8.

to make it do duty for a general organisation. Waller's cry for a national army[1] had as yet produced no results. The new troops either did not come into existence at all, or were drafted into various local regiments to fill up gaps caused by the stress of war. The difficulty of carrying on a campaign without a national army was quite as great as the difficulty of overthrowing the Royalists with Manchester in command.

Cromwell was doubtless in the right in thinking that the best way to get support from the Eastern counties was to besiege Newark, and thereby to show to the populations of those districts that the army was worth supporting. He was as openly and bitterly hostile to the Scots on account of their refusal of toleration to the sects as he was to Manchester on account of his inefficiency. "In the way they now carry themselves," he said on one occasion to the Earl, "pressing for their discipline, I could as soon draw my sword against them as against any in the King's army." "I will not deny," he said at another time, "but that I desire to have none in my army but such as are of the Independent judgment." Manchester asked his reason for so divisive a resolution. "That in case," replied Cromwell, "there should be propositions for peace, or any other conclusion of a peace, such as might not stand with the ends that honest men should aim at, this army might prevent such a mischief." Cromwell was not content with masterful words. He had weeded out from the regiments under his influence all who were opposed to the liberty of the sects or who hoped to end the war by negotiation rather than by victory.[2]

Cromwell's hostility to the Scots.

It was not only amongst the Scots that this language, audacious in its outspokenness, raised enemies. The sects were not popular with average Puritans, and there were not a few amongst the well-born officers of Manchester's army who jeered openly at the 'godly, precious men,' who 'had filled dung-carts before they were captains and since,' and who had now turned the Isle of Ely into 'a

Opposition to Cromwell.

---

[1] See p. 5.

[2] Manchester to the House of Lords. *Camd. Misc.* **viii.**

mere Amsterdam,' in which they troubled the churches with
their ravings, whilst the clergy, thrust from their pulpits, were
compelled to sit as silent auditors of such scandalous profanity.
Military saints, too, it seems, were not wanting, who professed
' to have seen visions and revelations.' [1]

With the contempt of the ordinary man for fanatical zeal
was blended the contempt of the man of social position for

Cromwell's attack on the nobility.
the tradesman and the farmer. Men with whom
distinctions of birth counted for much felt instinctively that Cromwell was their bitterest enemy. He
refused to recognise any distinctions save those arising from
services rendered to the common cause. He was fully aware
that the notion of coming to an understanding with the King
rather than with the sects found acceptance mainly with the
Puritan peers and with the wealthiest Puritan gentlemen. It
was a matter of common observation that the rental of the
Peace-party in the House of Commons had been enormously
in excess of that of the War-party, in the days when rents had
been actually received in full by those who claimed them.[2]
When Vane's proposal to deprive the King of authority had
been laid before the Generals at York, the ready answer had
been that the nobility would not endure it,[3] and it is therefore
no matter of surprise that Cromwell, though his aims were
directed towards a religious rather than a social revolution,
retorted that he hoped to ' live to see never a nobleman in
England,' or that he spoke of himself as loving certain persons
'better than others because they did not love lords.' [4] It
would not be well, he is even reported to have added in a
moment of rude familiarity to Manchester, till he was himself
' but Mr. Montague.' [5]

No wonder that before this boisterous energy the well-bred

---

[1] Statement by an opponent of Cromwell. *Quarrel of Manchester and Cromwell,* 71.

[2] The extreme difficulty in getting rents in is shown by the evidence of D'Ewes's Diary and the *Verney MSS.*

[3] See p. 369, note.

[4] Manchester to the House of Lords. *Camd. Misc.* viii.

[5] Holles, *Mem.* 14.

gentleman, the 'sweet meek man,' as Baillie styles him, shrank back as from a fiery lava stream. Failure, ultimate failure, no doubt there was in Cromwell's efforts to break through not merely the proprieties of ceremonial order, but to push aside the culture of the day with the help of men whose fanaticism was in his eyes more than compensated by their sincerity. For the immediate work of the day no other instruments could compare with these. There was in Cromwell a massive common-sense and a grasp on the realities of the present which raised him to a pre-eminence soon to be uncontested in the midst of a generation of dreamers.

In an army thus divided in mood fresh causes of dispute were certain to arise. The Committee of Both Kingdoms,

Aug. 6.
Manchester
asked to go
against
Rupert. disquieted at Rupert's energetic preparations at Chester, urged Manchester to march against him with all his available force. Manchester replied by sending the advice given by his principal officers to

Aug. 10.
Manchester
refuses to go. the effect that it was too late in the year to besiege Chester, and that it would be impossible to keep the army supplied at such a distance, especially as the provision carts would have to pass within easy distance of the hostile garrisons of Newark and Belvoir. Moreover, the Association would refuse any longer to support an army which left the Eastern counties at the mercy of the enemy.[1]

There is nothing to show that Cromwell disapproved of this advice as matters stood.[2] What he did disapprove of was

Nothing
serious done. the rejection of every possible plan of action. After a while a council of war was summoned, and a

Aug. 21.
A party of
horse to be
despatched
to Cheshire. resolution for an attack upon Newark was taken. Then came a fresh despatch from the Committee of Both Kingdoms urging Manchester to send at least a small party of horse to assist Brereton in Cheshire; yet, though Manchester appeared to be busy with his pre-

---

[1] The Com. of B. K. to Manchester, Aug. 6. Considerations. *Quarrel of Manchester and Cromwell*, 5, 9.

[2] He may not have been consulted. In his narrative he says that the only council of war held was one on the subject of Newark.

parations, he remained inactive at Lincoln whilst August slipped away.[1]

On September 1 the body of cavalry told off for the succour of Brereton was at last on the move. On the following day it

Sept. 1.
Cavalry ordered to go to Cheshire.

was recalled, partly because news arrived that Prince Rupert, carrying with him the Royalist horse which had come in from Lancashire and Westmorland,

Sept. 2.
Manchester receives orders to march southwards.

had turned southwards with the bulk of his forces, and partly because, though nothing as yet had been heard of the surrender at Lostwithiel, it was known that the army of Essex was in a critical position, and

that it was now of greater importance to maintain the balance in Southern England than to defend Lincolnshire against the garrison of Newark.[2]

On September 4 Manchester set out from Lincoln.[3] At Huntingdon, on the 8th, he heard of the surrender of Essex.

Sept. 4.
Manchester sets out.

His business now would be not merely to check Rupert, but to restore a falling cause. Manchester at once expressed his readiness to do his utmost.

Sept. 8.
Learns that Essex has surrendered.

"The Lord's arm," he wrote to the Committee of Both Kingdoms, "is not shortened, though we be

Offers to march and to make up disputes.

much weakened. I trust He will give us a happy recovery. I shall, with all the speed I can, march in observance of your former orders. Concerning

those differences which your Lordships take notice to be amongst some of this army, I hope your Lordships shall find that I shall take such care as, by the blessing of God, nothing of the public service shall be retarded."[4]

Manchester's zeal, perhaps real enough at first, soon cooled down. He lingered at Huntingdon instead of hastening to the rescue of the distressed Parliamentary armies. He would

---

[1] The Com. of B. K. to Manchester, Aug. 14. Manchester to the Com. of B. K., Aug. 21. Cromwell's narrative. *Quarrel of Manchester and Cromwell,* 14, 16, 81.

[2] Com. of B. K. to Manchester, Aug. 28, Sept. 1. Manchester to the Com. of B. K., Sept. 2. *Ibid.* 20, 22, 23.

[3] Manchester to the Com. of B. K., Sept. 4, 5. *Ibid.* 24.

[4] Manchester to the Com. of B. K., Sept. 8. *Ibid.* 25.

hang any one, he said, who advised him to march to the West.[1] Cromwell appears to have attributed his General's

Manchester soon cools down. vacillation to the influence of Crawford, and to have threatened that his colonels would resign in a

Threatened resignation of the colonels. body unless Crawford were removed from his command. Manchester strove in vain to effect a reconciliation, and, failing in this, betook himself to

Sept. 12. Manchester's visit to London. Westminster, accompanied by the two antagonists, in the hope that the Committee of Both Kingdoms would mediate between them better than he had been able to do.[2]

A few hours in London must have convinced Cromwell of the difficulties of carrying the extreme measure on which he

State of feeling at Westminster. was bent. Not only were the minds of all men averse to a course which seemed like a mere satisfaction of personal jealousy,[3] but the danger incurred by Essex's disaster had produced a strong feeling that it would be unwise to do anything to alienate auxiliaries so powerful as the Scots. A circumstance had lately occurred which went far to show that Vane and his allies had need to walk warily.

Aug. 30. The Elector Palatine in England. The Elector Palatine landed at Greenwich,[4] ostensibly on the errand of urging his claims to the restitution of the Palatinate. Little as was his share of wisdom, it is difficult to imagine that he could have considered it appropriate at this crisis of the Civil War to press in person his demands for men and money, or even for diplomatic assistance. On the other hand, though no evidence to that effect exists,[5] it is likely enough that when Vane suggested at

[1] Depositions of Cromwell and Hammond. *S. P. Dom.* diii. 56, vii. xv.

[2] Manchester's statement to the House of Lords, Dec. *Camd. Misc.* viii. *Baillie*, ii. 229.

[3] See the letter of the Com. of B. K. to the Commanders, Sept. 10. *Rushw.* v. 719.

[4] D'Ewes's Diary. *Harl. MSS.* 166, fol. 111b.

[5] I can hardly count as evidence the statements which occur in Agostini's despatches, to the effect that the Prince, after his arrival, was neglected by those who had encouraged him ; but they undoubtedly point in the direction of my suggestion.

York in June that Charles should be deprived of the royal
authority, he had taken some steps to ascertain whether the
Elector would be willing to occupy his uncle's place, as

What were
the motives
of his jour-
ney? William of Orange afterwards, under somewhat similar circumstances, occupied the place of his uncle
James. It was likely enough, too, if such overtures
had been made, that the young man, restless and impatient
with the dreary lot of an exile, should have thought fit to come
in person to see what would be the result of the proposal.
At all events, if this was the real course of events, it renders
explicable what otherwise is inexplicable, the fierce indignation with which Vane and St. John met the apparently harmless act of folly of which the Prince had been guilty. Naturally
they would wish him at a safe distance, where he could tell no
compromising tales, and they knew well that, much as they
might wish to give him their support, it was, for the moment at
least, utterly beyond their power to give effect to their wishes.

It was therefore the party of Vane and St. John which
carried through the House of Commons a message to the

Sept. 2.
He is at-
tacked by
Vane's party. Elector, in which he was told that the shorter his
stay in England was the better it would be for his
interests, and though these words were softened

The Elector
takes the
Covenant. down by the Lords, no material alteration was made
in their purport. The Elector, however, persisted in
remaining in spite of the rebuff, and ostentatiously took the
Covenant as an outward mark of his sympathy with the
Parliamentary party. He was lodged at Whitehall, where
he received all outward demonstrations of courtesy, but he
was made to understand that he had visited England to no
purpose.[1]

Vane, in truth, could not afford to weaken his position by
open talk about the dethronement of the King. Even when,

Sept. 7.
The Com-
mons sup-
port Essex. on September 7, the news of Essex's surrender
arrived, it was clearly shown that Essex still had a
hold on the majority of the members. A letter was
drawn up thanking the defeated commander for his conduct,
and assuring him that Manchester and Waller had been

[1] *C.J.* iii. 614, 615. *L.J.* vi. 695.

ordered to march to Dorchester,[1] in order to hold the ground till his own troops could be re-equipped. In the House blame was thrown, not on Essex, but on Middleton, who had failed to carry succour to him in time. Hazlerigg gave general offence by an inappropriate burst of laughter when the letter was read in the House.[2] Amongst Cromwell's troopers he would have found many to share his opinion. When the report of the disaster of Essex reached Huntingdon, not a few of the Independents in the army showed 'themselves so joyful as though it had been a victory new gained to themselves.'[3]

The view taken in the army.

In the battle-field it was Cromwell's special characteristic that, impetuous as he was in a charge, he never failed to pull up to look around him as soon as the purpose of the charge had been effected. It now appeared that his behaviour in the arena of politics was to be precisely the same as his behaviour in the field of war. He had not been long at Westminster before he had taken the measure of the situation. Abandoning as impracticable his demand for Crawford's dismissal, he contented himself with drawing from Manchester a declaration of his resolution to push on with all speed against the enemy.[4] As a member of the House of Commons he had an opportunity of gaining a step in the direction in which he wanted to go. On September 13 there was a debate on a form of ordination which had been presented by the Assembly for the approval of the House. Something in its wording gave offence even to members who had little in common with Vane and Cromwell. Not only did Selden play his accustomed part by asking how far the clergy might claim to rule over the souls of the people, but D'Ewes, who held the sects in utter abomination, expressed a hope that 'the clergy intended only the power

Sept. 12. Cromwell abandons his demand for Crawford's dismissal.

Sept. 13. Debate on ordination.

Language of Selden and D'Ewes.

---

[1] *L.J.* vi. 699.   [2] D'Ewes's Diary. *Harl. MSS.* 166, fol. 112b.

[3] Statement by an opponent of Cromwell. *Quarrel of Manchester and Cromwell,* 76.

[4] Manchester's statement to the Lords. *Camd. Misc.* viii. *Day Book of the Com. of B. K. Baillie,* ii. 230.

and purity of the ordinances, and not to introduce such a tyrannical power as the bishops had.'[1]

Cromwell saw his opportunity. At his prompting St. John, framing the wording of the motion which he was about to lay before the House in such a way as to give as little offence as possible, asked the Commons to vote ' that the Committee of Lords and Commons appointed to treat with the Commissioners of Scotland and the Committee of the Assembly do take into consideration the differences in opinion of the members of the Assembly in point of church-government, and to endeavour a union, if it be possible ; and, in case that cannot be done, to endeavour the finding out some way, how far tender consciences, who cannot in all things submit to the common rule which shall be established, may be borne with according to the Word, and as may stand with the public peace, that so the proceedings of the Assembly may not be so much retarded.'

The Accommodation order.

The phraseology of the clause which demanded consideration for 'tender consciences' was curiously like that which was to be found in those frequent proclamations on the subject which had been from time to time issued by Charles, but to which he had done so little to give effect. Whether Cromwell would be able to give effect to his policy in the face of the opposition which it would arouse remained to be seen, but at least it would not be his own fault if it failed. For the moment it was at least tacitly accepted by the whole House. It may be that, in that hour of peril, even those to whom toleration was a word of fear dimly perceived that it was a reconciling and not a dividing policy. At all events the Accommodation order, as it was afterwards called, was accepted without a division. There was something singularly appropriate in the scene which followed. Before the close of the sitting the Speaker, 'by command of the House,' gave 'thanks to Lieutenant-General Cromwell for his fidelity in the cause in hand, and in particular for the faithful service performed by him in the late battle near York, where

The order accepted.

Cromwell receives the thanks of the House.

---

[1] D'Ewes's Diary. *Harl. MSS.* 166, fol. 113b.

God made him a special instrument in obtaining that great victory.'[1]

Cromwell's efforts for accommodation were not likely to remain long unchallenged. Baillie gave expression to the irri-

Dissatisfaction of the Scots. tation of the Scots. "The great shot of Cromwell and Vane," he wrote, "is to have a liberty for all religions without any exceptions. Many a time we are put to great trouble of mind; we must make the best of an ill game as we can. . . . God help us ! If God be pleased to settle Scotland and give us Newcastle all will go well." Scottish victories in the North, it seemed, would relieve the Scots in London from the pressure brought to bear upon them by the ' very wise and active ' head upon Cromwell's shoulders.[2]

The party of toleration, however, was not without hope that an English victory in the South might redress the balance in its

Manchester favoured by Vane and Cromwell. favour. There can be little doubt that Vane and Cromwell had accepted Manchester's promises of energetic action as satisfactory, and it is certain that at this juncture they were disposed to rely on him rather than on Essex. On the 21st a querulous letter from

Sept. 21. A letter from Essex. Essex was read in the House, which to some extent justified the feeling against him. Writing from Portsmouth, where he was awaiting his defeated army, he declared it to be impossible for his cavalry to serve under Middleton, whose delay in relieving the army in Cornwall was

Manchester and Waller to join forces. the cause of their miseries. On this the House voted that Manchester and Waller should join forces against the King. Holles urged that Essex should be included in the combination, but he was unable to gain acceptance for his plea.[3]

It was the more necessary to have an army ready to take the field as the King was moving eastwards. On September 5

Sept. 5. The King at Tavistock. he reached Tavistock. To push on hastily before the enemy's forces could be reorganised was the course most clearly to his advantage, but it was either out of his power to do so, or at least he fancied it to be

---

[1] *C.J.* iii. 626.   [2] *Baillie*, ii. 230.
[3] D'Ewes's Diary. *Harl. MSS.* 166, fol. 123b.

out of his power. The Cornish levies of Maurice's army had
gone home to celebrate their victory, and the experience of the
last year's campaign had shown how hard it was to secure their

Sept. 8.
Asks for
peace.

services in the East as long as Plymouth was hostile
in the West. Having therefore sent after Essex one
more demand for peace, Charles made a futile at-

Sept. 10
Makes an
attempt on
Plymouth.

tempt to capture Plymouth, and then, leaving Sir
Richard Grenvile behind to block up the place so as

Sept. 23.
Arrives at
Chard.

to render it innocuous, began his eastward march. On
the 23rd he established himself at Chard. On his
way he learnt that his forces had gained possession
of Barnstaple and Ilfracombe, the former town having revolted
to Parliament shortly before the battle of Cropredy Bridge.

The King's army, in spite of its success at Lostwithiel, was
not in much better condition than Manchester's army had been
after Marston Moor. It had already been weakened by the
loss of the detachment left behind with Grenvile to block up
Plymouth, and its numbers were now still further reduced by
the necessity of sending detachments to block up Lyme and
Taunton. Charles had to remain at Chard for a week, till
fresh supplies could be drawn from Devonshire, however
impatient he may have been.[1]

Charles's plan of campaign was clearly marked out beforehand. Two of the fortresses by which the central strength of

Charles's
plans.

Oxford was girdled round—Banbury and Basing
House—were hard pressed by the enemy. It would
therefore be his first duty to relieve their garrisons, and he had
no expectation of being able to do this without a battle. With
this object in view he had ordered Rupert to join him as he
marched forward, and to bring with him some troops with
which Sir Charles Gerard had been unsuccessfully defending
South Wales. As soon as a victory was won—and in the distracted condition of the enemy Charles counted on nothing
less—he would press on against the Eastern Association. In
the Royalist camp it was fully believed that the King would
winter in Norfolk. Such a conclusion of the campaign of 1644
would make the work of the following year comparatively easy.[2]

[1] *Walker*, 80–88.   [2] Trevor to Ormond, Oct. 13. Carte's *Ormond*, vi. 205.

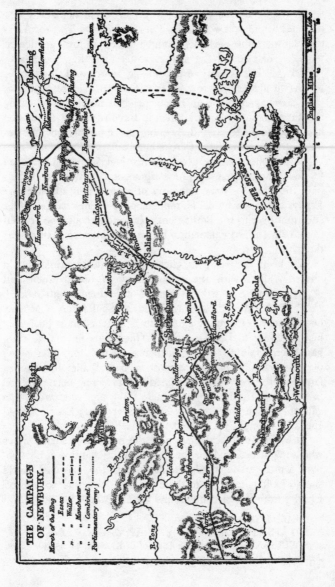

Tempting as the prospect was, there were not a few who doubted whether it was more than a dream. The royal exchequer was almost exhausted, and hundreds of loyal gentlemen had found the strain greater than they could bear "The poverty of our nobles, gentry, and those shires which we possess," wrote one of Ormond's correspondents, "is [1] so insufferable, that I fear we shall not hold out many months without yielding. Already three thousand gentlemen have compounded, and daily more go." [2] Wherever Charles was not in person things were going badly. Whilst the Royal army was engaged at Lostwithiel, Wareham had been recaptured by the Parliamentary levies in Dorsetshire. It was ominous of approaching disaster that Hurry, the betrayer of Hampden, once more changed sides and went over to the Parliament. If anyone could be trusted to make a shrewd calculation of his own interests, Hurry was the man.

Poverty of the King.

Aug. 4. Wareham retaken.

To keep the King in check till the other armies could arrive, Waller, with the strong body of horse which had been under the command of his Lieutenant-General, Middleton, was stationed at Shaftesbury. Money, he warned the Committee of Both Kingdoms, must be had if his men were to keep together. One of his majors, he said, had been 'fain to borrow sixpence to pay for the shoeing of his horse.' What was almost as bad, Waller had no infantry, all the foot which remained to him having been disposed in garrisons in the coast towns. "We are," he wrote, "a gallant forlorn hope." If Manchester and Essex arrived speedily all might yet be well. [3]

Waller at Shaftesbury.

It was no mere calculation of the number of square miles which might be saved for the Parliament by fighting at Shaftesbury which made Waller anxious that the expected battle should be fought so far to the west. His aim was to cut off Charles from the garrisons round Oxford, where his possession

---

[1] 'Are' in the text.

[2] D. O'Neill to Ormond, Oct. 3. Carte's *Ormond*, vi. 203.

[3] Waller and Hazlerigg to the Com. of B. K., Sept. 24, 25, 30. *Com. Letter Book.*

of the fortresses would enable him to fight at advantage. It was not, however, an easy task to comply with Waller's wishes.

Waller urges that Essex and Manchester may come up. Essex's horse indeed was available in case of necessity, but such of Essex's foot as had straggled to Portsmouth were still unarmed. Though there was now a revulsion of feeling in favour of Essex in the House, and orders were given to provide for his necessities,[1] some time must elapse before those orders could be put in force, and if Waller was to have speedy aid everything depended on the energy with which Manchester carried out the resolution announced by him when he was last at Westminster.

Essex's army to be equipped.

On September 22 Manchester was at Watford. On the 25th he reached Harefield, only four miles farther on. He

Sept. 22. Manchester's movements. Sept. 25. was ready to obey orders, he declared, but the bridge at Maidenhead was broken, and he could not cross the Thames till it had been mended. Moreover, he was still of the opinion which he had expressed in the late discussions. "If the King be upon his march," he

Sept. 28. wrote, "in that condition that I see those armies in, you do expose us to scorn, if not to ruin." The reply of the Committee was that orders had been sent to Waller either to stay at Shaftesbury or to move to Marlborough if the King marched that way, and that in any case Manchester was to join him with all possible speed.[2] On the 29th Man

Sept. 29. Manchester refuses to advance. chester wrote that he had arrived at Reading, but that he had heard that Waller had no infantry with him. It would therefore be unsafe for him to advance further 'with so inconsiderable a strength.' Manchester's resolution was probably not altogether due to his distrust of his own powers. He had recently learnt that the Newark

Sept. 30. Royalists had taken advantage of his absence and were ravaging Lincolnshire, and he was now inundated with letters from the counties of the Association 'expressing their great trouble that their forces are drawn from

[1] *C.J.* iii. 639.

[2] Manchester to the Com. of B. K., Sept. 22, 25. The Com. of B. K. to Manchester, Sept. 28. *Quarrel of Manchester and Cromwell,* 27–31.

them.' He could think of no better course than to lay the whole difficulty before the Committee of Both Kingdoms.[1]

As might be expected, the Earl was more outspoken in conversation than he was in his despatches. "My army," he said, "was raised by the Association, and was for the guard of the Association. It cannot be commanded by a Parliament without their consents." [2] "It is a pity," he said on another occasion, "we should leave those counties who have paid us and parted with their money so willingly to us all this while, now by our absence to be exposed [3] to the incursions of an enemy." The weather was adverse and the time of year unseasonable for operations in the field. The best thing to do would be for the armies of Essex and Waller to take up a defensive position about Reading and Basing House whilst his own army was quartered at St. Albans. The orders of the Committee to march westwards he treated as a mere concession to the importunity of interested persons whose estates lay in the districts threatened by the King. He never liked the war, he added, but was against it from the beginning. It was easy to begin a war, but no man knew when it would end.[4]

Manchester's conversation.

It is evident that this amiable nobleman was out of place at the head of an army. In a somewhat similar conjuncture in the preceding year, Cromwell, crying "It's out instantly all you can," [5] had sought for safety by dashing at the enemy. Manchester had no leadership in him either for politics or war. No wonder that Waller grew hopeless, and that Cromwell and his godly colonels settled down into grim despair of accomplishing aught as long as this man had the army at his command.

Manchester had appealed to the Committee of Both King-

---

[1] Manchester to the Com. of B. K., Sept. 30. *Quarrel of Manchester and Cromwell*, 32.

[2] Watson's deposition. *S. P. Dom.* diii. 56, xiv.

[3] 'And now by our absence be exposed' in MS. Pickering's deposition, Dec. 12. *Ibid.*

[4] Rich's deposition, Dec. 26. *S. P. Dom.* diii. 56, xviii.

[5] See vol. i. p. 191.

doms, and the Committee was doing what it could. It pushed

Activity of
the Com-
mittee of
Both King-
doms.

on the equipment of Essex's forlorn infantry, of whom some 4,000 had gathered round him at Portsmouth.[1] It applied to the City for a fresh loan of trained bands, and the City offered five regiments on condition that there should be no uncertainty about their pay. The Houses hardly knew where to turn for money. In their

Pardon sold
to Edmund
Waller.

distress they remembered that Edmund Waller had been in prison for more than a year, and was exceedingly anxious to escape from the trial which was impending. They therefore offered to pardon him on his engagement to leave the country and to pay 10,000*l*. Waller caught at the bargain, and his money was reserved for a first instalment of the pay about to fall due to the City forces.[2]

When the City regiments were ready it was to Manchester's army that they were to be added. On October 1 the Commons,

Oct. 1.
Essex to join
Manchester
and Waller.

rescinding their former decision, resolved that Essex's army should join Manchester's and Waller's.[3] If

Difficulty
about the
command.

the three Generals were to combine it would be more than ever necessary to come to some resolution about the command. Waller at least was not likely to stand in the way of harmonious co-operation. He had no wish to urge his pretensions against Manchester. "I am so heartily weary of this war," he wrote, "that I shall submit to anything that may conduce to the despatch of it."[4] It was useless to expect Essex to obey Manchester or Manchester to obey Essex. The Houses therefore left it to the Committee to take the matter in hand.[5]

Before the Committee succeeded in untying this tangled

Sept. 30.
Charles
leaves
Chard.

knot Charles had again entered upon his forward march. On September 30, sending before him a proclamation in which he called on his subjects to join him in settling the terms of peace in a full and free Parliament,[6]

---

[1] The Dutch ambassadors to the States-General. *Add. MSS.* 17, 677 R. fol. 440.

[2] *C.J.* iii. 639.　　　　　　　　　　[3] *C.J.* iii. 648.

[4] Waller to the Com. of B. K., Sept. 25.　*Com. Letter Book.*

[5] *L.J.* vii. 6.　　　　　　　　　　[6] *Rushw.* v. 715.

he set out from Chard. At South Perrot he was joined by Rupert,

His inter-
view with
Rupert. whose debaucheries at Bristol had excited the indignation of decent Royalists,[1] but who was always ready to fling himself into the saddle as soon as an opportunity of fighting occurred. The result of the Prince's conversation with his uncle was that he undertook to return to Bristol in order to bring up a reinforcement of 4,000 men to join

Oct. 2.
Charles at
Sherborne. the Royal army at Sherborne.[2]   Whilst Charles was waiting for this increase to his army he received a

State of his
negotiations
with France
and the
Prince of
Orange. visit from the French minister, Sabran.   Neither the negotiation with France nor that with the Prince of Orange had advanced far since the rejection of Charles's insane suggestion in June that Frederick Henry should come to an understanding with Spain.[3]   The Queen had been too ill since her arrival in France to give any personal assistance to her husband, but early in August she had de-

Aug. 6.
Jermyn
writes to
the Prince. spatched Jermyn to Paris to beg Mazarin to accord that armed succour which was to form part of the arrangements of the suggested marriage of the Prince of Wales with the daughter of the Prince of Orange.   Mazarin was courtesy itself, but though Gravelines had surrendered he did not think it possible to find either the men or the money till the issue of the campaign on the Rhine was decided.   The

Sept. 4.
The Prince's
answer. Prince of Orange was still more cool.   On September 4 he informed Jermyn that the best course which the King of England could pursue would be to make peace with his subjects at any price.[4]

In his conversation with Sabran Charles lowered his demands.   Of foreign soldiers, he said, he did not stand greatly

Oct.
Charles's
conversation
with Sabran. in need, and the arms which he had lately received from France were so bad that he preferred to have fresh ones made at Bristol ; but he was in the greatest straits for money.   To Sabran's reply that France

---

[1] Trevor to Ormond, Oct. 13. Carte's *Ormond*, vi. 205.

[2] *Walker*, 98. Digby to Rupert, Oct. 20. *Add. MSS.* 18, 781, fol. 297.   [3] See vol. i. p. 191.

[4] Jermyn to the Prince of Orange, Aug. $\frac{6}{16}$. The Prince of Orange to Jermyn, Sept. $\frac{4}{14}$. *Groen van Prinsterer*, Ser. 2, iv. 107, 117.

wanted money as much as he did, Charles had nothing to say ;
but he urged the ambassador to make it known that France
would take his part if the Parliament refused to come to terms.
This, he said, was the only way in which the war could be
brought to an end. Sabran had no instructions to do anything of the kind, and Charles, in writing to the Queen, did not
conceal his annoyance at the ambassador's profession of absolute neutrality.[1]

Charles's mysteries were seldom kept secret long. " The
Queen," wrote Baillie on September 16, " is very like to get
Charles's
diplomacy
not secret. an army from France." [2] Ill would it fare with an
English sovereign who sought to strengthen his
throne with the help of a French invasion.

Whilst Charles remained at Sherborne Waller reiterated his
cry for help. He pleaded that no local jealousy might stand
Oct. 4.
Waller calls
for help. in the way of Manchester's advance. It was better,
he urged, to hazard worse loss in a particular coun-
try than not to break the King's army. " Destroy
but this," he added, "and the work is ended. Were this land
but fit for mercy, there is means enough to do it." [3]

Waller's entreaties were seconded by the authorities at
Westminster. The Committee of Both Kingdoms unremit-
Oct. 5.
Essex un-
able to
march. tingly urged both Essex and Manchester to push on.
On the 5th Essex replied that he was prepared to
disregard ' all particular spleens or provocations of
those who were under his command '—he evidently considered
Oct. 7.
Manchester
ordered to
advance. both Manchester and Waller as his subordinates—
but that without money and arms he could not stir.[4]
On the 7th the Committee wrote to Manchester to
send forward all his horse to the West, and on the following

---

[1] Sabran to Brienne, $\frac{\text{Oct. 24}}{\text{Nov. 3}}$. *Add. MSS.* 5,460, fol. 325b. The King
to the Queen, Oct. 20. *S. P. Dom.* diii. 24. Charles's letter is undated,
but its date is fixed by a comparison of Sabran's despatch and the Queen's
reply of Nov. $\frac{8}{18}$. *Letters of Henrietta Maria*, 263.

[2] *Baillie*, ii. 230.

[3] Waller and Hazlerigg to the Com. of B. K., Oct. 4. *Com. Letter
Book.*

[4] Essex to the Com. of B. K., Oct. 5. *Com. Letter Book.*

day they enclosed an order to him from the House of Commons to march 'forthwith westward with all' his 'forces.' Manchester

Oct. 8.

Oct. 9.
He refuses to go to Waller's help.

had made up his mind to have nothing to do with so distant an advance. He replied, with scant respect to the Commons, that he had frequently received orders from them to march westward, but that they had never designated any place to which he was to march. He had often been ordered by the Committee to go with his infantry to Newbury. They were ready to set off at a moment's notice, on the understanding that they were there to meet the army of Essex and the City trained bands. He had ordered some of his horse, which was lying at Hungerford, to proceed to Salisbury to support Waller.[1] This was hardly the obedience which the Committee required. Yet Manchester's officers, who witnessed his petulant outbursts of temper, may well have doubted whether even this modified

Manchester's talk.

obedience would be rendered. " I would venture cashiering rather," he had said when he reported in the dining-room the orders which he had received to march to the West ; " still, they would have me march Westward and Westward Ho, but they specify no place. It may be to the West Indies or to St. Michael's Mount." Colonel Rich, who was present, enquired whether they were to take up their winter quarters at Newbury. " No," replied Manchester, with dull jocularity, " if we do, I will give them leave to new bury me."[2]

No doubt, in refusing to advance to the aid of Waller, and in resolving to make a junction with Essex his first considera-

How far was his hesitation justified?

tion, Manchester may have been arguing justly. His army was weak in foot, and there would probably have been some risk in his pushing on unaided. It was his entire refusal to take into consideration the interests at

---

[1] The Com. of B. K. to Manchester, Oct. 7, 8. Manchester to the Com. of B. K., Oct. 9. *Quarrel of Manchester and Cromwell*, 39, 40, 41.

[2] Hammond's deposition. Rich's deposition. *S. P. Dom.* diii. 56, xv., xviii.

stake, or to think of the mischief which would ensue if Charles were allowed to regain his circle of fortresses round Oxford, which stamped him as the incapable commander that he was. No wonder his officers, eager for the fight, were convinced that he was in reality a traitor to the cause which they at least, with all their hearts had espoused.

CHAPTER XXI.

THE SECOND BATTLE OF NEWBURY AND THE RELIEF OF DONNINGTON CASTLE.

THE approaching junction of Essex and Manchester seemed to make it imperative upon the Committee of Both Kingdoms to appoint a commander of the united armies. Yet on October 14 they resolved to evade the difficulty. The command was as it were to be placed in commission. There was to be a council composed of Essex, Manchester, Waller, and several of the principal officers, together with two civilian members of the Committee—Johnston of Warriston and Crew—who were to accompany the army in the field. No military operation was to be undertaken except by the vote of the majority of the Council, and no such vote was to be valid unless the two civilians were present. When a decision had been thus arrived at Essex was to have the credit of announcing it to the army.[1]

1644.
Oct. 14.
The command to be put in commission.

Waller's retreat from his exposed position at Shaftesbury had by this time become inevitable. On the 8th, when Charles, urged by Goring to strike a blow whilst his enemies were still divided, had broken up from Sherborne, Waller fell back before him, and on the 15th, when the King entered Salisbury, took up his quarters at Andover.[2] Hope of support from Manchester there was none, as Manchester was preparing to move in the direction of Basingstoke, where he had arranged to meet

Oct. 8.
Waller falls back before the King's advance.

Oct. 15.
The King at Salisbury.

[1] Instructions for the Lord General's army, Oct. 14. *Com. of B. K. Day Book.*

[2] *Walker*, 165. Waller and Hazlerigg to the Com. of B. K. *Com. Letter Book.*

Essex, who expected to be able to leave Portsmouth on the

Oct. 17.
Manchester
at Basing-
stoke.

16th. Manchester, in fact, reached Basingstoke on the 17th, and was quickly followed by four out of the five City regiments under the command of Sir James Harrington.[1]

In the meantime Charles was preparing to strike a blow at Waller. Through the mismanagement of Prince Maurice the

Oct. 18.
The King
attempts to
surprise
Waller.

Oct. 19.
Waller joins
Manchester.

design failed, and Waller, having succeeded, on the 18th, in making his escape from Andover, joined Manchester on the following day.[2] Not only had Manchester, by refusing to advance, allowed Charles to take up a stronger position than he would have been able to do farther westwards, but he had made it well-nigh impossible to carry to a successful end at least two of the three sieges which had been undertaken by the Parliamentary forces. Basing House indeed was still covered, but the sieges of Banbury and Donnington Castle could hardly be continued if Charles was master of the field in Oxfordshire. One indeed of Charles's objects was already attained. Don-

Oct. 18.
The siege of
Donnington
Castle aban-
doned.

nington Castle had been closely begirt for nearly three weeks. The means of resistance at the disposal of the Governor, Colonel Boys, were slight, but he had made up for all defects by his vigour and resource, and on the 18th the besiegers were frightened away

Need of Ba-
sing House.

by the King's presence at Salisbury.[3] The condition of Basing House cried aloud for succour. A

Oct. 20.
Charles at
Whitchurch.

small supply had been thrown into it by Colonel Gage from Oxford on September 9, but it was now again in distress. On the 20th, therefore, Charles arrived at Whitchurch, hoping to break up the siege. He was too late. On the morning of the 21st Essex and Manchester

[1] Manchester to the Com. of B. K., Oct. 19. *Quarrel of Manchester and Cromwell*, 47.

[2] Waller and Hazlerigg to the Com. of B. K., Oct. 19. *Com. Letter Book.*

[3] *Walker*, 107. I suspect that Walker is mistaken in thinking that Manchester was before Donnington in person on Oct. 9. He wrote a letter on that day from Reading, in which he says nothing about going.

effected their junction at Basing.[1] Together with Waller's

Oct. 21.
Junction of
Essex and
Manchester.

force and the City regiments, the united army was about 19,000 strong,[2] whilst the King, at the outside, could not number more than 10,000.

Finding the relief of Basing House for the present impracticable, the King drew off to Newbury, sending Northampton

Oct. 22.
Charles at
Newbury.

Oct. 25.
Banbury
relieved.

to drive off the besiegers from Banbury with the help of Gage and a party from Oxford—a commission which was successfully executed on the 25th. Charles himself entered Newbury with the intention of keeping on the defensive, and wearing out his

enemies by exposure to the miseries of a winter campaign if they ventured to attack him; but the Parliamentary army did not therefore come under Manchester's control.

Essex fell ill, and was of necessity left behind at Reading.[3] The Council of War, into whose hands authority had been

Illness of
Essex.

The Parliamentary
commanders
resolve to
fight.

News from
Lincolnshire.

placed, resolved to fight the King wherever he was to be found. As the troops marched westwards along the valley of the Kennet, they were gladdened by favourable news from other scenes of warfare. The ravages of the Newark garrison had been checked in Lincolnshire, and Crowland, which had again been seized by a party of Royalists, was now blocked up.[4] There was therefore no longer any-

thing to make Manchester anxious to fly to the succour of his Association. On the 25th, as the regiments were tramping

Oct. 19.
Newcastle
taken.

across Bucklebury Heath they were overtaken by a horseman, who brought news that on the 19th Newcastle had surrendered to the Scots. In an instant large

[1] Waller to the Com. of B. K., Oct. 20. Johnston and Crew to the Com. of B. K., Oct. 20, 21. *Com. Letter Book.*

[2] I take this number from Cromwell's narrative. *Quarrel of Manchester and Cromwell,* 85. *The True Informer* gives 18,000 or 19,000 for the Parliamentarians. This is borne out by Hammond's deposition (*S. P. Dom.* diii. 56, xv.), who counts Manchester and Waller, apparently before the junction with Essex, at 14,000.

[3] Johnston and Crew to the Com. of B. K., Oct. 25. *Com. Letter Book.*

[4] *The London Post.* E. 13, 18.

numbers of the soldiers fell upon their knees to give thanks
to God for the happy tidings.[1] Soon after Thatcham was
passed, they began to meet with resistance from the enemy,

Oct. 26.
The Par-
liamentary
army on
Clay Hill.

but no serious opposition was offered, and on the
morning of the 26th the Parliamentary army established itself on Clay Hill, to the north of the
Kennet, from which a full view of the Royalist position was to be obtained.

That position was a formidable one. A considerable force
was massed on the north side of the Kennet, between that

The Royal-
ist position.

river and the stream of the Lamborne, which flowed
from the north-west and joined the Kennet a little
to the eastward of the King's lines, offering a considerable
obstacle in the way of an attack from the north or east.
Beyond the Lamborne, on the north bank, was a mansion
known as Shaw House, and this, together with an entrenched
building and some cottages hard by, was occupied as an advanced post in front of the line. About a mile to the rear of
the Royalist left, but on high ground in a commanding position
on the north bank of the Lamborne, rose the towers of Donnington Castle. From that spot the ground sloped steeply
down to two open fields, known as Shaw Field and Newbury
Field, in which, to the north of Newbury itself, was quartered
the King's life-guard together with a strong body of horse,
under Sir Humphrey Bennet, behind the King's chief line of
defence. Further in the rear, at Speen, was Prince Maurice, a
detachment of whose force was established on the hill which
rose behind the village.[2]

As the Parliamentary commanders reconnoitred this position they rapidly came to the conclusion that it was useless to
attempt it in front. It was soon resolved to detach a portion

[1] Johnston and Crew to the Com. of B. K., Oct. 26. *Com. Letter
Book.* This castle at Newcastle did not surrender till the 21st. *Rushw.*
v. 650.

[2] The topographical details have been well given in Money's *Two
Battles of Newbury*, 151 ; but, relying on evidence which he has not seen,
I have drawn the line of the flank march as reaching Wickham Heath
before turning eastwards.

of the army, under Balfour and Skippon,[1] to whom were at-

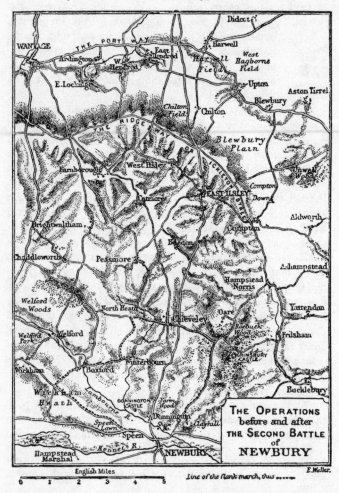

THE OPERATIONS
before and after
THE SECOND BATTLE
of
NEWBURY

English Miles

Line of the flank march, thus ......

E. Weller.

tached Waller and Cromwell—the most adventurous of the

Balfour and Skippon are named in the depositions as the commanders; I suppose because they represented the army of the absent
Lord General.

leaders—to pass round Donnington Castle, and to fall on the
rear of Prince Maurice at Speen. As soon as their
guns were heard Manchester was to attack Shaw
House, hoping that the distraction of the enemy would render
his task the easier.

A flank
march.

The troops told off for the flank march bivouacked on the
night of the 26th at North Heath, out of the reach of the guns
of the castle. Early in the morning of the 27th
Manchester delivered a false attack, to divert the
attention of the Royalists. The officer in charge of
the assailing column, however, pushed on further than had
been intended, and was roughly handled before he got clear.[1]

Oct. 27.
A false
attack by
Manchester.

In the King's quarters the tactics of the enemy were
thoroughly understood. Maurice was directed to face westwards at Speen, and to prepare to meet an attack
from that side. In a letter to Rupert, who had engaged to set out from Bristol on the 29th, and to
bring with him some 3,000 men,[2] Digby, writing after the
repulse of Manchester's attack, was full of confidence that if
Waller and Skippon attempted to storm the King's position
they would fail no less completely. If, on the other hand,
their intention was to blockade the King, their provisions
would fail them, and their men, lying unsheltered in the fields
so late in the year,[3] would be exposed to every hardship. "If
they remove," he continued, "we shall be able to move towards Oxford or Wallingford, which, if we can once gain, we
are then sure to join with you without impediment, and to get
very much the start of them through Buckinghamshire, towards the further object [4] which you propose in the Associated
Counties." [5]

Confidence
cf the
Royalists.

[1] *Walker*, 111.

[2] Rupert to Digby, Oct. 24. *Add. MSS.* 18,981, fol. 316. The date
is taken from Digby's answer.

[3] Oct. 27 is Nov. 6 according to the proper reckoning.

[4] The word 'object' is inserted by conjecture.

[5] Digby to Rupert, Oct. 27. *Add. MSS.* 18,981, fol. 312. The
ciphered part of the letter is omitted as unintelligible in Warburton's
Rupert, but it is easily read with the help of other deciphered letters in
the same volume.

If only Maurice could succeed in holding the high ground above Speen, the year might end with something like a triumph for Charles. All that morning Maurice was hard at work throwing up entrenchments on Speen Hill and placing behind them five guns, with which he hoped to master any attack that could be made on him.

Defensive works thrown up above Speen.

Maurice's preparations were not entirely finished when, about two in the afternoon, Balfour and Skippon arrived on Wickham Heath, at a point about half a mile from the Royalist position on Speen Hill. After leaving the heath they had for the next quarter of a mile to pick their way carefully through lanes and across hedges. When, at last, they came in sight of the enemy, the strength of his position became evident. The road towards it lay through a long narrow strip of open ground commanded by Maurice's guns, on either side of which the country was so cut up by hedges as to render it very difficult for the cavalry, in which arm the Parliamentary army was especially strong, to operate with any prospect of success. In spite of all obstacles, however, the assailants pushed steadily on. About a quarter-past three there was a forward rush.[1] After a sharp fight the breastwork was carried,

The opening of the battle.

---

[1] Waller in his letter in D'Ewes's Diary (*Harl. MSS.* 166, fol. 139) says that "after arriving on the heath, about a mile and a half from Newbury, at two, we fell into lanes and hedges, and marched not above one quarter of a mile before we came in sight of the enemy. . . . Upon our approach their cannon played hard upon us. The place being a narrow heath gave not leave to bring up our body. The hedges hindered our horse very much. Their cannon made our ground very hot. There was no way left but to fall on with horse and foot, and that without delay, which put in execution—the sun not being an hour high—his Excellency's foot . . . went on undauntedly." Oct. 27, the day of the battle, was equivalent to Nov. 6 in our calendar, when the sun sets at 4.23, so that Waller gives the time of this final attack at about 3.23. The depositions vary in their account of the time of attack from Hooper's statement that it was about two hours before sunset—*i.e.* 2.23—to Weaver's and Rawlins's, that it was about one hour, or 3.23. In the first place, timing an occurrence by the number of hours before sunset is necessarily vague, and, in the second place, it is probable that the various witnesses were not speaking of the same occurrence. Hooper, who seems to have been with Balfour and Skippon, may have meant that at 2.23 they came in sight

and Essex's old soldiers, recognising the guns which they had lost in Cornwall, 'clapped their hats on the touchholes on them to claim them as their own.'[1]   To the Cornish soldiers

Maurice's position stormed.

Speen taken.

who guarded them, remembering their own ill-treatment after the surrender at Lostwithiel, they showed scant mercy as they dashed down the hill, and drove the enemy out of Speen village, where four more guns fell into the hands of the victors. By the time the task was accomplished it was near upon four o'clock, and in another quarter of an hour the sun would be sinking below the horizon.[2]

All this while Manchester had made no sign, and Balfour and Skippon had been left to carry Speen Hill and Speen itself

Manchester inactive.

unaided. It is not likely that the Earl deliberately intended to betray his comrades, but he had no heart in the battle, and with timid indecision he feared to run a risk which might prove disastrous. As he often acknowledged, he was a civilian, not a soldier, and he was not, as Cromwell had been two years before, a civilian with the making of a soldier in him. In vain his own officers urged him to attack. Crawford was no friend of Cromwell's, but he was too good a soldier not to fret under the delay, and he too pressed Manchester in vain for permission to execute the movement which he had been told off to perform.[3]

of the enemy and were first under fire, which would pretty well agree with Waller's statement; whilst Weaver and Rawlins, who were on Manchester's side, would refer to the actual storming of the works, in which respect they agree with Waller as to the moment being an hour before sunset, or 3.23. Watson speaks of the attack as having been at an hour and a half before sunset, or 2.53; and Norton, who, as well as Watson, was with the eastern division of the army, saw great guns firing about 3. Such a difference is easily explicable as referring to a different stage of the proceedings. Symonds (*Diary*, 145) says that the Parliamentary troops approached about 3.

[1] *Ludlow*, i. 130.

[2] Symonds in his *Diary* (p. 145) says that at four the Parliamentarians were 'at the bottom of the hill near the church called ——' The editor fills the blank with 'Shaw,' but obviously Speen is meant.

[3] Cromwell's statement about Manchester's delay 'till almost half an hour after sunset' (*Quarrel of Manchester and Cromwell*, 86) has hitherto been treated with contempt. It is strongly supported by the depositions.

The troops which had carried Speen were thus left for the time unsupported. About a quarter of a mile of hedgerows still separated them from the open Newbury Field where the King's cavalry was posted, and if only their own horse could reach this point they might hope even yet to win the day, in spite of the sluggishness of their comrades. On the right Balfour, pushing on by the side of the marshy ground along the Kennet, almost reached the object of his desires, but just as he was at the last hedge an opportune charge delivered by Sir John Cansfield and Sir Humphrey Bennet drove him back in disorder. On the left Cromwell was even less successful.[1] On that side of the

The struggle for Newbury Field.

Captain Rawlins, who was with Manchester, says that 'he heard Major-General Crawford and the Scoutmaster General'—*i.e.* Watson—'earnestly to press the Earl of Manchester that, as those forces were now engaged in fight with the enemy on Speen side, so that his Lordship would fall on this side likewise ; and with that Major [General] Crawford did afterwards come again to persuade the Earl of Manchester to give him leave to fall on ; and the same day, about a little after sunset'—*i.e.* after 4.23, being not far from the time given by Cromwell—'Major-General Crawford being ready to engage with the enemy, the Earl of Manchester sent this examinate unto him to countermand his falling on the enemy.' Watson says that Manchester fell on about a quarter of an hour after sunset - *i.e.* 4.38. Watson had urged him to advance earlier, but he had replied 'that it would be time enough,' and had done nothing till the Speen forces had beaten the enemy. Further, the same witness 'saith that as the soldiers of the Earl of Manchester were drawn out, and ready to fall on upon the enemy, being then when the enemy was routed on Speen, and a little after sunset the Earl sent this examinate to Major-General Crawford to charge him that the Major-General should not fall on or now engage the regiments.' Crawford, a most unwilling witness against Manchester, practically corroborates this evidence. "So," he says, "that time the Earl of Manchester did continue in his very great toiling to prepare the falling upon the enemy in and near Dolman's House"—*i.e.* Shaw House—"and about 500 commanded musketeers, commanded for the falling on, first as forlorn hope, which, to the amazement of the enemy, were several times drawn on and off, and at last they fell on, seconded by the several brigades of foot." *Quarrel of Manchester and Cromwell,* 65.

[1] The assertions of Manchester and Ash that Cromwell did nothing of importance is borne out by Waller's silence, and is sufficiently accounted for by the position in which he was. No doubt he did his best in the

battle the Royalist Earl of Cleveland, mindful of the renown which he had gained at Cropredy Bridge, dashed forward into the very thick of the hostile ranks, and was led off the field as a prisoner. Such a success, however, could not enable Cromwell to renew the glories of Marston Moor amidst hedges lined with musketeers, especially as the part of the field in which he fought was commanded by the guns of Donnington Castle. It was for Skippon's foot to make their way across the obstacles before them. Slowly but resolutely they were accomplishing their task, yet when the sun had set the last hedge was still before them. An attempt was made to prolong the struggle by the faint beams of a moon still in its first quarter,[1] but the uncertainty of the light favoured the defence, and no further ground was gained from the Royalists.

Only during the last moments of the struggle did Manchester overcome his irresolution and give orders for the attack. The assault was carried out with intrepidity,[2] but Shaw House was too well fortified and too well defended to be carried by storm after sunset. Manchester's attempt was hopelessly repulsed. It may be, as some thought, that at this crisis of the battle it was a mistake to attack Shaw House at all. An hour before, when Skippon's

Manches-
ter's attack.

original attack, and is mentioned by Johnston and Crew amongst a number of others who 'did very good service.' Johnston and Crew to the Com. of B. K., Oct. 28. *Quarrel of Manchester and Cromwell,* 50.

[1] Mr. Hind informs a friend through whom I consulted him that on the day of the battle 'the moon was on the meridian at Newbury at 5h. 19m. P.M. at an altitude of 22°, and set at 10h. 1m., Newbury mean time.' We have to reconcile with this (1) the evidence that fighting continued by moonlight after the sun had set, and (2) the general consensus of authorities that the fighting was stopped by darkness long before 10 P.M. The moon had not quite completed its first quarter, so that in any case its light cannot have been very great, but the safest explanation of the darkness seems to be the coming up of clouds.

[2] Waller, who was not prejudiced in Manchester's favour, says that 'the Earl of Manchester fell on for the gaining of his passage, but it proved (answerable to our thoughts) very difficult. We hear great commendations of the gallantry of his foot. The enemy's works were well fortified, and Mr. Dolman's house,' *i.e.* Shaw House, 'was to him instead of a castle.'

men were crowning Speen Hill, an assault upon so vital a point might have served, according to the original design, to distract the attention of the enemy. Now that the enemy was being pushed back, the true course would perhaps have been to leave Shaw House alone, and to have poured in through the gap between that building and the village of Donnington, so as to fall on the rear of the King's defeated army.[1] Incapable as Manchester had been even of fulfilling the engagement which he had deliberately undertaken, it was hopeless to look to him for one of those sudden strokes of genius which mark a great commander.[2]

In spite of Manchester's incapacity Charles's position would indeed have been perilous if he had remained to tempt a renewal of the conflict when morning dawned. Hastily giving orders to withdraw the army during the night, he set off with three hundred horse for Bath to hasten Rupert's reinforcements. His stores, his ammunition, and his heavy guns he left at Donnington Castle. As soon as the moon had sunk below the horizon the whole army marched silently off in the direction of Wallingford, and when morning dawned it was beyond the reach of serious pursuit.

The King's army withdrawn.

With the dawn the Parliamentary commanders discovered that they were no longer in presence of the enemy. The greater part of the blame for permitting the King's escape justly fell upon Manchester, as it was far easier for him to ascertain even in the dark that a whole army was defiling past his position, than for Skippon and Balfour to discover that the same army was marching away from the front of theirs.[3] Yet, after all, the fault lay more with the Committee of Both Kingdoms than with any of the Generals. No one feels responsibility like a commander-in-chief, and the Committee had

---

[1] This was Captain Hooper's opinion, as given in his deposition (*S.P. Dom.* diii. 56, v.), and it is hinted at by other witnesses.

[2] For the Royalist account of the battle see *Mercurius Aulicus.* E. 18, 11.

[3] At Lansdown, for instance, Waller got away from Hopton without being detected.

taken good care that there should be no commander-in-chief at Newbury.[1]

When at last the escape of the enemy was known, Waller, with the greater part of the cavalry, hurried in pursuit. Twice

Oct. 29.
Pursuit of the cavalry.
during his march he received messages from Manchester urging him to return to take part in the council of war, but it was not till he and his fellow-commanders had reached Blewbury—a village lying at the foot of the northern slope of the downs which separate the valleys

The halt at Blewbury.
of the Thames and the Kennet—that they consented to draw rein. The Royal army, they there learnt, had passed the river in front of them at Wallingford, and, desirous as they were of advancing by way of Abingdon in pursuit, they could hardly expect to push on amongst the lanes and hedges on that route without the support of infantry. Waller and Cromwell, therefore, leaving their men behind, rode back to Newbury to urge Manchester to join them with all his foot in the pursuit of the flying enemy, or at least to allow a select body of 3,000 men to cross the Thames together with the horse, in order that, by establishing themselves round Burford and Woodstock, they might hinder Rupert from effect-

A council of war.
ing a junction with the army at Oxford. In the Council of War which was held to debate this proposal, Waller declared for a still bolder step. Let them follow the King and fight him after his junction with Rupert in the neighbourhood of Bath, or occupy the fertile ground of the valley of the Avon if he refused to fight. Manchester, perhaps not unnaturally, shrank from so hazardous an enterprise, and the majority of the officers present took his side. A convoy of provisions which was necessary for the army had not yet arrived. There had already been frequent desertions, and, if the soldiers were to be exposed to the hardships of a winter campaign, there would certainly be many more. The commanders who voted with Manchester probably thought that

---

[1] Ash's *True relation.* E. 22, 10. Cromwell's narrative. *Quarrel of Manchester and Cromwell*, 87. Waller and Hazlerigg to the Com. of B. K., Oct. 30. *Com. Letter Book.* Depositions of Hazlerigg and Waller. *S. P. Dom.* diii. 56, xix. xx.

the military reasons were sufficient for delay, but Manchester himself was one of those who wear their heart upon their sleeve, and he roused suspicion by his reply to some words which dropped from Hazlerigg. "Thou art a bloody fellow," he said. "God send us peace, for God does never prosper us in our victories to make them clear victories." It must have been impossible for some of those who heard the words to avoid asking themselves whether Manchester himself might not have been to some extent the cause of the failures which he thus piously ascribed to Divine Providence.[1]

On both sides there was a feeling that a long continuation of the war would be intolerable. Manchester could not bear to risk its prolongation by decisive action. The commanders who opposed him were as anxious to secure an early peace as he was, though they differed from him as to the means by which it was to be obtained. "We feel the season of the year," wrote Waller ; " we see the soldiers' wants and sufferings; yet our sensibleness of the desolation and utter ruin which falls upon all sorts of people where armies come makes us more earnestly desire to end the war than to enjoy our own ease."[2]

It seemed safer to Manchester to summon Donnington Castle than to pursue the King. The Governor, now Sir John Boys, was told that if he did not give up the fortress the besiegers would so destroy it as not to leave one stone on another. "If you do," was the sturdy answer, "I am not bound to repair it." A weak attempt to storm the place was repulsed, and Manchester, all too late, came round to the opinion of Cromwell and Waller. On November 2 he marched to Blewbury with the intention of making his way to Woodstock. As usual he was in no hurry. It took him two days to cover eleven miles. On the evening of the 3rd the inevitable council

Oct. 31.
Donnington
Castle summoned.

Nov. 2.
Manchester
leaves Newbury.

---

[1] Ash's *True relation.* E. 22, 10. Cromwell's narrative. *Quarrel of Manchester and Cromwell,* 87. Waller and Hazlerigg to the Com. of B. K., Oct. 30. *Com. Letter Book.* Depositions of Hazlerigg, Waller, Harrington, and Jones. *S. P. Dom.* diii. 56, ix. xix. xx. xxiv. xxv.

[2] Waller and Hazlerigg to the Com. of B. K., Oct. 30. *Com. Letter Book.*

of war was held at Harwell, not far from Blewbury. Though there were some who wished the greater part of the army

A council of war at Harwell. to push on and to occupy the Thames valley in order to cover the siege of Donnington Castle by troops left behind for the purpose, more hesitating councils prevailed, and it was perhaps in consequence of a threat from Manchester to return to the Eastern Association that even Cromwell agreed to a proposal to keep the army together in a retreat upon Newbury. Possibly Cromwell approved of this course as the lesser of two evils, unless, indeed, he did no more than express his formal concurrence with the vote of the majority.[1] At all events it was resolved that the army should remain in its position till Johnston and Crew had visited Westminster to lay the state of affairs before the Committee of which they were members. When, however, on November 6, orders arrived for the army to return to Newbury in pursuance of the vote of the council of war, the hardier project of interposing between the two divisions of the Royal army was no longer practicable, and the retreat was at once commenced.

[1] There is no doubt a discrepancy between Cromwell's statement (*Quarrel of Manchester and Cromwell*, 89) that 'all were against drawing back to Newbury save his Lordship only,' and a letter to the commanders (*ibid.* 52) in which the Committee of Both Kingdoms write that they understood 'by my Lord Warriston and Mr. Crew that it was the unanimous opinion of a council of war that the carriages necessary for the army cannot pass to Abingdon, and that the forces should continue united at Newbury and thereabouts till the King's army went into winter quarters.' This, it will be seen, lays stress on the armies continuing united, and Watson, in his deposition, says that about this time Manchester declared that 'if the Committee of the Association at London would call him back he would return, although he should receive a command to the contrary from the Committee of Both Kingdoms.' On the other hand, some members of the deciding body may, as I have suggested above, have been influenced by motives other than purely strategical ones, and have voted against their private opinions in order to secure Manchester's co-operation. It was not a General's council of war, but a council of Generals, and it may have been understood—as was the case, for instance, in the Privy Council—that the opinion of the majority should be regarded as unanimously adopted. For Manchester's case see Ash's *True relation*, E. 22, 10.

Charles, it was now known, had reached Oxford on the 1st, and Rupert, accompanied by Sir Charles Gerard and Sir Marmaduke Langdale, had brought with him from the West upwards of 5,000 men to swell the numbers of his uncle's main army.[1]

On November 6, the day of Manchester's retreat, Charles declared his nephew, at a general rendezvous on Bullingdon Green, General of all the Royal forces.[2] The old Lord Brentford, scouted by all, was no longer to employ his skill and experience in the service of the master whom, if results prove anything, he had saved from many a danger. For the time the new General seemed resolved to prove that he was not liable to the charge of rashness.

Nov. 6.
Rupert declared General.

On the 7th Charles and Rupert set out to relieve Donnington Castle. Manchester, who had foreseen nothing and provided for nothing when it was in his power to do so, now ordered Cromwell to advance with his horse to check the enemy's march. Cromwell, who would gladly have descended with the whole army into the valley of the Thames three days before, recoiled from a plan which it was now impossible to execute. " My Lord," he said bitterly, " your horse are so spent, so harassed out by hard duty, that they will fall down under their riders if you thus command them ; you may have their skins, but you can have no service."[3]

Nov. 7.
The King's march.

Everything was now making for Charles. Marching at the head of 11,000 men, he reached Donnington Castle on the morning of the 9th. Whilst provisions were being thrown into the fortress and the artillery, which had been left behind after the battle, was being removed, the King drew up his army on that very Newbury Field over which Cansfield and Bennet had charged at the crisis of the action. This time, a party of infantry having been left to guard Newbury, the bulk of the

Nov. 9.
Donnington Castle relieved.

The King's army in Newbury Field.

---

[1] *Walker,* 116.

[2] Diary of Rupert's marches. *Clarendon MSS.* 2,254.

[3] Ash, who reports this (*True relation,* E. 22, 10), heard the words spoken.

Parliamentary foot was drawn up behind a hedge to the west of Shaw House, facing westwards. Cromwell, with the greater part of the horse, was on Newbury Wash, on the south side of the Kennet and the town, waiting for the decision of the commanders whether the offered battle should be accepted or not.

The decision was perhaps necessarily adverse. The field chosen by the King was even more directly under the fire of the castle than the position which had been occupied by him in the previous battle. What decided the question with most who were present was the fear lest, if their whole army were drawn out to the north of the Kennet, the King might slip past them and possess himself of Newbury. The horse, too, had been scattered for the sake of forage, and it was only late in the day that Cromwell was able to bring it across the Kennet.[1] Yet, though a resolution was taken not to fight on that day, it was thought that an opportunity for a battle would offer itself when the King moved off on the following morning.[2]

The Parliamentary Generals resolve not to fight.

The 9th, therefore, passed away without any further incident, except the repulse of a rash attempt to carry the Parliamentary position by a charge of cavalry. When in the morning the King's retreat began there was the usual indecision at the Parliamentary headquarters. At last, about eleven o'clock, news arrived that Charles had halted on Winterbourn Heath, about two miles beyond Donnington Castle. Once more a council of war was held in a small house on Shaw Field. Not only was the risk of allowing the King to possess himself of Newbury still present to the commanders, but the low physical condition of the soldiers and their rapid diminution in numbers was a matter of common notoriety. Hazlerigg, who had attached himself to the party of action, now made

Nov. 10. The King's retreat.

A council of war on Shaw Field.

Hazlerigg declares against fighting.

[1] This was made an object of accusation against Cromwell, but the cause of his delay is explained in Skippon's letter to Essex of Nov. 10. *Rushw.* v. 730.

[2] Manchester, Waller, and Balfour to the Com. of B. K., Nov. 9. *Quarrel of Manchester and Cromwell,* 55. Depositions of Hazlerigg and Ireton. *S. P. Dom.* diii. 56, xix. xxii.

himself the spokesman of those who were on the side of caution. The Parliamentary horse, he said, was weak – no more than 4,500 strong now.[1] The King's army was evidently better than theirs. If they beat the King he would still be king, and they would be unable to overpower his garrisons. If the King beat them he would overrun the whole country up to the gates of London, and there would be nothing to stand against him south of Leven's army at Newcastle. It would therefore be best to draw back into Newbury to wait for better times.[2]

Hazlerigg was succeeded by Cromwell. No one knew better than Manchester's Lieutenant-General the deplorable

Cromwell's speech.

condition to which the Parliamentary army had been reduced in a single month, and it may be that in the course of his speech he acknowledged the difficulties of the task which the army was now called upon to accomplish with very insufficient means. Yet in the end he seems to have spoken strongly on the importance of fighting at all hazards. Rumours were abroad that a French army was to land in the

Altercation between Manchester and Cromwell.

spring to fight on Charles's side, and Cromwell argued that to beat the King now would be the surest way of hindering a French invasion.[3] Manchester, who was better informed on the state of Charles's French negotiations, replied that the danger did not

---

[1] That is to say that 3,500 had disappeared since the army started from Basing. Skippon says that in the force of the Lord General there was now only 800 horse and 1,200 foot, showing a loss of 1,000 or 2,000, according as Essex's force is taken at 3,000 or 4,000 at Basing. Skippon to Essex, Nov. 12. *Rushw.* v. 733.

[2] Crawford's assignment of this speech to Hazlerigg (*Quarrel of Manchester and Cromwell*, 68) is corroborated by Manchester. *Rushw.* v. 735. Crawford might retail gossip, but, in the face of an impending Parliamentary inquiry, it is unlikely that he and Manchester would have made Hazlerigg talk in this fashion if he had not done so.

[3] The last argument is given by Cromwell himself (Money's *Battles of Newbury*, 191), and confirmed by other depositions. Yet Crawford says that 'Cromwell, presently speaking, did in these very words'—*i.e.* in those of Hazlerigg—'make a speech very near a quarter of an hour long; so that, all joining, did presently order the foot to Newbury.' Manchester says (*Rushw.* v. 735) that 'there was not one present that delivered his

exist.[1] Cromwell having expressed surprise at the denial, Manchester took higher ground. Catching at the argument which Hazlerigg had already used, he expressed his opinion that a prolongation of the war was useless. "If we beat the King ninety and nine times," he said, "yet he is king still, and so will his posterity be after him; but if the King beat us once we shall be all hanged, and our posterity made slaves."[2] "My Lord," replied Cromwell, "if this be so, why did we take up arms at first? This is against fighting ever hereafter. If so, let us make peace, be it never so base."[3]

For the first time, except in private talk, that feeling against the war in general which underlay all Manchester's military hesitations flashed into light. Hitherto he had persuaded himself that, in spite of his dislike of the war, he had but argued on purely military grounds against each particular action as it arose; and that, at all events, he had resolutely determined to conform to the decision of the council of war, whatever it might be.[4]

Vexed as Cromwell was, he was not bereft of his usual power of recognising the whole of the actual situation. The

---

opinion for fighting with the King at that time.' The suggestion above that Cromwell recognised the difficulty of fighting would account for the divergent accounts of his speech.

[1] There were two ways in which Manchester may have known this. When he was near Basing House he had a long conversation with Sabran (Sabran to Brienne, $\frac{\text{Oct. 24}}{\text{Nov. 3}}$, *Harl. MSS.* 5,460, fol. 325b). Again, the letter in which Charles informed his wife of his disappointment (see p. 39) was intercepted. It is now in the Record Office (*S. P. Dom.* diii. 29), and is indorsed with a statement that it was read on Nov. 1. This probably means that it was read in the Com. of B. K., and if so its purport may have been communicated to Manchester by a fellow-member of the Committee.

[2] "These are the very words, as this examinate remembereth.' Hazlerigg's deposition. *S. P. Dom.* diii. 56, ix.

[3] *Ibid.*

[4] "In all precedent councils," said Ireton (Deposition, *S. P. Dom.* D iii. 56, xxii.), "where the examinate was present, his Lordship did never, to the examinate's remembrance, make the question in general whether we should fight if we might; but that being always supposed, as he under-

Committee of Both Kingdoms had been listening to the rumours in London, which assigned the late disasters to

Nov. 12.
Manchester
to conform
to the advice
of the coun-
cil of war. Manchester's wilfulness and neglect of advice. They therefore, in ignorance of the support which he had received from the other commanders, reiterated their instructions that nothing should be done except 'by common advice of a council of war.'[1] Manchester was naturally annoyed. "My Lord," Cromwell was afterwards re-

Nov. 13.
Cromwell's
remark. ported to have said, "I hold him for a villain and a knave that would do any man ill offices, but there was nothing done but what was justifiable, and by the joint consent of a council of war."[2]

At this time, indeed, so far as can be gathered from evidence which is both imperfect and conflicting,[3] Cromwell was weighed

Nov. 15.
The de-
spatch of the
Generals. down by a sense of the hopeless disorganisation of the army, even more than he was by his distrust of its principal commander. In a despatch signed by Manchester, Waller, and Balfour, and said to have been drawn up

---

stood, by all, his Lordship at former debates . . . did otherwise put off what tended to our engagement with other pretexts and remote expectances of one opportunity after another."

That the refusal to fight was approved of by the majority of the officers is evident, not only from the despatch of Nov. 10, signed by Manchester, Waller, and Balfour (*Quarrel of Manchester and Cromwell*, 55), but from Waller's words in a despatch signed by himself alone. "The relation of that business from my Lord of Manchester, Sir William Balfour, and myself," he writes, "will, in all likelihood, come to your hands, and I hope give your Lordships satisfaction that we could do no more than we did without a rash and precipitate engagement. . . . The continual duty and service we have been upon hath extremely weakened my troops ; . . . besides, my Lords, we are in such wants as there is a necessity of an instant supply." Waller to the Com. of B. K., Nov. 12. *Com. Letter Book.* On Manchester's desire to take advice, see his defence. *Rushw.* v. 735.

[1] The Com. of B. K. to the Commanders, Nov. 12. *Quarrel of Manchester and Cromwell*, 57.

[2] Crawford's narrative. *Ibid.* 69. If the word 'justifiable' be taken as meaning 'arguable,' there is nothing here that Cromwell may not have said.

[3] Soon after the King's retreat on the 10th the information of Depositions comes to an end.

by Cromwell,[1] the miserable plight of the troops is strongly insisted on. "The army," say the three Generals, "is much

State of the army. weakened both in horse and foot. The horse are very unable for marching or watching, having now for so long time been tired out with hard duty in such extremity of weather as hath been seldom seen; so that if much more be required at their hands you will quickly see your cavalry ruined without fighting. The foot are not in better case, besides the lessening of their numbers through cold and so hard[2] duty. We find sickness to increase so much upon them that we cannot in duty conceal it from you, nor indeed with that Christian consideration which we owe to them, whose extreme sufferings we daily look upon not with a little sorrow, the places we are in not affording firing, food, or covering for them; nor is the condition of the people less to be pitied, who both in our horse and foot quarters are so exhaust that they have so little left for themselves that we may justly fear a famine will fall upon them."[3]

With this misery hourly impressing itself upon him, it is likely enough that Cromwell was, at this time, far less set upon warlike enterprise than he afterwards imagined himself to have been. Five days after this despatch was written it was known that the King was on the move from Marlborough, and it was believed that his object was the relief of Basing House,

Nov. 17. The army leaves Newbury. which was again in distress. The Parliamentary army marched out of Newbury to Kingsclere, intending to meet him there. Manchester, however, deflected the course of his troops in the direction of Alder-

Nov. 18. The army at Mortimer's Heath. maston, from which he marched on the 18th to Mortimer's Heath, with the intention, as he gave out, of making his way to Basing. Basing, however, he never reached. His men were starving, and they ran away

---

[1] This is stated by Crawford, and the sentence about the horse looks very much like an official redaction of Cromwell's statement about having the skins of the horses.

[2] The word 'hard' is not in the MS.

[3] Manchester, Waller, and Balfour to the Com. of B. K., Nov. 15. *Com. Letter Book.*

by scores to Reading, where provisions were to be found in plenty.[1] Reluctantly or otherwise, a council of war came to the conclusion that it was impossible under such circumstances to protect the besiegers of Basing House. The whole army made the best of its way to Reading, and orders were given to abandon the siege. When Sir Henry Gage, who had been recently knighted, was sent by the King to relieve the steadfast garrison of that eastern outpost of his power, he found, on arriving on the ground, that no enemy remained to be over-powered or outmanœuvred.

On November 23 Charles entered Oxford in triumph, safe behind the girdle of fortresses which the efficiency of his army and the bad generalship and the bad management of his opponents had enabled him to retain intact, save where the indomitable Browne still guarded Abing-don. In the North of England indeed the tide of fortune was still setting against him. Liverpool had surrendered to Meldrum on November 1 ; Helmsley had given itself up on the 14th to Fairfax ; whilst Carlisle was so closely besieged by David Leslie, that there was little hope that its resistance would be prolonged for many weeks. Yet Charles may well have thought the recoil of the great army which had set forth against him with high hope, less than two months before, was a sure token that the success for which he had waited so patiently was at last coming within his grasp.

Nov. 23. The King in Oxford.

Affairs in the North.

Hopefulness of the King.

What was, in fact, really wonderful was not that Charles had accomplished so much; but that he had not accomplished more. During the three campaigns over which the war had

---

[1] That there was a great store of provisions in Reading is mentioned in the clauses added on the 18th to a duplicate of the despatch of the Committee of Both Kingdoms to Manchester and the other commanders of the 18th. Its attraction would explain the discrepancy between the statements of Cromwell and his opponents about this march. As a military movement, considered without regard to the fact that soldiers have mouths, it was as absurd as Cromwell said it was ; whilst Cromwell's disinclination at the time to go to the relief of Basing is too strongly testi-fied by Manchester, Crawford, and Ash to be passed over, and is just what might have been expected after the despatch of the 15th.

lasted strategical superiority had been entirely on the King's side. Not only had the movements of the Royalist forces been directed in accordance with a well-conceived plan, but the plan had been varied from time to time as circumstances required. In the first short campaign which ended at Turnham Green, the object of the person, whoever it may have been, who directed the Royal armies was to drive right at the heart of the enemy, and to deal him a mortal wound. When this proved impracticable, recourse was had in that second campaign which opened with the siege of Reading and closed with the battle of Cheriton, to a scheme in accordance with which combat was to be refused in the centre, whilst the two wings in Yorkshire and Cornwall pushed on to smother the weaker enemy between them. After this scheme, too, had been tried in vain, and when the balance of numbers had turned against Charles, the very opposite plan was tried. Abandoning the attempt to act from the circumference upon the centre, Charles resolved to act from the centre upon the circumference. Adopting the principle which was afterwards to be stamped with the mint-mark of Napoleon, he was to fling his forces first upon the Scots and their allies in Yorkshire, and then alternately upon the divided armies of the southern Generals in Oxfordshire and in Cornwall. When this was done he was to regain his position of vantage at Oxford, to wait safely there till the divisions of his adversaries gave him another opportunity.

The strategy of three campaigns.

To ascribe warfare so skilful as this to Charles is to suppose that he possessed a flexibility of mind and a readiness to adjust his actions to circumstances which was altogether foreign to his character. To ascribe it to the fluctuating majority of a council of war is equally impossible, and the silence of contemporaries seems to make it equally impossible to suppose that the Royalist plans were the suggestion of the old General who was honourably dismissed after the retreat from Newbury. The most probable explanation is that the operations which ended at Cheriton were either originally suggested by Rupert or derived by him from a plan sketched out by the Prince of Orange. As has been seen, the new and brilliant strategy of the campaign of 1644 had been

Brentford's place as a commander.

originally suggested by Rupert,[1] and Brentford, at the most deserved the credit of having modified it according to circumstances as they arose, and of carrying it out with the same ability which had marked his conduct of the operations after the relief of Gloucester in the preceding year,[2] and his superiority in the manœuvres which preceded the battle of Cheriton.[3]

Yet even the amount of skill shown by the old Scottish General—considerable as it was—was not likely to make him popular with his English subordinates. Apart from the prejudices of nationality, what they looked for was success, and undoubtedly Brentford had not been successful. It is useless for a General to direct a campaign unless he can fight a battle, and Brentford had none of the fire of battle in him. There was with him no prompt seizing of opportunities, no instantaneous detection of the weak points in the enemy. The dashing officers who served under him came to regard him as one who had no sympathy with a gallant exploit. They chafed under his control, and flung themselves into adventures in disobedience of his orders.[4] In Rupert they found the man after their own heart. Yet already Rupert had given signs of a temper which would be likely to disqualify him for the high post to which he had been raised. He had scarcely occupied it a week when he flung up the commission which he had coveted, because Charles, who had made him General of his army, would not also make him captain of his guard. It is true that his resignation was promptly withdrawn, but a commander-in-chief whose temper was so uncertain could hardly be trusted at a critical moment.[5]

Rupert's want of temper.

It was, however, no mere tactical inferiority which had deprived Charles of the benefit of Brentford's generalship. In

---

[1] See vol. i. p. 351. If this strategy was originally suggested by Rupert to Charles and subsequently accepted by Brentford, it would illustrate Clarendon's statement that Brentford always adopted the King's views.

[2] See vol. i. pp. 206, 207.

[3] See vol. i. p. 321.

[4] His extreme caution at Cheriton is a case in point.

This occurred at Marlborough on Nov. 15. Symond's *Diary*, 152.

the Puritan armies, together with much unpromising material there were men who were better soldiers than any who fought on the Royalist side. The horsemen of the sects who followed

Quaility of the Parliamentary army.

Cromwell at Marston Moor, the London trained bands, against whom the most splendid chivalry of Charles's army dashed in vain on Enborne Heath, the infantry of the old army of Essex who swarmed over Maurice's entrenchments on Speen Hill, could hardly be matched in the ranks of their opponents. Hitherto all their martial qualities had been neutralised by defective organisation. Unless military and financial centralisation could reduce the existing chaos to order, it was hardly likely that even Cromwell, splendid tactician as he was, could convert disaster into success.

CHAPTER XXII.

PRYNNE, MILTON, AND CROMWELL.

THE strife which had broken out in the army on the question of military efficiency was inseparably connected with a conflict of opinion which had long cleft Puritan society asunder. Manchester was the representative not merely of an unadventurous school of commanders, but of an unadventurous school of politicians. In Parliament and Assembly Presbyterianism maintained its ascendency. Yet between the Presbyterianism of England and the Presbyterianism of Scotland there was a great gulf. It is indeed possible to transfer the external institutions of a political or religious system from one nation to another, but it is not possible to transfer the spirit by which that system is animated. England might, if she chose, adopt from Scotland the parity of ministers and the lay elderships, but she would of necessity colour those institutions as soon as they were established with her own national traditions and modes of thought. The historical development of the Scottish nation favoured the predominance of the clergy, whereas the historical development of the English nation favoured the predominance of the laity.

1644.
Manchester and the Presbyterians.

English and Scottish Presbyterianism.

It was therefore from no zeal for Presbyterianism as a divine institution that its English supporters rallied round it. It was to them chiefly an ecclesiastical form of Parliamentarism, in which the Assembly was to work under the control of the Houses, and the parochial clergy were to work under the control of the lay elders.

The name ' Presbyterian,' in short, by fixing attention ex-

clusively upon the ecclesiastical aims of the party which bore
it, has been the source of much unintentional misunderstand-

The English ing. It is beyond dispute that the Presbyterian party
Presbyterian failed in establishing the Church polity which they
party. defended, and it is therefore easy to forget that they
succeeded in inspiring both Church and State with the spirit
which had impelled them temporarily to become the champions
of that polity. When at last the Restoration arrived, it was
parliamentary rather than monarchical, and though the bishops
returned to the sees from which they had been expelled, they
returned practically stripped of that uncontrolled jurisdiction
which had aroused opposition in the days of Laud. To make
King and Church responsible to Parliament was the real aim
of the Presbyterian party, and every year which passed after the
Restoration made it more evident that, for the time at least,
the most substantial gains of the long conflict had fallen to those
who had concentrated their efforts on this object.

It was inevitable that a party thus constituted should be
intensely conservative, for the very reason that up to a certain

Its conserva- point it had been driven to be revolutionary. A task
tism. which can only be accomplished by the energy of a
whole generation unconsciously calls up in those who devote
themselves to it a sullen indifference to changes which seem to
have no relation to the change which they themselves advocate,
even if they do not dread new proposals of reform as distract-
ing attention from the work which appears to them to be the
one thing needful. Of conservatism of this kind Prynne was,
if not the most convincing, at least the most self-sufficient and

1643-44. voluminous champion. During the progress of the
Prynne's Civil strife the stream of his vituperation had never
literary
activity. flagged. In 1643 he had proved, at inordinate
length, that Nathaniel Fiennes was a coward and a traitor;
that Charles had illegally scattered favours amongst disloyal
Papists, and that sovereign power resided in Parliaments.[1]
In the spring and summer of 1644 he was engaged in hunting

---

[1] *The doom of cowardice and treachery,* E. 251, 6; *The Popish Royal
Favourite,* 287, g, 20; *The sovereign power of Parliaments and Kingdoms,*
287, g, 19.

down his former oppressor, Archbishop Laud, but in the
autumn, sniffing a fresh quarry, he flung himself with all his
might into the dispute between the Presbyterians and the
His Presby-   Independents.   The support which he gave to the
terianism.   former party would indeed have given dire offence
to all true disciples of Calvin.   Not only did he refuse to allow
that any ecclesiastical institutions were of divine origin, but he
argued that every nation acting through its Parliament and
Assembly was at liberty to erect, within certain narrow though
not clearly defined limits, whatever kind of Church it pleased.
To this Church all persons were obliged 'in point of conscience
and Christianity to submit.'   Its discipline would no doubt be
exercised, as in Scotland, by Church Courts and Assemblies,
but it would be exercised under the supremacy of the State,
and with safeguards imposed by Parliament against clerical
self-will.   The doctrine that all ecclesiastical jurisdiction must
proceed from the lay State was as firmly grasped by Prynne as
it had been by Henry VIII., or by the framers of the Root and
Branch Bill of 1641.[1]

Against Independents and Sectaries of every kind the
censures of the Church were, according to Prynne, to be freely
Its intoler-   employed.   The congregational system, he held, was
ance.   not merely irrational, but would logically result in
that toleration of all heresies which had been proposed by the
author of *The Bloody Tenent.*   He was not, however, content
with denouncing the results of Independency.   He attacked it
in its substance when he asked triumphantly whether its root
were not 'a pharisaical spiritual pride, vainglorious singularity,
or self-conceitedness of man's own superlative holiness, as they
deem it, which makes them to deem themselves so transcen-
dently holy, sanctified and religious above others, that they
esteem them altogether unworthy of—yea wholly exclude them
from their communion and church society.'[2]

Spiritually, Prynne stood at a far lower level than Roger
Williams.   The claim to think and to feel, not after the fashion

---

[1] *Hist. of Engl.* 1603–1642, ix. 407.

[2] *Twelve considerable serious questions touching Church Government,*
E. 257, 1, p. 7.

of the world, but as each man's brain and heart might dictate to him, was not merely ignored by Prynne—it was treated with contemptuous scorn. For that very reason his doctrine was a great power in the land. It was Prynne's Presbyterianism which was welcome to a world which fancied itself necessarily intelligent because it was educated. It enlisted on the side of the average intellect of the day, which on the one hand dreaded the intolerance which is always latent in fanaticism, and, on the other hand, looked with suspicion on ideas not yet stamped with the mint-mark of custom, the feeling, which unconsciously exists in the majority of mankind, of repugnance against all who aim at higher thinking or purer living than is deemed sufficient by their contemporaries, and who usually, in the opinion of their contemporaries, contrive to miss their aim.

Cause of Prynne's influence.

Prynne found controversialists enough ready to take up his challenge. The only reply which attracts the modern reader is one never intended by its author to be a reply to Prynne's arguments at all. Not any deep interest in the war between the rival forms of church government, but strange domestic experiences of his own, led the poet of *Comus* to stand forward in defence of intellectual liberty.

Prynne and Milton.

In May 1643 Milton visited the home of the Powells, a Royalist family living at Forest Hill, near Oxford, and after a month's stay brought back with him as his bride Mary Powell, a girl of seventeen, his own years numbering thirty-four. The month of courtship was followed by a month of marriage, waxing ever gloomier as the days passed by. The young wife soon discovered that her elderly husband devoted himself during the livelong day to his books and his studies; and that his conversation, when she was admitted to share in it, turned upon subjects which were to her scarcely intelligible. One thing alone was clear to her, that her life's companion held opinions which, so far as she could understand them, resembled those which she had learnt to regard as detestable and profane. The husband, on the other hand, found that the child whom he had wedded had no sympathy with him in his pursuits, no power of encouraging

1643. Milton's marriage.

or cheering him in his appointed task. To both alike the yoke
of matrimony was an intolerable burden. At the end of a

July.
month the young wife asked leave to visit her parents,
and, finding herself once more happy, refused to
return to her tormentor. The husband, even before he was
deserted,[1] had sat down to write a tract on *The doctrine and*

Aug. 1.
Publication
of *The doc-
trine and
discipline of
Divorce.*
discipline of Divorce, in which a noble argument on
behalf of true marriage as an association of soul and
intellect was made to lead up to the conclusion that
it was the just prerogative of every husband to dismiss the wife who failed to answer his craving for mental and
spiritual companionship, though he refused to make any provision for the case of a woman burdened with a boorish or
unsympathising husband.

Those who have conjectured—for nothing but conjecture
is possible—the motive of the poet in making so untoward a

Was Milton
true to him-
self?
selection, have usually been of opinion that he was
thrown off his balance by the bright eyes and grace-
ful figure of the cavalier maiden, and that he thus
became false to that ideal of an inward beauty of soul em-
bodying itself in the outward form which had given inspiration to *Comus*. It may have been so ; but, though Milton's silence is far from being conclusive, there is at least no
hint in all his voluminous writings on the subject of divorce
that he had been ensnared by beauty, or that he considered that
a sober and sedate man was in any danger of being fascinated
by the outward appearance. Even if, as is by no means unlikely, physical beauty revenged itself on its scorner more than
he cared to acknowledge, is it not probable that, in this instance
as in all others, Milton was in the main true to his nature?
May he not have dreamed, as many another sensitive idealist
has dreamed, that it would be well for him to choose some
rustic, uncultured maiden to educate for worthy companionship? Something of this is perhaps implied in the only phrase
in which he ever referred to his own courtship, when he complained that 'the bashful muteness of a virgin may ofttimes

[1] The evidence has been collected and judicially weighed by Prof.
Masson in his *Life of Milton*, ii. 502 ; iii. 42.

hide all the unliveliness and natural sloth which is really unfit for conversation.' As in so much else Milton had set his ideal too high for realisation ; too high, in the first place, because in his day women were never educated to be the intellectual companions of men of independent thought ; too high, in the second place, because he had not learnt to pay due honour to womanhood, or to understand that true companionship can never be had from one who is treated as an inferior, to be moulded and fashioned at the pleasure of a master.

It may be that Milton was not yet prepared to write, as he afterwards wrote upon bitter and diversified experience, the harsh sentence that

> " God's universal law
> Gave to the man despotic power
> Over his female in due awe,
> Nor from that right to part an hour ; "

but, in some modified form, the feeling was with him from the beginning. He had too little dramatic instinct to enter into the secret of a woman's heart, and too great contempt for all that was unlike himself to be happy in his marriage. His noble conception of wifely virtue was unaccompanied by any equally noble conception of manly self-surrender.

That Milton's tract should arouse opposition was unavoidable. Even in an age in which almost every received doctrine

Opposition aroused.

was subjected to question, an attack on the received doctrine on marriage was regarded with unqualified detestation. Milton met the storm which his tract had raised by defiantly re-asserting his opinion. On February 2,

1644. Feb. 2.

July 15. *The judgment of Martin Bucer.*

June. *On education.*

1644, he issued a new and enlarged edition of his pamphlet, and in July he appealed in a new work to the authority of Bucer as justifying the position he had taken up. He had already in the previous month put forth a tract on education, in which there is not the slightest allusion to the education of girls. It is not given to any man, however high-minded and far-sighted, to foresee the whole solution which a future age may apply to a complex difficulty, and if Milton's answer to the eternal problem of the relation between the sexes was a blundering one—only, in truth, less blundering than the answer given by the Cluniac monks of the eleventh century—it was because he had failed to understand the conditions under which his high ideal of marriage as 'the soul's union and commixture of intellectual delights' could be rendered attainable. So far as Milton was not personally at fault, the root of his error, like the root of the error of Hildebrand, lay in the complacency with which he regarded the existing low standard of female education. The women of the seventeenth century were well skilled in all housewifely arts, and were as capable as women of other centuries of patient and self-forgetful heroism ; but, except on the ground of religious consolation, they had very little intellectual companionship to give. In households in which the sons of the family were subjected to severe mental discipline it was usually thought a waste of time to allow a girl to learn more than to scrawl an almost illegible letter, in which the spelling, even in those days of vague and uncertain orthography, might fairly be characterised as abominable.[1]

Milton's consciousness that his main position was sound led him to embark on a yet higher argument. His persistence in the publication of his opinions naturally brought upon him a storm of obloquy daily increasing in volume and in force. Prynne tersely characterised his doctrine as 'divorce at pleasure.' Preachers and pamphleteers assailed him as the advocate of all license and depravity. By issuing his tract without the permission required by the licensing ordinance of 1643 [2] he had contravened the Parliamentary law, and at one time it seemed likely that he would be called to account for the offence.[3]

Aug.
Attacks on Milton.

Dropping for a time the subject of marriage and divorce,

---

[1] This is distinctly to be recognised in the correspondence of the Verney family.

[2] See vol. i. p. 149.

[3] The particulars, in far greater detail than I can spare room for, can be traced in Masson's *Life of Milton,* iii. 262-275.

Milton turned to the vindication of each man's right to assert unpopular opinions. On November 24 he issued, under the title of *Areopagitica*, a defence of 'the liberty of unlicensed printing.' Less concerned with practical politics than the author of *Liberty of Conscience*,[1] and less careful of sectarian religiosity than Roger Williams, Milton's spirit soars aloft in a purer air. The one lasting conviction of his life, that the free development of the individual—or at least of male individuals—was the indispensable condition of a healthy commonwealth, found its noblest expression here. Milton perceived that the liberty which all professed to be ready to accord to good books could only be secured if it was also accorded to books which were reputed to be evil. Not only was it impossible to prevent the circulation of bad books,[2] but it would be actually injurious to attempt to do so. The presence of evil, thought Milton, tests and hardens the resistance offered to it by the good. He could not 'praise a fugitive and cloistered virtue unexercised and unbreathed, that never sallies out and sees her adversary, but slinks out of the race, where that immortal garland is to be run for, not without dust and heat.'

Nov. 24. Areopagitica.

The principle of liberty.

Holding such views, Milton was not likely to be well satisfied with the conduct of the Assembly of Divines or of the laymen who had fallen under its influence. "There be," he writes, "who perpetually complain of schisms and sects, and make it such a calamity that any man dissents from their maxims." To him every sign of mental activity was welcome. "Now, once again, by all concurrence of signs," he vehemently declared, "and by the general instinct of holy and devout men, as they daily and solemnly express their thoughts, God is decreeing to begin some new and great period in His Church, even to the reforming of reformation itself. What does He then but reveal Himself to His subjects, and as His manner is, first to His Englishmen? . . . Behold now this vast city, a city of refuge, the mansion-house

Mental activity in England.

[1] See vol. i. 290.

[2] Milton reminds his readers that *Mercurius Aulicus* was in everyone's hands.

of liberty, encompassed and surrounded with His protection;
the shop of war hath not there more anvils and hammers waking
to fashion out the plates and instruments of armed justice in
defence of beleaguered truth than there be pens and heads there,
sitting by their studious lamps, musing, searching, revolving
new notions and ideas wherewith. to present, as with their
homage and their fealty, the approaching reformation : others
as fast reading, trying all things, assenting to the force of
reason and convincement. . . . Under these fantastic terrors
of sect and schism, we wrong the earnest and zealous thirst
after knowledge and understanding which God hath stirred up
in this city.   What some lament of, we rather should rejoice at,
should rather praise this pious forwardness among men, to re-
assume the ill-deputed care of their religion into their own
hands again.   A little generous prudence, a little for-
bearance of one another, and some grain of charity
might win all those diligences to join and unite in
one general and brotherly search after truth, could we but
forego this prelatical tradition of crowding free consciences and
Christian liberties into canons and precepts of men."

Organisa-
tion through
liberty.

The buoyancy of heart with which these words were written
was characteristic of Milton in those days.   Like the French
revolutionists, he was slow to measure the difficulties in the
way of the realisation of his ideal, and as they fancied that
organisation through law was readily attainable, so did he
fancy that organisation through liberty was within easy reach.
The idealist, usually in the right as to the thing which he
desires, is always wrong as to the time within which the obstacles in his path can be swept away, and in thinking it
possible in an instant to create a home of liberty out of the
England of Laud and Prynne, Milton did but exhibit his own
ignorance of the actual ways of men.

No doubt the yoke of the Long Parliament upon the press
was less grievous than the yoke of the Star Chamber had been.
Milton, suiting the action to the word, had published
Areopagitica without a licence, and no attempt had
been made to punish him for his audacity.   Men of
note, like John Goodwin or Henry Burton, had no difficulty in

The Long
Parliament
and the
press.

obtaining a licence for their arguments on behalf of toleration,[1] but less respected authors were not so fortunate. "The truth is," wrote one to whose pamphlet a licence had been refused, "if the book bear Independent upon its front, and be thought to speak for that way . . . it is silenced before it speaks."[2]

In fact, it was only by connecting itself with some more widely-spread desire that this struggle for intellectual liberty could be crowned with even temporary success for many a

Sept.
Feeling in
the Houses.

year to come. In both Houses the current of feeling ran strongly in favour of Presbyterian restraint. No single step was taken to give effect to that Accommodation Order which Cromwell had wrung from

Sept. 18.
A City
petition.

the Commons.[3] On September 18 the thanks of the House were given to a body of petitioners from amongst the City clergy, who had asked that 'erroneous opinions, ruinating schisms, and damnable heresies'

Oct. 23.
Request of
the Lords.

might be suppressed.[4] On October 23 the Lords urged the Assembly to 'hasten the settling of the government of the Church,' and on the next day the

Oct. 24.
The Commons ask for
a Directory.

Commons requested the divines to apply themselves to the preparation of a Directory which might take the place of the Book of Common Prayer.[5] On

Nov. 1.
A Scottish
request.

November 1, a few days after the capture of Newcastle was known in London, a letter was received from the Committee of the Estates of Scotland with the northern army, imploring the English Parliament so to settle the government of the Church as to remove 'those great prejudices raised against our cause by the abundance of variety of sectaries, separatists, and schismatics.' This time the Commons took the lead in the work of repression, asking the

[1] Goodwin, Θεομαχία, E. 12, 1; Goodwin, *Innocency's Triumph*, E. 4, 10; Burton, *Vindication of Churches commonly called Independent*, E. 17, 5.

[2] *Inquiries into the causes of our miseries*, E. 22, 1. In the third section (E. 24, 3, p. 22) the author states that the impression of the second section had been seized.

[3] See p. 30.

[4] *Rushw.* v. 780.

[5] *L.J.* vii. 31; *C.J.* iii. 675.

Lords to join in recommending this letter to the consideration of the Assembly.[1]

The Assembly was not slow to take the hint. On the 8th it presented to the Houses a recommendation in favour of Presbyterianism as the only fitting government for the Church.[2] On the 15th the Commons passed a resolution—which was indeed easier to announce than to enforce—'that no person be permitted to preach who is not ordained as a minister,'[3] and though consideration of the further question of the establishment of Presbyterianism was postponed till the objections of the dissenting brethren, now seven in number, had been heard, enough had been done to show that there was no intention of tolerating the preaching of a layman.[4]

Nov. 8.
Advice of the Assembly.

Nov. 15.
No one to preach who is not ordained.

In most questions relating to church government the Houses were ready to follow the lead of the Scots. On the still more pressing subject of opening negotiations with the King, the influence of the Scots was no less discernible. On November 8 propositions for peace which had been drawn up under Scottish influence were, with some slight alteration, unanimously adopted, and on the 20th were despatched to Oxford.

Nov. 8.
Peace propositions adopted,

Nov. 20.
and sent to Oxford.

With respect to the Church, the demand made by the Houses was, that 'the reformation of religion according to the Covenant be settled by Act of Parliament in such manner as both Houses shall agree upon after consultation had with the Assembly of Divines,' and this demand was accompanied by a recitation of the clause of the Covenant in which both kingdoms had bound themselves 'to endeavour the nearest conjunction and uniformity in

The religious propositions.

---

[1] Sinclair and others to the Com. of B. K., Oct. 23. *L.J.* vii. 44 ; *C.J.* iii. 684.

[2] *L.J.* vii. 61 ; *C.J.* iii. 691.   [3] *C.J.* iii. 697.

[4] In the course of some debate some inquiry seems to have been made as to the effect of the words ' No person ' in excluding women. "*Acriter disputatum* if the word ' Person ' were ' Man '—No person in holy orders, *ut prævenirent mulieres.*" D'Ewes's Diary, *Harl. MSS.* 166, fol. 161.

matters of religion.' That this demand was framed in an
exclusively Presbyterian sense hardly admits of doubt; but
in giving at least a tacit approval to it, Vane and
his allies might comfort themselves with the knowledge that nothing definite had as yet been legis-
latively settled, and that, even within the lines now laid down,
some expansion was still possible. Yet, though no evidence
exists on the point, it is most probable that the absence of any
resistance on the part of the Independents was mainly due to
the conviction that Charles would save them the trouble of a
fruitless opposition by peremptorily rejecting the proposal.

Part taken by the In-dependents.

To Charles, indeed, the political propositions would be as
offensive as the ecclesiastical. Not only were all Papists who
had taken up arms against the Parliament, and all
persons who had had a hand in the Irish rebellion,
to be excluded from pardon, but the names of fifty-seven of
the King's most trusted supporters, including those of his two
nephews, Rupert and Maurice, were placed on the list of proscription, whilst an immense number of his less important
supporters were to be excluded from office. The whole of the
estates of those to whom pardon was refused was to be applied
to the payment of the expenses of the war, whilst the forfeiture
of a third part was to suffice as a penalty on those whose
names appeared in the second category. Besides this, a crowd
of unnamed delinquents were to be called upon to sacrifice a
tenth of their property. Not even a semblance of royal power
was to be left to Charles. The militia and the navy were to
be placed permanently under commissioners to be named by
the Houses, and the nomination to all posts of importance
was to be transferred to the Houses themselves, or to commissioners acting in their name.

The political propositions.

The transference of power thus sketched out was certainly
not to be effected in favour of liberty. The propositions relating to the Church were of the most stringent and
intolerant kind. Not only was an oath to the Covenant to be exacted from every subject in the three kingdoms,
but, at the express desire of the Scots, the King himself was to
be required to swear to it. It was almost certain that the

Liberty dis-regarded.

system proposed to be substituted for Episcopacy would, as
far as ecclesiastical institutions were concerned, be Presby-
Aim of the   terianism of the most rigid kind. In short, the aim
Peace-party. of the great Peace-party, so commanding in Parliamentary authority, but so fatally deficient in intelligence, was
to treat Charles much as Milton had treated Mary Powell.
They asked him for his hearty co-operation in a course of
action which he regarded with loathing.[1]

As a matter of Parliamentary tactics, those who believed
that the Peace-party needed only to be left to itself to work its
Military re-   own destruction were doubtless in the right. Other
organisation. considerations than those of Parliamentary tactics
concurred in suggesting to the leaders of the War-party the
wisdom of allowing the negotiation to take its course. Believing as they did that a slackening of military effort would enable
the King to dictate his own terms, they preferred to work with
their Parliamentary opponents rather than against them. The
recent events at Newbury had brought about a remarkable
consensus of opinion that, if the war was to be carried on,
the army must be reorganised, and both Cromwell and Vane
were sufficiently shrewd to be aware that the sooner a practical
attempt was made to procure Charles's acceptance of the
Presbyterian terms, the sooner Manchester and Holles would
discover the truth which they had been so slow to learn, that
the war could only be brought to an end by victory. Even
now it was generally understood that the present military
anarchy must be dealt with at once, as it would be too late
to reduce the army to discipline when the time arrived for
taking the field.

The stone was set rolling on November 19 by the presentation of a petition in which the Eastern Association complained
Financial   that they were no longer able to bear the charge of
revolt of the maintaining their troops, and called on Parliament to
Eastern As-
sociation.   provide a remedy.[2] The system of maintaining an
army for general purposes by local contributions had broken
down where it was strongest, and the Commons, in referring

[1] *L.J.* vii. 54 ; *Acts of the Parl. of Scotland*, vi. 129.
[2] *C.J.* iii. 699 ; *Perf. Diurnal*, E. 256, 40.

the petition to the Committee of Both Kingdoms, not only
instructed it to take into consideration the whole state of the
Parliamentary armies, but, on the 23rd, reinforced
their order with directions to the Committee to 'consider of a frame or model of the whole militia.'[1] An
effort, it seemed, was at last to be made to give practical effect
to Waller's suggestion of an army wholly at the disposal of
Parliament.[2]

Nov. 23.
A New
Model to be
considered.

It is possible that the promptness with which these orders
were given was in some degree owing to the return of Cromwell
to his place in Parliament. The 23rd had been fixed
as the day on which he and Waller were to make
their statements on the proceedings at Newbury, the
House not having been satisfied with an official defence which
had been offered by Hazlerigg on the 14th.[3] Some members,
however, were of opinion that further inquiry would only lead
to useless recrimination, and the report of the two generals was
therefore postponed to the 25th, perhaps in the hope that it
might be altogether dispensed with as injurious to the maintenance of military discipline.[4]

Cromwell at
Westmin-
ster.

If such was the expectation of those who had urged delay,
it was likely now to be disappointed. Cromwell was already
beginning to show himself a leader of men as well as
a commander of armies. Political assemblies are
always impatient of far-reaching schemes which embrace the future as well as the present, and there can be little
doubt that if *Areopagitica* had been delivered as an actual
speech in Parliament, it would have been received with icy
coldness. Then, as now, the House of Commons liked to be
led on step by step, and took a peculiar pleasure in imagining
that each move in advance was absolutely final. Cromwell,
alike by temperament and calculated prudence, was the very

Cromwell
as a states-
man.

[1] *C.J.* iii. 703.   [2] See p. 5.

[3] *Perf. Diurnal*, Nov. 14. E. 256, 36.

[4] *C.J.* iii. 703 ; Whitacre's Diary, *Add. MSS.* 31,116, fol. 175b. According to Whitacre the report was postponed ' because it was feared by
many that the relating of it might tend to the increasing divisions in the
army, which were now well quieted and appeased.'

man to afford the guidance which the House required. Widely as his sympathies extended, he knew how to single out amongst many objects the one which was supremely important because most easily attainable at the moment, and whilst throwing himself with all the energy of his character upon the achievement of his immediate purpose, to maintain a complete silence on subjects which would have divided him from those whose help he needed.

The combination of the power of enthusiasm with the power of reticence was the distinguishing note of Cromwell's character as a statesman—a note which, under malignant interpretation, led easily to charges of hypocrisy. Such charges appeared to have the better foundation in the uncertainty with which he felt his way to a great decision. Alike as a commander, as a speaker, and as a politician, Cromwell stands apart from those whose life-work has been moulded by self-sustained effort in pursuit of a regularly formed plan. The inward doubts and wrestlings, the instant urgency with which he sought God in prayer for a Divine light which should determine his course amidst the darkness around him, were the truest expressions of the hesitation with which he approached each turning-point in the path of duty. The involved sentences of his oratory—if, indeed, oratory it can be called—and the absence of any strategical plan in his warfare are closely akin to the open-mindedness with which he gauged each political difficulty as it arose. There were so many evils which needed remedy, so many healing measures to be applied, that it was hard to choose a course. When the moment of decision came at last, all previous hesitation vanished. Cromwell needed the impact of hard fact to clear his mind, but when once it had been cleared he saw his way with pitiless decision of purpose. Old friends who crossed his path were thrown aside, and hopes which he had once held out to them were withdrawn. The need of the moment was all in all to him, and what that need was he saw with unrivalled accuracy of vision.

On his return to Parliament Cromwell instinctively perceived that the reorganisation of the army was the one thing needful. It was no time to be wrangling over the discipline

Cromwell's reticence.

of the Puritan Church when the very existence of Puritanism was at stake, or to criticise the terms offered to the King *Cromwell's aims.* when the opening of a negotiation could be avoided by no art of his. On these points Cromwell preserved for many months a resolute silence. The time would come when it might be useful to speak of them, but the time had not come yet. When the King had been beaten in the field other objects would be easier of attainment, and, like all true leaders, Cromwell fixed upon an aim which would unite rather than upon one which would distract.

Cromwell's superb presence of mind boded no good to the ascendency of the Presbyterian leaders. They might safely have contemned the idealism of Milton, but their inability to make war or to conclude peace would before long deliver them over to the man whose capacity for practical action was unrivalled in his generation.

CHAPTER XXIII.

THE FIRST SELF-DENYING ORDINANCE.

IF it was in Cromwell's nature to avoid flying at abuses in general, whilst he singled out some particular abuse which it was in his power to remedy, it was also in his nature to connect that abuse with some particular person. As a soldier, deserted by his comrades in the stress of battle, and surrounded by a ring of foemen, chooses instinctively some one hostile face at which to dash for dear life's sake, so Cromwell dashed at Manchester. Whatever might be pleaded on the part of that general—the difficulties arising from the deficiency of the commissariat, the inclemency of the weather, or the unwavering support of the majority of his fellow-commanders—was all forgotten now. Yet if Cromwell swayed the details of the past to his own side, the charge which he was about to bring was true in its application to the central fact of Manchester's conduct. Manchester, he rightly held, had erred not from mere inertness or incapacity, but from unwillingness to win such a victory as would stand in the way of a reconciliation with the King—a reconciliation which, to Cromwell's mind, would involve the abandonment of everything worth fighting for at all.

When on November 25 Cromwell took his seat in the House, prepared to make the statement which had been fixed for that day,[1] he had first to listen to the adoption of a motion for a request to the Lords 'to consider of bringing up the Scottish army southwards.'[2] A Scottish army, to form a nucleus round which the scattered fragments of the English forces might gather, would

1644.
Cromwell prepares to attack Manchester.

Nov. 25.
The Scottish army invited to move southwards.

---

[1] See p. 79.   [2] *C.J.* iii. 704; *L.J.* vii. 73.

be fatal to the realisation of Cromwell's aim. What he wanted
was that the English army might be strong enough to act independently of the Scots. There was, therefore, all the more
reason for proceeding with the attack on Manchester, because
it was only after the removal of Manchester that it would be
possible to send into the field an English force such as Cromwell desired to see.

When at last the two generals were called on to declare
their knowledge of the causes of the late miscarriages, Waller

Statements by Waller and Crom-well. was the first to speak. No record of his words has
reached us, but there is some reason to suppose that
he confined himself to a complaint of Manchester's
failing to come to his assistance at Shaftesbury.[1] Cromwell
followed with a far more sweeping attack. With every sign of
bitter irritation he ascribed every mistake that had been committed to the personal wrong-headedness of Manchester.[2] The
affair was referred to a committee of which Zouch Tate was the
chairman.[3]

As might have been expected, Manchester took fire. On
the 26th he asked leave of the Peers to defend himself in

Nov. 26. Manchester asks to de-fend himself. the House of which he was a member. On the
28th, having obtained the required permission, he
assailed Cromwell in return. On December 2 the
Nov. 28. His defence, Earl, by the direction of the Peers, produced his
Dec. 2. communi-cated to the Commons. counter-statement in writing, and the Lords, adopting his cause as their own, not only sent his narrative
to the Commons, but named seven peers to examine
the affair, and asked the Commons to appoint some members
of their House to join them in the committee which was to
take part in the inquiry.[4]

The narrative thus laid before the Commons consisted of
two sections. In the first, which related entirely to the military

---

[1] This, at least, is the burden of his first subsequent deposition. *S.P.
Dom.* diii. 56, vii.

[2] Cromwell's narrative, *Quarrel of Manchester and Cromwell,* 78.

[3] *C.J.* iii. 704.

[4] *L.J.* vii. 73, 76, 79, 80.

side of the dispute, Manchester passed lightly over his own part in the recent failure, painted Cromwell as a factious and somewhat inert officer, and laid stress upon his own habit of conforming himself to the resolutions of the Council of War, and upon Cromwell's acknowledgment that this had been the case. As a personal reply this section of the narrative was to a certain extent effective, but it offered no serious defence of those errors which had ruined the last campaign. In the second section Manchester attacked his accuser on the political side. After urging that Cromwell's own position in the army was sufficient evidence that no attempt had been made in it to depress Independents, he held him up to scorn as the despiser of the nobility and the contemptuous assailant of the Assembly of Divines. Cromwell, it seemed, had actually spoken of those reverend gentlemen as persecutors. What was still worse, he had expressed a desire to have an exclusively Independent army, with the help of which he might be enabled to make war on the Scots if they attempted to impose a dishonourable peace on honest men.[1]

Manchester's narrative.

On both sides the larger political dispute threatened to swallow up the question of military action. The Scots were especially irritated by Cromwell's attack upon themselves, now for the first time revealed to them. "This fire," wrote Baillie, "was long under the embers; now it's broken out, we trust, in a good time. It's like, for the interest of our nation, we must crave reason of that darling of the sectaries, and, in obtaining his removal from the army, which himself by his over-rashness has procured, to break the power of that potent faction. This is our present difficile exercise: — we had need of your prayers."[2]

Anger of the Scots.

To break the power of Cromwell it was necessary to have a policy at least as practical as his. The success of the peace negotiation, which was especially the work of the Scots, was

[1] The first part of the narrative has long been accessible in *Rushw.* v. 733; the second is printed in vol. viii. of the *Camden Miscellany*, from a copy amongst the *Tanner MSS.* See also a note by Major Ross in the *Engl. Hist. Review*, for July, 1888.

[2] *Baillie*, ii. 245.

already becoming doubtful. The commissioners sent in charge of the propositions entered Oxford on November 23 amidst the execrations of the crowd, and were personally insulted by a party of officers after they reached their quarters. On the 24th, the King, who had returned on the previous day from the relief of Donnington Castle, listened with dignity to the long list of demands, each one of which insisted on a surrender of some point which he was absolutely pledged to make good. The names of Rupert and Maurice on the list of proscription were received by the courtiers with contemptuous laughter. When at last the reading was finished, Charles briefly asked the commissioners whether they had power to treat. They replied that they had only authority to receive his answer. That answer, they were told, they should have, with all convenient speed.

Nov. 23. The peace commissioners at Oxford.

The short interval which had thus been gained was used by Charles to sow division amongst his antagonists. In the evening, taking Rupert with him, he dropped in at the lodging occupied by Holles and Whitelocke, complimented them on their pacific dispositions, and flattered them by asking their advice on the best means of ending the war. After some fencing, the two commissioners retired into another room, and, committing their opinion to paper, left it on the table. Whitelocke also took the precaution of disguising his hand.[1]

Charles tries to win over Holles and Whitelocke.

Whatever may have been the contents of the paper itself, the mere fact that two of the commissioners were ready to enter into a private negotiation with the King was enough to show him that some of them at least did not entirely approve of the harsh demands which they had been sent to lay before him. On the 27th he offered a sealed packet to the commissioners. As it bore no address, they at first objected to receive it. "You must take it," said the King sharply, "were it a ballad or a song of Robin Hood." "You told me twice," he continued, on their repeating their objection, "you had no power to treat. My

Nov. 27. The King's reception of the commissioners.

---

[1] *Whitelocke*, 113; *L.J.* vii. 82.

memory is as good as yours. You were only to deliver the propositions. A postillion might have done as much as you."[1]

Nov. 30.
Charles offers to send his answer.
On this the commissioners gave way, and when, on November 30, the packet which they carried was opened by the Houses, it was found to contain a request that a safe-conduct might be sent for Richmond and Southampton to bring the King's formal answer to Westminster. On December 3 both Houses concurred in assenting to the King's demand.[2]

Significance of the step taken.
Although the resolution thus adopted did not bind the Houses to anything, it undoubtedly pointed in the direction of further concession. "There are three things," Charles had said, in taking leave of the commissioners, " I will not part with— the Church, my crown, and my friends ; and you will have much ado to get them from me."[3] Although these words were not included in the official report of the deputation, it can hardly be doubted that they were privately circulated, and the resolution to allow the negotiation to proceed was therefore taken with a full knowledge that there was no chance of obtaining the King's consent to anything which, in the most distant way, resembled the propositions offered to him for acceptance.

Anxiety of the Scots to overthrow Cromwell.
Whatever might be the ultimate result of the vote taken on the 3rd for carrying on the negotiation, it could not fail to be received by the Scots as an indication that the influence of the War-party was declining. Following, as it did, closely upon the charges delivered by Manchester against his Lieutenant-General on the 2nd, it stirred the hopes of all whose minds were set upon the destruction of the influence exercised by Cromwell in Parliament and the army.

To prepare the way for the intended onslaught, a conference was held at Essex House on the night of the 3rd.[4]   In this

---

[1] Holles's narrative, *Tanner MSS.* lxi. fol. 203 ; *C.J.* iii. 710.

[2] *C.J.* iii. 710, 712.

[3] Holles's narrative, *Tanner MSS.* lxi. fol. 203.

[4] The account of this conference given by Whitelocke (116) has no date, but the position which he gives to it seems to fix it to the 3rd. It

conference Essex himself, with Holles, Stapleton, and other leaders of the English Peace-party, met the Scottish commis-

Dec. 3.
A conference at Essex House.

sioners, with Loudoun at their head, whilst White-locke and Maynard, who always voted steadily for peace, were present to give advice upon any legal questions that might arise. Already Essex and Holles had been

Proposal to accuse Cromwell.

won over by the Scots to look favourably on a plan for accusing Cromwell as an incendiary between the two nations, under the clause of the Covenant which provided for the bringing to justice of those who divided 'the King from his people, or one of the kingdoms from one another.'

To Scotchmen accustomed to see their courts of justice used for political ends there was nothing repulsive in this pro-

The English lawyers questioned by Loudoun.

posal. In his broadest Scotch Loudoun denounced Cromwell as an obstacle to 'the gude design,' and as one who, if he was permitted to go on as he had begun, might endanger the cause on which they had embarked. By the law of Scotland such a one was an incendiary who kindled coals of contention to the damage of the public. The question which Loudoun had to ask of the English lawyers was whether he was also an incendiary by the law of England, and, if so, in what manner was he to be brought to trial ?

Loudoun and his supporters had probably counted on the attachment of Whitelocke and Maynard to their political party.

Reply of Whitelocke and Maynard.

They had forgotten to take into account the irre-sistible bias of English lawyers to subordinate politi-cal to legal considerations. The cautious Whitelocke

follows the order about the safe-conduct, which was made on the morning of the 3rd. Other notices, it is true, intervene, but in Lord Bute's MS. this is not the case. In itself this argument is very far from being con-clusive, but it is reinforced by the appropriateness of the time. Holles had to make, in the House of Commons, his report of Manchester's charges, and the Scots would naturally wish that arrangements might be made to follow it up by an accusation of Cromwell, if such was to be brought. On the other hand, a later date is impossible. At the conference at Essex House Maynard and Whitelocke disclaimed all knowledge of the positive facts charged against Cromwell, which they could not have done after the report made on the 4th.

replied that, though he was of one mind with Loudoun in his definition of the word incendiary, he should like to see the evidence against Cromwell before pronouncing him to be one. If that evidence was sufficient to warrant an accusation, the accusation could only be brought in Parliament. To this opinion Maynard adhered, but he added words which must have opened the eyes of those who heard him to the risk they were incurring. "Lieutenant-General Cromwell," he said, "is a person of great favour and interest with the House of Commons, and with some of the Peers likewise, and therefore there must be proofs, and the most clear and evident against him, to prevail with the Parliament to adjudge him to be an incendiary." [1]

No impeachment of Cromwell on vague and uncertain charges was possible after this. When the Commons met on the morning of the 4th, Holles contented himself with making a bare report of the charges which had been brought by Manchester in the House of Lords; and Cromwell, who had heard from someone—probably from Whitelocke himself [2]—of the danger which he had escaped, replied by a fierce attack on the military inefficiency of the Presbyterian general. In a long speech, of which all that is known is that it contained an absolute denial of the accusations brought against himself, [3] he criticised Manchester's narrative with excessive severity. He had on his side the strong feeling which the Commons always exhibited whenever a member of their House was attacked by a Peer, and the conviction which must have spread amongst the ranks of the Peace-party itself, that Manchester was undeniably an unsatisfactory commander. The Commons not only refused to set aside their order for referring to Tate's Committee the original narratives of Waller and Cromwell; but, entirely passing over the proposal of the Lords that a joint committee

Dec. 4.
Holles's report.

Cromwell's reply.

---

[1] *Whitelocke,* 116.

[2] Whitelocke states that Cromwell received information, but does not give the name of the informer.

[3] "Ipse omnia capita absolutè negabat." D'Ewes's Diary, *Harl. MSS.* 483, fol. 120.

should be appointed to consider the charges against Crom-

The Commons take umbrage at the Lords' proceedings.

well, they directed the formation of a committee of their own House to consider whether their privileges had not been infringed upon by the support which the Lords had given to an attack upon a member of the House of Commons. At its first meeting the new committee placed John Lisle in the chair.[1]

Formation of Lisle's Committee.

Successful as Cromwell had been, it may well be that his very success made him uneasy. He was hardly likely to pro-

Cromwell's hesitation.

mote military efficiency by bringing about a rupture between the Lords and the Commons, between the English and the Scots, between the Presbyterians and the Independents. If he really felt anxiety, it was not long before an opportunity was given him of retracing his steps and of realising his aim in a more promising manner.

On December 9 Zouch Tate made the report from the committee of which he was the chairman[2] to a House of 200

Dec. 9. Report of Tate's Committee.

members,[3] who had come in unwonted numbers to listen to his statement. Instead of entering at length into the truth or falsehood of the accusations against Manchester, he contented himself with asserting in conclusion 'that the chief causes of our division are pride and covetousness.'[4]

As soon as Tate had sat down Cromwell rose. Though the suggestion that the commanders had ruined the army by their covetousness and jealousy was not likely to proceed from himself, he could not but know that the belief that this explanation was the true one was widely entertained. Unless

Cromwell's speech.

the war was speedily brought to an end, he declared, the kingdom would become weary of Parliament. "For what," he continued, "do the enemy say? Nay, what do many say that were friends at the beginning of the Parliament? Even this, that the members of both Houses have got great places and commands, and the sword into their hands;

[1] *C.J.* iii. 714; Whitacre's Diary, *Add. MSS.* 31,116, fol. 178.

[2] See p. 83.

[3] *Perfect Occurrences.* E. 258, 1.

[4] Whitacre's Diary, *Add. MSS.* 31,116, fol. 178.

and, what by interest of Parliament, and what by power in the army, will perpetually continue themselves in grandeur, and not permit the war speedily to end lest their own power should determine with it. This I speak here to our faces is but what others do utter abroad behind our backs." He would not, he added, reflect upon any, but, unless the war could be more vigorously prosecuted, the people would endure it no longer and would force Parliament to conclude a dishonourable peace. It would be imprudent to insist on the oversight of any particular commander. He himself, like all military men, had been guilty of oversights. "I hope," he ended by saying, "we have such true English hearts and zealous affections *Proposes* towards the general weal of our mother-country, as *that officers* no members of either House will scruple to deny *shall deny* *themselves.* themselves and their own private interests for the public good; nor account it to be a dishonour done to them whatever the Parliament shall resolve upon in this weighty matter."[1]

The debate rolled on, and at last Tate rose again to move in the sense indicated by Cromwell, "That during the time of *Tate moves* this war no member of either House shall have or *the Self-* execute any office or command, military or civil, *denying* *Ordinance.* granted or conferred by both or either of the Houses of Parliament, or any authority derived from both or either of the Houses."[2] The motion was seconded by Vane, and was warmly commended by many who usually acted in opposition to Vane. Those who wished to be rid of Cromwell were as ready to support it as those who wished to be rid of Manchester.[3]

Conjecture has busied itself with the question whether

---

[1] *Rushw.* vi. 4.   [2] *C.J.* iii. 718.

[3] Baillie, it may be remarked, was pleased with the suggestion. At some time in the course of the debate Cromwell made a second speech (*Perfect Occurrences*, E. 258, 1), expressing his assurance that the change would not affect the fidelity of the army. In *The Perfect Diurnal* is what appears to be an abstract of the opinions expressed in the debate. They are not of a high order, being in consonance with the language of Tate's report, rather than with that of Cromwell's speeches.

Tate was from the beginning in collusion with Cromwell.
Though certainty on this point is unattainable, it is very un-
Did he act in collusion with Crom-well? likely that he was. Himself a Presbyterian of the
narrowest type,[1] he was hardly the man to play into
Cromwell's hands. It is more probable that he did
but repeat the platitudes about the selfishness of the generals
which had of late been heard out of doors with increasing
frequency, and that Cromwell, by a happy inspiration,[2] utilised
the prevalent feeling for his own purpose. However this may
have been, it is in the highest degree unlikely that Cromwell
craftily expected to retain his own command whilst Essex and
Manchester descended to a private station. As circumstances
stood at the moment when Tate's final proposal was made,
Cromwell would have been more than a sagacious statesman—
he would have been an inspired prophet—if he had foreseen
the course which events ultimately took. He had against him
the Scots, the House of Lords, and a considerable minority of
the House of Commons. If he wished personally to retain his
command whilst expelling Manchester, he would surely have
continued the prosecution of his adversary in the face of all
obstacles, sooner than have sought to force his way back into

[1] He was afterwards one of two members who brought in the bill
against blasphemy and heresy which is the high-water mark of Presbyterian intolerance.

[2] Clarendon's account (viii. 191) of an intrigue conducted by Vane to
influence the decision of the House in favour of the Self-Denying Ordinance by stirring up the preachers on the day before to urge it is plainly
inaccurate. He says that this took place on a fast-day instituted by the
Houses. In the first place, no institution of a fast is to be found in the
journals, and, in the second place, the day named was a Sunday, on which
no fast was ever appointed. It is likely enough that political sermons
were preached on it, but some other evidence than Clarendon's blundering account is needed to show that they anticipated Cromwell's speech
rather than Tate's. Unless they did there would be nothing to show
premeditation on Cromwell's part. Clarendon was, as far as London was
concerned, at the mercy of Oxford gossip. It may be noted that Rushworth (vi. 3) says that the House 'took into consideration the sad condition of the kingdom,' after which it went into committee. Neither the
journals nor any other authority gives sanction to this statement, which
was probably found by Rushworth in some ill-informed pamphlet.

military office in the teeth of the opposition he would have to encounter, after the doors had been closed against him as much as against Manchester by positive legislation. It is hard to avoid the conclusion that he was prepared to sacrifice not only his attack upon the commander whom he despised, but even his own unique position in the army.[1]

The Self-Denying Ordinance—it is convenient to use the name by which it was ultimately known—was passed rapidly

Progress of the Self-Denying Ordinance.

Dec. 18. Essex not to be excepted from the Ordinance.

through the preliminary stages. On December 18 it was proposed in committee to except Essex from its operation ; and, though the motion was rejected, it was only lost by a majority of seven. A similar fate attended a proposal that no one should be employed who refused to take the Covenant or to promise submission 'to such government and discipline in the

Dec. 19. The Covenant not to be required of officers.

Church as shall be settled by both Houses of Parliament upon advice with the Assembly of Divines.' Military proficiency was to take precedence of ecclesiastical propriety. On December 19 the Ordinance without further alteration was sent up to the Lords.[2]

On the question of military organisation Cromwell had thus gained a commanding position in the House of Commons. It was purchased by the abandonment of all criticism upon the conduct of the negotiations with the King, and upon the neglect which had befallen the order adopted at his motion in September for the accommodation of the differences between the Presbyterian and the Independent divines.

No skill or self-sacrifice of Cromwell's could win the House

The Self-Denying Ordinance laid aside by the Lords.

of Lords to his side. The Peers justly regarded the proposed ordinance as directed against themselves, and for some time they quietly laid it aside as threatening the rights and privileges of their order. They might have known that a policy of mere resistance would

---

[1] Those who hold the contrary opinion have, I think, been unconsciously influenced by a confusion between the terms of the first and second Self-Denying Ordinances. Here, as in everything else, there is nothing which clears up difficulties so much as a strict attention to chronology.   [2] *C.J.* iii. 726.

avail them little, and that their position in the State was threatened, not so much because their authority was questioned, as because they had shown themselves incompetent guides alike in the council and in the field.

It is possible that the Lords were encouraged in their resistance by the knowledge that, in spite of the failures at

The military situation. Lostwithiel and Newbury, the military situation was by no means desperate. In September Lord Herbert of Cherbury, whose philosophic religion would have been

Sept. Montgomery Castle surrendered to Parliament. equally denounced by the divines of Oxford and by the divines of Westminster, and in whom the vaingloriousness of youth had passed insensibly into the valetudinarian timidity of age, surrendered Montgomery Castle to the Parliamentary commander, Sir Thomas

Sept. 18. An attempt to retake it fails. Middleton. On September 18 an attempt made by Lord Byron and Sir Michael Ernely to regain the fortress was signally defeated by a combination of Parliamentary forces under the command of Sir John Meldrum. The gate of the upper valley of the Severn thus remained in Parliamentary keeping, and the brilliant and versatile owner spent the remainder of his days as a pensioner of that Parliament with which he was in little sympathy, but which at least appeared to be stronger than its opponents.

Middleton was left behind to secure the fruits of victory. Meldrum had other work on hand. For some time previously

The siege of Liverpool. he had been engaged in the siege of Liverpool, whither he hurried back in order to be on the spot

Nov. 1. Its surrender. to receive the surrender of the town. On November 1, when the place was no longer capable of resistance, the English soldiers of the garrison deserted in a body to Meldrum, while the Irish who were left behind, fearing that they would receive no quarter, seized their officers, and, offering them as prisoners to the Parliamentary commander, completed the surrender.[1]

The Irish soldiers were only just in time in bargaining for

---

[1] *Rushw.* 747. The later part of the life of Lord Herbert of Cherbury has been carefully traced by Mr. S. L. Lee, in his edition of Lord Herbert's Autobiography.

their lives.   There was one point on which English parties were unanimous, and on October 24 an ordinance had been

Oct. 24.
Ordinance
against the
Irish. passed directing that every Irishman taken either at sea or on land in England or Wales should be put to death without mercy.[1]   Meldrum, however, had consented to spare the lives of the Irish soldiers at Liverpool before this murderous command had been notified to him.

Important as was the capture of Montgomery and Liverpool, the maintenance of Taunton was of even greater importance.

Sept.
The siege of
Taunton. When the King's army, after its success at Lostwithiel, swept in triumph over the West, Taunton alone amongst the inland towns refused to acknowledge defeat.   There was a stout Puritan spirit within its walls, and its governor was the lion-hearted Blake, who had contributed so powerfully to the defence of Lyme.   After the weakness of the Parliamentary armies had been demonstrated by the operations round Newbury, grave anxiety was felt at Westminster for the safety of this isolated post, the more so as its continued resistance would give employment to royalist forces which might otherwise be available for Charles's next campaign in

Nov. 6.
Waller
ordered to
relieve
Taunton. central England.   Waller was therefore ordered early in November to send a detachment to its relief.[2] Waller, however, was too fully employed to allow him to carry out these orders, and the promised help was long delayed.   It was not till December that Major-General Holborn was directed to push westwards through Dorset towards Taunton.

In accomplishing this task Holborn had the assistance of a man who, whatever he chose to do, did it with all his might.

Sir Anthony
Ashley
Cooper. Sir Anthony Ashley Cooper, a young man of wealth and position in the county of Dorset, had just come

1642–43.
He remains
neutral at
the begin-
ning of the
war. of age when the Civil War broke out.   He was, if any man ever was, a born party leader.   As a lad at Oxford he had headed a revolt of the freshmen of Exeter College against the custom which prescribed submission to the indignity of having their chins skinned by the

---

[1] *L.J.* vii. 34.

[2] The Com. of B. K. to Waller, Nov. 6.   *Com. Letter Book.*

older undergraduates, and of swallowing a compulsory draught of a nauseous compound of salt and water. He had subsequently headed another revolt against an attempt made by the College authorities to weaken the undergraduates' beer.[1] Such a youth, it might be thought, would have been amongst the first to take arms on one side or the other when the war broke out, especially as he happened to be accidentally present at Nottingham on the day on which the King's standard was raised. Yet he returned unmoved to his own county, and during the first months of the war remained quietly at home.

If Cooper's neutrality is to be judged in the light of his later career, it may be thought probable that his vehement His probable spirit was held in check by his want of sympathy motives. with the enthusiasms of either party. Pugnacious as he was, he could not find either in Puritanism or in its opposite a fitting cause for taking up arms. His was the zeal for an ordered secular freedom, which counted as impertinence the claims of presbyter or bishop to interfere in temporal affairs, and it is, therefore, little wonder that he should have felt disinclined to side with either.

It was impossible for any man of Cooper's position to maintain neutrality long. The invasion of his county by 1643. the Royalists after the battle of Roundway Down His temporary Roy- compelled him to take a side. The example of his alism. neighbours, and perhaps the fact that the Parliamentary party was the more distinctly religious of the two, decided his course for him. He raised a regiment for the King, and 1644. was appointed Governor of Weymouth and Portland. He goes over to the Yet he remained a Royalist for little more than six Parliament. months. In January 1644, abandoning all his earthly possessions, he presented himself at Westminster as a convert to the Parliamentary faith.

It may fairly be believed that, in making this change, His motives Cooper was in the main actuated by conscientious discussed. motives. Much as he distrusted presbyters and bishops, he distrusted the Pope still more; and Charles's attempts

[1] Christie's *Life of Shaftesbury,* i. 17.

to strengthen himself with the aid of the French Catholics had disquieted others besides the young baronet. In his own words, he had become fully satisfied 'that there was no intention of that side for the promoting or preserving of the Protestant religion and the liberties of the kingdom.' Yet it does not follow that a sense of personal slight did not mingle with more public sentiments in his breast. In the preceding August Charles had written to Hertford signifying his intention of conferring on Cooper the governorship of Weymouth, and, after speaking of him in slighting terms as a youth without experience in war, had suggested that he should be induced to resign the post after a brief tenure.[1] If, as there is strong reason to believe, Cooper's resignation was already demanded before the end of the year, he would be likely to take deep offence even though the stately glories of the peerage might be offered as a sop to his wounded vanity. He imagined himself capable of rising to distinction in active life, and he can hardly have been well pleased with the prospect of hanging about Oxford as the useless ornament of a discredited court.[2]

Whatever Cooper's motives may have been, he threw himself with all possible energy on the side which he had now adopted. On August 3 he was appointed to the command of a brigade, and took an active part in the reduction of Wareham. He was then placed on the committee by which Dorset was governed, and in September was

Aug. 3.
He commands a brigade at Wareham,

---

[1] The King to Hertford, Aug. 10. *Christie*, i. 45.

[2] The whole subject has been discussed by Mr. Christie (i. 40–53) in a sense favourable to Cooper. The feeling about the grant of a peerage as no consolation for the loss of military position, which I have supposed to be that of Cooper, was undoubtedly that of Gerard under similar circumstances in the following autumn. Of one piece of evidence showing that Cooper was actually dismissed Mr. Christie was not aware. There is a letter from Cooper to Hyde, written from Weymouth on Dec. 29, 1643 (*Clarendon MSS.* 1,734), in which he asks permission to leave the county. If he had still been Governor of Weymouth he would either not have requested leave of absence or would have added reasons for so doing. The rest of the letter is filled with complaints of the low state of the King's affairs in Dorset, from which it may be gathered that he considered Charles's cause in the county to be almost hopeless.

appointed to the chief command of the forces of the country.
During the remainder of the autumn he took an active part

Sept.
and is put
at the head
of the
Dorsetshire
forces.

in the local operations. His most distinguished
success was the storming of Sir John Strangways'
fortified house at Abbotsbury. Yet it was owing to
no merit of his own that the blackened walls of
Abbotsbury did not stand up as the monument of his shame.
It is the glory of our Civil War that the stern laws of war
which allowed the conqueror to put to the sword a garrison
which had once rejected a summons were rarely put in practice.

His in-
tended
cruelty at
Abbotsbury.

If exceptions to the merciful custom of England undoubtedly existed, Cooper stands out as the one
commander who boastfully recorded that, with no
plea of necessity to urge, he had commanded that, after the
house which he attacked was ablaze, quarter should be refused, and the gallant soldiers, whose only crime was that
they had manfully performed their duty, should be thrust back
into the flames to perish by a death of torture. Fortunately,
his subordinates were too inured to the chances of military
life to be carried away, like their young commander, by the
excitement of the strife, and Colonel Sydenham, riding hurriedly
round to the back-door, admitted the garrison to quarter.[1]

When Holborn moved through Dorset on his way to

Accom-
panies
Holborn.

Taunton, Cooper was put in charge of the contingent drawn from the garrisons on the Dorsetshire
coast to accompany the expedition.[2] On December 14 the

---

[1] Cooper to the Committee of Dorset. *Christie,* i. 62.

[2] Mr. Christie (i. 72) makes him commander-in-chief of the whole force
on the ground of Cooper's distinct statement ' in his thoroughly reliable
autobiographical sketch.' Certainly Cooper's statement is distinct enough.
He says that he ' received orders to attempt the relief of Taunton, and a
commission from . . . the Earl of Essex to command in chief for that
design, which, having received the addition of some forces, under the command of Major-General Holborn . . . was . . . happily effected ' (*Christie,*
i. App. xxxi.). That this assertion is not ' thoroughly reliable ' appears
from Essex's commission (*Shaftesbury Papers, R.O.* ii. 46), which appoints
him commander-in-chief, but only over the troops drawn from the garrisons of Weymouth, Wareham, and Poole. Essex adds that Cooper is to
obey orders ' from myself, both Houses of Parliament, or the Serjeant

relieving force reached Taunton, and, having scattered the besiegers before them, threw in the necessary supplies. Cooper's fertility of resource and his hold upon the men of Dorset must have been of the utmost use to Holborn. So completely indeed does he seem to have taken the upper hand, that it was by him and not by Holborn that the despatch announcing the success of the enterprise was penned.[1] In a diary written about two years afterwards—apparently, it is true, without any thought of publication—he audaciously claimed for himself the title of commander-in-chief of the expedition.

Dec. 14.
Taunton relieved.

Cooper's part in the success.

Whatever may have been the respective merits of the commanders, the importance of the work performed by them was beyond dispute. It was not merely that they had given fresh vigour to Blake and his gallant crew. It might well be that Taunton would play the part in the operations of 1645 which had been played by Hull in the operations of 1643. Local feeling was as strong in Somerset as it had been in Yorkshire, and if Taunton could hold out, its resistance could hardly fail to detain for local purposes those western levies on which the King was counting. Charles must have been the more provoked as the place was not one before which failure was to be expected. It had no regular fortifications, and it was from behind wooden palings and earthworks thrown up on the emergency that Blake had bidden defiance to his assailants.[2]

Importance of the relief of Taunton.

Major General of the Western Counties,' *i.e.,* Waller, whose letter of Nov. 11 states that Holborn is 'to command all in chief.' See *Hist. Rev.* July, 1889, p. 521.

[1] Cooper to Essex, Dec. 15. *Christie,* i. 72. The date of the relief of Taunton is supplied from D'Ewes's Diary, *Harl. MSS.* 166, fol. 169b. Compare *Perfect Passages.* E. 22, 7.

[2] " It is almost a miracle," wrote Cooper in the letter just quoted, "that they should adventure to keep the town, their works being for the most part but pales and hedges, and no line about the town."

CHAPTER XXIV.

THE EXECUTION OF ARCHBISHOP LAUD.

AMIDST the strife of armies and of parties the negotiation with the King dragged slowly on. On December 17, two days before the Self-Denying Ordinance passed through the Commons, Richmond and Southampton appeared at Westminster as the bearers of a letter in which Charles requested the Houses to appoint commissioners to agree upon reasonable terms of peace with others named by himself.[1] The proposal was accepted on the 20th, but an excuse was found for sending the two peers back to Oxford, to hinder them from placing themselves in communication with the London Royalists.[2] In spite of the opposition of the Lords, who wished that the instructions to be given to the Parliamentary commissioners should be referred to a joint committee of the two Houses, the Commons succeeded in referring them to the Committee of Both Kingdoms, which was not likely to frame them in any more conciliatory spirit than had been shown in the propositions recently despatched to Oxford.[3]

It was, in truth, of very little importance whether the little knot of twelve or thirteen peers which now made up the House of Lords succeeded in softening the terms which were to be offered to the King. They were themselves engaged upon a work which made reconciliation with him almost absolutely hopeless. Week after week during the spring and early summer of the year which

Marginal notes:

1644
Dec. 17.
The negotiation with the King.

A letter from Charles.

Dec. 20.
Negotiations to be opened.

Dec. 28.
Instructions to be drawn up.

March 12–
July 29.
The trial of the Archbishop.

[1] *L.J.* vii. 103 ; *C.J.* iii. 726.

[2] *L.J.* vii. 113, 116; *C.J.* iii. 731; Whitacre's Diary, *Add. MSS.* 31,116, fol. 181b,   [3] See pp. 76, 85.

was now passing away, Archbishop Laud had stood at their
bar to listen to the voluminous evidence of treason which had
been elaborated by Prynne, and which was now adduced
against him by a committee of the House of Commons. Reiterated attempts were made to show that the old man had
deliberately attempted to change the religion established by
law, and even to subvert the law itself. It is unnecessary once
more to argue here that, in one sense, the charge was historically true, and that, in another sense, it was historically false.
Nor is it needful to inquire whether, even if the worst construction of Laud's conduct be made, his case was a fitting one to
submit to a judicial tribunal. The Lords who formed that
tribunal neglected to preserve even the semblance of judicial
impartiality. They strolled in and out of the House as fancy
took them, and it was seldom that, with the exception of the
Speaker, Lord Grey of Wark, any single peer who had listened
to the accusation in the morning thought it worth while to
remain in his place to hear the answer given in the afternoon.[1]

Under such circumstances, it is no wonder that modern
opinion, unfavourable as it has been to the Archbishop, should
have been still more unfavourable to his accusers.
The case of
Laud com-
pared with
that of
Strafford.
Why, it is said, should they not have allowed an old
man who, if not innocent, was at least harmless, to
descend into the grave in peace? Between the cases
of Laud and Strafford, it has been urged, there was no
similarity. Strafford had been put to death, not so much
because he had been criminal as because he had been dangerous. No one could say that Laud was personally dangerous.
His death would not check by one hair's-breadth the onward
march of the royal army. Yet if the object of the Commons
had been to mark with a sentence of infamy for example's sake
the root of the evils under which they had suffered, it is hard
to say that they were in the wrong in singling out Laud as their
victim. Strafford had offered his brain and arm to establish a
system which would have been the negation of political liberty.
Laud had sought to train up a generation in habits of thought

[1] History of the troubles and trial, *Laud's Works*, iv. 49.

which would have extinguished all desire for political liberty. Strafford's power was like a passing storm ; Laud's like a stormy torrent from the mountain flank on which no verdure can grow.

To give every man his due, it must be remembered that whilst the Independents probably shared the modern feeling that Laud was intolerant, the charge of intolerance counted but little against him in the eyes of the Presbyterians. It is true that, if Laud had been intolerant, the majority in the two Houses were no less intolerant. If he had striven to suppress religious liberty, so did they. If he had attempted to force the whole of the English Church into an Episcopalian mould, they were attempting to force it into a Presbyterian mould. In truth, the charge which was brought against him was not that he was intolerant, but that he was an innovator. Yet here, too, his accusers appear to have been no less guilty than himself. What innovation can have been greater than the overthrow of episcopacy, and the substitution of extempore devotions for the Book of Common Prayer ? Yet it is certain that the Presbyterians in Parliament and Assembly would have been the last to admit the charge which, in our eyes, is fatal to their claim to sit in judgment upon Laud. They held that, whilst Laud's changes had been in contradiction with the spirit of the English Church, theirs were no more than the development of its truest life. Nothing was further from their minds than to establish a new church in the place of an old one. They were, as they firmly believed, but dealing with the historic Church of England as their fathers had dealt with it a century before. As one generation had rid itself of the Papacy and the Mass, another generation was ridding itself of episcopacy and the Prayer-Book. In their eyes, Laud's crime was that he had gone backwards, and their own virtue that they were willing to go forwards.

With no feeling of injustice, therefore, in their hearts, the Commons pushed the charges home. On October 11, the evidence on matters of fact having been exhausted, Laud's counsel was heard on points of law. As in Strafford's case, the obvious argument was urged that, whatever the Arch-

Marginal notes:

Laud's intolerance not questioned by the Presbyterians.

His innovations attacked.

The Presbyterians hold that they are no innovators.

bishop might have done, he had not committed treason under the Statute of Edward III.[1] It is not unlikely that the argument had some influence on the Peers, always exposed more than others to impeachments for treason, and having amongst their number those who were unwilling to exasperate the King at a time when it was proposed to open negotiations with him.

Oct. 11.
Laud's counsel heard on points of law.

So apparent was the hesitation of the Lords, that the Archbishop's enemies resolved at last to threaten a renewal of that popular pressure which had proved so effective in Strafford's case, and on October 28 a petition for the execution of Laud and Wren, having been largely signed in London, was presented to the Commons. On the 31st the Commons, waiving their impeachment, resolved to proceed, as they had done in Strafford's case, by an Ordinance of Attainder, which, however, was not sent up to the Lords till November 22. On the 28th, though only six days had elapsed, the Commons lost patience, and bade the Lords execute justice on a delinquent so notorious. "The eyes of the country and City," said Strode, who bore the message, "being upon this business, the expedition of it will prevent the demanding of justice by multitudes."[2] "Is this," asked Essex indignantly, "the liberty which we promised to maintain with our blood? Shall posterity say that to save them from the yoke of the King we have placed them under the yoke of the populace?"[3] The House itself returned a dignified answer[4] in defence of its own independence; but it had no strong ground of reason on which to fall back on the main question at issue. The Lords, therefore, could but interpose a brief delay. On December 17 they voted that the ordinance might be accepted as true in matter of fact,[5] that is to say, that Laud

Oct. 28.
A London petition.

Oct. 31.
An Ordinance of Attainder.

Nov. 22.
Its discussion by the Lords.

Nov. 28.
A message to the Lords.

---

[1] *Laud's Works*, iv. 386.

[2] *L.J.* vii. 76. Whitacre (*Add. MSS.* 31,116, fol. 176) says that the word 'multitudes' was introduced by Strode without authority.

[3] Agostini to the Doge, Dec. $\frac{6}{16}$. *Venetian Transcripts, R.O.*

[4] *L.J.* vii. 76

[5] Laud (*Works*, vi. 416) says that though there were twenty Lords

had really endeavoured to subvert the fundamental laws, to alter religion as by law established, and to subvert the rights

Dec. 17.
The Lords
agree to the
ordinance in
matter of
fact.

of Parliaments. Of the arguments used on both sides little is known, but it is said that Pembroke supported his denunciation of Laud with reasoning which, if it meant anything at all, implied something not far short of Papal infallibility in the House of Commons. "What," he said, "shall we think the House of Commons had no conscience in passing this ordinance? Yes, they knew well enough what they did."[1] No one, indeed, expected wisdom to flow from the lips of Pembroke.

It might be thought that, with the decision of their own House in Strafford's case before them, the Lords, having once

The Lords
prolong the
struggle on
the question
of law.

settled the question of fact, would have speedily proceeded to settle the question of law by qualifying Laud's action as treasonable. With them, however, resistance was an affair of feeling and passion rather than of argument. On December 19, only two days after their first vote on the Ordinance of Attainder had been taken, the Self-Denying Ordinance was brought up from the House of Commons, and its appearance was sure to increase the irritation of the Peers.

With the two Houses in such a temper, questions which at other times might have been disposed of without difficulty were

Sentences
by the Court
Martial.

certain to lead to a conflict between them. Occasion for ill-will was now furnished by a series of condemnations pronounced by the Court Martial out of the hands by which the comrades of Edmund Waller had been sent

Dec. 23.
Execution
of Sir A.
Carew.

to execution.[2] No one, indeed, was found to take up the case of Sir Alexander Carew, who was executed on December 23 for his attempt to betray Plymouth to the enemy.[3] It was otherwise with Sir John Hotham, who

---

present on the day before, only sixteen took part in the vote on the 17th. The journals give twenty-two and twenty respectively, but some may have left the House before the end of the sitting.

[1] *Laud's Works*, vi. 416.

[2] See vol. i. p. 157.

[3] See vol. i. p. 207.

had been sentenced to death on December 7. On the 24th his son, Captain Hotham, was sentenced to the same fate, though he had done his best to throw the blame of his own misconduct upon his father's orders.[1] There was a general belief that the Houses would be content with a single victim, and the friends of Sir John, who were numerous among the Presbyterians,[2] were anxious that he should not be that victim.[3] It was at their instance that the trial of the son had been hurried on, and it was again at their instance that on December 24, as soon as the sentence on the younger Hotham was known, the Lords requested the Commons to grant a reprieve to the father till January 6, in the hope that before the time of the reprieve had expired the son, whose execution was fixed for January 2, might be no longer alive. The Commons indeed granted the reprieve, but they absolutely refused to extend their favour beyond December 31. When that day arrived the Lords, without consulting the other House, ordered execution to be respited for four days more, and on the morning of January 1, when Sir John was led out to die, the order of the Peers for his reprieve

Dec. 7.
Sir J.
Hotham
sentenced.

Dec. 24.
Captain
Hotham
sentenced.

Father and son.

Dec. 31.
The Lords extend the reprieve.

---

[1] *Rushw.* v. 798–802.

[2] Cromwell acted as teller in two divisions (on Dec. 24 and 30) against reprieving Sir John. *C.J.* iii. 734 ; iv. 4.

[3] In the long account of the affair of the Hothams in the *Clarendon State Papers*, ii. 181, the whole of the manœuvre to save Sir John at the expense of his son is attributed to the friends of the elder prisoner, and the name of Hugh Peters is not even mentioned. Clarendon, who had this paper before him, throws the blame on Hugh Peters, who, being sent as chaplain to prepare them for death, told them 'that there was no purpose to take away both their lives, but that the death of one of them would suffice, which put either of them to use all the inventions and devices he could to save himself ; and so the father aggravated the faults of the son, and the son as carefully inveighed against the father.' This may be a mere piece of Oxford gossip ; but, even if it is true, it does not tell against Hugh Peters. He may very well have known, what seems to have been a matter of common talk, that both were not to die, and it was no fault of his if, by conveying the information, he set them on mutual accusations.

was handed to Alderman Pennington, who now acted as Lieu-

Jan. 1.
Sir John
returned to
the Tower. tenant of the Tower. The unfortunate man was restored to his prison, being not without difficulty snatched from the hands of the infuriated multitude who had come to witness his execution.

At this proceeding of the Peers the Commons naturally took umbrage. If the younger Hotham had ever any chance of escape—and he had freely offered 10,000*l.* as the price of his life, as Waller had done before him—all hope was now at

Jan. 2.
Execution
of Captain
Hotham. an end. On the 2nd he was beheaded on Tower Hill. In order to secure obedience in future to the sentences of the Court Martial, the Commons issued instructions to all ministers of justice warning them against paying attention to reprieves issued by a single House. On

Jan. 3.
Execution
of Sir John. the 3rd Sir John was once more taken to execution. After he had mounted the scaffold it was observed that he spent an unusually long time in prayer, and it was maliciously suggested that the prolongation of his devotions was owing to a lingering hope that the Peers might again intervene in his favour. The Lords, however, did not venture to repeat their audacious step, and Sir John followed his son to a blood-stained grave, unpitied alike by either party.[1] The

The Lords
refuse to
renew the
ordinances
for martial
law. Lords asserted their independence in the only way open to them. The ordinance establishing a court of martial law expired on January 2, and on the following day they rejected the request of the Commons to revive it.[2]

During the ensuing year ordinances were passed from time to time giving the power to execute martial law to the commanders of armies under special circumstances; but it was not till the spring of 1646 that a court with authority to judge by martial law was re-established in London.[3]

---

[1] *L.J.* vii. 118; *C.J.* iii. 734, iv. 4–7. Whitacre's Diary, *Add. MSS.* 31,116, fol. 183; *Merc. Civ.*, E. 24, 9; *Parl. Scout*, E. 24, 10. When Pontefract Castle was taken in the following summer, fresh evidence against the Hothams was discovered. *A new discovery of hidden secrets.* E. 267, 2.

[2] *L.J.* vii. 121.   [3] *L.J.* viii. 252.

In refusing to renew the ordinance for martial law the Peers had exhausted their power of resistance. Constitutional scruples were not likely to stand in the way of those who now led the Commons, should the Peers persist in their attempt to

Plan for
uniting the
Houses.

save Laud from the scaffold. For some days a plan had been freely discussed for rendering them innocuous by uniting the Houses in one body after the fashion of a Scottish parliament.[1] One more appeal, however, was first made to their reason or their fears.

On the 2nd a conference was held on the subject of Laud's attainder. The Commons boldly urged that there

Jan. 2.
The Commons' argument against Laud.

were treasons by the common law which were not treasons by statute; and that, even if this rule did not apply to the case in question, Parliament had the right of declaring any crimes it pleased to be

Jan. 4:
The Ordinance of Attainder passed.

treasonable. On January 4 the resistance of the Lords was at last brought to an end, and their assent to the Ordinance of Attainder was given in due form.[2]

Before the sentence could be carried out Laud made an effort, which he could hardly have expected to be successful,

Jan. 7.
A pardon tendered and rejected.

to save his life. He tendered a pardon from the King, sealed as long ago as in April 1643. Upon its rejection, he asked that the usual penalty of the gallows, with its accompanying butchery, might be

Laud's request that he may be beheaded refused,

commuted for the more merciful axe. Though his request was backed by the Lords, the Commons not only rejected it, but rejected it without a division.

Jan. 8.
but ultimately granted.

Presbyterians and Independents were of one mind in the bitterness of their hatred to Laud. Yet even in this case night brought counsel, and on the 8th the easy concession to humanity was made. Laud had already

---

[1] Letter from London, Jan. $\frac{2}{12}$, *Arch. des Affaires Étr.* li. fol. 223 ; Salvetti to Gondi, Jan. $\frac{3}{13}$, *Add. MSS.* 27,962 K, fol. 392b ; Agostini to the Doge, Jan. $\frac{3}{13}$, *Venetian Transcripts, R.O.*

[2] The extracts from the journals relating to the proceedings against Laud are conveniently collected in the notes to his History of the troubles and trial, *Laud's Works*, iv. 384-425.

asked that three divines of his own selection might accompany him at the last scene. The Commons struck out two of the names, substituting for them those of two Puritan ministers in whose pious exhortations they could confide.[1]

On the morning of the 10th the old man who had once seemed to hold the destinies of the Church of England in his hand prepared for his death. "I was born and baptized in the bosom of the Church of England," he asserted once more on the scaffold: "in that profession I have ever since lived, and in that I come now to die. This is no time to dissemble with God, least of all in matters of religion; and therefore I desire it may be remembered I have always lived in the Protestant religion established in England, and in that I come now to die. What clamours and slanders I have endured for the labouring to keep an uniformity in the external service of God according to the doctrine and discipline of the Church all men know, and I have abundantly felt." Then, in praying for himself, he prayed for the land of his birth as well. "O Lord," he cried, "I beseech thee give grace of repentance to all bloodthirsty people; but if they will not repent, O Lord, confound their devices . . . contrary to the glory of Thy great name, the truth and sincerity of religion, the establishment of the King and his posterity after him in their just rights and privileges, the honour and conservation of Parliaments in their just power, the preservation of this poor Church in her truth, peace, and patrimony, and the settlement of this distracted people under their ancient laws, and in their native liberty." Troublesome questioners attempted to interrupt the last moments of the dying man with inquiries into the basis of his religion, but, after vain endeavours to satisfy their importunity, he laid his head on the block. "Lord, receive my soul," he cried. The words were preconcerted with the executioner as the sign that he was to do his duty. The axe fell and all was over.[2]

Jan. 10. Laud's execution.

Laud's last prayer.

[1] *L.J.* vii. 127, 128; *C.J.* iv. 12, 13.
[2] Heylyn, *Cyprianus Anglicus*, 527.

Little as those who sent Laud to the block imagined it, there was a fruitful seed in his teaching which was not to be

Fruit of Laud's teaching.

smothered in blood. If the Church of England was never again to assume a position of authority independent of Parliament, and if the immediate object for which Laud had striven—uniformity of worship for all subjects of the Crown—could never be permanently realised, his nobler aims were too much in accordance with the needs of his age to be altogether baffled. It is little that every parish church in the land still—two centuries and a half after the years in which he was at the height of power—presents a spectacle which realises his hopes. It is far more that his refusal to submit his mind to the dogmatism of Puritanism, and his appeal to the cultivated intelligence for the solution of religious problems, has received an ever-increasing response, even in regions in which ·his memory is devoted to contemptuous obloquy.

For the moment those who had been most bitter against Laud were the heirs of his errors. Whilst the Archbishop was preparing for death, Parliament was giving its assent to a scheme for erecting a uniformity as absolute as that which it had

Jan. 4. The Directory to be established.

censured when proceeding from him. On January 4 the Lords finally accepted the Commons' amendments to the ordinance which was to declare the Book of Common Prayer abolished for ever, and to set up in its place a Directory of Worship after the most approved type of Puritanism.[1] Parliament and Assembly were now face to face with the grave question of the enforcement of uniformity. The Dissenting Brethren, indeed, with whom the championship of liberty rested in the Assembly, had already thrown away what chance they ever had of convincing those to whom they

1644 Dec. 23. Arguments of the Dissenting Brethren.

appealed. On December 23 their arguments against the establishment of Presbyterianism were produced before the House of Commons ; but they proved to be so voluminous that the House sarcastically ordered that no more than three hundred of their reasons should be

[1] *L.J.* vi. 121, 125; *Rushw.* v. 839.

printed. On the main question the House was decidedly against them. The basis on which ordinary Presbyterianism rested was parochial. Every person living within certain geographical limits was to take his place in the parochial organisation, and to submit to the parochial authorities. Each parish was to take part in the choice of representatives to sit in the superior assemblies of the Presbytery or of the national Church, and no ecclesiastical community except that of the parish was to be allowed to exist. It was now urged on behalf of the Dissenting Brethren that the basis of the Presbyterianism to be established should be congregational ; that is to say, that, in addition to the parochial churches, there should be a toleration of congregations voluntarily formed by persons living in different parishes, and that such congregations should be exempted from parochial jurisdiction, but should be subordinated to presbytery and assembly, to which larger gatherings they were to send their representatives.[1]

Parochial and congregational Presbyterianism

The scheme thus proposed was one which, at least for a time, might have bridged over the gulf which separated the two Puritan parties. Neither of them, however, would have anything to say to it. It was too lax for the Presbyterians, too strict for the more pronounced Independents. On January 6 its acceptance was negatived without a division. On the 13th the House gave its assent to to the ordinary Presbyterian system by a resolution that parochial congregations should be combined in groups under presbyteries, though as yet it did not proceed to embody its resolution in an ordinance.[2] Outside the House Prynne was clamouring in a pamphlet which bore the name of *Truth Triumphing* for the complete establishment of the ecclesiastical discipline foreshadowed in this vote, and for the absolute suppression of all heresies and schisms whatsoever.

Jan. 6-13. Adoption of parochial Presbyterianism.

Jan. 2. Prynne's Truth Triumphing.

---

[1] *C.J.* iii. 733 ; Whitacre's Diary, *Add. MSS.* 31,116, fol. 181b.

[2] *C.J.* iii. 733, iv. 12 ; Whitacre's Diary, *Add. MSS.* 31,116, fol. 181b, 186b.

Though the motives of the Independent members for failing to offer opposition in the House to a vote which seemed to crush their hopes can only be matter of conjecture, it is probable that they preferred to take their stand on a wider and more complete toleration than would have satisfied the Dissenting Brethren, and that they thought it wiser to allow the establishment of the Presbyterian organisation to take its course whilst reserving to themselves the right to plead at some future day the cause of such as sought to worship entirely outside it. As the Parliamentary Independents were far in advance of the Independent members of the Assembly, they were in turn outstripped by men who in the army or elsewhere pushed the doctrine of Individual liberty to the extreme. Of these men the mouthpiece was John Lilburne, who had been a fellow-sufferer with Prynne in the days of Laud's supremacy, and who, with all Prynne's doggedness, possessed the power, which Prynne never had, of presenting his arguments in such a way as to impress themselves upon the vulgar understanding.

The Presbyterian organisation not resisted by the Independents in the House.

Lilburne and Prynne.

The two men were in fact opposed to one another by their whole habits of thought. Prynne was the narrowest of conservatives, Lilburne the most extreme of revolutionists; more dangerous, it might seem, than Milton, because he dwelt in the world of action rather than in the world of thought. To Prynne the very notion of individual liberty was hateful. Lilburne was so enamoured of it that he advocated something like the negation of law. Prynne regarded the ancestral rights of Englishmen as fully safeguarded if improper opinions were suppressed by Parliament instead of being suppressed by the Star Chamber and the High Commission. Lilburne had come with no less vehemence to the conclusion that it was the birthright of every Englishman to refuse obedience to the law whenever it commanded him to do anything to which he had a conscientious objection. In his reply to Prynne's *Truth Triumphing*, he explained that it had been his original intention merely to inform him that he 'did err, not knowing the Scriptures.' He

Jan. 7. Lilburne's Letter to Prynne.

now found it necessary to be more explicit. "Being,"[1] he continued, "that you and the Black-coats in the synod have not dealt fairly with your antagonists in stopping the press against us while ·things are in debate, yea, robbing us of our liberty . . . in time of freedom, when the Parliament is sitting, who are sufficiently able to punish that man, whatsoever he be, that shall abuse his pen,[2] so that while we are with the hazard of our dearest lives, fighting for the subjects' liberty, we are brought into Egyptian bonds .. . . by the Black-coats . . . and, truly, it argues no manhood nor valour in you nor the Black-coats by force to throw us down and tie our hands, and then to fall upon us and buffet us ;[3] for, if you had not been willing to have fought with us upon equal terms, namely, that the press might be open for us as for you, and as it was at the beginning of this Parliament, which I conclude the Parliament did on purpose that so the free-born English subjects might enjoy their liberty and privilege." This lengthy sentence never came clearly to an end, but Lilburne finally announced his readiness to argue that no Parliament or any earthly authority had any jurisdiction over the kingdom of God, and that persecution for conscience' sake is of the devil. He would concede to Parliament the right to establish a State church if it pleased, but he refused to allow that he could be compelled to pay tithes in its support. Such payment, he affirmed, would 'be a greater snare than the Common Prayer to many of the precious consciences of God's people, whose duty is, in

[1] 'Being' is a word frequently used in the seventeenth century where we should use 'seeing.'

[2] The anonymous author of *Inquiries into the causes of our miseries* (see p. 75) was ready to impose some limitations on the liberty of printing. "Truly," he writes, after saying that truth and reason were the old licensers, "my spirit could never go forth with any other way of licensing, or midwifing such births as are books into the world, . . . and, if so be our conceptions and births want either one or both, let the parent smart for his lie, and be fast locked in Bedlam till he recover his wits again : and if he be libellous, as too many are, let his own place, the pillory, instruct him to better manners, but if he hath blasphemed God . . . let him die."

[3] This is almost a reproduction of Bastwick's language in the Star Chamber.

my judgment, to die in a prison before they act or stoop unto so dishonourable a thing as this is to their Lord and Master, as to maintain the Black-coats with tithes, whom they look upon as the professed enemies of their annointed Christ.'[1]

Some sympathy may be due even to the 'Black-coats' if they were afraid of the consequences of Lilburne's doctrine that his conscience was to be the measure of his obedience to the law. 'Freeborn John,' as he was nicknamed—from his persistent appeal to the rights of the 'freeborn Englishman,' whom he supposed to have derived from the medieval law a claim to almost unfettered liberty, may fairly be regarded as a rough unpolished successor of Eliot in the ranks of those who have shown that, alongside of those precursors of human progress who think imaginatively, there is a place for those who dare to suffer rather than bend before injustice. Lilburne in the course of his career was, indeed, in prisons oft, and it is easy to condemn him as a fanatic who suffered on behalf of opinions which, even when they were true, were exaggerated by him out of all proportion to their value. The fact of his readiness to suffer was—irrespective of the causes of his suffering—the offering which he had to make to a generation which was striving to break the bonds which law and custom had imposed on the energies of the individual.

Importance of Lilburne's views.

At the time Lilburne's utterances were regarded with special apprehension. He was not merely a private enthusiast. He was Lieutenant-Colonel Lilburne in the army of the Eastern Association, and there was a strong probability that men who shared his views would have even more influence over the soldiery than they had hitherto possessed.

Lilburne as yet not a private person.

Upon these conflicts, political and religious, Charles founded his hopes. Having failed to capture the fortresses of the enemy by open attack, he had lately been attempting to use treachery with equal ill-success. On November 28 he issued a commission to young Roger L'Estrange to reduce the town of Lynn with the co-operation of the in-

Nov. 28. Commission to reduce Lynn.

[1] *Copy of a Letter.* E. 24, 22.

habitants. L'Estrange, who offered money and rewards freely,

Dec. 28.
L'Estrange
sentenced,

was detected in the conspiracy, and was sentenced to death as a spy. The Royalists strongly protested that he had been engaged in an act of war, and

1645.
Jan. 1.
and re-
prieved.

Parliament, perhaps from fear of reprisals, spared his life.[1] He remained long in prison, and lived to acquire more notoriety with his pen than he had succeeded in acquiring with his sword.

The attempt on Lynn was paralleled by an attempt on Abingdon. Major-General Browne, who was in command of

1644.
Nov.-Dec.
Digby's
negotiation
with
Browne.

the place, was known to be discontented in consequence of the neglect of Parliament to furnish him with supplies, and Digby, always awake to the possibilities of an intrigue, opened a secret negotiation with him in the hope of persuading him to deliver up Abingdon to the King. Browne met craft with craft, professed to be

Dec. 19.

inclined to betray his trust, and so gained time for strengthening his fortifications. As soon as his new works were completed he defied Digby to do his worst.[2]

On January 10 Charles, finding that he had been mocked,

1645.
Jan. 10.
The
Royalists
repulsed at
Abingdon.

despatched troops to surprise the place. Browne was quite ready to receive them, and the Royalists were driven back with heavy loss. Amongst the slain was Sir Henry Gage, the energetic Governor of Oxford.[3]

The failure at Abingdon was not the only evidence of Charles's military weakness. During the first days of January

Jan. 9.
Goring at
Farnham.

Goring, now Lord Goring through his father's creation as Earl of Norwich, at the head of a considerable body of horse, swept over Hampshire, and on the 9th he even entered Surrey, and occupied Farnham. It was, however, easier for him to seize upon a post so far in advance of the main Royalist lines than to maintain himself in it, and he was soon in full retreat, not in consequence of the superiority of the enemy, but because his men were exhausted and he was left without means to pay them.[4]

---

[1] *Rushw.* v. 804.　　　　　[2] *Ibid.* v. 803.
[3] Browne to the Com. of B. K. Jan. 11. *Com. Letter Book.*
[4] Goring to the King, Jan. 9. *Warburton,* iii. 46.

The poverty of the King was no greater than the poverty of the gentlemen and noblemen who surrounded him in Oxford. Poverty at Oxford. Whether their estates lay in the enemy's country or not, their rents remained unpaid, and the distress amongst this loyal class was marked by the increasing number of those who made their way to Westminster, took the Covenant, and compounded for their own property by the payment of a heavy fine. Amongst those who remained staunch at Oxford distress had almost led to a mutiny. The Oxford Parliament was in session, and its members called loudly for peace. Charles could bear the opposition no longer. On the Jan. 11. Arrest of three peers. 11th he ordered the arrest of three peers, of Percy, of Andover, and of the Lord Savile who, in 1640, had forged the letter of invitation to the Scots, and had recently been created Earl of Sussex. The grounds assigned for their imprisonment were that they had held intelligence with the rebels and had spoken disrespectfully of the King,[1] but it is probable that the original cause of Charles's displeasure was the persistency with which Percy and the other lords had urged him not merely to open negotiations with the Parliament, but to treat in person in London.[2]

With his usual sanguine assurance Charles was quicksighted to perceive every sign of weakness in the enemy and Charles still sanguine. blind to every indication of his own. "Likewise," he had not long ago written to his wife, "I am put in very good hope—some hold it a certainty—that, if I could come to a fair treaty, the ringleading rebels could not hinder me from a good peace; first, because their own party are most weary of the war ; and likewise for the great distractions which Jan. 9. at this time most assuredly are amongst themselves, as Presbyterians against Independents in religion, and general against general in point of command."[3] His

---

[1] *Dugdale's Diary* ; The King's answer, *Clar. MSS.* 1,814 ; Reply of the Earl of Sussex, *Camden Miscellany*, viii. Compare for rumours in London, *The London Post*, E. 25, 13 ; *Perfect Passages*, E. 25, 17.

[2] The King to the Queen, Feb. 15. *King's Cabinet Opened*, p. 7. E. 292, 27.

[3] The King to the Queen, Dec. *Ibid.* p. 11. E. 292, 27.

expectations were indeed of the highest. "The settling of religion and the militia," he again wrote, "are the first to be treated on ; and be confident that I will neither quit episcopacy nor that sword which God hath given into my hands." [1]

Yet above all these reasonings Charles found his principal encouragement in the execution of the wronged Archbishop.

Jan. 14.
Strafford's
blood
appeased.

"Nothing," he assured the Queen, "can be more evident than that Strafford's innocent blood hath been one of the great causes of God's just judgment upon this nation by a furious civil war, both sides hitherto being almost equally guilty, but now this last crying blood being totally theirs, I believe it is no presumption hereafter to hope that the hand of justice must be heavier upon them and lighter upon us, looking now upon our cause, having passed through our faults." [2]

[1] The King to the Queen, Jan. 9. *The King's Cabinet Opened*, p. 1.
[2] The King to the Queen, Jan. 14. *Ibid.* p. 23.

CHAPTER XXV.

WHEN, on January 4, the conflict between the Houses on the subject of the punishment of the Archbishop was brought to a close by the passage of the Attainder Ordinance through the Upper House, the conflict on the subject of military organisation seemed to be no nearer to a settlement. Three times during the preceding week [1] the Commons had called for the report of their committee on the charges brought against Manchester. Nothing, however, was done, and the proposal was probably only intended as a strong hint to the Lords that if they did not wish an impeachment brought against the Earl, they must take the Self-Denying Ordinance into speedy consideration. Cromwell, indeed, seems already to have abandoned any serious thought of pursuing the attack upon which he had entered. In the senate as in the field, he was always ready to draw up when his charge was at the fiercest, and to vary his methods in accordance with the necessities of the moment. He knew far better than to become a mere 'Rupert of debate,' and a prospect of gaining all that he wanted, without the friction which would have attended an impeachment of Manchester, now opened itself before him.

For some weeks the Committee of Both Kingdoms had been employed discussing the scheme for the remodelling the army which had been referred to it in November.[2] It was

margin notes: 1645. Jan. 4. The conflict between the Houses on military organisation.

---

[1] On Dec. 26, Dec. 30, and Jan. 1. *C.J.* iv. 2, 4, 6.
[2] See p. 79.

universally acknowledged to be necessary, not merely because Essex was sluggish or Cromwell factious, but because the arrangements for paying the troops had entirely broken down.

The New Model dis-cussed in the Committee of Both Kingdoms.

Jan. 6. Resolution of the Committee.

At last, on January 6, the committee came to the conclusion, that, irrespectively of local forces, the army ought to consist of 21,000 men, and that its pay, which was the all-important matter, should be dependent on the monthly payment of taxes regularly imposed, and not on the fluctuating attention of a political assembly, or the still more fluctuating goodwill of county committees. These taxes were to be assessed on the counties least exposed to the stress of war, whilst those in which the conflict was raging might be left to support the local garrisons and any special force which they might think good to employ in their own defence.[1]

The plan thus sketched out furnished the Lords with a fresh motive for opposing themselves to the Self-Denying Ordinance. On January 7, abandoning the calcu-

Jan. 7. The Lords state their objections to the Self-Denying Ordinance.

lated silence which they had hitherto observed, they informed the other House of their objections. After an expression of dissatisfaction at the proposal to incapacitate the Peers—whose part in war had always been the foremost—from military service, they took the practical ground that it would be unwise to throw the army out of gear till the New Model had actually come into existence, especially as its creation would evidently be a work of time.[2] The obvious answer to this final argument was to make the greater speed, and the New Model, which was

Jan 9. The New Model in the House of Commons.

Jan. 11. It is adopted.

sent by the Committee of Both Kingdoms to the House of Commons on the 9th, was adopted without a division on the 11th.[3] Already signs were visible that there were other than Parliamentary reasons for dealing swiftly with the army. The divisions of the senate had spread to the camp, and on the 10th Cromwell informed the House that no less than forty of

---

[1] Com. of B. K. Day Book, Jan. 6.
[2] *L.J.* vii. 129.
[3] *C.J.* iv. 15, 16.

Manchester's officers had subscribed a petition asking Parliament to continue him in his command, and that at
Henley a colonel, to whom orders had been sent to
change his quarters, had refused to obey till he had
heard what answer had been given to this demand.[1]

Jan. 10.
News of
distractions
in the
Parliamen-
tary army.

The Lords resolved at last to stand firm. On the 13th,
with only four dissentient votes—those of Kent, Nottingham,
Northumberland, and Say—they threw out the Self-
Denying Ordinance.[2] If there was to be a New
Model they wished their own members to be at the
head of it. Their motives were intelligible enough.
Their prudence was less discernible.

Jan. 13.
The Lords
throw out
the Self-
Denying
Ordinance.

The first thought of the chiefs of the Independents, in
whose hands the leadership of the Commons now was, seems
to have been to fall back on the old attack upon
Manchester. On the 15th the two committees
charged with the investigation of the points raised
in the course of the dispute[3] were ordered to make
their report. On the 20th Lisle, speaking, as it
would seem, on behalf of both committees, reported
that the Lords, in nominating peers to take part in
the examination of a member of the House of Commons[4] without previously obtaining leave from the House to
which he belonged, had been guilty of a breach of privilege.
At the same time he recommended that the charges brought
on both sides should be thoroughly investigated, Manchester
being allowed every opportunity of conducting his defence.[5]

Jan. 15.
Report
ordered on
the dispute
between
Manchester
and Crom-
well.

Jan. 20.
Lisle's
report.

It needs no evidence to show that the revival of the attack
on Manchester was bitterly resented by the Peers. Yet one
piece of evidence there is which paints their exasperation to the life. On the day of Lisle's report,
perhaps in consequence of the prolonged sitting of
the House of Commons, no member of that House
was present at the Committee of Both Kingdoms. The
six peers who were in their places—Northumberland, Essex,

Incident at
a meeting
of the
Committee
of both
Kingdoms.

---

[1] Whitacre's Diary, *Add. MSS.* 31,116, fol. 185b.
[2] *L.J.* vii. 136.   [3] See pp. 83, 89.
[4] See p. 83.   [5] *C.J.* iv. 25.

Warwick, Manchester, Say, and Wharton—passed a resolution 'that the business of the opinion of some in Lieutenant-General Cromwell's regiment against fighting in any cause whatsoever, be taken into consideration to-morrow in the after-noon.'[1] When, on the following afternoon, the Commoners mustered in strength, no more was heard of this strange proposal, which was doubtless never intended to be more than an elaborate joke.

Jan. 21.

On the other hand, the blow of the Commons was well-timed. They did not bind themselves to proceed with the inquiry into Manchester's conduct, but they would be ready to do so if the Lords rejected the New Model as they had rejected the Self-Denying Ordinance. In that case what was now but a reconnaissance in force might be converted into a real attack.

Intentions of the Commons.

For the present the New Model Ordinance was to be pushed on. On the 21st, by a vote of 101 to 69, Cromwell and the younger Vane acting as tellers for the majority, the House resolved that the commander-in-chief of the new army should be Sir Thomas Fairfax. Skippon was then named as Major-General. The post of Lieutenant-General, carrying with it the command of the cavalry, was significantly left unfilled. By rejecting the Self-Denying Ordinance the Lords had torn down the barrier which the best cavalry officer in England had erected in the way of his own employment.

Fairfax to command the New Model.

Skippon to be Major General.

The Lieu-tenant-General-ship vacant.

Yet, on the other hand, there were grave reasons against according the highest military position to one who had taken so prominent a part in political strife. No such reason could be assigned against the promotion of Fairfax, who had no seat in the House. He had already shown himself patient in disaster and full of vigour to turn disaster into victory. His rapid blows delivered in the fight for the Yorkshire clothing towns at the opening of the war, and repeated on a larger scale when he threw himself upon the Royalists at Nantwich, marked him out as a general who would

Cromwell and Fairfax.

[1] *Com. of B. K. Day Book*, Jan. 20.

never wander aimlessly like Essex into Cornwall, or loiter, like
Manchester at Newbury, on a stricken field.   If he had a fault
as a soldier, it lay in his habit of plunging unthinkingly into
the thick of the fight, regardless of his duties as a commander.
What was specially to the purpose was that he possessed to the
full the civic virtue of obedience to the State, and that he
had stood entirely aloof from the recent disputes.   Most likely
no one in England—probably not Fairfax himself—knew
whether he was a Presbyterian or an Independent.

On the 28th the New Model Ordinance was despatched to
the Lords.   The Lords were well aware that the charges
against Manchester were held in reserve, to be
proceeded in or dropped as circumstances might
demand.   If, however, Cromwell, in his controversy
with the Peers, held the sword in one hand, he extended the olive branch with the other.   Between him and
the Scots there had long been bitter antagonism.   Yet it was
Cromwell who on the 30th appeared in the House
of Commons as the spokesman of the Committee of
Both Kingdoms to urge the necessity of bringing the
Scottish army southwards.[1]   If, as must surely be
the case, this implies that he was favourable to the proposal, it
looks as if he wished to reassure the Lords by giving them
security that the New Model would not occupy the whole
field.   If the New Model would be in a special sense the army
of the House of Commons, the Scottish force would be in a
special sense the army of the House of Lords.   When once
the negotiations at Uxbridge were at an end—and it did not
need a tithe of Cromwell's shrewdness to give certainty that
they would not produce a peace—the Scots would bear their
part in the war as readily as the newly organised English army.
Everything which Cromwell had done, as well as everything
which he had deliberately omitted to do, would thus conduce
to his primary object of defeating the King.   When that was
accomplished it would be time to think of that which was to
follow.

There can be little doubt that, to Cromwell and the Inde-

[1] *C.J.* iv. 37.

*Jan. 28.
The New
Model
Ordinance
sent to the
Lords.*

*Jan. 30.
Cromwell
supports
the advance
of the Scots.*

pendents, the negotiation which was now opening at Uxbridge was but one more step towards victory over the King.

The Independents expect the Treaty of Uxbridge to fail.

They were far more likely to be able to prolong the war if they allowed the Scots to try their hands at making peace. As a record of futile proposals and abrupt rejections of those proposals the Treaty of Uxbridge deserves but scanty recognition. Its importance in the history of the war lies in this, that it brought the Scots into line with the English War-party in the decisive campaign which

The treaty of Uxbridge a Scottish negotiation.

was about to open. To all intents and purposes the Treaty of Uxbridge was a Scottish negotiation. The propositions offered to the King had originally been drawn up under Scottish influence. It was Henderson and no English divine who was appointed as the chief clerical assistant to furnish the needful theological arguments in favour of Presbyterianism, whilst Loudoun and Maitland—who now bore the title of Earl of Lauderdale in consequence of the recent death of his father—were foremost amongst the lay Parliamentary commissioners in supporting the pleadings of Henderson. As far as our knowledge reaches, Vane and St. John, who represented the Independents at Uxbridge, if they were not absolutely silent, took as little part in the debates as possible, and it is doing them no injustice to suppose that, like Cromwell at Westminster, they were keeping themselves in reserve till the Scots had played their game and lost it.

The commissioners from both sides arrived at Uxbridge on January 29. Amongst those sent by the King were some, such

Jan. 29. Arrival of the commissioners.

as Hertford and Southampton, who were sincerely desirous of peace; but they were bound by their instructions, and they could only toil in vain round the impossible task of reconciling the King's unbending devotion to Episcopacy with the equally unbending Presbyterianism of the Scots.

To do Loudoun and Lauderdale justice, it was not by

Motives of the Scottish commissioners.

Presbyterian fanaticism that they were impelled. They did not feel towards bishops as Prynne or Henderson felt towards them. The Scottish revolution had been political as well as ecclesiastical, and though the nobles who had put themselves at its head had, with more or less conscientiousness, appropriated the ideas of the ecclesiastical wing of their party, they were principally concerned in maintaining the dominant position which their share in the revolution had given them. There are no signs that they were animated by the crusading spirit, or that they were conscious of a Divine mission to exterminate Episcopacy in the British Isles. They knew, however, that Scotland was a poorer and weaker country than England, and they believed that Scotland, or, to speak more plainly, their own authority in Scotland, would be secure only when a government was established in England which was homogeneous with that which they themselves wielded in Scotland. An Episcopalian and monarchical England or an Independent and republican England would be constantly tempted to interfere with that peculiar compound of ecclesiastical democracy and political aristocracy which was the temporary outcome of the historical development of their own country.

Such motives naturally led the Scottish commissioners to strive after the impossible. They knew that a restored monarchy in England, surrounded by Presbyterian institutions, would be a weak monarchy as far as Scotland was concerned, and they knew too little and cared too little about the wants of England or the mental characteristics of Charles to ask whether the object of their desire was practicable. They were not likely to reveal their whole secret to men of their own speech. In the presence of Sabran they felt no hesitation. Before setting out from Westminster they told him plainly that, though it was unnecessary to destroy Episcopacy in England on religious grounds, its overthrow was an indispensable condition of the union and peace of the two kingdoms. If Charles would give way on this point, they would throw their weight into his scale on all other matters.[1]

Their aims acknowledged to the French ambassador.

[1] "Touttes leurs responces ont concouru que S. M. de la Grande Bretagne ayant consenty en Escosse la forme de Religion, par l'eschange des Evesques au Presbiteriat, laquelle n'estant point essentielle pour la foy l'estoit pour l'union et respos des deux Royaumes, S. M. de la Grande

This attitude of the Scots, so far as it was known, could not fail to excite dissatisfaction in the War-party. It was the wish of the Scots and of the majority of the Peers that the question of religion should be settled first,[1] but to this the Lower House, now under the leadership of the Independents, opposed an unshaken resolution. It was finally decided that the three points of religion, of the militia, and of Ireland should be discussed in rotation, three days being assigned to each subject. If, after nine days, no conclusion had been reached, three days more were to be devoted to religion, and so on with the other points. If at the end of twenty working days the two sides were still unable to agree, the negotiation was to be at an end.[2]

Dissatisfaction of the War-party.

Conditions of the treaty.

Bretagne ne la pouvant reffuser, et qu'ils me pouvoient assurer que le Roy d'Ang^re y consentant touttes sortes de propositions seroient bientost accommodeés au gré de S. M."—Sabran to Brienne, $\frac{\text{Jan. 30}}{\text{Feb. 9}}$. *Add. MSS.* 5,461, fol. 65b.

[1] "J'ay sçeu que les Escossois et la Chambre des Communes, ou plustost les Independants qui en sont, ont debattu longuement entre eux si l'on commenceroient ou fineroit par la Religion, les Escossois ont desiré de commencer par là ou est leur principal interest et attachement à leur Convenant, pour, s'ils obtiennent leur fin, se trouver puis arbitres du different par le poids qu'ils donneront du costé ou ils voudront pancher, qui sera des lors celuy du Roy, et des Pairs, pour ne tomber dans un changement de forme de gouvernement qui leur prejudicieroit. Les autres voulloient finir par là, et voir tous les autres articles vuidez auparavant ou ils s'interessent plus qu'en celuy de la Religion, et ceux de la Chambre Haute (qui ne parlent qu'apres les Escossois, et qui ne trouvent plus de salut à leur prerogatives qu'en l'espoir que les Escossois disputants pour l'authorité du Roy, ils le feront aussy pour leur dignité particuliere et de tous) s'attachent entierement auxdits Escossois, et s'opiniastrent pour l'amour d'eux au poinct de la Religion, affin que ce contentement le acquiere au Roy et à eux. En sorte que j'en tire cette consequence que si S. M. de la Grande Bretagne se relasche de la Religion, les Escossois n'ayants plus d'interest qu'en une paix qui asseure ce qui leur est deub, et leur pays, auront grand desmelé avec la Chambre des Communes et Londres ; et si le Roy d'Angleterre s'obstine à sa Religion et de ne la vouloir contester que tous articles ne soyent consentys, la dite Chambre des Communes est pour en estre d'accord, et s'opposer au desir des Escossois."—Sabran to Brienne, Feb. $\frac{6}{16}$. *Ibid.* fol. 76.

[2] *Rushw.* v. 861.

That any one should have expected a favourable result from this negotiation is indeed marvellous. The Three Pro-

The Three Propositions of Uxbridge. positions of Uxbridge, as the terms which the Parliamentary commissioners were empowered to offer on these three heads were afterwards called, showed that the incapacity of the leaders of the Peace-party to understand the excellence of compromise equalled if it did not surpass that of Charles himself. In the first, they asked that the King should take the Covenant, should assent to the abolition of Episcopacy and the Prayer-book, to the establishment of Presbyterianism and the Directory. In the second, they demanded that the militia and the navy should be permanently controlled by commissioners named by Parliament, joined by a body of Scottish commissioners not exceeding in number a third part of those of England, whilst the Scottish militia was to be at the orders of commissioners named by the Scottish Parliament, joined by English commissioners, not exceeding a third part of their own body. In the third, they insisted on the passing of an Act to make void the Irish Cessation, and on Charles's permitting the war in Ireland to be prosecuted by the English Parliament without hindrance from himself.[1]

After a few preliminary arrangements had been made, the main proceedings were opened at Uxbridge on January 31.

Jan. 31. The religious difficulty. A rhetorical discussion between Henderson and a doctor from Oxford, on the respective claims of Presbyterianism and Episcopacy to Divine authority, called forth from Hertford the blunt remark that he believed neither the one nor the other to be of Divine right. The laymen then proceeded to business. Little was gained by the change. The Parliamentary commissioners had been instructed to insist that the King should take the Covenant and consent

The abolition of Episcopacy demanded. to the abolition of Episcopacy. On the other side, Hyde, knowing that there were differences of opinion amongst his opponents, did his best to stir up strife in their ranks by asking subtle questions on the nature of the Presbyterian system. It was not diplomacy of a high order, but, perhaps, nothing better was possible, unless Charles was

[1] *Rushw.* v. 865, 879, 897.

honestly prepared to meet the adverse proposal with something more than a blank negative.[1]

Charles's intellect was not flexible, and he had recently shown how little he was able to enter into the feelings of

A form of prayer sanctioned by the King.

the nobler spirits among his antagonists. He had authorised the use of a form of prayer in which the Divine assistance in bringing the war to an end was to be implored by all loyal subjects, and in which God was to be asked to 'let the truth clearly appear who those men are which under pretence of the public good do pursue their private ends.'[2] In a letter which he despatched to Nicholas, who was one of his commissioners at Oxford, he clothed the

Feb. 6. A free-spoken letter.

same idea in freer language. "I should think," he wrote, "if in your private discourses . . . with the London commissioners you would put them in mind that they were arrant rebels, and that their end must be damnation, ruin, and infamy except they repented and found some way to free themselves from the damnable way they are in . . . it might do good."[3]

Untoward as Charles's language was, there were influences around him in favour of peace which it was almost impossible

Feb. 10. Toleration scheme of the Oxford clergy.

for him directly to resist. The clergy at Oxford were consulted as to the limits of possible concession, and the result was a joint declaration, which has the merit of containing the first scheme of toleration on a national basis assented to in England by any public body.[4] A

Feb. 13. A scheme of Church reform.

plan of Church reform was, in consequence, brought forward on the 13th by the King's commissioners at Uxbridge. At least, it compared favourably with anything produced on the other side. Episcopacy was to be maintained, but the bishops were not to exercise coercive jurisdiction without the consent of presbyters chosen by the clergy

[1] *Rushw.* v. 861 ; *Whitelocke*, 128; *Clarendon*, viii. 221.

[2] *A form of Common Prayer*, p. 11. E. 27, 4.

[3] The King to Nicholas. *Evelyn's Diary* (ed. 1879), iv. 149.

[4] The clergy's paper tendered concerning religion, Feb. 10. *Clarendon MSS.* 1824. Printed in *The English Historical Review* for April 1887, p. 341.

of the diocese. Abuses were to be remedied by Act of Parliament. The Book of Common Prayer was to be retained subject to such alterations as might be agreed on, and—far more important than all this—freedom was to 'be left to all persons of what opinions soever in matters of ceremony, and . . . all the penalties of the laws and customs which enjoin those ceremonies' to 'be suspended.'[1]

The Oxford clergy had, at least, made their intention clear. "We think it lawful," they had declared, "that a toleration be given—by suspending the penalties of all laws—both to the Presbyterians and Independents." There is evidently here the germ, or more than the germ, of the great policy of 1689. In passing through Charles's mind the phrase had become more hazy, as it does not appear whether he meant to permit the clergy to vary the ceremonies in the one Church, or to allow the existence of congregations outside the Church, provided that, however much they might differ from it in ceremony, they agree with it in doctrine. Yet for all that, it is to him, and not to his antagonists, that the honour belongs of being the first to propound the terms of peace which ultimately closed the strife. The bid was one for the support of the Independents against the Presbyterians, and was perhaps the easier for him to make if, as may have been the case, he had no expectation that it would ever be accepted, and had only consented to the step in order to gratify his importunate supporters.

It is not a matter for surprise that the Independents made no sign of accepting the proposed terms. Of Charles, and of all that came from Charles, they were profoundly suspicious. Nor is it likely that even if their distrust had been removed they would have closed with the present offer. Tolerationists as they were, they were not yet prepared to admit that the ceremonies of the Church of England were within the pale of toleration. They had suffered too much from Episcopal authority to regard its retention in any form as part of a possible solution of the difficulties of the country.

What was the meaning of these words?

The offer rejected by the Independents.

[1] *Rushw.* v. 872, 873.

If the Independents were not to be won, Charles's proposal was doomed. The Scots, and the supporters of the Scots, still

A Presbyterian settlement urged,

fancied that it was possible for them to drive the King to assent to the establishment of the Presbyterian system. Pembroke, who was always blurting out what other men were ashamed to say, and who was entirely indifferent to forms of church government, reminded one of the Royal commissioners that if Charles would give way now, it would be easy for him to recover his power hereafter.[1]

but rejected.

Such counsels of treachery were addressed in vain to Charles. He was an intriguer, but he was not a hypocrite. He was ready to bribe his opponents by offering to deserters offices, 'so that they be not of great trust';[2] but he refused to abandon that Episcopacy which was in his eyes both a Divine institution and one of the strongest buttresses of his own authority.

On the question of the militia a difference of opinion had manifested itself as distinctly as on the question of religion.

The militia.

The Parliamentary commissioners asked that it should be commanded in perpetuity by persons named by the Houses, whilst Charles was only ready to place it temporarily under a body, one half of which was to be named by Parliament and the other half by himself. At the end of three years this compromise was to be abandoned, and the entire authority over the militia was to revert to himself. As for

Ireland.

Ireland, the discussion soon degenerated into a wrangle on the question whether the Cessation had been accepted to save the Protestants or to encourage the Papists ; and for those who took the latter view, it was an easy step to argue that Charles's proposed religious compromise was only intended to secure toleration for Papists.[3]

The growing divergence of opinion at Uxbridge could not fail in producing its effect at Westminster. As early as February 4, when it was known that difficulties had been thrown

---

[1] *Clarendon*, viii. 243.

[2] Memorial for Nicholas, Feb. 17. *Evelyn's Diary* (ed. 1879), iv. 152.

[3] *Perfect Passages.* E. 269, 5 ; E. 270, 23.

in the way of the abolition of Episcopacy, the Peers offered
to pass the New Model Ordinance with the addition of certain

Feb. 4.
The Peers
pass the
New Model
Ordinance
with pro-
visoes.

provisoes [1] which would, as they hoped, render it innocuous.   They asked, first, that all officers above
the rank of lieutenant might be nominated by both
Houses, thus securing to themselves a veto upon every
appointment ; and, secondly, that both officers and
soldiers should not only take the Covenant, but should submit
'to the form of Church Government that is already voted by
both Houses of Parliament.'

To the first proviso Cromwell offered a steadfast opposition.
He asked that the appointment of the officers should rest with

Feb. 7.
The pro-
visoes
modified
by the
Commons.

the commander-in-chief alone.   The Parliamentary
spirit was, however, too strong for him, and the
Commons, adopting a compromise, resolved by a vote
of 82 to 63 that, though the appointment of officers
should be made by the commander-in-chief, the approval of
the Houses should in all cases be necessary ; an approval
which, unless in very exceptional cases, it would be difficult to

. Feb. 8.

refuse.   With respect to the second proviso, the
Commons agreed that officers and soldiers should
take the Covenant, but they absolutely refused to enforce submission to the form of Church Government voted by both
Houses, on the plea that if the Covenant were taken such a
submission would be unnecessary, and that the votes of the
Houses on the subject were not yet complete. [2]

On the 12th the Commons argued before the Lords in
favour of their amendments.   On the same day news reached

Feb. 12.
Bad news
from Wey-
mouth.

Westminster that a party of Royalists under Sir
Lewis Dyves had seized one of the forts which
guarded Weymouth. [3]   Waller was at once ordered to
relieve the town, but though he would gladly have

Feb. 14.
Mutiny of
Waller's
cavalry.

obeyed, his cavalry, which had formerly served under
Essex, broke out into mutiny at Leatherhead.   "We
will rather go," they said, "under any the Lord General

[1] L.J. vii. 175.
[2] C.J. iv. 43, 44; L.J. vii. 191.
[3] C.J. iv. 46 ; The True Informer, E. 269, 21.

should appoint than with Sir William Waller, with all the money in England." [1]

When this mishap was known in Westminster, it was also known that the King's commissioners at Uxbridge had presented a scheme of Church reform, which, in spite of its intrinsic merits, was hateful alike to the Presbyterians of both nations. That scheme fused for a time the Peace-party and the War-party into one. Both alike declared for war, which,

Feb. 15.
Passing of the New Model Ordinance.

as the mutiny at Leatherhead gave evidence, it would be impossible to carry on with a disorganised army. The Lords gave way at once, and on the 15th they passed the New Model Ordinance as it had last come from the Commons without any further difficulty. [2]

Formally at least the negotiations at Uxbridge still dragged on. An attempt which led to nothing was made to discover

Continued discussions at Uxbridge.

some compromise on the question of the command of the militia. Time was running short when Charles's commissioners made an unexpected proposal. Let the armies on both sides be disbanded, and His

Feb. 20.
Charles proposes to go to Westminster.

Majesty would then repair in person to Westminster. [3] To this fresh suggestion the Parliamentary commissioners returned a deaf ear. They were certainly in the right. "As for trusting the rebels," Charles had only the day before written to his wife, "either by going to London or disbanding my army before a peace, do no ways fear my hazarding so cheaply or foolishly; for I esteem the interest thou hast in me at a far dearer rate, and pretend to have a little more wit—at least by the sympathy that is betwixt us—than to put myself in the reverence of perfidious rebels." [4] Charles now, it seems, imagined that after a complete disbandment on both sides he would be able to secure the restoration of the excluded members to their places at Westminster,

---

[1] *Com. of B. K. Day Book*, Feb. 15.

[2] *L.J.* vii. 195.

[3] *Rushw.* v. 920.

[4] The King to the Queen, Feb. 19. *The King's Cabinet Opened*, p. 6. E. 292, 27.

and would thus be able to impose his own conditions on the reunited Parliament.[1]

On February 22, as the days fixed for the negotiation were running to an end, the royal commissioners made a final attempt to reopen the religious question. The King, they said, was ready to discuss the future settlement of the Church with Parliament and a National Synod summoned for the purpose. Neither this nor a repetition of the proposal to disband the armies met with any favourable response from the representatives of the Houses.[2]

Feb. 22. National Synod proposed.

The negotiation, or, as it was commonly called, the Treaty of Uxbridge, was thus brought to an end. No one except Cromwell and his adherents had gained anything by it. The active support of the Scots in the war against the King was secured now that they had made the discovery that Charles was unwilling to become a Presbyterian. The modern reader, indeed, is apt to brush aside the long argument on which the thoughts of contemporaries were fixed, and to concentrate his attention on the scheme of Church reform proposed by the Oxford clergy as the one object of interest in the whole dreary futility. Charles was himself the first to show how little he cared for it, by throwing it over in favour of another scheme for calling a National Synod. Yet if ever there was an idea which an earnest man would have cherished, it was that of toleration. To preach it in season and out of season, to render it palatable where it was unpalatable, to meet objections and suggest modifications, would have been a task for the highest statesmanship and the firmest courage. Even if Charles had possessed the necessary qualifications for the task, there was a fatal bar to its accom-

End of the Treaty of Uxbridge.

[1] " Le Roy de la Grande Bretagne desire venant ici, que toutes personnes Parlementaires soient admises ez chambres, ce que le Parlement n'a garde de permettre, parce que le parti de S. M. seroit le plus puissant à cause des divisions et de l'affection que plusieurs y ont pour le Roi de la Grande Bretagne."—Sabran to Brienne, $\frac{Feb\ 27.}{March\ 9.}$. *Add. MSS.* 5,461, fol. 124ᵇ.

[2] *Rushw.* v. 922.

plishment by him. The convictions to which he clung with all the tenacity of his nature were opposed to the scheme which he had allowed to be put forward in his name. Not much more than two years was to pass when the same scheme was to be offered to him by some of the very men who now rejected it, to be rejected in turn by himself.

CHAPTER XXVI.

TIPPERMUIR, ABERDEEN, AND INVERLOCHY.

ON February 19, when the negotiations at Uxbridge were drawing to a close, Charles received news [1] which, though without influence upon the resolution which he had already formed to reject the Parliamentary offers, undoubtedly inspired him with a fresh hope of gaining the mastery in the campaign about to open. In the Scottish Highlands a soldier of genius was carrying all before him in the name of the King.

1645.
Feb. 19.
News from
the High-
lands.

Though Montrose was an idealist capable of believing in his heart of hearts that Charles was indeed 'great, good, and just,' it was not for the restoration of a dead past that he drew his sword. He stood up for that which was, in some sort, the hope of the future. He detested the bigotry of the Presbyterian clergy ; and he detested still more the despotic sway of the great nobles who had banded themselves with Argyle, and had risen to power by flattering the prejudices of the clergy. Though there can indeed be little doubt that his own buoyancy of self-reliance, with its accompanying love of pre-eminence, urged him forward in the path which he had chosen, yet his ambition was closely intertwined with a nobler sentiment. To him the King whom he served was not the actual Charles, but an imaginary being who was eager to free Scotland from a stern and relentless tyranny, and to make possible again the free and joyous life of old. A clergy restraining themselves to their spiritual functions, and a nobility devoting themselves to

1644.
Montrose's
idealism.

His aims.

[1] The King to the Queen, Feb. 19. *The King's Cabinet Opened,* p. 5. E. 292, 27.

their country without self-seeking, filled in the picture of the future as it was reflected in Montrose's mind, and it was to be realised, not by raising the king to absolute power, but by the support which he would derive from the gentry and the nobility of secondary position. Montrose, in short, was the champion, so to speak, of a diffused aristocracy, rather than of that monarchy the name of which was so frequently on his lips.[1]

Unhappily for Montrose, the means of realising such aims were not to be found on Scottish soil. Argyle's Presbyterian supporters left much to be desired, but at least they had given to Scotland that discipline which had enabled the laborious middle class to assert itself in the face of what had but a short time ago been an anarchical nobility. The well-founded belief that the restoration to power of a nobility hostile to the ecclesiastical organisation of the middle class boded no good either to order or to liberty rendered Montrose's cause practically hopeless.

Obsstacles in his way.

Of all this Montrose saw nothing. He did not, like Cromwell, estimate at their true value the means with which he proposed to gain his ends. He dashed at his high aim like a Paladin of romance, conscious of the purity of his intentions, and trusting to his own genius to mould to useful purposes the intractable forces which chance might throw in his way. Self-confidence, indeed, he had to the full, but it was a self-confidence of which only noble spirits are capable, because it was founded on the belief that in the presence of a great effort base spirits would change their natures, and join with one heart in es'ablishing the reign of truth and justice. His dream was more of a 'devout imagination' than any that had ever entered into the mind of the most fanatical Calvinist.

His weakness.

Montrose's failure in his attempt upon the Lowlands in the spring of 1644[2] seemed at first to render hopeless the realisa-

[1] In this respect he occupies much the same position in Scottish history as the authors of the petition of the Knights Bachelors to Edward, after the Provisions of Oxford, occupy in English history. In both cases the Crown was to be strengthened against the higher nobility, with no intention of restoring the old absolutism.

[2] See vol. i. p. 336.

tion of his projects. When Rupert burst into the North,
Montrose rode off to him to beg for troops. He found him
at York, the day after his ruinous defeat at Marston
Moor. Rupert carelessly offered a thousand horse,
but night brought counsel, and on the following
morning he declared that he could not spare a single man.

*July 3.
He asks
Rupert for
help.*

Montrose now knew that he must depend on himself alone.
He was aware that Antrim had been commissioned to bring
over to the Highlands 2,000 Irishmen, but for some
time he had heard nothing of him. He therefore
despatched young Lord Ogilvy, the heir of the Earl
of Airlie, and Captain Rollock to Scotland to spy out the
country in disguise. In a fortnight his messengers returned
with tidings that the Presbyterian Government was supreme,
and that no man dared to move a hand against it. Yet Montrose, in spite of the adverse report of his own spies, could not
throw off the belief that at least in the Lowlands beyond the
Tay he might find support ; and in the spirit of his own lines—

*Montrose
and An-
trim.*

> " He either fears his fate too much,
>   Or his deserts are small,
> Who dares not put it to the touch,
>   And win or lose it all,"

he resolved to try what might be effected in those quarters by
the magic of his presence. On August 18, sending
away all of his remaining adherents except Rollock
and an officer named Sibbald, he set out from Carlisle disguised as a groom in attendance upon his companions.
On the 22nd he reached Tullybelton, a house near Perth, which
belonged to Patrick Graham, a kinsman of his own. His first
eager inquiries were directed to the condition of the loyal
gentry of the North. The news which he received was as dis-
couraging as that which had been brought him by Ogilvy and
Rollock. Huntly had given up all hopes of resisting the pre-
dominant party, and had fled to the hills, leaving the Gordons
without a leader.[1]

*Aug. 18.
Montrose
sets out for
Scotland.*

[1] *Wishart,* ch. iv. See vol. i. p. 336.

Montrose's intention, there can be little doubt, had been to rouse to action the Gordons together with the gentry of Angus and the Mearns.[1] It is true that the past history of Scotland did not give much reason to think it possible to overcome with their help the sober population of Fife and the Lothians, which was the real centre of the political life of Scotland. Montrose, however, had come temporarily to reverse the stream of history, and was not likely to be turned back by such considerations. It was more ominous that the gentry of the North gave no signs of being prepared to accept him as a leader. Everything around him boded failure, when a letter fell accidently into his hands which changed the whole current of his enterprise. If the gentry of the northern Lowlands refused to stir, he could appeal to the Highlands.

Montrose changes his plan.

Antrim, it seemed, had not been unmindful of his promise. Before the end of June he had overcome the scruples of the Supreme Council, and had shipped off some 1,600 men to the Western Highlands.[2] This force was probably composed of his own Macdonalds, who had served in the Irish war, intermingled with a sprinkling of the northern Irish. Its leader was Alaster Macdonell or Macdonald, whose father, known as Coll Keitache, the man who fought with either hand—in Lowland corruption, Colkitto[3]—had been the stoutest champion of his race, the Macdonalds of Islay and Kintyre,

June. Antrim sends men to the Highlands.

Alaster Macdonald.

[1] See vol. i. p. 298, note. It may also be remarked that the news brought to Montrose at Tullybelton turned on the condition of Huntly and the Gordons, not on the condition of the Highlands.

[2] Ormond put the number at 2,500 (Ormond to Nicholas, July 22, Carte's _Ormond_, vi. 178), but it appears from Antrim's own letter to Ormond of June 27 (_Carte MSS._ xi. fol. 301) that only 1,600 actually sailed.

[3] This appellation has popularly been given to the son, the meaning of Mac Coll Keitache being overlooked. It seems, on the whole, to be better in speaking of him and his men to call them Macdonald, than Macdonell or Macdonnell. Otherwise the unity of the clans of the name and the connection between them and their kinsmen in Ireland is apt to drop out of sight.

against the territorial aggrandisement of the Campbells. His stalwart son, an impetuous warrior but a bad general, had inherited the passions of the fierce old clansman.

Early in July Alaster Macdonald landed in Ardnamurchan. He came to bring Highland vengeance upon a Highland foe.

His ravages in Ardnamur- chan.
The Campbell tenants dwelt on the soil which had once been counted as the inheritance of the Mac- donalds, and for forty miles their land was now wasted with fire and sword. In order to keep open a way of retreat, Macdonald seized upon the castles of Mingary and Loch Alyne on the coast. Continuing his devastations, he called on his kinsmen, the Macdonalds, to join him, but the Macdonalds dared not stir against the overwhelming power of Argyle. Of Montrose he had no tidings, and he therefore

He proposes to return to Ireland.
resolved to content himself with the desolation which he had spread around him, and to carry his men back to Ireland. When he reached the place of

Aug. His retreat cut off.
embarkation he found that his retreat was cut off, as his ships had been burnt or captured by the Camp- bells. Nothing daunted, he made his way across glen and mountain to Lochaber, the westernmost of the districts which

His wanderings in the Highlands.
acknowledged the authority of Huntly. Like Mont- rose, he placed his chief hope in the support of the Gordons, and, like Montrose, he now learnt that the Gordons had made their submission to the covenanting Government. Headed back in his march to the east, he turned in a north-westerly direction towards the lands of the Mac- kenzies of Kintail on the shores of Loch Alsh and Loch Duich.

The Mac- kenzies and the Mac- donalds.
Little more than forty years ago the Mackenzies had been at deadly feud with the Macdonalds of Glen- garry. In 1603, in revenge for the slaughter of their chieftain's son, the Macdonalds set fire to a church which was crowded with a congregation of Mackenzies. Men, women, and children perished in the flames, whilst the Glengarry piper stirred the hearts of his clansmen to their deed of vengeance. Pitilessly the Macdonalds barred the doors with their claymores and thrust back their shrieking foes into the fire. In vain agonised mothers threw their children out of the windows in

the vain hope that these innocent ones at least might be spared. The Macdonalds knew no mercy, and the sword destroyed the infant lives which had escaped the flames.[1] Since that day of horror peace had been made between the Mackenzies and the Macdonalds, but the Mackenzies were hardly likely to welcome one who bore the Macdonald name. Their chieftain, the Earl of Seaforth, who was a man of uncertain politics, apt to throw himself on the strongest side, steadily refused to ally himself with the roving strangers. It was only on compulsion that he allowed them to pass through his territory. Macdonald, finding himself rejected of all, made for Badenoch on the upper Spey, which, like Lochaber, owed allegiance to Huntly, and took upon himself to call on the chieftains there to rise in the name of Huntly and the King. In this way he secured about five hundred recruits. It was in vain, however, that he attempted to push his way down the Spey to the immediate territory of the Gordons. The way was barred against him by the Grants and the Lowland gentry of Moray, who lived too near the Gordons to be other than good Covenanters, and who were on this occasion supported by a thousand of Seaforth's Mackenzies.[2]

Seaforth refuses to receive Macdonald.

Macdonald in Badenoch.

He fails to join Huntly.

Highlanders might indeed be counted as Royalists, but they were clansmen first and Royalists afterwards. The necessities of local warfare had early enforced the lesson of discipline in its only possible shape, that of absolute submission to the chieftain's will. To the chieftain each clan owed the military compactness which alone could give safety to those who were girt about by foes. The worst penalty in his power to inflict was to expel them from his obedience, that they might go forth as ' broken men,' wanderers over the face of the earth, with their hand against every man, and every man's hand against them. In return for the salutary despotism of the chieftain, the clansmen owed to him the most absolute obedience and the most absolute devotion. Between neighbouring clans there was often a bitter feud, and the hatred handed

The Highland clans.

[1] Mackenzie's *History of the Mackenzies*, 157.
[2] Patrick Gordon, *A short abridgment of Britain's distemper*, 65-69.

down from father to son not rarely showed itself in deeds of inhuman cruelty. The instincts of savage life in which strangers are counted as enemies were still strong within the Highlander, though in the seventeeth century there had been some progress, especially amongst the clans dwelling on the edge of the Highland line. In that region the chieftains mingled more readily with the nobles and gentry of the Lowlands, and their dependants were settling down into a position not unlike that of the tenants of the Lowland nobility. Yet even here the poverty of the soil made it difficult to find sustenance for all the dwellers upon it, and any excuse to enrich themselves at the expense of their Lowland neighbours was always gladly welcomed.

To bind the clans together for a political object was an impossible task. Neither any one chief nor any one clan would *Difficulties of uniting them.* agree to serve under a neighbouring chief.[1] It was on this rock that Macdonald's enterprise had split. He had summoned the clans in the name of Huntly and the King, but whatever he might say, he had failed to induce them to serve under a Macdonald.

But for Montrose Macdonald's position would have been hopeless. Montrose, however, was as prompt as Cromwell to *Montrose summons Macdonald to Blair Athol,* seize the chances of the hour, and he no sooner heard of Macdonald's arrival in Badenoch than he summoned him to join him at Blair Athol. On his way to the place of meeting Montrose met a Highlander speeding forward with the fiery cross which was to rouse the whole country to oppose the irruption of the strangers. He *and saves him from destruction.* hurried forward, and it was well for him that he was not too late. He found the Stuarts and the Robertsons gathered from the valleys of the Garry and the Tummel, and prepared to draw their swords against Macdonald's Irish.[2] At the voice of Montrose all jealousies were

---

[1] I need not refer to Lord Macaulay's elucidation of this simple thesis.

[2] It is perhaps necessary to designate them by this name. Yet though the word 'Irish,' was often employed in Scotland to designate a Celt

hushed, and the Highlanders as well as the new-comers from Antrim placed themselves at the disposal of the Lieutenant of the King.[1]

Macdonald was snatched from the jaws of death. Something of the sudden change was no doubt owing to the personal glamour of Montrose's presence, but it was in the main the result of his appearance as a visitor from another world than that of the Highland glens. It was probably fortunate for his cause that he made the first experiment so near the border of the Lowlands. The Athol chiefs shared to a great extent the feelings of the gentry farther south. The component factors in Scottish royalism were hatred of Argyle and hatred of the equalising pressure of the Kirk, and Argyle and the Kirk found little favour amongst the gentry on either side of the Highland line.

Montrose accepted as a leader.

There could be no doubt that Montrose had fighting before him. The apparition of Macdonald in the Highlands had stirred the apprehension of all whose property was exposed to plunder, and already three armies had been gathered by the national Government to make his escape impossible. Argyle was on his march from the West, on the track of his hereditary foe. A second force was gathering at Aberdeen to stop Deeside against him, whilst Lord Elcho collected a third from the men of Fife and of the lower lands of Perthshire, to keep him in check if he attempted to break out along the valley of the Tay.

Three Covenanting armies.

Montrose had to choose his enemy, and he chose the nearest, the army under Elcho at Perth. On his way thither he came upon a body of some five hundred men marching under Lord Kilpont and Sir James Drummond to join Elcho against the proscribed Macdonald. When the two commanders learnt that they had to do with Montrose, they followed their instincts and rallied to the royal standard.

Montrose's march to Perth.

Even after this reinforcement Montrose had scarcely more

generally, its present use tends to obscure the fact that many, if not most, of Macdonald's followers were of Scottish descent.

[1] *Wishart*, ch. v. ; *Patrick Gordon*, 72.

than 3,000 men on foot.[1] Cavalry he had none, save the three worn-out horses which had borne himself and his two companions from England. On the other side Elcho's army fell

Comparison between the two armies.

little short of 7,000, including at least 700 horse,[2] and accompanied by a park of artillery. Inferior in numbers and equipment, Montrose was vastly superior in the quality of his men. Every one of them was a man of his hands, inured from boyhood to war and to the hardy exercises which are the school of war. On the other side were townsmen and peasants who had gone through no such training, and who had never been carried on, like their countrymen who fought at Marston Moor, to the higher discipline of civilised

Sept. 1. The Battle of Tippermuir.

warfare. On the afternoon of Sunday, September 1, they were drawn up in the open valley about three miles west of Perth to oppose themselves to the approach of Montrose. All that could be done to stir up enthusiasm in their ranks was attempted, and one of their preachers even took upon himself to prophesy assured success. "If ever God," he declared, " spake word of truth by my mouth, I promise you in His name certain victory this day."

Montrose knew his adversary. Well aware that appearance goes far to intimidate an untried enemy, he stretched out his own line as far as possible, drawing them up only three deep, so as to present a front as long as that which was opposed to him. He had but little powder to spare, and his orders were that his men should march up close to the enemy before those who were provided with muskets fired a shot. Those who had no muskets must content themselves with pelting the Covenanters with stones. As soon as the enemy had been thrown into confusion they must all do their best with their swords. A battle fought under these instructions was not likely to last long. Elcho's raw soldiers took alarm at the first volley. Then there was a yell and a rush from behind the smoke, and

[1] Patrick Gordon makes them 3,200, but this can only be done by giving 1,500 to Macdonald. He must have lost more than 100 since his landing.

[2] Gordon makes the horse 1,000 and the foot 6,000. Wishart agrees with him as to the foot, but makes the horse only 700.

in an instant the Covenanting infantry was converted into a
flying mob.   The horses of the cavalry, terrified by the shower

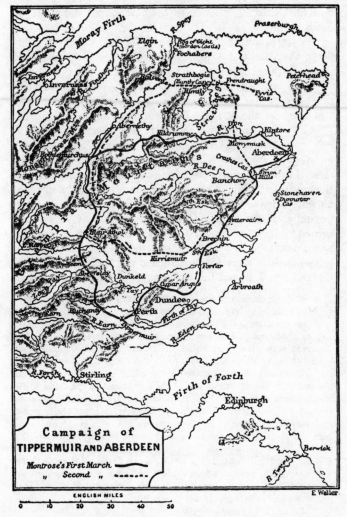

Campaign of
TIPPERMUIR AND ABERDEEN

Montrose's First March ———
    "   *Second*   " ------

ENGLISH MILES

of stones to which they were exposed, dashed from the field in headlong panic. The pursuit was hot, and two thousand of the fugitives were cut down before they reached a place of safety. Nine or ten died unwounded from the effects of the unwonted exercise. Before nightfall Montrose was master of Perth.[1]

As yet Montrose had his men under control. They plundered the slain, and stripped the suburbs of every thing that they could carry off; but neither cruelty nor robbery was permitted within the walls.[2] Montrose had two other armies to meet, and on the 4th he started for Aberdeen.

Montrose at Perth.

On the way Lord Kilpont was murdered, and the assassin, James Stewart of Ardvoirlich, fled to Argyle. The belief in the camp, in all probability erroneous,[3] was that Kilpont was put to death because he refused to join in murdering Montrose. The favourable reception given by Argyle to the supposed murderer was a sign that all who joined in a Highland rising might be assassinated with impunity, as far as the Covenanting authorities were concerned.[4] It is seldom indeed that a civilised community metes out to a less civilised one the measure by which it judges itself. When Argyle desolated the Highland glens with fire and sword, he was but inflicting due punishment on bar-

Sept. 7. Murder of Lord Kilpont.

---

[1] *Wishart*, ch. iv. v. ; *Spalding*, ii. 385, 402 ; *Patrick Gordon*, 65.

[2] Depositions in Napier's *Memorials of Montrose*, ii. 149.

[3] See the letter in the postscript to Sir W. Scott's introduction to the *Legend of Montrose*. It is from a descendant of Stewart and looks as if it preserved a true family tradition. It is there stated that Stewart challenged Alaster Macdonald, and that Montrose, at Kilpont's advice, arrested them both and enforced a reconciliation. A quarrel between Stewart and Kilpont arising out of the part taken by the latter in the arrest, sprang up in the midst of a drinking bout, and ended in the assassination. Some details of the story, however, are plainly incorrect, especially the statement that Stewart's quarrel with Macdonald arose from the plundering by the latter of the lands of Ardvoirlich, and that these lay on his line of march before he joined Montrose. This is certainly wrong, as Ardvoirlich lies on the south of Loch Earn, and the plundering, if effected at all, must have been carried out by some straggling parties of Macdonald's men on the way between Blair Athol and Perth, as Montrose's own line of advance did not approach it.

[4] *Acts of Parl. of Scotl.* vi. 359.

barians. When Montrose gathered the Highlanders to the slaughter of the burghers and the farmers of the Lowlands, he

Sept. 12.   placed himself outside the pale of civilised warfare.
A price set   On September 12 the Government of Edinburgh set
on Mont-
rose's head.   a price on his head. He was to be brought in dead or alive on the ground that he had 'joined with a band of Irish rebels and mass-priests, who had, this two years bygone, bathed themselves in the blood of God's people in Ireland, and in a traitorous and perfidious manner has invaded this kingdom, taken possession of some of the royal burghs thereof, apprehended, killed, and cruelly murdered divers of His Majesty's subjects.' [1]

It was easier to denounce Montrose than to lay hands on him. As he marched on rapidly towards Aberdeen the

Changes in   character of his army changed. The greater part of
Montrose's   his Highlanders returned home, as their manner
army.   was, to deposit their booty in their own glens. The Irishmen were always with him, and he was now also joined by the old Earl of Airlie with some of the gentry of Angus and the Mearns, who brought with them, in addition to a body of

Montrose   foot, a small party of forty-four horse. Montrose
and the   would gladly have welcomed the great Gordon fol-
Gordons.   lowing, but Huntly was far away; and two, at least, of his sons, Lord Gordon, the eldest, and Lord Lewis, the youngest, were still bound to the Covenanters as the nephews of their mother's brother, Argyle. Aboyne was in England, doing his duty on the King's side in the garrison of Carlisle.

It was not merely their connection with Argyle which made it difficult for the Gordons to rally to Montrose's standard. Montrose was longing to gather the feudal aristocracy around him, and he had to discover that in a feudal aristocracy it was the possession of broad acres and a numerous following of vassals which gave repute, not military genius or the authority

Lord   of the King. Huntly was in his own district a king
Gordon.   in all but the name, and he scorned to take orders from one whose estates were insignificant when compared to

[1] Declaration by the Committee of Estates, Sept. 12. Napier's *Memorials of Montrose*, ii. 163.

his own. He had received, too, from the King the Lieutenantship of the North, and he could not make up his mind

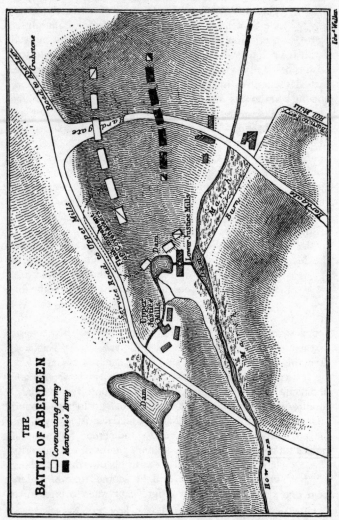

THE
BATTLE OF ABERDEEN

☐ *Covenanting Army*
■ *Montrose's Army*

to subordinate himself to the new Lieutenant of all Scotland.

Yet it was hard for him or his sons to desert the King's cause.
Their neighbours, the Frazers, the Forbeses, the Crichtons,
and the rest had adhered to the Covenant as a protection
against Huntly's power, and when Lord Gordon called on
them to follow him against Montrose, they with one voice
refused to place themselves under the command of their
hereditary enemy.[1] Some eighteen or twenty horse, under the
Lord Lewis orders of Lord Lewis, a youth gallant indeed and
Gordon. daring, but without steadiness of character, formed
the only contingent furnished by the Gordons to the Covenanting
Nathaniel army at Aberdeen. On the other hand Montrose was
Gordon. joined by a small force under Nathaniel Gordon, a
tried and hardy warrior who had supported Huntly's abortive
rising, and had refused to share in his submission.

Thus it was that when on the morning of September 13
Montrose approached Aberdeen from the west, he found
Sept. 13. himself at the head of an army very different from
Montrose that which had followed him at Tippermuir, inas-
before
Aberdeen. much as it was more suited to the exigencies of the
regular warfare of the day. The Highlanders were fewer and
the trained men more numerous. On the other hand the
enemy was strongly posted on the side of a hill in advance of
the town,[2] having not only the advantage of the slope and of
the possession of superior artillery, but the possession of a few
scattered houses and gardens abutting on the lane which led
to the centre of their position. Numbers too were on their
side. They had 2,000 foot and 500 horse, whilst 1,500 foot
and 44 horse made up the army of Montrose.

Prudence as well as dislike to cause unnecessary slaughter
led Montrose to try the effect of negotiation. He summoned
He the magistrates to surrender, adjuring them at least
summons to send their women and children to a place of
Aberdeen.
safety. The magistrates, though they governed a
town which had very little of the Covenanting spirit, had been

---

[1] *Patrick Gordon,* 79.

[2] The town then ended at the Den Burn, which ran in the bottom of
the valley now occupied by the line of railway and the Central Station.

chosen through the influence of the Covenanting party, and
they decisively rejected the offer.[1]   A horseman in their ranks
His drum-mer killed.   wantonly slew a drummer-boy who had accompanied
Montrose's messenger.[2]   Montrose was wild with
fury on hearing of the poor lad's fate, and he promised to
his followers the plunder of the town.   Yet he did not omit
the precautions of the coolest tactician.   He placed his scanty
Montrose's dispositions.   body of forty-four horse on the wings, according to
the practice of the day, but he knew that such a
handful would be incapable of charging the overwhelming
numbers of the enemy without disaster themselves.   At the
very time when Rupert and Cromwell were making the cavalry
charge the chief factor in battle,[3] Montrose, with the instinct
of genius, suiting his tactics to his conditions, adopting an
older practice known to commanders in the Thirty Years' War,
guarded his insignificant cavalry with musketeers interspersed
amongst them, so as to reserve it for use at a later period of
the fight.   Such adaptation of means to ends would have been
of little avail if he had not possessed in Macdonald's men a
highly disciplined force which was armed with muskets and
could be counted on to fight in a very different manner from
the wielders of the Highland broadsword.

[1] Facsimiles of the letters are given in *Spalding*, ii. 406.   The gap in
the sixth and seventh lines in Montrose's letter is caused by a drop of
rain falling on the paper as he was writing, as appears on inspection of
the original in the possession of the Town Council of Aberdeen.

[2] *Spalding*, ii. 407, note 1.

[3] The invention of the replacement of the old cavalry tactics, according
to which a charge was preceded by the firing of pistols and carbines, by
the shock of horse and man, is attributed by Captain Fritz Hoenig in his
Oliver Cromwell to Cromwell.   Colonel Ross, however, has pointed out
to me a passage in Bulstrode's *Memoirs* (81) which assigns it to Rupert
at Edgehill.   "Just before we began our march, Prince Rupert passed
from one wing to the other, giving positive orders to the horse to march
as close as possible, keeping their ranks with sword in hand to receive
the enemy's shot, without firing either carbine or pistol till we broke in
amongst the enemy and then to make use of our fire-arms as need should
require, which order was punctually observed."   Here, therefore, if Bulstrode is to be believed, Cromwell, as in other matters, appears as an
adapter and improver rather than an inventor.

Yet even Montrose's skill would hardly have availed him if there had not been an entire absence of command on the other side. Lord Balfour of Burleigh, who bore the name of general, knew nothing of war, and each of his subordinates, knowing equally little, did as he thought right in his own eyes.

Montrose began the attack by driving the enemy out of the houses and gardens occupied by them. After a while Lord The Battle Lewis Gordon charged with the small party of of Aberdeen. eighteen horsemen at his disposal on the right wing of the Royalists ; but the boy knew of no tactics other than those which had long been abandoned in England. His men advanced, fired their pistols, and retreated to load again, instead of sweeping down on the enemy with all the weight of man and horse. When Lord Lewis had retired, Lord Frazer and Lord Crichton attempted a fresh charge on the same wing, but being ill-seconded they failed to make any impression on the Royalists. The remainder of the cavalry on the left wing of the Covenanters, partly from their own ignorance of war, and partly because their general sent them no orders, remained fixed in the position in which they had originally been drawn up.

On his left wing, however, Montrose was near to a grave disaster. The Covenanters had sent a party of a hundred horse and four hundred foot to sweep round to their own right by a mill road out of sight, by which they reached a position in the rear of Montrose's left flank. Had they made up their minds to attack at once they could hardly have failed to roll up the whole of the enemy's line. But they hesitated and held back, though Nathaniel Gordon, who was on that side, had but thirty horse and a hundred musketeers to oppose to them. Montrose had thus time to bring over Rollock with his twenty-four horse from the right wing to Gordon's succour, and to push forward a fresh party of a hundred musketeers in support. The opportunity of the Covenanters was thus lost. Gordon took the offensive, and, falling upon them on the hillside, put their horse to flight and cut their foot to pieces.

On the other side of the battle, however, Sir William Forbes of Craigevar, taking advantage, it would seem, of Rollock's absence, charged right upon the enemy. Horsemen there were none to resist him, the storm therefore fell upon Macdonald's musketeers. With cool discipline the trained men opened their ranks, and Forbes's horse swept through Massacre in the midst of them doing no damage as they passed. the town. Macdonald faced round and pursued the flying rout with a fire which emptied many a saddle. Rollock was now able to return to his original post.

The Covenanting horse on both wings being thus disposed of, the battle was continued on more equal terms. The force of superior discipline prevailed, and the main battle of the Covenanters broke and fled.[1] In the chase which followed the victors burst into the open town with the flying rout. Then followed a scene of horror, the like of which had never been witnessed in the English war. Montrose, angered by the murder of his drummer, had promised his followers the plunder of the town. The wilder elements of barbarism were all let loose. Unarmed men were cut down in the streets; and, by a refinement of cruelty, those who were somewhat better clothed than others were stripped before they were slain, lest the coveted garments should be soiled with their blood. Women who ventured to bewail the slaughter of a husband or a father were killed on the spot or dragged off for outrage worse than death.[2]

It was not amidst a Covenanting population that this wickedness was wrought. Again and again, during the first years of the troubles, the townsmen of Aberdeen had shown that they were no meek disciples of the Kirk, as none knew better than Montrose himself.[3] It is true that through the

[1] Wishart's account of the battle is miserably poor as compared with Patrick Gordon's. The latter, too, stands the test of an acquaintance with the locality. Wishart places Rollock on the left wing, and Nathaniel Gordon on the right, which is plainly wrong. But he can hardly be wrong in bringing Rollock from one side to the other, and the view that Rollock was really moved from the right to the left is borne out by the fact that when Forbes charged nothing is said of horse resisting him. On this account I have placed this charge after the flank march on the other side.

[2] *Patrick Gordon*, 80; *Spalding*, ii. 406.

[3] Spalding (ii. 411) gives a list of 118 men killed in the battle, and

remainder of his career he showed himself merciful and generous to all who came personally in contact with him, and sparing of the bloodshed of unarmed populations whenever it was in his power to check the violence of his followers. Yet on this occasion he does not seem to have had any desire to avert the consequences of a rash promise made in a moment of exasperation.

The savagery of the captors of Aberdeen heightened, as might well be, the violent hatred with which Montrose was regarded in the Lowlands. Rollock, having been despatched to carry the news of the victory to the King, was captured on the way and condemned to death. Life was offered him on condition that he would engage to murder his commander. Rollock gave the required promise, and then hastened back to Montrose. On his arrival he told of the shameless engagement which had been extorted from him, and which he thought it no shame to break.[1]

Rollock asked to murder Montrose.

Startling as was the intelligence from Tippermuir and Aberdeen, it did not create any immediate sense of danger at Edinburgh or in England. Not a man was withdrawn from the Scottish army which was then lying before Newcastle. It was known that Argyle was in pursuit of Montrose, and it was firmly believed that Argyle would succeed where the untrained levies of peasants and shopkeepers had failed.

Once more Montrose appealed to the Gordons ; but the Gordons refused to move against the positive orders of Huntly, and no course was open to Montrose but to take to the hills. Darting hither and thither with his lightly equipped force, he was soon beyond the reach of Argyle, who was no soldier, and who carried with him the impediments of Lowland warfare.

Montrose in the Highlands.

Montrose marched westwards to Rothiemurchus, where he buried the cannon which he had taken at Aberdeen, and then made his way to Blair Athol, whence he had set out on his career of victory. He did not linger here. With Argyle lumbering

says that ninety-eight of them were ' no Covenanteris, but harllit out sore against their willis to fight against the Kingis livetennant.'

[1] *Wishart*, ch. xviii.

behind him, he started once more eastwards, then northwards across the Dee and the Don, and at last stood at bay at Fyvie Castle. Argyle fancied he had now a fair opportunity of crushing his deft antagonist, as Macdonald, with the bulk of his followers, was far away by the western sea, whither he had gone to secure from attack the two castles which he had seized on his landing. Montrose now showed himself as skilful in defence as he had shown himself at Aberdeen to be skilful in attack. Fyvie Castle, in itself incapable of holding out long against a formal siege, was surrounded to the north, the west, and the south by bogs through which only a narrow strip of hard ground allowed approach to an enemy. Argyle therefore proposed to attack the eastern side, where there were no such obstacles. On this side, however, a long but not very high bank interposed a natural barrier, on which Montrose drew up his men. The pewter utensils of the castle were melted into bullets; the powder had for the most part to be obtained from the pouches of slain enemies. Young O'Cahan, an Irish officer, left by Macdonald in command of such of his followers as remained with Montrose, animated the defenders by his high spirits and his courage. Argyle was warmly received, and after a prolonged struggle driven back. Before the Covenanters could again come within striking distance Montrose had slipped away; Argyle following heavily from east to west till he had tracked Montrose to Blair Athol and back again from west to east, losing men in every march, amidst the autumn rains. He failed to come up with his active foe; perhaps, indeed, he thought it better not to be too near him. At last, weary of his task, he turned his face to Edinburgh, and delivered up his commission to the Committee of Estates.[1]

Oct.

The defence of Fyvie Castle.

December had now arrived, and with it all expectation of war came to an end. Even Montrose doubted whether campaigning was possible in the Highlands, when the snow gleamed white on the mountain tops and choked the mountain passes. His heart was set on the conquest and organisation of Southern Scotland, and, sum-

Dec.

A council of war.

[1] *Wishart*, ch. vii.

moning a council of war, he suggested a descent into the
Lowlands. The chieftains would not hear of it. Macdonald
had now returned, bringing with him five hundred Highlanders

of the Macdonald name and blood. To Montrose flocked
Camerons from Lochaber, Macdonalds of Clanranald, Macdonalds from Keppoch, Glengarry, and Glencoe. Every man
of them hated Argyle with a bitter hatred, and they told

Montrose that the time was come to track the Campbell to his lair in the valleys round Inverary. Those valleys, they said, were rich in herds of cattle, and within the memory of man had never known the presence of the spoiler. It had long been held by every Campbell as an incontrovertible truth that the mountain ranges which guarded their homes were even in summer impassable by a hostile force. "I would rather," Argyle had been heard to say, "lose a hundred thousand crowns than that any mortal man should know the way by which an army can enter into my country."

Montrose, after some resistance, accepted the proposal. A few horsemen from Angus under Sir Thomas Ogilvy were with him, as well as a certain number of Gordons who had been roused to join him by Argyle's ill-advised plunderings in the Gordon lands; but the bulk of his force consisted of Macdonalds from whichever side of the Irish Sea they came. For them there was but one object of the war, the destruction of the Campbells, whose march through their glen had been ever marked in fire and blood. Before these hardy warriors every natural obstacle gave way. Clambering over rocks and wading through snowdrifts, the Highland host poured down upon the Campbell valleys. Argyle, leaving his clansmen to their fate, sought refuge in his fastness at Inverary. The vengeance of many generations was accomplished. Every head of cattle was destroyed, every homestead burnt to the ground. It was but dealing to the Campbells the measure which they had dealt to others, nor was the wrath of the Macdonalds to be satiated with the destruction of property. No quarter was given,[1] and every Campbell of age to bear arms who was unlucky enough to fall into their hands was butchered without mercy.

Dec. Montrose in Argyle.

On December 13 Montrose had burst into Argyle. January had almost closed when, leaving a desert behind him, he marched leisurely northwards, spoiling as he went. His track

[1] 'Although out of a generous disposition, he,' i.e. Montrose, 'would have spared the people, yet the Clan Donald, wheresoever they found any that was able to carry arms, did without mercy despatch them.'—*Patrick Gordon*, 98.

lay through the valley of the great lakes. When he reached
Loch Ness he learnt that his way was barred by Seaforth at
Jan.
Montrose
leaves
Argyle. the head of some 5,000 men gathered from the
northern shires. Seaforth had long professed himself
a Royalist, but his policy was always dictated by
the personal interests and feelings of the moment.

If Montrose had Seaforth before him, he had Argyle in his
rear. Argyle had summoned two hastily formed Lowland regi-
Argyle at
Inverlochy. ments to his assistance, and with these and such of
his own clansmen as had escaped he took up his
post with 3,000 men at Inverlochy, where the great glen reaches
the salt waters of Loch Eil. Montrose, it might seem, was
caught in a trap. His Highlanders were for the most part far
away storing up their plunder in their mountain homes. But
for Macdonald's regiments his force would have been scanty
indeed. As it was, he had no more than 1,500 around him.

Weak as he was in numbers, Montrose flew at Argyle.
His chief fear was that Argyle would shun the fight. He
Montrose's
march. therefore avoided the easy route down the valley,
lest the knowledge of his approach might drive the
Campbells to retreat. Turning to the left, he climbed the
rugged pass of Corryarrick. Onward the Highland host made
its way through clefts in which a hundred men could easily
have stopped the progress of an army. At last, after nightfall
Feb. on February 1, as they pressed on in the bright light
of the moon under the shoulder of Ben Nevis, they
caught sight of the Campbells in front of them between the
mountain and the shore.

For the Campbells there was no escape from the next day's
battle ; but Argyle was persuaded, too easily for his honour, to
Argyle takes
refuge in a
vessel. take refuge in a vessel lying in the loch. He had
recently dislocated his shoulder in consequence of a
fall from his horse,[1] and even if he had been more
of a warrior than he was he could have taken but little
personal share in the actual combat. Yet there have been
men who, even in such a case, would have thought it shame to

---

[1] Balfour's Annals, *Hist. Works,* iii. 256. I do not see any reason
foi disbelieving the fact.

look on from a position of security whilst their followers were exposed to wounds and death.

It is possible that Argyle expected not disaster but victory. His men were numerous and well equipped. Montrose's were few and fasting. "The most part of them had not tasted bread these two days." The next morning Montrose himself, with the Earl of Airlie, 'had no more to break their fast before they went to battle but a little meal mixed with cold water, which out of a hollow dish they did pick up with their knives for want of spoons.'

The command of Argyle's army had been given to Sir Duncan Campbell of Auchinbreck, a tried soldier from the Irish war. The Campbell Highlanders he placed in the centre with a newly-levied Lowland regiment on either wing. Such an army had too little coherence to be really formidable, and Sir Duncan was, it would seem,[1] compelled to hold back his Highlanders, lest, if they were allowed to charge, they might disorder the ranks of their un-trained and unwarlike comrades. Montrose had therefore the advantage of the attack. Nor was that all. He had contrived to bring a small body of horse under Sir Thomas Ogilvy over the mountain passes, and he knew that the fear of a cavalry charge would work wonders amongst infantry who were without cavalry to guard their flanks. His first order, therefore, was to Ogilvy's trumpeter to sound the charge. A peal long and loud carried dismay into the enemy's ranks. Then he let loose his whole force. Alaster Macdonald on the right and O'Cahan on the left wing dashed at the Lowland regiments, and the Lowland regiments, not knowing how soon the horsemen might be trampling them down, broke and took to flight. The whole weight of Montrose's army bore upon the Campbells in the centre. For some time they resisted stoutly, but at last they wavered and fled. For the Lowland runaways there was mercy, but there was none for any man who bore the name of Campbell. Out of 3,000 of which the army was composed when the battle began, no less than 1,700 perished under the

Feb. 2.
The Battle of Inver-lochy.

---

[1] This is not directly stated, but it may be gathered from the position of defence taken up by the Campbells.

very eyes of Argyle, and of these, by far the greater part were his own clansmen. For a time the Campbells ceased to be a power in the western Highlands.[1]

No wonder that after such an exploit Montrose overrated the possible results of his achievement, and fancied that be-

Montrose's hopes.

cause the Macdonalds had combined enthusiastically to crush the Campbells they would be ready to combine with equal enthusiasm to reconstitute the King's government in the Lowlands. In announcing his success to Charles he adjured him to abandon that negotiation with his rebellious English subjects which he was then opening at Uxbridge.

Feb. 3.
Montrose's despatch.

"Give me leave," he urged, "with all humility to assure your Majesty that through God's blessing I am in the fairest hopes of reducing this kingdom to your Majesty's obedience, and, if the measures I have concerted with your other loyal subjects fail me not—which they hardly can—I doubt not before the end of this summer I shall be able to come to your Majesty's assistance with a brave army, which, backed with the justice of your Majesty's cause, will make the rebels in England as well as in Scotland feel the just rewards of rebellion. Only give me leave, after I have reduced this country to your Majesty's obedience, and conquered from Dan to Beersheba, to say to your Majesty then, as David's general did to his master, 'Come thou thyself, lest this country be called by my name.'"[2]

---

[1] *Wishart*, ch. vii., viii. ; *Patrick Gordon*, 85–102. Compare Napier's *Memoirs of Montrose*, ii. 460–488.

[2] Montrose to the King, Feb. 3. Napier's *Memoirs of Montrose*, ii. 484. On the genuineness of this letter, see Mr. Napier's note at p. 488.

CHAPTER XXVII.

THE PROJECTS OF THE EARL OF GLAMORGAN.

IN Scotland the Saxon distrust and abhorrence of the Celt had been quickened into new life by the cruelties of Mont-

1645.
The Saxon
and the
Celt.

rose's followers at Aberdeen and in Argyle. In England they had, three years before, received a fresh impulse from the tale of the Ulster massacre. In London at least, just as the news from Inverlochy arrived, that tale was once more in all mouths. Two of the leaders of

1644.
Aug. 17.
Maguire
and Mac-
mahon
escape from
the Tower,

the Irish rebellion, Lord Maguire and Hugh Macmahon, had been transferred to England soon after their arrest in 1641,[1] and had been lodged in the Tower, where they long remained forgotten. Unluckily for them, in the summer of 1644 they drew attention to their existence by effecting their escape. For more than a month they concealed themselves in the house of a Catholic in Drury Lane. Their impunity made them care-

Sept. 19.
and are re-
captured.

less, and one of the pair, being attracted by the cry of an oyster-woman, looked out of window to call for her wares. His face was recognised, and together with his companion he was carried back to prison.

Nov. 17.
Macmahon
tried,

On November 17 Macmahon was indicted as a traitor, and being found guilty, was executed on the 22nd. Maguire pleaded that as an Irish peer he

Nov. 22.
and ex-
ecuted.

could only be tried by his peers in his own country. He obtained nothing more than a short delay. His plea was overruled, and on February 10, 1645, he was brought to the bar before an English jury.

[1] *Hist. of Engl.* 1603–1642, x. 52.

A trial thus conducted could have but one end. What was patriotism in Ireland was treason in England, and the admission of the prisoner that he had plotted to seize Dublin Castle as a pledge for the redress of certain grievances, amongst which the denial of toleration to the Catholics occupied the first place, was quite enough to secure his conviction. It would, however, have been little in accordance with the passions of the hour if the prosecution had contented itself with adducing the technical evidence of treason. The whole tale of the Ulster massacres, adorned with all those exaggerations which had become an essential part of the accredited story, was once more unrolled in the hearing of Londoners, though the proof which connected Maguire with those massacres was of the slightest, as he was himself in prison when the mischief was done. The jury naturally took the view that to set going the movement which had culminated in the unhallowed work of slaughter rendered Maguire responsible for all that followed, whilst the prisoner no less naturally saw in his own scheme for a national uprising a legitimate act of warfare against an alien domination.

Feb. 10. Maguire's trial.

The inevitable sentence was passed, and on February 20 Maguire was drawn on a sledge, as so many had been drawn before him, to taste the bitterness of a death at Tyburn. Sheriff Gibbs, whose duty it was to see to the execution of the sentence of the law, considered it to be his duty to weary the unfortunate man with questions intended to draw from him an acknowledgment in the first place that the Irish were murderers, and in the second place that these murders had been committed with the complicity of the King. Maguire pleaded in vain for a few moments of peace that he might prepare himself for death. Gibbs pursued him with his questionings to the very end.

Feb. 20. Maguire at Tyburn.

"Had you not engaged yourself by oath to the King?" was the one amongst the Sheriff's demands which revealed in the clearest light the belief which had sunk deeply into the popular mind. At the very time of Maguire's death, Charles was doing all in his power to strengthen that belief. For nearly a twelvemonth he had

The popular feeling about the King's complicity with the Irish.

entertained hopes of forming a vast combination in which the Irish Celts would play a leading part.   In March 1644, when

1644. the Agents of the Supreme Council arrived at Oxford, he was already in close communication with the Catholic son of the Marquis of Worcester, Lord Herbert of Raglan.   It was impossible for Charles to forget how, in the early days of the war, Herbert and his father had poured their wealth into his empty treasury; and he had recently acknowledged to them a debt of no less than 250,000*l.*[1]   Although Herbert had hitherto proved unsuccessful as a commander,[2] Charles listened eagerly to his sanguine anticipation of future

March (?)
Herbert to
be Earl of
Glamorgan. achievements, and conferred on him the title of Earl of Glamorgan by warrant.   Apparently in order to avoid drawing attention to the service on which Charles contemplated employing him, the warrant, though presented at the Signet Office, was allowed to stay there, no further steps being taken to procure the patent which alone would confer validity on the new title.

Glamorgan's plans were indeed such as it would be prudent to veil in profound secrecy.   His royalism, genuine as it was,

Glamor-
gan's aims. was very different from that of Hyde, or of any English statesman.   He lived and moved in the idea of vindicating his own Church from the bondage of the law, and he knew well that it was impossible to effect that object without also vindicating the authority of the King from the bondage of Parliaments.   His fantastic imagination took no account of the social and political forces which made against the realisation of this complex project, whilst his chivalrous

---

[1] I have, in an article in *The English Historical Review* for Oct. 1887, not only given the references to the evidence on which I rely for my account of Glamorgan's relations with the King, but have argued at length on the credence to be given to the various documents quoted. Last time I was at the Museum I began an examination of Mr. Round's criticism of my arguments contained in his *Studies in Peerage and Family History*, but I had then not time to complete my investigation, and am now too ill to enter into any discussion on the questions raised by him.

[2] See vol. i. p. 104.

devotion to Charles's person was blended in his mind with his no less chivalrous devotion to his Church.

It was nothing to Charles that Glamorgan was as incapable of executing a commission with discretion as he was of conceiving a plan which had any serious chances of success. Flighty and sanguine, the new Earl had no difficulty in persuading Charles that any one thing was possible, because he believed in his heart that all things were possible. Under his influence, the plan for bringing over an Irish army grew into a plan for rousing half Europe to take arms on behalf of Charles and the Catholic cause. Naturally in such a scheme Glamorgan was to play the leading part. Scarcely had the Irish Agents arrived in the spring of 1644, when, on April 1, a commission was drawn up authorising him to take the command of the 10,000 Irish soldiers whose appearance in England was expected to be the result of the negotiation at Oxford. Moreover, if, as every indication leads us to believe, we may refer a later statement, by Glamorgan, to this date, Sir Henry Gage, then a Catholic officer in the Spanish army in Flanders, who was afterwards killed at Abingdon,[1] was to command a force which was to be raised in South Wales, where the Herbert influence was powerful; whilst another army of 6,000 men composed of levies from Lorraine and Liege—and of such recruits of all nations as could be swept up in the Low Countries—were to be brought over to Lynn, where the officer in command for the Parliament was ready to betray his trust.[2] The whole of these armaments were to be placed under Glamorgan as commander-in chief.

Charles had no funds at his disposal wherewith to meet the expenses of so huge an undertaking. To some extent the difficulty was to be met by a grant to Glamorgan of authority to raise money by the sale of wardships, customs, and other property of the Crown, as well as by a lavish distribution of peerages and baronetcies. Glamorgan's chief reliance, however, was on the Pope and other Catholic

*April 1.
His commission.*

Money to be raised.

---

[1] See p. 113.

[2] L'Estrange's subsequent attempt on Lynn gives probability to this. See p. 112.

princes, who were expected to contribute largely to an enterprise from which their Church was to reap such extensive
benefits.

If it had been necessary to veil in secrecy the grant of an
earldom to Charles's new champion, it was still more necessary
to conceal the commission which placed him in command of
armies not yet in existence. Not only were the usual official
conditions preliminary on a grant under the great seal not
fulfilled, but the Lord Keeper himself had to be kept in ignorance of the whole proceeding. We know that in the case of
another patent a seal was imposed by Glamorgan himself and
Endymion Porter, probably either cut off or imitated from
some genuine patent, and it seems likely that the same course
was now adopted. A document of this kind could never
indeed be received as genuine in any court of law, but the
stake for which Glamorgan was playing was a victory which
would have reduced all courts of law to impotence. The
parchment he now possessed was good enough to exhibit
to Irish Confederates and to foreign courts.

In return for the services which he expected, Charles was
prepared to confer signal honours, and even to confer them by

May 4.
Glamorgan
to be Duke
of Somerset.
anticipation. He offered the hand of the Princess
Elizabeth to Glamorgan's eldest son, and on May 4
he conferred on Glamorgan himself the dukedom of
Somerset. This patent, unlike the commission, was sealed in
the usual way with the attestation of the proper officer of the
Court of Chancery. As, however, it was not to be immediately
produced, and as it was desirable to avoid drawing attention to
its existence, the usual preliminaries had been again avoided,
so that there might be some difficulty in substantiating its
validity, if at any future time it were called in question. In
short, the procedure in conferring the earldom was exactly re-
versed. In the one case the first step had never been followed
up ; in the other cases,—in conferring the commandership-in-
chief and the dukedom,—the final step was taken with nothing
to lead up to it.

The dukedom had not been granted many days when Glamorgan's elaborate plan practically broke down. Its backbone

was the project of bringing over the Irish army, and when, towards the end of May, the Irish Agents were dismissed from

Glamorgan's plan frustrated.

Oxford, and the negotiation was placed by Charles in Ormond's hands,[1] all present hope of obtaining the services of that army was extinguished. Of all

Ormond unfit to carry on the negotiation.

men living Ormond was perhaps the least fitted to conduct that negotiation even to the temporary success of which it was alone capable. His virtues and his defects alike stood in his way. He was too loyal to throw off his shoulders the load which Charles had placed upon them, but he was at the same time so completely wanting in initiative power that he never thought—as Strafford under similar circumstances would assuredly have thought—of suggesting a policy of his own, or even of criticising adversely the one imposed on him by his master.

Yet it ought to have been evident to Ormond that an Irish army was not to be gained by haggling over the privileges to be accorded to the true Irish Parliament and the true Irish Church. Even if the 10,000 men had really been forthcoming, they would have been of little avail unless the hearts of the Irishmen who composed it were engaged in Charles's cause ; and already before the breach of the Oxford negotiations an event had occurred which put Charles's power of winning the hearts of Irishmen to the test. On May 13 Monro,

May 13. Monro seizes Belfast.

who had been appointed by the English Parliament to the command of the English as well as the Scottish forces in Ireland, proceeded to vindicate his authority by treacherously seizing Belfast and turning out Ormond's garrison.

The Supreme Council offers its army to Ormond.

The Supreme Council immediately offered to place its whole army under Ormond's command if he would only engage to lead it against Monro.[2] Ormond was too scrupulous to accept the overture unless he received positive orders from Charles, and those orders Charles never gave.

No doubt there were good reasons why Charles should turn

[1] See vol. i. p. 347.

[2] Carte's *Ormond*, iii. 118. The numerous documents on which the narrative is founded are amongst the Carte MSS.

his back on the proposal, as acceptance of it would probably have cost him the service of nine-tenths of his army in England. What is, however, to be thought of a policy which based itself on the co-operation of an Irish army in England, when it was impossible to grant to the Irish the co-operation of an English army in Ireland?

Accordingly, the old path which led to nothing had once more to be trodden by the weary Lord Lieutenant. On July 26 Ormond received information that a commission had been sent to him, empowering him to recommence that negotiation with the Supreme Council which had utterly broken down at Oxford. "I have little ground of hope," he wrote despairingly to Digby, "that the commission will effect that for which it was sent; to wit, the concluding of a peace as may be for his Majesty's honour, or for the just and reasonable satisfaction of his Protestant subjects."[1]

July 26. Ormond again takes up the negotiation.

July 30. He has little hope.

The cost of that summer's war was such as to bring home conviction to every Irishman that he had but little cause for gratitude to Charles. In the north there was a long desultory warfare between Monro and the Confederates, in which Ormond's garrisons maintained a strict neutrality. In the south, Inchiquin, angry because Charles had refused to him the presidency of Munster,[2] had declared for the English Parliament, and was leading an attack on the Confederates which threatened to be more serious than any to which they had hitherto been exposed in that part of Ireland.[3]

Campaign in Ulster.

Inchiquin in Munster.

On September 6 the peace conferences were reopened at Dublin. It soon appeared that even if the political difficulties could be removed, the ecclesiastical difficulties were well-nigh insuperable. The Irish demanded the repeal not only of all statutes impeding the freedom of their worship, but of others, such as that of Appeals and of a portion of the Act of Præmunire quoted in that statute, which restricted the exercise of the Papal jurisdiction. The

Sept. 6. The conference at Dublin.

---

[1] Ormond to Digby, July 30.   Carte's *Ormond*, vi. 185.
[2] See vol. i. p. 333.   [3] Carte's *Ormond*, iii. 118.

King, on the other hand, though he was willing to engage that
the laws against freedom of worship should not be put in
Obstacles in
the way of
an under-
standing. execution, was not prepared to consent to their
repeal, and, for the present at least, he was absolutely determined to leave untouched the Acts of
Appeals and Præmunire.[1]

For the time, however, it appeared as if Charles would be
allowed to have his way. Differences of opinion were already
Parties
amongst the
Confede-
rates. making themselves manifest amongst the Confederates, and the lay peers were drifting apart from the
ecclesiastics. A party, of which Lord Muskerry was
the chief, declared in private to Ormond that they were ready
Oct.
Muskerry's
proposal. to accept the King's terms, if only ample security
were given that the lives and property of Irishmen
would be safe. They would not press for the immediate repeal of laws which they expected would fall of themselves whenever Charles was in a position to carry out his real
intentions. On the question of the repeal of the statutes
affecting the King's jurisdiction they were entirely silent, a
silence which probably implied an undertaking that Charles
should not be troubled further in the matter.[2]

With this proposal Charles was highly pleased. He, too,
now moved a step in advance, and commanded Ormond to
Dec. 15.
It is ac-
cepted by
the King. promise that the penal laws should be suspended as
soon as peace was made, and that whenever he was
restored to his rights with Irish help they should
be absolutely repealed ; 'but all those,' he added, 'against
appeals to Rome and Præmunire must stand.'[3]

The transmission of Muskerry's proposals had been accompanied by a private message from Ormond, in which the Lord
Lieutenant offered his resignation. In the first place he pleaded
the straits to which he was reduced by poverty ; but his
second reason doubtless had greater weight. If an English-

---

[1] Gilbert, *Hist. of the Irish Confederation*, iii. 289.

[2] Browne's note, in Carte's *Ormond*, v. 10.

[3] The King to Ormond, Dec. 15. Printed from a duplicate with a later
date in Carte's *Ormond*, v. 9. Compare Digby to Ormond, Dec. 16. *Ib.*
vi. 219.

man, he said, were to do what he was required to do in the

Nov. 14.
Ormond
offers his
resigna-
tion.

Dec. 15.
Charles
refuses to
accept it.

King's service, he would be subject to less misconstruction than an Irishman like himself in the same position. In other words, Ormond felt uncomfortable at the prospect of having to connive at the constant breach of unrepealed laws.[1] Charles gaily replied that the Irish peace would remedy all complaints, and must be despatched out of hand.[2]

Yet though Charles did not think fit to displace Ormond, he resolved to find him an assistant. His thoughts naturally reverted to Glamorgan, who might now, if the peace was at last procured, carry out those wider plans which had been laid aside in the spring. Glamorgan's wife was a daughter of the Earl of Thomond, and it was easy to discover a reason why he should wish to visit Ireland at this conjuncture of affairs. On

Dec. 27.
Glamorgan
com-
n.ended to
Ormond.

December 27 Charles informed Ormond of Glamorgan's intended journey on private business, and assured him that the Earl would be ready to do everything in his power to promote the cause of peace. "His honesty or affection to my service," the King added in a postscript, "will not deceive you, but I will not answer for his judgment."[3]

Charles was too often in the habit of employing those for whose judgment he could not answer. Yet even Charles was

Purpose of
Glamor-
gan's
mission.

hardly likely to send a man whose judgment he distrusted to conclude secretly a peace on terms which he had positively forbidden Ormond to listen to. The best explanation of an intricate mass of evidence is always that which raises the least difficulty, and for those who know the circumstances under which Ormond's resignation was offered the explanation lies on the surface. Charles was now bent on procuring an understanding with the Confederate

---

[1] Instructions for Barry, *Carte MSS.* xiii. fol. 162. They are undated, but there is a later copy in the same collection, xvi. fol. 211, dated Nov. 14, 1645. The year is plainly wrong, as we know from other sources that Barry was sent towards the end of 1644.

[2] The King to Ormond, Dec. 15. Carte's *Ormond*, v. 9.

[3] The King to Ormond, Dec. 27. Carte's *Ormond*, v. 7.

Catholics upon the terms offered by Muskerry. It was with a full knowledge of these terms that Ormond had wished to shift the burden of complying with them from his own shoulders to those of an Englishman. Charles refused to supersede him, but he sent an Englishman to do the work, to use his power of persuasion with those amongst the Confederates who were not in Muskerry's councils, and to give assurance that the laws would not be put in force against them, even though they remained unrepealed. What was needed was energy and sincerity of purpose rather than judgment, and if, as there is every reason to believe, Charles instructed his agent to conform in everything to the advice of Ormond,[1] his lack of judgment might not under Ormond's supervision be of much consequence Yet so bent was Charles on driving on the peace that he actually gave to the feather-brained Glamorgan a commission to succeed Ormond as Lord Lieutenant in the event of the death or misconduct of the latter ; in other words, in the event of his persisting in his refusal to carry out the negotiation on the lines indicated by his last instructions.[2]

With Charles eagerness to give peace to Ireland was altogether subordinated to his eagerness to obtain for the coming campaign in England those military succours which he had once hoped to obtain through Glamorgan for the campaign of 1644. It was this which had led him to entertain the idea of placing Glamorgan in Ormond's seat. Yet it is evident from

[1] " If you had advised with my Lord Lieutenant (as you promised me) all this had been helped." The King to Glamorgan, Feb. 3, 1646. Dircks, *Life of the second Marquis of Worcester*, 134.

[2] " For to endear myself to some, the better to do his Majesty service, 'tis true I did declare a promise from the King of his assent that after your Excellency's time he would make me Lord Lieutenant ; but 'tis no meaning of mine but to keep your Excellency in during your life, and not really to pretend unto it, or anything in diminution of your Excellency's honour or profit, or derogating from the true amity and real service which I have professed and will ever make good towards your Excellency. And my intention was ever to acquaint your honour herewith ; and I once intended to do it before my going to Kilkenny, but never to conceal it totally from you." Glamorgan to Ormond, Sept. 29, 1645. *Carte MSS.* xvi. fol. 396. But compare Rinuccini to Panfilio, Sept 29, 1646: *Nunziatura*, 166.

the instructions which he gave to the Earl that he only contemplated the necessity of change as a remote possibility, and that he much preferred that his two representatives should act in hearty co-operation. "You may engage your estate, interest, and credit," he wrote in the instructions which on January 2 he gave to Glamorgan, "that we will most readily and punctually perform any our promises to the Irish, and as it is necessary to conclude a peace suddenly,[1] whatsoever shall be consented unto by our Lieutenant the Marquis of Ormond, we will die a thousand deaths rather than disannul or break it ; and if upon necessity anything be to be condescended unto, and yet the Lord Marquis not willing to be seen therein, or not fit for us at the present publicly to own, do you endeavour to supply the same."

1645.
Jan. 2.
Glamorgan's instructions.

Read apart from the correspondence between Charles and Ormond, this clause might possibly be subject to a variety of interpretations. Read in its proper chronological sequence, it can bear but one meaning. Glamorgan was to act in strict subordination to the Lord Lieutenant, and to assure the Irish that the penal laws would be suspended after the signature of a treaty of peace, and repealed as soon as victory made it safe for Charles to take that course. It was the prospect of having to complete the negotiation on these terms which had driven Ormond to send in his resignation. More than this Charles was for the moment determined to refuse. The remainder of the instructions were taken up with directions for the management of the army, which was soon to be under Glamorgan's command,[2] couched in terms which imply that, as far as Ireland was concerned, the commission of the preceding April was still in force.[3] The informal patent conferring a dukedom on Glamorgan was allowed to fall asleep. There is reason to believe that his father was displeased that his son should be a duke whilst he himself remained a marquis,

Their meaning.

---

[1] *i.e.* soon.

[2] Instructions to Glamorgan, Jan. **2.** Dircks, *Life of the Marquis of Worcester,* 72.

[3] See p. 159.

and though the steps of the process cannot be distinctly traced, it is plain that the intention was already formed of making the old man a duke instead of his son. In February a warrant to that effect was actually sent to Worcester; but, as in the case of his son's earldom, complete secrecy was both enjoined and observed, no attempt being made to carry the grant beyond the initial stage.

Feb. 12.
Worcester
to be a
duke.

On January 12 the King's confidence in Glamorgan received a fresh attestation. "So great," he wrote, "is the confidence we repose in you, as that whatsoever you shall perform, as warranted under our signature, pocket signet, or private mark, or even by word of mouth, without further ceremony, we do, on the word of a king and a Christian, promise to make good to all intents and purposes, as effectually as if your authority from us had been under the great seal of England, with this advantage, that we shall esteem ourself the more obliged to you for your gallantry in not standing upon such nice terms to do us service, which we shall, God willing, reward. And although you exceed what law can warrant, or any powers of ours reach unto, as not knowing what you have need of, yet it being for our service, we oblige ourself, not only to give you our pardon, but to maintain the same with all our might and power; and though either by accident, or by any other occasion, you shall deem it necessary to deposit any of our warrants, and so want them at your return, we faithfully promise to make them good at your return, and to supply anything wherein they shall be found defective, it not being convenient for us at this time to dispute upon them; for of what we have here set down you may rest confident, if there be faith and trust in men. Proceed, therefore, cheerfully, speedily, and boldly, and for your so doing this shall be your sufficient warrant."[1]

Jan. 12.
The King
promises to
confirm
Glamorgan's
actions.

Perilously wide as these words were, it is not likely that they referred to the conclusion of the Irish peace. They are more appropriate to the other negotiation with which Glamorgan was entrusted, the negotiation with the Pope and the Catholic powers for money to pay the

Explanation
of these
powers.

[1] *Dircks*, 79.

armies which were to be brought from the Continent in support of the troops from Ireland.

"The maintenance of this army of foreigners," wrote Glamorgan in explanation many years afterwards, "was to have come from the Pope and such Catholic princes as he should draw into it, having engaged [1] to afford and procure 30,000*l.* a month, out of which the foreign army was first to be provided for, and the remainder to be divided among other armies. And for this purpose had I power to treat with the Pope and Catholic princes, with particular advantages promised to Catholics for the quiet enjoying of their religion, without the penalties which the statutes in force had power to inflict upon them. And my instructions for this purpose, and my powers to treat and conclude thereupon, were signed by the King under his pocket signet, with blanks for me to put in the names of the Pope or princes, to the end the King might have a starting hole to deny the having given me such commissions, if excepted against by his own subjects; leaving me as it were at stake, who for his Majesty's sake was willing to undergo it, trusting to his word alone." In all probability the powers referred to in this explanation are the warrants mentioned by Charles as those which he was ready to make good, the names comprised in which would have to be filled in by Glamorgan in accordance with the instructions which had been given him by word of mouth.

Glamorgan's explanation.

This interpretation of the meaning of Charles's warrant of the 12th is the more probable as that warrant followed closely on a commission granted on the 6th under the great seal—though without the customary formalities of sign-manual and privy-seal—by which Glamorgan was empowered to levy troops not only in Ireland but on the Continent as well.[2]

Jan. 6. Commission to Glamorgan to levy troops in Ireland and on the Continent.

Much as Charles trusted Glamorgan, he had another agent abroad even more devoted to his service and bound to him

---

[1] *i.e.* I having engaged.

[2] Commission to Glamorgan, Jan. 6. *Lord Leicester's MS.* fol. 713. The levies were to be made 'vel in nostro Iberniæ regno aut aliis quibusvis partibus transmarinis.'

by nearer ties. When, early in November 1644, Henrietta Maria arrived in Paris she was still weakly, but sufficiently recovered from her long illness to apply herself intermittently to business. Mazarin, for the time, kept her at a distance, but the Queen Regent welcomed her with all the effusiveness of her nature. Kindly words, however, were not closely followed by helpful deeds. Anne, it is true, presented her distressed sister-in-law with a small quantity of arms, which Henrietta Maria at once converted into money; but she frankly explained that she could do no more. The only comforting word which the Queen of England could send to her husband was that so soon as a cargo of Cornish tin, which was believed to be on its way, arrived at a French port, she would be able without difficulty to sell it, and would forward the purchase money to England.[1]

1644.
Nov.
The Queen at Paris.

France, in fact, was in no position to expend money from a sentimental interest in the fortunes of Charles. She was engaged in a struggle which taxed her resources to the uttermost. In the early summer of 1644, when the siege of Gravelines was drawing to an end,[2] Mazarin launched Enghien to the succour of Turenne, who was outnumbered by the Imperialist general, Mercy, on the Upper Rhine. After a week of battles round Freiburg in the Breisgau, Mercy drew off the shattered remains of his defeated army. Before the end of October the Rhine valley from Basel to Bacharach was in the hands of the French. The design of Richelieu was at last accomplished.

The campaign on the Rhine

July 24-30,
Aug. 3-9.
Battles of Freiburg.

Oct.
The Upper Rhine occupied by the French.

No slight exertions would be needed to maintain so vast an achievement, and, for some time to come, Mazarin was unlikely to have the power, even if he had the will, to do much for the English Queen. His policy with regard to England was to perpetuate its distractions, and to render it too weak to be an obstacle to the designs of France on the Continent,

---

[1] The Queen to the King, Nov. $\frac{11}{21}$. *Letters of Henrietta Maria*, 266, 267.

[2] See vol. i. p. 349.

especially if he could attain his object without much trouble
or expense to himself.[1]

Under these circumstances Mazarin was therefore quite
willing to listen favourably to the proposals which were at this
O'Hartegan time made to him by Father O'Hartegan, a Jesuit
at Paris. who represented at Paris the Confederate Catholics
of Ireland, and who was anxious that the protection of France
should be extended to his native country.[2] Neither Mazarin
nor O'Hartegan wished too openly to avow the support given
by France to a policy which, if successful, would practically
result in Irish independence. What was to be done must be
done in the name of Charles, and with the full approbation of
Nov. 24. the Queen. That approbation they had no difficulty
The Queen in securing. On November 24 O'Hartegan was able
supports
O'Hartegan. to report that the Queen had thrown herself vehemently on his side, and that Mazarin had promised him a
considerable sum in money.

Henrietta Maria, in listening to O'Hartegan's proposals,
was true to the only objects for which she really cared—the
restitution of her husband's authority and the concomitant
liberation of her Church. At Paris she found herself in the
midst of influences which carried her on insensibly in the path
which she was willing to tread. A joint committee of English
Sept. and Irish Catholics had been formed in that city in
A joint September, and had ever since been busily engaged
committee
of English in formulating its designs. The first resolution of
and Irish
Catholics. this committee had been that, though the cause of
the Catholics of both countries should be treated as indivisible,
its first efforts should be directed to the establishment of the
Catholic Church in Ireland, as a preliminary to the commence-
ment of operations in England. Sir Kenelm Digby was to be
despatched to Rome to lay the state of affairs before the Pope.
If O'Hartegan is to be trusted—and he had doubtless reason
to exaggerate the amount of support he was likely to receive—
money would not be wanting when the time for the great

---

[1] I derive my view of Mazarin's policy from his correspondence with
Montreuil, at a somewhat later date.

[2] Letter from Paris, Dec. $\frac{5}{15}$, 1645. *Carte MSS.* xvi. fol. 292.

enterprise arrived. Lady Banbury promised 10,000*l.*; Lord Montague and others had offered largely. The Nuncio, Cardinal Bagni, offered to pledge all that he was worth. Father Wadding wrote from Rome that he had 'the Pope's word for a considerable sum.' In giving hopes to the Supreme Council of powerful succour, O'Hartegan recommended that after the enemy had been expelled from Ireland, and the greater part of the strongholds of the land had been placed in Catholic hands, the long-talked-of Irish army might be sent across the sea to replace Charles on the English throne.[1] Practically there was to be an Irish conquest of England.

O'Hartegan's scheme was not the only one to which Henrietta Maria lent her ear. Amongst the enemies of

Nov. 23.
The Duke
of Lorraine
to be gained.

France was Charles, Duke of Lorraine. He had been expelled from his duchy by Richelieu, and the exile, as a Catholic prince of the Empire, had placed his sword at the disposal of the Emperor. Having no territorial army at his command, he fought—like Mansfeld at an earlier stage of the war—at the head of a band of adventurers who subsisted on plunder alone. Rapacious as his followers were, they bore themselves well in the day of battle, and at Freiburg they had contributed much to the tenacity of Mercy's resistance. Mazarin was therefore anxious to divert their energy to other fields, and he now informed Henrietta Maria that if she could induce the Duke to transfer his services to England, there would be no difficulty in finding the money necessary to enable him to carry on the operation.[2]

Little recked the French-born Queen of England of the cruelty of letting loose such a pack of wolves upon the soil

1645.
Jan. 2.
Goffe's
mission to
the Hague.

of that England which she regarded as the inheritance of her husband and her children. She at once closed with the proposal, and on January 2, before the Duke's answer could be received, she instructed Dr. Goffe, her agent at the Hague, to urge the Prince of Orange

---

[1] O'Hartegan to the Supreme Council, $\frac{\text{Nov. 24}}{\text{Dec. 4}}$. Carte's *Ormond*, vi. 216. Bagni to Barberini, Sept. $\frac{13}{23}$. *Roman Transcripts, R. O.*

[2] The Queen to the King, $\frac{\text{Nov. 23}}{\text{Dec. 3}}$. *Letters of Henrietta Maria*, 268.

to take a forward step in the marriage treaty which had been
the object of negotiation in the preceding summer.[1] Frederick
Henry was to pay dearly for the honour of having the Prince
of Wales as a son-in-law. The States General and France—
the Queen acted as though the consent of Anne of Austria
and Mazarin had been already secured—were to send a joint

Dutch assistance demanded.

embassy to London to inform Parliament that armed
assistance would be given to Charles unless he were
restored to his rights. The Prince was also to be
asked to make compensation for the massacre of Amboyna, to
state the amount of the portion which he intended to give with
his daughter, to lend 3,000 soldiers for service in England, and
to supply vessels in sufficient numbers, not only to transport
this contingent, but also to carry across the sea such forces as
might be obtained from France or Ireland.[2]

In less than a fortnight after these requests had been forwarded to the Hague the answer of the Duke of Lorraine

Jan. 16.
The Duke of Lorraine promises to come.

reached Paris. To the Queen's great joy, it was
entirely favourable. The Duke engaged to enter
Charles's service with 10,000 men.[3] Goffe was
therefore bidden to urge the Prince of Orange to

Jan. 17.
The Prince of Orange asked to help in their transportation.

find shipping to transport this army as well as the
other forces, and to commute the suggested loan of
3,000 soldiers for that of a fleet of warships to be
employed in an attack upon the Parliamentary navy
in the Downs or in the Medway. The help of the Dutch
transports would be especially needed in another quarter, as
the Queen had been assured by private persons in France that
an army of 5,000 men would be placed at her disposal.[4]

It is now possible to understand why powers had been

---

[1] See vol. i. p. 348.

[2] Note by Jermyn, $\frac{\text{Dec. 30}}{\text{Jan. 9}}$; Jermyn to the Prince of Orange, Jan. $\frac{2}{12}$;
instructions for Goffe, Jan. ; Note on the negotiation, Jan. ; *Groen van
Prinsterer*, Ser. 2, iv. 118.

[3] The Queen to the King, Jan. $\frac{17}{27}$. *The King's Cabinet Opened*,
p. 31. E. 292, 27.

[4] This we learn from a note by Goffe, Feb. ? *Groen van Prinsterer*,
Ser. 2, iv. 125.

given to Glamorgan to raise troops on the Continent as well
as in Ireland.   Charles indeed discovered before long that

O'Harte-
gan's
despatch
intercepted. O'Hartegan's projects had not sprung merely from a
loyal devotion to the throne. The Irishman's despatch
in which he artlessly expressed his real hopes was
intercepted by a Parliamentary cruiser, and was for obvious
reasons forwarded by the captors to Ormond.[1] Charles accord-

Feb. 19.
Charles
warns the
Queen
against him. ingly warned the Queen that O'Hartegan was a knave,
but he does not seem to have drawn the general
inference that the Dutchmen, Frenchmen, and Irishmen who professed themselves willing to assist him
were more likely to provide for their own interest than for his.
He recorded with satisfaction a message which he had recently

He learns
that the
Prince of
Orange will
lend ships. received from Goffe, to the effect that the Prince of
Orange had consented to furnish shipping for the
transport of the Lorrainers,[2] and his correspondence
with Ormond shows that he had no intention of
dropping his negotiation with the Supreme Council at Kilkenny
because their agent at Paris had written unadvisedly.

On January 22 Charles once more urged on Ormond the
necessity of concluding a peace. If nothing less would serve,

Jan. 22.
Charles
repeats his
terms to
Ormond. Poynings' Act might be suspended. As to the penal
statutes, he would not go a step further than he had
gone already, that is to say, than the promise of their
suspension when the treaty was concluded, and of
their repeal when victory had been secured with the help of an

Feb. 27.
The penal
laws to be
repealed if
help be
given, Irish army.[3] On February 27, however, when the
Treaty of Uxbridge was fairly at an end, he did go a
step further. " If," he wrote to the Lord Lieutenant,
" the suspension of Poynings' Act for such bills as
shall be agreed on between you there, and the present taking
away of the penal laws against Papists by a law will do it, I
shall not think it a hard bargain, so that freely and vigorously

---

[1] Ormond to Clanricarde, Feb. 3.   Carte's *Ormond*, vi. 241.

[2] The Queen to the King, Feb. $\frac{18}{28}$, *Letters of Henrietta Maria*, 290 ;
the King to the Queen, Feb. 19, *The King's Cabinet Opened*, p. 5, E.
292, 27.

[3] The King to Ormond, Jan. 22.   Carte's *Ormond*, vi. 233.

they engage themselves in my assistance against my rebels of
England and Scotland." Yet the concession was not to be
frankly made. Ormond was to conceal the fact that these new
powers had been sent to him, and was to make the best bargain he could.[1] The attempt to hold back what he was ready
to give was likely to be the more injurious to the course of
Ormond's negotiation, as it would convey to the Irish the idea
that he was not in earnest in the matter.

Charles, however, was by this time reconciled to the idea of
a repeal of the penal laws as soon as he was strong enough to
carry it out with impunity. On March 5 he authorised the Queen to consent in his name to the repeal
of the laws against the Catholics in England as well as
in Ireland, 'so as, by their means, or in their favours,
I may have so powerful assistance as may deserve so great a
favour and enable me to do it.'[2]

*March 5.
and the
favour to be
extended to
England.*

It was now time for the despatch of Glamorgan to Ireland.
Primarily the object of his mission was to take the command
of that Irish army which Charles now counted on obtaining,
and to organise the forces which were to be raised by the
Queen's supporters in France. He would also be useful in
smoothing the way of Ormond's negotiation. That he had
any secret instructions to abandon the Acts of Appeal and
Præmunire is an idea which may be rejected as incredible.
Charles in his last letter to Ormond had alluded to their abandonment as prejudicial to the royal authority, and when once a
notion of that kind had fixed itself in his head it was hopeless
to expect him to change his mind. For all that, there would be
need of an adroit negotiator in Ireland. Ormond's diplomacy
was carried on with the help of councillors of State, who did
not regard Charles's concessions with a favourable eye. It was
to be feared that he might not make the promise about the
repeal of the penal laws at the right moment—might not, it
was possible, even care to make it at all. Glamorgan must
therefore have powers not merely to command but to treat,

---

[1] The King to Ormond, Feb. 27. *Ibid.* vi. 257.
[2] The King to the Queen, March 5. *King's Cabinet Opened*, p. 7.
E. 292, 27.

not indeed without Ormond's knowledge, but in substitution for him if it proved to be necessary.

"We," wrote Charles in the commission which he issued on March 12 under his private signet, ". . . do by these as firmly as under our great seal, to all intents and purposes authorise and give you power to treat and conclude with the confederate Roman Catholics in our kingdom of Ireland, if upon necessity any be to be condescended unto wherein our Lieutenant cannot so well be seen in, as not fit for us at present publicly to own. Therefore we charge you to proceed according to this our warrant with all possible secrecy, and for whatsoever you shall engage yourself upon such valuable considerations as you in your judgment shall deem fit, we promise on the word of a king and a Christian to ratify and perform the same that shall be granted by you and under your hand and seal, the said confederate Catholics having by their supplies testified their zeal to our service."[1]

March 12. Glamorgan's commission to treat.

If there were still any doubt whether Glamorgan was intended to act independently of Ormond, it would be removed by the explanations which accompanied this commission. "On the word of a king," wrote Charles, after begging Glamorgan to deal with Ormond 'with all freedom and ingenuity,' "I will make good anything which our Lieutenant shall be induced unto upon your persuasion ; and if you find it fitting, you may privately show him these, which I intend not as obligatory to him, but to myself; and for both your encouragements and hopes, not having in all my kingdoms two such subjects; whose endeavours joining, I am confident to be soon drawn out of the mire I am now enforced to wallow in."[2] If this be not enough, it must be remembered that Glamorgan was still bound by the instructions of January 2,[3] which contemplated no independent action on his part, and which had never been superseded or changed.

An accompanying explanation.

It was mainly on military action that Glamorgan's heart was set. On the 21st, after making preparations in South

---

[1] Commission, March 12. *Dircks*, 80.
[2] The King to Glamorgan, March 2. *Dircks*, 75.
[3] See p. 166.

Wales for raising a force to join his levies from beyond the sea, he despatched a messenger to assure Charles 'that, God

March 21.
Glamorgan's
message to
the King.

willing, by the end of May or beginning of June, he will land with 6,000 Irish.'[1] On the 25th he sailed from Carnarvon on this hopeful enterprise. A

March 28.
He is
wrecked.

storm drove him northward, and on the 28th he was wrecked on the Lancashire coast, whence, slipping past the Parliamentary forces in the neighbourhood, he made his way to the safe refuge of Skipton Castle.[2] The burden of Ireland remained, where it had been before, on the shoulders of Ormond.

[1] Glamorgan's instructions to Bosdon, March 21. *King's Cabinet Opened*, p. 19. E. 292, 27.

[2] J. Bythell to his father, April 6. *Dircks*, 88. Dircks's notion that Glamorgan was lodged in Lancaster gaol arose from his mistaking a note by an ignorant scribe for part of the original document. See *Add. MSS.* 11,331, fol. 535.

CHAPTER XXVIII.

THE SECOND SELF-DENYING ORDINANCE AND THE NEW MODEL ARMY.

MONTROSE and Glamorgan were subjects after Charles's own heart, but, for all that, he had no worse enemies. Montrose's successes gave point to the feeling of exasperation which was uniting the Scottish Lowlander with his English kinsman against the King who was striving to recover his crown with Celtic aid, whilst Glamorgan's wild projects, if ever they came to be fully disclosed, would go far to merge the struggle between King and Parliament in a struggle between Englishmen and aliens. "We have no reason to lay down arms," declared a London newswriter, in reference to the proposal for a mutual disarmament which had recently been made by Charles,[1] "till the King yield to peace ; for so indeed the French and Irish may surprise us when they please."[2] The national spirit, always potent when it is stirred, was roused by Charles's bargainings with foreigners, and with races which the English looked down upon as inferior to their own. The proposed New Model army was no longer regarded as the instrument of the Independents. It was a national body raised for national ends.

There was no longer any question that a new and highly disciplined force was necessary. The existing army was falling to pieces from sheer disorganisation. On February 20 a mutiny broke out at Henley.[3] In

Marginal notes:
1645. Result of Montrose's victories and Glamorgan's schemes.

Feb. 25. The national feeling roused in England.

Feb. 20. Mutiny at Henley,

---

[1] See p. 129. [2] *Perfect Passages.* E. 270, 23.
[3] Grymes to Montague, Feb. 20. *S. P. Dom.* The valuable series of letters received by the Committee of Both Kingdoms unfortunately comes to an end on Feb. 17.

Buckinghamshire Crawford's men were stinging the county into angry protest by living at free quarters.[1] The cavalry, and of Waller's cavalry. which had recently been transferred from Essex to Waller, continued to cry out for Essex,[2] and refused obedience to their new general. They deserted their posts and moved off northwards, finally quartering themselves Feb. 28. at Beaconsfield. A fortnight's pay was sent down to quiet them, but they refused to return to their duty unless they were paid for another month as well.[3]

At such a crisis men's thoughts turned instinctively to the tried warriors of the Eastern Association. "For Colonel Good character of Cromwell's soldiers. Cromwell's soldiers," boasted a London newswriter, "it was informed that in what posture so ever they were, that were it at midnight, they were always ready to obey any ordinance of Parliament, and that there was none of them known to do the least wrong by plunder or any abuse to any country people where they came, but were ready to advance with Sir William Waller."[4] Yet even upon these trusted soldiers the general disorganisation produced its effect. The Feb. 21. They refuse to march. Eastern Association, seeing that the troops which it had raised for its own defence were quartered in Surrey or Hampshire, grew unwilling to bear the expense of supplying them. The men were left penniless, and an order to be ready to march with four days' provision was received with sullen murmurs. They declared that they must have money, pistols, and recruits before they could take the field.[5]

March 3. Cromwell to join Waller. It was felt at Westminster that Cromwell was the only man capable of allaying the storm, and the rejection by the Lords of the Self-Denying Ordinance had made Cromwell's services once more available. The necessary money and arms were quickly found, and Cromwell was ordered to place himself at the head of the cavalry which had formerly been his own, and with them to attach himself to

[1] Com. of B. K. to Crawford, Feb. 21. *Com. Letter Book.*
[2] See p. 128.
[3] Whitacre's Diary, *Add. MSS.* 31,116, fol. 196b.
[4] *Perfect Passages.* E. 270, 5.
[5] Whitacre's Diary *Add. MSS.* 31,116, fol. 195.

Waller's army.[1] Difficulties were smoothed away on his arrival, and in a short time Waller was placed in a condition to set out for that Western campaign for which he was designed.

If the Parliamentary troops round London were in a state of distraction, the local forces at a greater distance had

Feb. 22. Shrewsbury surprised.

acquitted themselves well. In the early morning of February 22 Colonel Mitton surprised the Royalist garrison of Shrewsbury. An invaluable position on the Severn was thus acquired for the Parliament. Unfortunately the victory was stained by the execution of a dozen Irish prisoners, in accordance with the recent ordinance [2]—a barbarity for which Rupert retaliated by hanging an equal number of his Parliamentary prisoners.[3] Almost at the same

Scarborough taken.

time the town of Scarborough fell into the hands of Meldrum, though the castle held out for some weeks

The surprise and recovery of Weymouth.

longer. In the South, on the other hand, Weymouth was surprised by a party of Royalists under Sir Lewis Dyves. They did not, however, long enjoy their success. Melcombe Regis, the adjoining town, was still held by a Parliamentary garrison, which, having been reinforced by a party from Portland under Captain Batten

Feb. 28.

assumed the offensive and stormed one of the captured forts of Weymouth. By February 28 the Royalist intruders had been completely expelled from the whole place.[4]

Whatever might be Charles's hopes from Celtic Scotland and Celtic Ireland, from France, or the Netherlands, it was

Charles's plan of campaign.

plain that before help could reach him from afar he would have once more to fight for his crown with such forces as England could supply. His principal army, now under Rupert's command, had served him well in the last campaign, and he resolved to pursue once more the strategy which had already stood him in good stead in the past

---

[1] *Com. of B. K. Day Book*, Feb. 27 ; the Com. of B. K. to Cromwell, March 3, *Com. Letter Book*.

[2] See p. 94.

[3] *Shrewsbury taken*, E. 270, 26 ; *L.J.* vii. 329.

[4] Sydenham to Essex, March 1. *L.J.* vii. 262.

summer. Once more Oxford was to be the basis of operations from which Rupert might dash out from time to time to relieve beleaguered garrisons, and to swoop down upon any weak point in the enemy's defences. Excellent as the plan would have been if Oxford had been sufficiently supplied with provisions and warlike stores to be a true basis of operations for an army on the march, it might easily break down if this central fortress should prove a source of weakness rather than of strength. How weak it was no one knew better than Charles. Far from the sea, and, unlike London, having no trade or commerce of its own, it depended for supplies upon the district, ever growing narrower, in which the Royalist commanders of garrisons were still able to enforce the payment of contributions and the levy of supplies.

Weakness of Oxford.

Hence it was that the eyes of Charles and his counsellors turned wistfully towards the West. South Wales had for some time been the chief recruiting ground of the Royalist infantry, and it was now thought possible to establish a fresh basis of operations to the south of the Bristol Channel. During the winter there had been much talk of the formation of a Royalist Western Association, which was to comprise the counties of Cornwall, Devon, Somerset, and Dorset, to counterbalance the Eastern Association on the Parliamentary side.

Proposed Western Association.

From the first the scheme was not a hopeful one. Not only had nature interposed difficulties of communication between the western peninsula and the other Royalist districts further north, but experience has shown that local forces were not to be trusted to advance beyond their own borders, unless their homes were freed from all danger of an attack in their absence from the enemy's garrisons. It would therefore be necessary, before the troops of the new association could be utilised for general purposes, to render Plymouth, Lyme, and Taunton innocuous. Plymouth and Lyme could only be blockaded, but hopes were entertained amongst the Royalists that Taunton might even yet be reduced.

To give encouragement to the new association, as well as to avert the danger of his falling into the hands of the enemy at the same time as his father, the young Prince of Wales, who had nearly completed his fifteenth year, and who, as Duke of Cornwall, was closely connected with one of its counties, was despatched to hold his court at Bristol.[1] The boy was accompanied by a body of councillors, amongst whom Hyde, Capel, Hopton, and Culpepper were the most eminent. It is possible that their services at Oxford were the more easily dispensed with as they were notoriously opposed to Charles's Irish schemes.

March 5. The Prince of Wales to go to the West.

Five days after the departure of the Prince, Charles adjourned the Oxford Parliament till October 10.[2] Before and during the Treaty of Uxbridge its members had subjected him to considerable pressure by their urgent entreaties that he should come to terms with the Parliament at Westminster,[3] and he now resolved to be cumbered with them no longer. In the next letter which he wrote to the Queen he congratulated himself on being 'freed from the place of base and mutinous motions—that is to say, our mongrel Parliament here.'[4] He had already rid himself of some of those who had been the loudest in their cry for peace.

March 10. Adjournment of the Oxford Parliament.

Lord Percy and the Earl of Sussex were now set free on an engagement to transport themselves at once to France, as Wilmot had done before.[5] Percy complied with the condition affixed to his liberation, but Sussex made his way to Westminster and professed himself a convert to the true Parliamentary faith. As his new associates refused to acknowledge the earldom recently conferred on him, he sank once more into the Lord Savile of earlier days. After his frequent changes he found himself as much distrusted at Westminster as he had been at Oxford.

Percy and Sussex liberated.

[1] *Clarendon*, ix. 6, 7. See also the suppressed passage in a note.

[2] *Dugdale's Diary*, March 10.

[3] See p. 114.

[4] The King to the Queen, March 13. *King's Cabinet Opened*, p. 12, E. 292, 27. The records of this Parliament were burnt before the surrender to Fairfax in 1646, and we have therefore no knowledge of its proceedings, and scarcely any notice of it after its first session; but there are occasional indications which show that it met from time to time.

[5] See p. 12.

When the Prince arrived at Bristol he found everything in confusion. The Western Association, of which so much had been expected, was still to be formed. The Committee of Somerset had promised much, but had performed nothing. The Prince could only obtain bread by borrowing it of Hopton, who was in command of the garrison of Bristol. Not a horse nor a man had been levied, and the gentry of the county were occupied in quarrelling amongst themselves. Goring, self-sufficient and licentious, though he had no authority from the King to exercise command in the West, was practically master of the country. After his retreat from Farnham in January,[1] he had settled down at Salisbury, 'where his horse committed such horrid outrages and barbarities as they had done in Hampshire.' It was to his negligence that the Royalists ascribed the capture of Weymouth. As soon as the quarters round Salisbury were exhausted he moved westward, ravaging the country as he went. Early in March he was at Exeter, where he and his principal officers 'stayed three or four days in most scandalous disorder, a great part of his horse living upon free quarter, and plundering to the gates of Exeter.'[2]

March 6. The Prince at Bristol.

Feb. Goring in the West.

March.

To the local commanders Goring gave personal offence which they resented almost as much as the tillers of the soil resented the exactions of his troopers. Having made up his mind to lay siege to Taunton, he wanted infantry for the purpose, and therefore summarily called on Sir John Berkeley, the governor of Exeter, to send him as many men as he could spare. He also gave orders to Sir Richard Grenvile, the most insubordinate of generals, to come in person with the bulk of the forces with which he was then besieging Plymouth, leaving only sufficient men before the town to block it up. The orders may have been good in themselves, but Goring had no commission empowering him to give them, and he had no idea of condescending to entreat a favour where he had no right to command. Berkeley, an honourable and loyal

He resolves to besiege Taunton.

His treatment of Berkeley and Grenvile.

<hr>

[1] See p. 113.   [2] *Clarendon*, ix. 7-9.

soldier, did as he was bidden ; but Grenvile, at least for a
time, hung back.[1]

On March 11 Goring appeared before Taunton, where
Blake had made every preparation to stand a second siege.

March 11.
Goring
before Taun-
ton.
As his supplies were inadequate for the maintenance
of a large garrison, he dismissed Holborn and the
force which had relieved him in December.   Holborn contrived to make his way safely through the open
country, and finally succeeded in joining Cromwell, who was
now serving under Waller, and was watching for an opportunity
to succour Taunton.[2]

The news of Holborn's safety was not the only disquieting
intelligence which reached Goring.   On the 11th a Wiltshire

Royalists
surprised
at Devizes.
party on its way to join him was surprised by Waller
and Cromwell near Devizes.   " Of 400 horse," wrote
Waller, "there escaped not thirty." [3]   In spite of
this success, however, want of supplies forced the small Parlia-

Waller falls
back.
mentary army to fall back through Dorset.   There
was constant manœuvring on both sides and occasional skirmishes.   Whenever Goring suffered loss he discreetly
avoided mentioning it in his despatches.   Whenever he gained

March 22.
Goring's
boast.
a success he magnified it into an important victory.
" For pursuing Waller," he characteristically boasted,
" if he go as fast as Cromwell, I cannot overtake
him." [4]   Waller indeed had brought off Holborn safely, but
it was impossible to deny that he had abandoned not only

March 27.
Wa ler's
complaints.
Somerset, but Dorset as well.   On the 27th he
wrote from Ringwood to Lenthall.   " I cannot but
advertise you," he complained, "that, since my coming
hither, I have observed a great smoke of discontent rising

[1] Digby to Berkeley, March 11 ; Goring to the Prince of Wales,
March 12 ; Berkeley to Digby, March 23 ; *Clarendon MSS.* 1833, 1834,
1842.

[2] *The Moderate Intelligencer.* E. 277, 14.   Clarendon (ix. 9) speaks
of these men as being under the command of Vandruske, but Vandruske
seems to have been Holborn's subordinate.

[3] Waller to Lenthall, March 13.   Sanford, *Studies of the Rebellion*,
616.

[4] Goring to Culpepper, March 22-30. *Clarendon MSS.* 1841, 1856.

among the officers. I pray God no flame break out. The ground of all is the extremity of want that is among them, indeed, in an insupportable measure." [1]

The failure of the Parliamentary army of the West arose from financial disorganisation at Westminster. The failure of

Causes of failure on both sides.

the Royalists arose from the defects of the character of their commander. "Dear general," wrote Digby

March 29. Digby's warning to Goring.

from Oxford to Goring, "I have nothing to add but to conjure you to beware of debauches; there fly hither reports of the liberty you give yourself, much to your disadvantage." [2]

If Charles's main army was relieved from the burden of a Goring in command, the pressure of financial need was felt

The King's main army.

Financial distress.

there as strongly as it was by Waller. The best planned schemes had to be abandoned because the money needed for the purchase of arms and ammunition was not forthcoming. Even when arms and ammunition could be had, there was irregularity of pay, followed by its inevitable consequence, irregularity of discipline. Detached parties were especially liable to be left to their own resources, and consequently to become a scourge to the country. Early in March Sir Marmaduke Langdale successfully relieved Pontefract,[3] but the outrages committed by his followers, especially upon the women who were so unfortunate as to live on his line of march, must have effectually quenched any spark of loyalty which remained in the districts through which he passed.[4] Prince Maurice had been sent to hold out

Maurice's plunderings.

a hand to the beleaguered Royalists in Cheshire, but he too was reported to be 'plundering and impoverishing the country extremely.'[5]

On March 11 Rupert was at Ludlow, hoping to join his

[1] Waller to Lenthall, March 27. Sanford, *Studies of the Rebellion*, 618.

[2] Digby to Goring, March 29. *Ibid.* 620.

[3] On the military history of Pontefract in the Civil War, see Holmes, *The Sieges of Pontefract.*

[4] *Merc. Civicus*, E. 273, 5; Whitacre's Diary, *Add. MSS.* 31,116, fol. 198; Luke to Massey, March 20, *Egerton MSS.* 785, fol. 59b.

[5] Maurice's Diary, *Arch. Cambrensis*, i. 39.

brother and raise the siege of Beeston Castle. Brereton, who
commanded the besiegers, called on the Committee of Both
March 11.
Rupert
hopes to
join him.
Kingdoms for assistance. The Committee, knowing the importance of barring Rupert's way into
that Lancashire recruiting ground which had served
Preparations
to resist him.
him so well in the campaign of Marston Moor, hurried up troops from all quarters, whilst Leven despatched David Leslie from Yorkshire with a strong party of
Scots to assist in stopping the career of the formidable Prince.[1]

Important as these succours were, they did not reach
Brereton in time to prevent the breaking up of the siege of
Beeston
Castle
relieved.
Beeston Castle. More than that Rupert was unable
to accomplish. Yet it was not fear of the enemy by
Rupert's
retreat.
which his forward march was checked. The country
in his rear was in flames, and he was compelled to
hurry back to stamp out the conflagration.[2]

The grievous exactions of the Royalist garrisons in Herefordshire and in the neighbouring districts of Worcestershire
March 18.
A rising in
Hereford-
shire.
were the origin of the mischief. On March 18 some
15,000 countrymen gathered outside the gates of
Hereford. They fired upon the soldiers, and called
upon the citizens to admit them into the town. On the following day Massey appeared on the scene, pleading
March 19.
Massey
attempts
to win the
insurgents.
with the insurgents to join their cause with his, and
warning them, truly enough, that there was no room
for a third party in England. The men of Herefordshire were, however, no Puritans, and they could ill brook
the domination of a Puritan Parliament. They turned a deaf
ear to Massey's exhortations, and, contenting themselves with
promises of better treatment from the Governor of Hereford,
most of them withdrew to their homes, whilst those who
remained were dispersed by Rupert's returning squadrons.[3]
Byron, the Governor of Chester, had hoped much from

---

[1] *Com. Letter Book*, March 11-25.

[2] Williams to Ormond, March 25.   Carte's *Ormond*, vi. 270.

[3] Declaration of Scudamore, March 19 ; Massey to Luke, March 22 ;
Webb, *Civil War in Herefordshire*, ii. 154, 369 ; *The Kingdom's Weekly
Intelligencer*, E. 276, 3 ; *The Moderate Intelligencer*, E. 277, 8.

Rupert's coming; the retreat of the Prince filled him with
dismay. Once more he turned his eyes wistfully
across the Irish Sea. "If," he wrote, "considerable
forces come forth of Ireland in any reasonable time,
I doubt not but with God's blessing they may quickly clear
these parts." [1]

April 1.
*Byron looks
to Ireland
for help.*

It may be doubted whether the Irish troops for which
Byron called would really have carried all before them in a
country where their presence would have been
equally detested by both parties. The spirit which
had brought the Herefordshire peasants into the
field might easily in that case have thrown them entirely on
the side of the Parliamentary commanders. As it was, the
weariness of the prolonged struggle, which had taken a
special form in Herefordshire, was everywhere to be traced,
and though it showed itself at the moment in a rooted
distrust of both parties, it might be counted as certain ultimately to throw its weight into the balance in favour of that
party which was most capable of maintaining discipline and
ensuring order.

*Lesson of
the Here-
fordshire
rising.*

Of the two sides, there could be little doubt which would
be the first to meet the exigencies of the situation. What the
King was unable to do the Parliament could do if it
would. For some time the temper of all parties at
Westminster had been as warlike as Charles's own.
On February 24 the Dutch ambassadors appeared
before the Houses to urge them to accept Charles's
proposals for the settlement of ecclesiastical difficulties.[2] The only result of such interference was
that the minds of Englishmen were knitted together
in resenting it. The opposition of the Scots to a prolongation
of the war had come to an end since the breaking
up of the conferences at Uxbridge, and the Scots
necessarily drew the English Presbyterians in their
train. On February 25 the Commons appointed a
committee to draw up a fresh Self-Denying Ordinance.

*Feb.
Warlike
feeling at
West-
minster.*

*Feb. 24.
The Dutch
ambassa-
dors urge
the Houses
to accept
the King's
terms.*

*Feb. 25.
A New Self-
Denying
Ordinance
to be
prepared.*

[1] Byron to Ormond, April 1. *Carte MSS.* xiv. fol. 342.
[2] *L. J.* vii. 240.

It was only natural that the proposal should irritate those amongst the Lords who were for peace at any price, but they had no longer the Presbyterian feeling at their service.

March 4.
A demand
on the City.

When, on March 4, the City was asked to lend 80,000*l.* to cover the initiatory expenses of the New Model till the taxation out of which the advance could be repaid had been gathered in, Loudoun was no less urgent in supporting the demand than Northumberland or Vane himself.[1]

In the meanwhile the organisation of the New Model was steadily making way. On March 3 Fairfax's list of officers

March 3.
The list of
officers sent
to the Lords.

March 10.
Names
struck out.

was sent up to the Lords for their approbation. The list was little to their taste. They knew that they had before them a final struggle against military Independency, and they struck out the names of two colonels, Pickering and Montague, as well as those of more than forty captains.[2] Though for some days the Peers maintained their ground, there was no longer any decisive majority even in their own House. When

March 17.
A close
division.

on the 17th a division was taken, the numbers were equal. On this Say tendered the proxy of the absent Mulgrave, to be used in favour of the restoration of the names struck out. Essex, on the other side, produced the proxy of his brother-in-law Clanricarde.[3] Clanricarde, it was now urged, was a Catholic, and his vote was therefore worthless. An attempt was then made to dispute the validity of Mulgrave's

March 18.
The names
restored.

proxy, but it was found impossible to maintain the objection, and on the 18th, Clanricarde's proxy having been ruled to be of no avail, the names of the Independent officers were restored by a single vote.[4]

So well were the Commons satisfied with their victory that

The Lords
to be
thanked.

they appointed a committee to draw up a declaration expressive of their gratitude to the Lords, and of their own wish to preserve the liberty and indepen-

[1] *Three Speeches.* E. 273, 3.

[2] *L.J.* vii. 268 ; Whitacre's Diary, *Add. MSS.* 31,116, fol. 198, 198b.

[3] He was Earl of St. Albans in the English peerage.

[4] *L.J.* vii. 268, 272–277 ; Sabran to Brienne, $\frac{Mar. 27}{April 6}$, *Harl. MSS.* 546, fol. 151b ; D'Ewes's Diary, *Harl. MSS.* 165, fol. 193.

dence of the Peers.[1] Now that the Peers were ready to comply with the wishes of the Commons, the Commons had no longer any object to gain by reducing the two Houses to a single assembly.[2]

On March 24 the new Self-Denying Ordinance was brought into the House of Commons by the committee appointed to

March 24.
The second Self-Denying Ordinance.

draw it up. Its form had probably been affected by the termination of the conflict between the Houses. The question whether Essex and Manchester should retain their commands had virtually been settled by the appointment of Fairfax and Skippon. Whatever might be the military titles of the two peers, they would no longer have armies to follow them to the field.[3] Such a position would be not only irksome to themselves, but it might under unforeseen circumstances be troublesome to the community. It was therefore desirable that the two lords should be removed from their nominal commands, and if members of the Upper House were displaced members of the House of Commons could hardly expect to remain in office. Yet if the new Ordinance was to be drawn up on the lines of the old one, it must avoid the objection which the Lords had taken to the terms in which the original Ordinance had been couched. Members of either House were no longer to be disqualified from office ; they were simply to be required, within forty days after the passing of the Ordinance, to resign any post conferred by the existing Parliament. Not a word was said to prevent their re-employment, and recent experience had shown that, whenever the Commons were in earnest about a matter, it was not hard for them to force the hand of the Peers.[4]

---

[1] *C.J.* iv. 83.   [2] See p. 106.

[3] Especially as, on March 11, the Lords had consented to an ordinance empowering Fairfax to take what officers or soldiers he pleased out of the armies of Essex, Manchester, or Waller. Fairfax had it, therefore, in his power to leave all the three without a single soldier. *L.J.* vii. 269.

[4] *L.J.* vii. 302. The name, *Self-Denying Ordinance,* was never applied by contemporaries to the first Ordinance. The first notice I have found of it as applied to the second is in *The Scottish Dove* of April 4. E. 276, 15. "The Self-Denying Ordinance—for so I may call it— is passed."

Before the new Ordinance was ready to be despatched to the Lords, the declaration which was to smooth away all

March 25.
Declaration
of the
Commons.

asperities was transmitted to them. The Peers were told that the Commons detested the very idea of overthrowing their order, and that they held themselves as much bound to uphold their liberties as to preserve their own. Unluckily this declaration was

An ordi-
nance for
granting a
commission
to Fairfax.

accompanied by an ordinance for granting to Fairfax a commission authorising him to carry on war. A close scrutiny revealed the omission of the directions which had been given to Essex in his original commission to wage war for the preservation of the King's person. To this

Objection of
the Lords.

omission the Lords objected. Parties were, however, too equally balanced in their House to enable them to maintain the objection. According to the rumours of the day, personal as well as political rivalries were engaged in the

March 18.
Northum-
berland
guardian of
the King's
children.

struggle. Northumberland, who took the side of the Commons,[1] had recently been appointed to the guardianship of the King's two youngest children, who were in the custody of Parliament, a post which was before long rewarded with a salary of 3,000*l.* a year.[2] At

Rumour of
an intention
to depose
the King.

the same time a report gained credit that, in case of the King's protracted refusal to come to terms, the Parliamentary leaders would place the crown on the head of the Duke of Gloucester, and would confer on Northumberland the office of Lord Protector.[3]

---

[1] Those who shared the views of the Commons sufficiently to re-cord their protests were Northumberland, Kent, Pembroke, Nottingham, Salisbury, Say, Wharton, North, and Howard. That Pembroke's name should appear on this list is the strongest evidence of his want of prin-ciple.

[2] *L.J.* vii. 279, 327.

[3] "Veramente se si considera bene il procedere del Parlamento, si concluderà che habbino volontà a poco a poco di smascherarsi con cambiar il Re nella persona di questo Duca," i.e. the Duke of Gloucester, "et fare durante la sua minorità il Conte di Northumberland, hora suo nuovo Governatore, protettore del popolo et di quelli che aderiscono al cambia-mento del governo." Salvetti to Gondi, March $\frac{21}{31}$. *Add. MSS.* 27,962. K, fol. 417.

On April 1 the transference of a single vote, that of the Earl of Bolingbroke, brought with it the submission of the

April 1. The Lords give way.

Lords on the question of Fairfax's commission.[1] The Self-Denying Ordinance, which had been brought up the day before, passed rapidly through all its stages, and was finally accepted on the 3rd.[2] On the

April 3. The Self-Denying Ordinance passed.

2nd, even before it passed, Essex, whose example was followed by Manchester and Denbigh, anticipated its effect by laying down the generalship which was still formally his. In a few well-chosen and

April 2. Essex, Manchester, and Denbigh resign their commands.

dignified words he vindicated his honesty of purpose, and commended his officers, whose pay had fallen much into arrears, to the favourable consideration of the Houses. On the 9th Warwick, who had been

for some time absent from the House, gave in his resignation

April 9. Warwick's resignation.

of the office of Lord High Admiral,[3] and on the 19th a commission of six lords and twelve members

April 19. The Admiralty in commission.

of the House of Commons was appointed to fulfil the duties of the post.[4] The two Houses found it

more difficult to arrive at an understanding as to the actual command of the fleet. The Commons not very wisely wished it to be undertaken by a committee of three persons.

May 7. The Lords wish the fleet to be commanded by a peer.

The Lords replied that it would be better to entrust it to a single person, and added a recommendation that the single person should be one of themselves,[5] being, thus the first of the two Houses to call atten-

tion to the fact that the second Self-Denying Ordinance did not, like the first, permanently exclude from office. The

May 15. Batten to command the fleet.

Commons in reply directed the new Admiralty Commission to appoint Captain Batten to command as Vice-Admiral. They took this step without consult-

ing the Upper House. As there were twelve commoners to six peers on the commission, they were able to count on their orders being obeyed.[6]

[1] *L.J.* vii. 289–298 ; Salvetti's Newsletters, April $\frac{4}{14}$, *Add. MSS.* 27,962, K. fol. 425b ; D'Ewes's Diary, *Harl. MSS.* 166, fol. 197.

[2] *L.J.* vii. 302.　　　[3] *Ibid.* vii. 311　　　[4] *Ibid.* 327.

[5] *Ibid.* 357.　　　[6] *C.J.* iv. 144.

Thus closed the long struggle which had at one time threatened to rend the Parliamentary party in twain, and to
Nature of lay it dishonoured and degraded at the feet of the
the struggle. King.[1] If the authors of the Self-Denying Ordinance and of the New Model had gained the upper hand, it was because from first to last they had an intelligent conception of the conditions of action. The stern logic of facts had driven the Presbyterians to follow in the track marked out beforehand by the Independents.

There was no delay in using the powers which had at last been fully given to Fairfax. The first attempt to embody the
April 5. old soldiers in the new army was made at Reading,
Essex's where Essex's five regiments were quartered together
army re-
duced. with a few companies which had formerly served under Robartes. The men had of late been giving signs of a mutinous disposition, and it was not without apprehension that, on April 5, Skippon, to whom the work of reorganisation had been entrusted, summoned them before him. His declaration that justice should be done to all claims produced a favourable effect. The whole of the rank and file consented willingly to the terms of the new service, and even some of the sergeants and corporals agreed to enlist as privates. In his report to Parliament Skippon attributed the bad spirit which had hitherto prevailed to the necessitous condition of the officers, and to the evil effect of their discontent upon the men.[2]

---

[1] There is an entry in the *Commons Journals* (iv. 96), under the date of April 2, to the effect that the Earl of Manchester's answer to the charge relating to Newbury and Donnington should be reported. It might be inferred from this that some of Manchester's opponents still intended to prolong the personal attack upon him. The true explanation is given by D'Ewes (*Harl. MSS.* 166, fol. 117). Compensation for their losses in consequence of the war had been voted to Essex and Denbigh, but a proposal to compensate Manchester was resisted on the ground that his estates had not been ravaged by the enemy. It was Manchester's ally, Sir William Lewis, who moved that the report on Manchester's answer should be read, evidently with the intention of giving him the opportunity of attacking the Independents in return. The matter, however, proceeded no further.

[2] *Several Letters.* E. 277, 8.

There could be little doubt that the change from destitution to regular pay would be as welcome to the regiments of the other commanders as it was to those of Essex. On April 16 a letter from Waller was read in the House of Commons. He piteously complained of his unhappy condition. His soldiers, for want of pay, were deserting in large numbers, and those who remained refused obedience to his orders. His wretched plight, he added, 'made him desirous rather to give his Yea and No in the House of Commons than to remain amongst his troops so slighted and disesteemed by them.' [1]

April 16.
Waller's
complaints.

Waller had his wish. His men were either sent to garrison the fortresses of the southern coast or enrolled in the new army.[2] In obedience to the Self-Denying Ordinance he quietly took his place on the benches of the House of Commons. If he had not the highest qualities of a commander, he came short of them as much through want of force of character as through defect of military skill. As a master of defensive tactics he was probably unequalled on either side, and if he had not Cromwell's gift of compelling attention to his wants, and of forcing the necessary supplies out of the hands of negligent officials, he was the first to discern the real cause of the weakness of the Parliamentary armies, and to propose the remedy which ultimately proved efficient. Of his steadfastness in action and his patience in adversity there can be no question. The ferocity of all-controlling genius was lacking to him.

April 17.
End of
Waller's
command.

Waller as a
commander.

Of the readiness of Manchester's soldiers, the veterans of the Eastern Association, to take arms under the new conditions there could be little doubt. Yet the old soldiers even of Manchester's army were not all sectaries or Independents. On April 20 Colonel Pickering, a zealous Independent, arrived at Abingdon to command one of the newly-formed regiments. The men had no objection to take military orders

Manchester's
soldiers.

April 20.
Resistance
to a preach-
ing colonel.

[1] Whitacre's Diary, *Add. MSS.* 31,116, fol. 205. A petition from Waller's officers stated that during a service of two years they had received but six weeks' pay. *Perfect Passages.* E. 260, 20.

[2] The Com. of B. K. to Waller, April 17. *Com. Letter Book.*

from him, but when their new colonel proceeded to preach a sermon to them they broke into mutiny.[1]

At Westminster the general feeling was startled by the proceedings at Abingdon. Both Houses concurred in passing rapidly an ordinance which prohibited laymen from preaching, and these injunctions were forwarded to Fairfax with strict orders to see that they were observed in the army.[2] He was told that he was expected to enforce obedience 'now that the State hath been so careful to provide constant pay.'[3]

April 25. Laymen prohibited from preaching.

'Constant pay' might indeed be expected to work wonders. Without it all hope of maintaining discipline must be abandoned. If the old soldiers were not all under the influence of Puritan zeal, what was to be said of the new recruits? As many as 8,460 were needed to fill the ranks, and no attempt was made to obtain them by voluntary enlistment. The Committee of Both Kingdoms ordered the county committees to impress the required number, taking special care that the recruits were 'of able bodies, and of years meet for their employment, and well clothed'[4] in those scarlet coats which from henceforth became the uniform of the English soldier.[5] Of their spiritual condition not a word was said. In London, at least if the statements of the French ambassador are to be trusted, young men were seized in the streets and carried off forcibly to serve against the King.[6]

Constant pay.

March 19. Recruits pressed.

It would take much to reduce such elements to order. The Kentish recruits rose upon their conductors, seized on a gentleman's house near Wrotham, and bade defiance to all comers. It was only after they had been attacked

April 10. A mutiny in Kent.

---

[1] Whitacre's Diary, *Add. MSS.* 31,116, fol. 207 ; D'Ewes's Diary, *Harl. MSS.* 166, fol. 204b.

[2] *C.J.* iv. 123; *L.J.* vii. 337. [3] *C.J.* iv. 126.

[4] The Com. of B. K. to the Deputy Lieutenants and Committee of Essex, &c., March 19. *Com. Letter Book.*

[5] *Perfect Passages.* E. 260, 32. The fact was first pointed out by the Hon. J. W. Fortescue in *Macmillan's Magazine*, Sept. 1893.

[6] Sabran to Brienne, April $\frac{4}{14}$. *Add. MSS.* 5,461, fol. 174.

in form by a military force that they submitted to their fate.[1]
Parties of Hertfordshire men roamed about the county, com-

April 18.
Outrages in
Hertford-
shire.
mitting outrages wherever they came. A dozen of
the offenders were brought before the justices at
St. Albans, and two of the number were condemned
to death. By the direction of the House of Commons the
sentence was put in execution.[2]

In spite of facts such as these, the popular belief that the
New Model was not merely a Puritan but an Independent

The officers
of the New
Model.
army is not without foundation. An army is to a
great extent moulded by its officers, and the officers
of this army were men of a pronounced, and especially of a tolerant, Puritanism. The officers too had on their
side, if not the whole of the old soldiers, at least those who
were most energetic and most amenable to discipline, more
particularly the sturdier Puritans of the Eastern Association who
were especially numerous in the ranks of the cavalry. It was
by such as these that the whole lump was ultimately leavened.

No attempt was made even to exact the taking of the Covenant from the common soldiers. A clause in the New Model

The officers
only re-
quired to
take the
Covenant.
Ordinance, it is true, had directed that the Covenant
should be tendered to them in accordance with instructions to be hereafter issued by the Houses. No
such instructions were ever issued, possibly because
to refuse entrance to the ranks to those who were unwilling to
take the Covenant would have opened an easy door of escape
to the pressed men who were driven unwillingly into the army.
As far as the officers were concerned, the Covenant was almost
entirely useless as a test of Presbyterianism. It was capable
of various interpretations, and the conscience of a Puritan
must have been scrupulous indeed had he found any difficulty
in placing his own construction upon it. Only one member of
the House of Commons amongst those who remained at their
posts at Westminster after the first months of the Civil War,
Sir Ralph Verney, refused the Covenant at the end of 1643,
preferring the miseries of exile to the soiling of his conscience.

[1] *The Kingdom's Weekly Intelligencer.* E. 278, 8.
[2] *C.J.* iv. 119.

Only one of those chosen by Fairfax to take a command in
the new army rejected, in 1645, the condition of taking the
Lilburne
refuses to
take the
Covenant. Covenant, which Parliament had imposed upon the
officers. It is hardly necessary to say that the one
who gave no heed to the convenient interpretations
with which others quieted their consciences was John Lilburne.
Cromwell liked the man, and pleaded hard with him to reconsider his determination ; but Cromwell pleaded in vain, and
Lilburne was necessarily excluded from all share in the warfare
of the New Model.[1]

That the New Model would, under the guidance of Independent officers, become ultimately a support to the Inde-
Pay of the
army. pendent party was probable enough. For the present,
the matter of supreme importance was that it should
be paid regularly. Paid highly, indeed, it never was. The
foot-soldier received but eightpence a day—a sum which was
at that time only a penny more than the daily remuneration of
the agricultural labourer, and which was no more than had been
paid by Elizabeth to her soldiers at the end of her reign, and
by Charles in his expeditions against the Scots.[2] That eightpence, however, was no longer to be at the mercy of the
spasmodic efforts of reluctant committee-men, or of scarcely
March 31.
It is
secured on
county
taxation,
and on an
advance by
the City. less spasmodic efforts of a popular assembly. It was
to be secured on a fixed taxation, for the full amount
of which the counties were to be responsible, and,
lest there should be any difficulty in the first starting
of the new financial machinery, the City had agreed
to advance no less a sum than 80,000l.[3] In a time of scarcity
and distress, when employment was hard to find, the punctual
payment of even agricultural wages was not to be despised. In
the case of the cavalry, each horseman received two shillings a
day, with the obligation of providing for his horse. One-quarter
of this sum was, however, retained to be paid at some future

---

[1] *Innocency and Truth justified*, p. 46. E. 314, 21.

[2] Grose, *Military Antiquities*, i. 291, 296 ; Rogers, *Six Centuries of
Work and Wages*, 427 ; *Com. of B. K. Day Book*, Jan. 6.

[3] *L.J.* vii. 293.

date, and the gradual accumulation of arrears served as an additional security against desertion.

It was not only through the religion of its officers that the New Model bade ·fair to be Independent in its character. No distinction of rank in the New Model. Independency was something more than the proclamation of a religious principle. It implied a contempt for distinctions of rank unaccompanied by merit or public service. "I had rather," Cromwell had once said, "have a plain russet-coated captain that knows what he fights for, and loves what he knows, than that which you call a gentleman, and is nothing else. I honour a gentleman that is so indeed." [1] Cromwell's principle was carried out in the selection of officers for the New Model. No distinction of rank was recognised, as there was no minute inquiry into diversities of creed. Amongst the new military leaders were Hewson the cobbler and Pride the drayman ; but the gentry of England were largely represented in the list of officers. It has been calculated that 'out of thirty-seven generals and colonels' who took part in the first great battle, 'twenty-one were commoners of good families, nine were members of noble families, and only seven were not gentlemen by birth.' [2]

Such was the army sent forth in the hope of wresting victory from the King. If there was in it a danger to political liberty, Political danger not thought of. it was a danger which no one suspected at the time, and which, so far as it is inherent in all military organisation, dated from 1642 rather than from 1645.

It is well for those who are opening the floodgates of civil war to ask themselves whether the attainment of the objects at which they aim is worth the risk of military intervention in affairs of State. It can never be worth while, when war has once been commenced, for either side to keep its army weak and disorganised merely to avoid the danger of its throwing its sword into the balance of political parties.

---

[1] Cromwell to Spring and Barrow, Sept. 1643. *Carlyle*, Letter XVI.
[2] Markham, *The Great Lord Fairfax*, 199.

CHAPTER XXIX.

THE NEW MODEL ARMY IN THE FIELD.

IMPROVED as was the financial outlook at Westminster, there was still much to be done to meet the ever growing expenses of the war. Local forces and garrisons had to be provided for, and the engagement of the Houses for the payment of the Scottish armies in England and Ireland had, if possible, to be met. Every source of revenue was largely anticipated, and no fresh means of raising money came amiss. On April 23 the Committee of Both Kingdoms reported to the Commons that there were pictures at York House which had been collected by the late Duke of Buckingham, and which were now valued at 12,000*l.* If half of these were sold, 6,000*l.* would be available for the forces in Ireland. A squeamish member, indeed, objected that 'most of those pictures were either superstitious or lascivious, and that it was not fit to make benefit of the superstitious ones, but rather to have them burnt.' Possibly, but for an unexpected obstacle, the House might have decided to sell the pictures which were merely lascivious—especially as even the objecting member does not appear to have thought of asking that these should be committed to the flames. Northumberland, who was the tenant of York House, and whose vote, in the balanced state of parties in the House of Lords, was too precious to be lost, stopped the proposed sale of the Titians and Rubenses which had been acquired by Buckingham in the days of his splendour, by declaring that without them the rooms occupied by himself would be unfit for habitation, and that, if he had to

Marginal notes:

April.
The financial position.

April 23.
Proposed sale of pictures.

Northumberland stops the sale.

remove to another house, he should expect the House of
Commons to pay his rent.[1]

Low as was the Parliamentary treasury, its contents were
wealth itself when compared with the deplorable destitution of

The
Royalist
system of
raising
supplies.

the King. In the early part of the war some advantage had been procured to the royal cause by the
system under which local contributions had been
paid over, not to county committees, but to the local
military commanders, who were most deeply interested in
enforcing payment in full. As the exhaustion of the country
increased this system recoiled on those who employed it.
When money was not forthcoming, houses were sacked and
their inmates exposed to every species of indignity. In the
West Grenville and Goring were earning for themselves a
specially evil name by their cruelty and extortion.

To authority of every kind Goring was essentially un-
amenable. On April 11 Rupert appeared at Bristol to take

April 11.
The Prince's
orders to
Goring.

counsel with the Prince. As a result of the consultation, a letter was written to Goring in the
Prince's name, proposing that he should place his
infantry and artillery at the disposal of Grenvile, who was now
in the neighbourhood of Taunton, and was preparing to besiege
the place. Goring himself at the head of his cavalry was to
sweep over the Wiltshire downs, thus covering the siege operations against a possible advance of the enemy.[2] Goring replied

Goring
refuses
obedience.

in a long sulky letter,[3] objecting to the whole scheme.
He then, without waiting for an answer, sent off his
foot towards Taunton, and rode off to Bath to
recruit his health, there being, as he said, nothing else left for
him to do. His conduct was the more extraordinary as he
had himself previously signified his approbation of the very
proposal which he now refused to execute. "Well," was
Hyde's reply, "you generals are a strange kind of people. . . .

---

[1] *C.J.* iv. 121 ; Whitacre's Diary, *Add. MSS.* 31,116, fol. 206b.

[2] The Prince's letter has not been preserved, but its purport may be
gathered from the ensuing correspondence, and from *Clarendon*, ix. 13.

[3] Goring to Culpepper, April 11. *Clar. MSS.* 1866. Clarendon in-
accurately calls it a 'short sullen letter.'

For God's sake, let us not fall into ill humours which may cost us dear. Get good thoughts about you, and let us hear

THE FIRST OPERATIONS
OF THE
NEW MODEL ARMY
Route of Fairfax ------
" " Cromwell -·-·-·-

speedily from you to a better tune."[1]   The probable explanation of Goring's fit of ill-temper is that he was aware that

[1] Hyde to Goring, April 12. *Clar. MSS.* 1868.

Rupert had been consulted by the Prince, and that he was jealous of any military authority higher than his own.

At this crisis of the western campaign, when one military system on the Parliamentary side had broken down and that which was to replace it was being slowly brought into existence, the leaders at Westminster were well served by Goring's insubordination. They could not hope that Rupert would give them as much assistance. Since his return from Bristol he had been hanging about Gloucester and Hereford, pressing soldiers and preparing for vigorous action. It was known that Charles was making ready at Oxford to join his nephew, and there was no slight alarm at Westminster lest the enemy might be ready to take the field before the New Model was in a position to stir.

Rupert recruits his army.

Naturally the thoughts of all who dreaded this result turned to the only soldier who had beaten Rupert in the field. It can hardly be doubted that some at least had already formed the intention of retaining Cromwell's services in that lieutenant-generalship of the New Model for which he was so eminently qualified. For the present it was possible for Parliament to avail itself of his skill as a cavalry officer without in any way infringing upon the Self-Denying Ordinance, as the forty days over which his command was extended after the passing of that measure had not yet expired.

Cromwell to be opposed to him.

On April 20, therefore, Cromwell received orders to throw himself to the west of Oxford, stationing himself so as to interrupt the passage of the King's train of artillery which Maurice was about to convoy from Oxford to his brother at Hereford.[1]

April 20. Cromwell's orders.

In carrying out these instructions Cromwell was certain to do all possible damage to the enemy on the way. On the 23rd he was at Watlington at the head of 1,500 horse, whence pushing forwards in a north-westerly direction, he eagerly interrogated every passenger whom he met. He soon learnt that Maurice had not yet arrived at Oxford to take charge of the artillery, but that

April 23. Cromwell at Watlington.

[1] The Com. of B. K. to Cromwell, April 20. *Com. Letter Book.*

Northampton was quartered at Islip with a strong body of horse. He at once made for Islip, only to find that Northampton had been warned in time and had ridden off to a place of safety. The next morning, however, Northampton returned with reinforcements, but only to be routed with heavy loss. A party of the defeated Royalists took refuge in Blechington House. The place was strongly fortified, and Cromwell, though he sent in a peremptory summons, was fully aware that, being without either foot or artillery, he was powerless to enforce the acceptance of his demand for surrender. The governor, young Windebank, a son of Charles's former Secretary of State, shaken, it is said, by the terrors of his young wife, and of a party of ladies from Oxford whom he was entertaining, lost heart and surrendered the fortress entrusted to his care. On his arrival at Oxford he was hurried before a council of war and condemned to death. This time Charles, often so merciful, was obdurate, and on May 3 the young officer was shot in the Castle garden.[1]

April 24. Skirmish at Islip.

The surrender of Blechington House.

April 25. The governor tried,

May 3. and shot.

After this exploit Cromwell swept round Oxford, defeating Sir William Vaughan at Bampton, and attempting by sheer force of audacity to drive Faringdon Castle to surrender. The commander of the castle, unlike young Windebank, kept his head cool, and Cromwell not having the means at hand to suit the action to the word, was compelled to leave the achievement unaccomplished. Yet, in spite of this rebuff, his raid had been completely successful. By sweeping off all the draught horses in the country through which he passed, he had rendered it impossible for Maurice to remove the heavy guns from Oxford for some days to come. Charles's plan for an early opening of the campaign was entirely disarranged, and Cromwell, knowing that it was no longer necessary for him to expose himself to Rupert's attack by remaining between Oxford and Hereford, rode off towards Fairfax's army, pre-

April 27. Cromwell defeats Sir William Vaughan.

The King's plans disarranged.

---

[1] Cromwell to the Com. of B. K. April 25; Cromwell to Fairfax, April 24; *Carlyle*, Letter XXV. and App. No. 5; *Dugdale's Diary.*

pared to hand over the command of the cavalry to his successor as soon as his own term of office was at an end.[1]

It was not Charles's military projects alone which were baffled. The fine web of diplomacy in which he took delight *Failure of his diplomacy.* was giving way in all directions. The Prince of Orange, indeed, still professed his readiness to serve him, but Frederick Henry was but the first magistrate of a republic. The Dutch statesmen set themselves strongly against *The army of Lorrainers not to pass through the Netherlands.* a proposal which Charles's agent, Goffe, had been instructed to make, that the Duke of Lorraine's army should pass through Dutch territory, and be transported to England in Dutch shipping.[2] Goffe was accordingly bidden to ask Mazarin to allow the Duke to embark at Dieppe; but there was not much probability that Mazarin would agree to a scheme which would compromise him with the English Parliament.[3] Nor was much more to be expected from the Queen's machinations at Paris. Henrietta Maria was driven to acknowledge that her husband was in the right when he described O'Hartegan as a knave. The Royal-*Despondency of the Royalists in Paris.* ists of her court were far more despondent than she was herself. "I cannot see," wrote one of them to a friend in England, "that you can expect any considerable help from abroad." The French clergy, indeed, had promised large contributions; but it was more than doubtful whether they would fulfil their engagements. "The Irish," he continued, "promise great matters. They are false, and your condition there will be little better than in England."[4]

Irish, French, Dutch, or Lorrainers were all one to Charles if only they would help him to regain his crown. Born of a

---

[1] *Perfect Occurrences*, E. 260, 27; Cromwell to Burgess, April 29; *Carlyle*, Letters XXVI. and XXVII.; Digby to Rupert, April 29, *Add. MSS.* 18,982, fol. 46.

[2] See p. 172.

[3] Jermyn to Digby, $\frac{\text{March 29}}{\text{April 8}}$; Goffe to Jermyn, April $\frac{6}{16}, \frac{7}{17}, \frac{14}{24}$, *S.P. Dom.*

[4] The Queen to the King, $\frac{\text{March 23}}{\text{April 2}}$, *Letters of Henrietta Maria*, 299; Wood to Webb, $\frac{\text{March 30}}{\text{April 9}}$, *S.P. Dom.* dvi. 83.

Scottish father and a Danish mother, with a grandmother who was half French by birth and altogether French by breeding,

Charles's
want of
national
feeling.

with a French wife, with German nephews and a Dutch son-in-law, Charles had nothing in him in touch with that English national feeling which is too often the mother of much narrowness of view and of much cruelty and injustice to alien races, but which no ruler of England can afford to despise.

Of all the hopes which Charles set upon distant aid, his expectation of assistance from Montrose was the one upon

His hopes
from
Montrose.

March.
Charles
sends a
message to
Montrose.

which he counted the most. Scarcely had he received the despatch which announced the defeat of Argyle at Inverlochy before he sent off a letter to the victor. The bearer was a Scottish gentleman named Small, who made his way safely through England and the Lothians in the disguise of a beggar. The letter has not been preserved, but so far as its purport can be discovered, it seems to have held out hopes that Charles would make his way northward at the head of his army, and that he expected Montrose to join him in the Lowlands.[1] A body of 500 horse under Sir Philip Musgrave was to be despatched to strengthen Montrose in the arm in which he was most deficient.[2]

Whether Montrose were successful or not in breaking through into the Lowlands, he had already affected the course of the English war. Neither Tippermuir nor Aberdeen had so

[1] "By these letters"—*i.e.* by Montrose's reply which was intercepted —"the Committee came to know, what they never had thought on, viz. how (the King's business being so forlorn in England that he could not make head against his enemies there) his Majesty designed to come with his army to Scotland, and to join Montrose : that so this country being made the seat of war, his enemies might be forced to an accommodation, to free their land from a burden which it could not stand under." *Guthry's Memoirs*, 147.

[2] "Had I but for one month," Montrose wrote subsequently to Charles, "the use of those 500 horse, I could have seen you before the time that this could come to your hands with 20,000 of the best this kingdom can afford." Montrose to the King, April 20. *Merc. Aulicus.* E. 286, 17.

alarmed the Scottish Government as to induce them to withdraw troops from England. Inverlochy was a defeat of far
greater proportions. Leven was accordingly directed to despatch part of his force under Baillie and the double
renegade Hurry to deal with Montrose as only disciplined soldiers could deal with him. Leven's army
in England was thereby weakened and an opportunity was afforded to Charles of striking a blow in the North
of England at the diminished forces of the Scots before
Fairfax was ready to stir.

Baillie and Hurry despatched to oppose Montrose.

It was this hopeful plan which had been frustrated by
Cromwell. On April 24 Rupert adjured his uncle to join him
at once, in order that the combined armies might
march to deliver Chester and Pontefract, as well as
the other garrisons of the North. To defeat Leven's
army was an almost necessary preliminary to the
accomplishment of this task. Whether Rupert intended to
follow up this enterprise with a march into Scotland or with an
attack upon the isolated New Model army in England must
remain uncertain, though as far as can be judged from his subsequent conduct, the latter plan would have had his personal
preference.[1]

April 24. Rupert urges Charles to join him.

However this may have been, an immediate start from
Oxford was out of the question. Charles mournfully answered
that the draught horses on which he had relied to
drag his artillery had all been carried off, and that
more than four hundred were needed for his heavy
guns and waggons. Rupert must therefore hasten to Oxford
collecting the necessary horses on the way. As even Rupert's
cavalry would be insufficient to protect the King's march when
at last it was undertaken, Goring must be directed to abandon
the operations round Taunton, and to come to the support of
the royal army.[2]

April 29. The King cannot stir.

---

[1] Rupert's letter is only known through Digby's answer. Digby to
Rupert, April 29. *Add. MSS.* 18,982, fol. 46.

[2] "The late ill accidents here by Cromwell . . . have for the present
totally disabled the King to move towards your Highness, both by want
of a strength to convoy him and the train safe [to ?] you and by making

When the King's orders reached Goring they found him once more at his duty. The prospect of relieving the King in

April 30.
Goring sets
out for
Oxford. his difficulties may have tickled his vanity, and he probably counted on the favour likely to accrue to him in case of success to bring him within easy reach of the chief object of his ambition, the supreme command in the West. On the 30th he announced that in two days he would be between Faringdon and Oxford with 2,000 horse.[1] It is by no means unlikely that Goring's alacrity was quickened by his knowledge that steps were being taken to levy an army in the West under influences other than his own.

April 23.
The Prince
of Wales at
Bridgwater. On the 23rd the Prince of Wales arrived at Bridgwater, where he was met by the commissioners of the four western counties. On the next morning the

April 24.
An army to
be raised in
the West. commissioners declared their readiness to raise an army of 8,000 men in addition to the guard which was to accompany the Prince and to the forces in the garrison towns.[2] Even if this army never came into

it impossible to get draught horses in these parts . . . we wanting as yet, though all diligence hath been used, four hundred, though we should leave the four field pieces behind us. The first difficulty of convoying the King and train safe, I hope, may be removed by Goring's advance with his horse, who is sent for; but how to be supplied with teams unless you furnish them out of those parts, I cannot imagine. Upon the whole matter, Sir, I do not think it possible for the King to move towards you, unless you can advance such a body this way as may make us masters of the field, and sweep before you these necessary draught horses through the countries which you pass, or that you can find means for raising and convoying them safe to Oxford with a less force, whilst Goring, coming up to us, shall entertain this field power of the rebels, in either of which cases we shall be ready at a day's warning to move which way soever you shall judge advantageous; whereas otherwise the reputation of Cromwell's successes is already likely to draw such swarms out of London upon us, and the King will be in hazard of being suddenly besieged in this place." Digby to Rupert, April 29. *Add. MSS.* 18,982, fol. 46. The greater part of this quotation is in cipher. Compare Digby to Rupert, April 27; *Warburton*, iii. 77; and Nicholas to Rupert, April 29, *Add. MSS.* 18,982, fol. 48.

[1] Goring to Berkshire, April 30. *Clarendon MSS.* 1870.

[2] Minute of the commissioners' declaration, April 24. *Warburton,* iii 80.

existence, there were forces in Somerset over which Goring
found it difficult to exercise control. Sir Richard
Grenvile had at last arrived to besiege Taunton,
and though he was seriously wounded in an attack
on Wellington House and forced to leave the field,
the Prince's council disappointed Goring by conferring upon Sir John Berkeley the command over the besieging
force.[1]

Sir R.
Grenvile
wounded.

Sir J. Berke-
ley besieges
Taunton a
second time.

The opening of a second siege of Taunton was too serious
a matter to be passed over lightly at Westminster. Fairfax was
at once ordered to relieve the town with as many
regiments of the New Model as he was able to muster. On April 30 the ' rebels' new brutish general,'
as Charles contemptuously styled him,[2] set out from Windsor
at the head of 11,000 men. On the evening of
May 2 he met Cromwell at Newbury.[3] On the
same night a party of Cromwell's horse was surrounded in the dark by Goring's advancing troopers, and a
loss inflicted on them which was magnified at Oxford into a considerable disaster.[4] Whilst Goring
halted at Faringdon, Rupert and Maurice with 2,000
horse and foot made their appearance at Burford.
On the following morning the two princes rode into
Oxford to confer with the King.[5]

April 30.
Fairfax
sets out to
relieve it.

May 2.
Meeting of
Fairfax and
Cromwell.

May 3.
Goring at
Faringdon.

May 4.
Rupert at
Oxford.

The movements of Goring and Rupert had changed the
whole military situation. For some weeks Charles had been
strong in Somerset and on the Welsh border, and
weak at Oxford. He was now strong at Oxford and
weak in Somerset and on the Welsh border. A
general worthy of the name holding an independent command
over the Parliamentary army would not only have seen at a
glance that the alteration of the enemy's dispositions necessi-

Change in
the military
situation.

---

[1] *Clarendon*, ix. 15.

[2] The King to the Queen, May 4. *King's Cabinet Opened*, p. 3. E.
292, 27.

[3] Yonge's Diary, *Add. MSS.* 18,780, fol. 15.

[4] Sprigg's *Anglia Rediviva*, 18 ; *Clarendon*, ix. 28.

[5] *Dugdale's Diary*.

lated an alteration of his own, but would at once have acted

Fairfax
continues
his march,

May 7.
and arrives
at Blandford.
upon his knowledge. Yet Fairfax plodded on with
his whole force to the relief of Taunton as if it still
needed the presence of 11,000 men to set free
the beleaguered town. On May 7 he arrived at
Blandford.[1]

It was not, however, the fault of Fairfax that so great a folly
was committed. He had no real control over the movements

Fairfax has
no control
over the
movements
of his army.
of his army. The Committee of both Kingdoms,
indeed, had not repeated its blunder of the preceding year by placing the actual command in commission, but it had retained the management of the
campaign in its own hands. With Essex and Manchester as

He is sub-
jected to the
Committee
of Both
Kingdoms.
members of their body they were hardly likely to err
in the direction of rashness ; but even if their generalship had been all that was to be desired, it was
impossible for a body fixed at Westminster to keep
touch of the enemy or to provide for those sudden changes
which task the alertness even of a general in the field. Al-

May 3.
Orders to
Fairfax to
halt.
though it was known to the Committee on April 29
that Goring was setting out for Oxford,[2] they did not
take alarm till May 3, when they prepared orders
for Fairfax to halt. Even then the official delays in communi-
cating their decision to the Houses were such that it was not

May 5.
Positive
orders sent
to him.
till the 5th that positive directions were transmitted
to him to hasten back eastwards, sending forward a
mere detachment for the relief of Taunton.[3] In the
meanwhile the King was left at Oxford unembarrassed by the
presence of any enemy whom he dared not face.

From Blandford a body of five or six thousand men under
Colonels Weldon and Graves were despatched to Taunton.
There was no time to be lost. On the 8th the besiegers

---

[1] *Sprigg*, 332.

[2] The Com. of B. K. to Cromwell, April 29. *Com. Letter Book.* The
Committee must have had secret intelligence from Oxford to have known
it so early, or Goring must have been on the move before he wrote from
Wells on the 30th.

[3] Com. of B. K. to Fairfax, May 3, 5. *Com. Letter Book.*

delivered a general assault and scaled the wall. Blake had

May 7.
A relieving
force sent
to Taunton.

already prepared for the misfortune, and the assailants found themselves confronted by an inner line
of defence. Unable to pass over the obstacles in

May 8.
An assault
repulsed.

their way, they contrived to set fire to some houses;
but the wind blew the flames into their faces and
compelled them to withdraw. On the following

May 9.
Partial
success.

morning a fresh attempt was more successful, and a
third part of the town perished in the flames. Yet,
in desperate case as he was, the indomitable Blake continued
his resistance. Whether he knew or not that relief was at hand,
the besiegers knew it, and even exaggerated the numbers of the

May 11.
End of the
second siege
of Taunton.

approaching force. On the 11th, just as Blake had
exhausted his ammunition, the Royalists, for the
second time, broke up the siege and moved hastily
away.

Outside the walls the relieving force was saddened by the
spectacle of devastated fields and deserted villages. Inside
was the heroic garrison under its trusty leader.[1] Blake's
achievement had been no useless display of chivalry. To preserve Taunton was to paralyse the royal forces in the West,
and to paralyse those forces was to deprive Charles of that help
without which he could hardly hope to preserve himself from
desperate failure.

Charles was now able to march whither he would. On
May 7, three days before the fate of Taunton was decided, he

May 7.
The King
leaves
Oxford.

rode out of Oxford with Rupert and Goring. A
courtly astrologer predicted a splendid victory for
him, and announced the desolation which was about
to fall on the rebellious city of London.[2] Yet even after the
accession of the forces under Rupert and Goring, the King could
count in his army no more than 11,000 men, and it was only by
the ablest generalship that such an army could be made available against the far superior forces amidst which it was placed.

---

[1] Weldon to Fairfax, May 11, *Two Letters*, E. 284, 9; *A great
victory*, E. 284, 11; Culpepper to the King, May 11; Sir J. Digby to
Digby, May 18, *S.P. Dom.* dvii. 70.

[2] Wharton, *An Astrological judgment.* E. 286, 31.

How little authority Charles possessed to control the discordant purposes of his generals was seen at the first council of war, held at that same Stow-on-the-Wold where Essex and Waller had agreed to part nearly a year before.[1] He was now urged to postpone his northern march, and to throw himself with his whole force upon Fairfax, who was still believed to be marching upon

May 8.
The council of war at Stow-on-the-Wold.

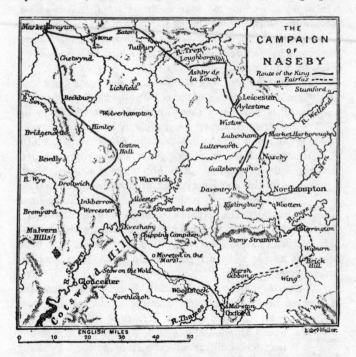

THE CAMPAIGN OF NASEBY

Route of the King ————
„ Fairfax -----

ENGLISH MILES

Taunton. The advice may have been good, and the hope that it might be with Fairfax as it had been with Essex weighed with the greater part of the commanders to press for its adoption. Rupert, who had conceived the other plan, and Sir Marmaduke Langdale with the officers of his northern horse,

[1] See vol. i. 353.

who longed to free their own homes from the enemy, were eager for a northward march. The old local spirit which had been exorcised from the Parliamentary ranks was still as strong in the Royalist armies as when in 1643 it held back Newcastle from advancing southwards after his victory at Adwalton Moor, or when it fixed the King before the walls of Gloucester. Charles, finding no concurrent eagerness in favour of either scheme, weakly consented to try both. He and Rupert would turn to the North, whilst Goring was despatched to prove his fortune in the West, with directions to return to the main army as soon as he had achieved the victory which he was ready to claim by anticipation.

Fatal as the division of forces was, it was made more fatal by the personal jealousies of the commanders. Goring, unless the evidence of those who knew him well is to be distrusted, was far more anxious to obtain an independent command than to advance the King's service, whilst Rupert supported him in gaining his object because he feared the presence with the King of so glib-tongued a rival. However this may have been, Goring returned to the West with authority virtually to exercise the supreme command. The Prince's councillors were now to be his humble servants, unable to withstand his pleasure. Charles's knowledge of mankind must indeed have been scanty if he thought that good would result from such an arrangement.[1]

Rupert and Goring.

Goring to have supreme command in the West.

As Charles marched northwards with diminished numbers, it became necessary for him to gather reinforcements from every available quarter. He drew off the garrison from Campden House as he passed, and the stately mansion, built at an expense of 30,000*l.* by King James's silk mercer, the first Lord Campden, was burnt by Rupert's orders, lest it should afford a shelter to the enemy.[2] On the eleventh the King arrived at Droitwich. Those who were about him felt, or affected to feel, the strongest confidence. "We have

May 9. The King's march.

Campden House burnt.

May 11. The King at Droitwich.

---

[1] *Walker,* 125; *Clarendon,* ix. 31. [2] *Walker,* 126.

great unanimity amongst ourselves," wrote Digby, "and the rebels great distraction." Charles was more despondent. On the day on which Digby wrote these words he despatched to Ormond an order once more commanding him in more positive terms than before,[1] to consent to the repeal of the penal laws rather than frustrate his hope of an Irish peace. "The Irish peace," he added, in a private letter accompanying this despatch, "is of so absolute necessity that no compliments nor particular respects whatsoever must hinder it."[2]

May 13. Digby's confidence.

The Irish penal laws to be repealed.

If there was not—in spite of Digby's assertion—great unanimity amongst the Royalists and great distraction amongst their adversaries, there was at least a failure in adequately conceiving the military position on the part of the Committee by which the movements of the Parliamentary armies were controlled. If there was one lesson more than another taught by the past history of the war, it was the uselessness of undertaking sieges whilst the enemy's main army was unbeaten in the field. It was the victory at Marston Moor which had delivered almost every northern fortress into the hands of the Parliamentary generals, whilst the want of any similarly decisive victory in the South had rendered the sieges of Donnington Castle, of Basing House, and of Banbury of no avail. Yet the Committee of Both Kingdoms now proposed to employ Fairfax and the New Model army in the siege of Oxford, leaving to Leven and the Scots the main burden of marching southwards to meet the King in the field. It is true that orders were given to reinforce Leven by a combination of detachments from various counties—a combination which it might be somewhat difficult to effect—and by a force of 2,500 soldiers of Fairfax's army to be sent under the command of Colonel Vermuyden It was expected that Vermuyden would meet the Scots on their advance southwards, somewhere in the neighbourhood of

Condition of the Parliamentary armies.

Necessity of defeating the King.

May 10. Oxford to be besieged by Fairfax.

May 13. The Scots to march southwards.

---

[1] He had already given permission on Feb. 27. Carte's *Ormond*, v. 13.

[2] The King to Ormond, May 13. *Clarendon MSS.* 1875, 1876.

Nottingham.   Cromwell and Browne were to join Fairfax in the projected investment of Oxford.[1]

A plan depending for its success upon the rapid concentration of forces of two different nationalities and of local levies
Weakness of the plan. which had never yet worked together, whilst the main English army was fixed immovably round Oxford, needs only to be stated to be condemned.   Yet, strange
It is supported by the Independent leaders. as it may appear, the plan was supported in the teeth of the opposition of the Scottish commissioners [2] by those very Independent leaders who had shown themselves most anxious to bring the war to a close by a victory in the field.

The fact was that the extraordinary directions given by the Committee were the result of the not uncommon tendency of
Lord Savile's intrigues. politicians to subordinate military action to political intrigue.   That old schemer Savile had been at his accustomed work.   It is unnecessary to deny that Savile had a genuine desire for peace, but it is no less certain that he sought it in the dark and underhand ways which befit a conspirator.   No sooner had he arrived at Westminster, a fugitive from Oxford, than he sought to come to an understanding with the Scots.   Finding himself coldly received by them, he turned to the Independents.   His chief correspon-
Newport's information. dent at Oxford was Lord Newport, and Newport was eager to throw himself upon the winning side.   He now informed Savile—if at least Savile is to be believed—that, could he be assured that the monarchy would be preserved, there would be no difficulty in bringing about such a military defection in the King's ranks as would bring the war to a
Improbability of its truth. speedy end.   Goring would transfer his services and those of the cavalry which he commanded to the Parliament, and Legge, who had recently been appointed Governor of Oxford, would open the gates of the city to a besieging army.

---

[1] Com. of B. K. to Fairfax, May 10; Com. of B. K. to Leven, May 13; Com. of B. K. to Cromwell and Browne, May 13; Com. of B. K. to Vermuyden, May 13.   *Com. Letter Book.*

[2] The remonstrance of the Scottish commissioners.   *L.J.* vii. 390.

What truth there may have been in Newport's tale about Goring it is impossible to say. That Legge ever thought of betraying the trust reposed in him is in the highest degree improbable. Yet in spite of the improbability of Savile's information, Say, who was an influential member of the Committee of Both Kingdoms, obtained the appointment of a sub-committee to receive propositions for the surrender of the King's fortresses. Though this sub-committee never met for business, Say, speaking in its name, encouraged Savile in his treachery. It was also, according to all appearance, on the ground of hopes founded on that treachery that Say carried with him his colleagues of the Committee itself in sending Fairfax to besiege Oxford.[1]

Whatever risk the Parliamentary authorities might be running from a defective plan of campaign, they had no longer any to fear from the indiscipline of their army. Deserters, mutineers, and plunderers were freely hanged. A blasphemer had his tongue bored through with a hot iron. The commander was as prompt to obey as he was to exact obedience. Uncongenial as his task was, Fairfax submissively carried out his instructions. On May 22 he joined Cromwell and Browne at Marston. The preparations for surrounding the Royalist stronghold were promptly made. During the following days shots were exchanged, but it was impossible to commence the attack in earnest till the necessary siege artillery arrived from London.[2]

Discipline in the army.

Fairfax obeys orders.

May 22. Oxford besieged.

On the 14th, long before Fairfax arrived before Oxford, the King moved forward from Droitwich. Good news greeted him on either hand. In Wales Sir Charles Gerard had routed Laugharne, had gained Haverfordwest, and was in good hope of making himself master of Milford Haven itself. At Scarborough, Cholmley had sallied out of the castle. In the fight which ensued Sir John Meldrum,

May 14. The King's movements.

---

[1] Compare Savile's examination, *Add. MSS.* 32,093, fol. 211, with the documents printed in *Baillie*, ii. 487.

[2] *Sprigg*, 17, 21; *A copy of a letter*, May 24, E. 285, 17. *The Weekly Account*, E. 285, 19; *A Diary*, E. 286, 10.

who, after the reduction of Liverpool, had been sent to com-

mand the besiegers, received a wound of which he
ultimately died.[1] Charles's own march impressed

with dismay the Parliamentarians in Cheshire. On
the 18th Brereton hurriedly raised the sieges of

Chester and Hawarden Castle. This important
news reached Charles on the 22nd just as he was
leaving Drayton.[2] The first part of his scheme was
thus successfully accomplished.

Whilst Charles was reaping the fruits of his own energetic
action, the plan of the Committee of Both Kingdoms was

ignominiously breaking down. No sign of treachery
had manifested itself at Oxford, whilst the Scots in
the North had shown no eagerness to measure
swords with Charles. For some days Lord Fairfax,

who was in command of the Parliamentary forces in
Yorkshire, had been appealing to Leven to hurry to

Manchester in support of Brereton.[3] On May 21 Leven re-

plied that he intended to take a circuitous route by
way of Westmoreland. By no other road could he
drag his cannon across the hills. The King, he
said, probably intended to invade Scotland, and
when once the Scottish army was in Westmoreland,

it might support Brereton and cover Scotland as well. Whatever ground was lost by his present course might be sub-

sequently recovered. By marching in any other
way, he added, in a letter written on the following
day, 'we should have left our country altogether
naked.'[4] Leven's anxiety, strange as it appeared to Fairfax,
was not merely assumed. Tidings had reached him from
Scotland which were of such a nature as to impose caution
upon the most adventurous commander.

[1] Whitacre's Diary, *Add. MSS.* 31,116, fol. 211; D'Ewes's Diary, *Harl. MSS.* 166, fol. 211.

[2] Resolutions of the council of war, May 17; Brereton to King, May 20, *Add. MSS.* 11,331, fol. 119b, 138; *Walker*, 127; Digby to Nicholas, May 25, *S.P. Dom.* Walker's statement that the King heard the news at Stone on the 23rd is plainly wrong.

[3] Lord Fairfax and the Committee at York to Leven, May 20. *S.P. Dom.* dvii. 72.   [4] Leven to Lord Fairfax, May 21. *Ibid.* dvii. 75.

CHAPTER XXX.

DUNDEE, AULDEARN, AND LEICESTER.

THOUGH the proud boast with which Montrose had closed his despatch from Inverlochy [1] was not yet fulfilled, he had not loitered over his task. Scarcely was the battle won, when he turned sharply back upon Seaforth and the northern clans who had blocked his way at the north-eastern end of the great lakes. Not a man of them ventured to await the coming of the warriors who had smitten down the Campbells in their pride.

1645. Feb. Montrose after Inverlochy. Seaforth's army dispersed.

When Montrose reached Elgin he was rejoiced at the arrival of Huntly's eldest son, Lord Gordon, and also of Lord Lewis Gordon, who had fought so ineffectively at Aberdeen.[2] If Huntly still kept aloof, his absence was more than compensated for by the presence of his heir. Lord Gordon had attempted to lead the Covenanters, and had found that they would have none of him.[3] He now threw himself heart and soul on the side of Montrose, and became one of his warmest personal admirers. His coming, however, was more than the gain of a gallant comrade. The gentry of the name and following of Gordon supplied Montrose with a small but efficient body of cavalry. To Montrose this was everything now. However eager he might be to press forward into the South, and to come to the help of Charles, he was incapacitated from playing a serious part in Lowland warfare with infantry alone, especially as a disciplined force, far different from the raw

Lord Gordon joins Montrose.

Baillie and Hurry on the way.

[1] See p. 155.   [2] See p. 147.   [3] See p. 145.

levies which he had crushed at Tippermuir and Aberdeen, was on the way against him under Baillie and Hurry.

The submission of Lord Gordon was an example not lost upon waverers. Seaforth and Sir James Grant followed Mont-
Submission of Seaforth and Grant. rose to Elgin as supplicants for pardon, and did not sue in vain. At least they saved their estates from *Plunder of the North.* plunder. Montrose, as he passed into the South, had no pay to give his followers, and let them loose upon the lands of the Covenanters of the North. From Inverness to Kintore their farms and houses were given over to the spoiler.[1]

Montrose's, like Argyle's before him, was a calculated cruelty. In the Lowlands, however, Argyle's wasting of High-
Montrose and Argyle. land glens and burning of the houses of Royalist noblemen aroused no resentment, whilst the suffer-
ings of the farmers and burghers of the northern counties excited fear and indignation in the same classes in the South. Of their anger the Kirk was the mouthpiece. On the *Montrose excommuni-cated and declared a traitor.* first news from Inverlochy it hurled its excommu-nication at Montrose's head. On February 11 the Scottish Parliament declared both him and his chief supporters to be guilty of treason. From that time Montrose was styled at Edinburgh 'that excommunicated traitor, James Graham.' In the eyes of the clergy and of the Parliament he was not merely the assailant of the ecclesiastical and political institutions of the realm. He was also the man who threatened, with the help of Celtic barbarism, to blot out the long results of patient toil.

It was, in all probability, at some point in his southward march that Montrose received the message in which Charles *Montrose receives Charles's message.* promised him the aid of 500 horse under Musgrave, and conjured him to hasten his march to the *He is op-posed by Baillie and Hurry.* Lothians.[2] Day after day, however, passed away without further intelligence of Musgrave's coming, and when Montrose reached Forfarshire he found his way to the South blocked by Baillie and Hurry. Many

---

[1] *Wishart*, ch. ix. ; *Spalding*, ii. 446 ; *Patrick Gordon*, 105.
[2] See p. 203.

days were spent in manœuvring. Hurry's cavalry was on one occasion driven in headlong flight, but it was a more difficult matter to overpower Baillie, a methodical soldier, who avoided an engagement, and sought to wear his opponent out

Campaign of
DUNDEE & AULDEARN

March of Montrose before the taking of Dundee ——
March of Montrose after the taking of Dundee ------

ENGLISH MILES

0   10   20   30   40   50

Edwᵈ Weller

by forcing him to keep on the defensive. One day when the two armies were posted near Cupar Angus on opposite banks of the Isla, Montrose, in the chivalric fashion of the antique world, sent Baillie a challenge. He would allow his antagonist to cross the river unassailed if he wished

A challenge to Baillie

to take the offensive, or he would himself cross the stream on the same conditions. Baillie replied that he would fight when he thought fit, not when it pleased the enemy.[1]

In the end Baillie marched away in full retreat for Fife. Instead of following him across the Isla, Montrose turned aside Montrose at to Dunkeld. By crossing the Tay there he would Dunkeld. have a straight course southwards. If he were once over this obstacle, the Forth would hardly keep him back. Already in imagination he saw thousands of Lowlanders weary of the yoke of the Kirk flocking to his standard as it streamed across the Border.[2]

Montrose was too sanguine. His antagonist had almost gained his object without firing a gun. The Highlanders understood a warfare which consisted in a fierce charge and a hasty pursuit followed by a speedy return with their plunder to their native glens. They did not understand a war of manœuvre, of the weary occupation of posts, and of patient endurance of Montrose's suffering. At Dunkeld Montrose's host melted away army melts almost as rapidly as a Highland host was wont to do away at Dunkeld. after the winning of a signal victory. Even the Gordons were discontented, and not a few of them deserted a leader who had led them so far from home and who had not as yet repeated the marvels of Inverlochy.[3]

Before long Montrose had with him no more than 200 horse and 600 foot upon whom he could count. The march into the Lowlands must be for the present abandoned. His little force must not be left longer without that booty which was its

[1] *Wishart*, ch. ix.

[2] "Taum versus tendit : Fortham etiam, si qua fieri posset, transgressurus, unde auxilia Regi non defutura sperabat." *Wishart*, ch. ix.

[3] Patrick Gordon (115) denies that Lord Lewis caused the movement by his own desertion, as is asserted by Wishart, but he acknowledges that he wanted to leave the army temporarily on private business, though he stayed for a time and was present at the retreat from Dundee. W. Gordon, in his *History of the illustrious Family of Gordon*, ii. 453, asserts, on the authority of one who was present, that Lord Lewis fought well in the retreat from Dundee. Wishart cannot be considered accurate, and I suspect that Lord Lewis left after Montrose had taken and abandoned Dundee.

best reward. News—false, as it afterwards appeared—that the enemy had crossed to the western side of the Tay, led him to suppose that all to the east of the river was at his mercy.

April 3.
He leaves
Dunkeld.

Taking with him a picked force of 600 musketeers and 150 horse, he started from Dunkeld before dawn on the morning of April 3. Crossing the Isla, he marched through Cupar Angus on Dundee. On the 4th he was outside the walls. The citizens, being surprised,

April 4.
Dundee
taken.

opposed but a feeble resistance. Houses were fired, the market-place was occupied, and the sack begun. In the midst of the tumult a messenger brought tidings that Baillie and Hurry with their whole army were hastening to the relief of the town. To fight them was madness, but those advisers who urged Montrose to consult his own safety by flight little knew the man to whom they addressed such unworthy counsels. Cutting off the spoilers from the prey on which they had flung themselves—a feat beyond the power of any other

A hasty
retreat.

commander in Europe—he marched out of the eastern gate almost as Baillie was entering the western. Keeping his 150 cavalry as a rearguard, he placed 200 of the best appointed musketeers in the last ranks of the foot, with orders to face about in support of the horse in case of an attack.[1]

Night was drawing on, but before its shadows fell Baillie, who had continued his pursuit through the town, ventured a charge. His charge was repelled, and he deemed it the better part to outmanœuvre an enemy so hard to defeat. Whilst Montrose's 750 were hurrying onwards in the dark in the

Baillie's
manœuvre.

direction of Arbroath, Baillie was pushing forward to the left of their line of march, anxious to cut them off from the hills to the north-east, and to pin them against the sea when they reached Arbroath. With many

---

[1] Napier turns Montrose's wonderful performance into a miracle by saying that these men in front were drunk. All that Wishart says is that the soldiers after the taking of Dundee were 'vino paululum incalescentes.' Afterwards he speaks of them as 'vino prædâque graves.' At all events drunken men cannot march as these did.

antagonists Baillie's plan would have been successful, but it
did not succeed with Montrose. Divining his ad-

Montrose's
counter-
manœuvre.

versary's strategy, he halted his men before Arbroath
was reached, and bade them retrace their steps.
After a while he wheeled to the right, slipping past Baillie,
who was now well in advance still heading towards

April 5.

the east. Montrose reached Careston Castle on the
South Esk as the sun was rising.

At last Baillie discovered his error, and started in pursuit
with his cavalry on the right track. When he caught sight of

Montrose
escapes to
the hills.

the enemy, only three miles separated Montrose
from the shelter of the hills, but it seemed for a
moment as if those three miles would be enough to
destroy him. His men had been marching, fighting, and
plundering for three whole days and the two intervening
nights. They had fallen on the ground in a sleep so dead,
that when Baillie's horse approached, the officers could not
rouse more than a very few of them. Yet those few were
sufficient to show a front to the enemy. The hostile cavalry
drew off, and as soon as the sleepers could be awakened, they
were speedily led to a place of safety. Horsemen were not
likely to follow them amongst the hills.

Never had Montrose's skill as a commander been more
clearly manifested. In the camps of Germany and France,

His skilful
generalship.

when his name was mentioned, soldiers of no mean
authority were heard to extol his retreat from
Dundee above all his victories.[1]

Though Montrose's last achievements might bring glory to
himself, they augured ill for the help which he had counted on
being able to afford to Charles. His Highlanders, perhaps
even the Gordons, could not be trusted for the purposes of
warfare in the South, and now, if not earlier, Lord Lewis
Gordon rode home with a considerable following. With his
reduced numbers, Montrose, in spite of his masterly generalship,
could not hope, till fresh reinforcements had joined him, to
effect anything considerable in Scotland.[2]

[1] *Wishart*, ch. ix.
[2] Montrose to —— ? April 20. *Merc. Aulicus.* E. 286, 16.

At Oxford little was for some time known of these achievements of Montrose. It was difficult to open up communications between the two armies. Though Small, who had borne the tidings of the victory of Inverlochy, had reached Charles in safety, he had been captured by the Covenanters on his return. The letters seized upon his person revealed the King's plan of campaign to his enemies. On May 1 the unfortunate messenger was hanged at Edinburgh as a traitor and a spy.[1]

Charles's plan of campaign revealed.

For some days Montrose had little that was hopeful to impart. The old weary work of collecting forces had to be begun afresh, and Lord Gordon was despatched home to undo the mischief caused by his brother's desertion. Montrose himself, wandering about Perthshire, wrote again to the King, and, by whatever channel it passed, this letter reached Oxford uninjured. In it he expressed his regret that he had heard nothing of the promised succour of cavalry, and contented himself with holding out hopes of being able to neutralise such of the enemy's forces as were in Scotland. He no longer spoke of marching to join the King in England.[2]

April 10? A letter from Montrose.

At Balquhidder Montrose's spirits were cheered by the arrival of Aboyne, who had cut his way out of Carlisle through the besiegers' lines. Scarcely less acceptable was the news which reached him on the shores of Loch Katrine a day or two later, that the enemy had divided his forces. Whilst Baillie was watching the Highlands from Perth, Hurry had gone north to collect the Covenanting forces for an attack upon the Gordons. For Baillie Montrose with his scanty following was no match, though if he could effect a junction with Lord Gordon he would be again in a condition to fight a battle. Swiftly, as his manner was, he

April 20. He is joined by Aboyne

---

[1] *Guthry's Memoirs,* 147.

[2] The letter was published in *Merc. Aulicus.* E. 286, 17. It arrived in Oxford on May 10, and is dated April 20. On this day, however, according to Wishart, Montrose was at Balquhidder receiving Aboyne. Wishart may be wrong, but it is, on the whole, more probable that the date on the newspaper is a misprint, perhaps for the 10th.

sped northwards, slipping past Baillie on the way. Macdonald rejoined him on the march, and on the banks of the upper Dee he found Lord Gordon at the head of a body of horse, raised amongst the gentry of the Gordon name. He was now between the two hostile armies, and could choose his antagonist. To save the Gordon lands from plunder, he singled out Hurry as his victim.

Montrose marches northwards,

and resolves to attack Hurry.

Hurry, though he had retired to Inverness to gather his forces round him, imagined himself to stand in no need of Baillie's help. Seaforth had once more changed sides, and was ready to bring up his Mackenzies, whilst Sutherland had marched with his followers from the extreme North. The Frazers, too, and others of the Covenanting gentlemen of Moray, were on Hurry's side, in addition to Hurry's own trained soldiers from the army in England. The numbers in both armies are variously given, but there can be no doubt that Hurry far outnumbered Montrose. Few as Montrose's horse were, it was the first time that he had horsemen enough to use as a cavalry force should be used in battle.

Hurry's forces.

As soon as Hurry heard that Montrose was descending the valley of the Spey, he formed a plan which was at least worthy of a commander trained in a better school of warfare than that of the Elchos and the Balfours. With the object of luring Montrose into a hostile country, the Covenanting general advanced to meet him near Elgin, and upon his approach conducted his retreat so skilfully that Montrose, though following hard, was never able to do him any serious damage. On the evening of May 8 Montrose reached the village of Auldearn, expecting to follow Hurry on the following morning through Nairn to Inverness. In the meanwhile he sent out sentinels to guard against surprise. He was, as Hurry intended him to be, in the midst of a hostile population, from which not a word of intelligence was to be had.

Hurry's plan.

Before dawn on the morning of the 9th, Hurry had fronted round, hoping by a night march to surprise the Royalists. He almost effected his object. The night was wet and gusty, and Montrose's sentinels did not care to go far afield. Fortu-

May 9.
An
attempted
surprise.

nately for Montrose, the rain which drove them in wetted the powder in the muskets of Hurry's soldiers, some of whom—they can hardly have been found in his own disciplined regiments—fired a volley to clear the

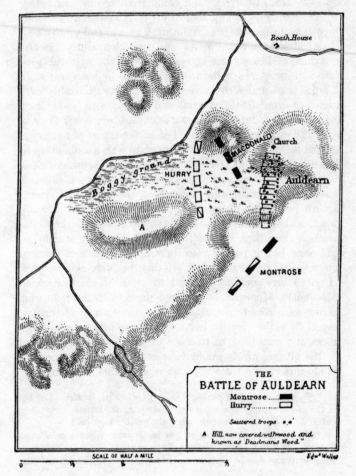

Boath House

MACDONALD

Church

HURRY

Auldearn

Boggy ground

A

MONTROSE

THE
BATTLE OF AULDEARN

Montrose _____
Hurry _____ ▭

Scattered troops •,•'

A *Hill now covered with wood and known as Deadman's Wood.*"

SCALE OF HALF A MILE

Ed.ª Weller

barrels. They were still four or five miles from the enemy,
and they fancied that the noise of the discharge would not be
heard.

As it happened, some of Macdonald's sentinels caught the
sound. Montrose had scarcely time before the enemy arrived

Montrose's
arrange-
ments.

to draw up his little force in battle array. No long
study of the ground could have served him better
than his swift glance in the early morning. The line
of cottages in the village of Auldearn lay north and south along
a ridge at right angles to the road by which Hurry was approaching.[1] Below these cottages, towards the west, the gardens and inclosures of the villagers fenced by low stone walls
afforded a natural fortress, beyond which was a tolerably level
stretch of ground, at first rough and covered with bushes, and
then sinking gradually into a marsh caused by a brook away at
some distance from the slope. The northern part of the rough
ground behind the bog he entrusted to the guardianship of
Macdonald and the Irish, giving them the royal standard, in
order that the enemy might imagine that the King's Lieutenant
was there in person, and might direct the bulk of his forces
against so defensible a position. The remainder of his infantry
and the whole of his cavalry he kept aloof out of sight to the
south of the village behind the crest of the ridge. Centre he
had none, but he posted a few men in front of the cottages in
order to lead the enemy to believe that they were held in force.
If only Hurry could be induced to make his chief attack on
Macdonald, Montrose, by sweeping down upon the right wing
of the assailants, might easily decide the fortune of the day,
especially as the Royalist horse would have firm ground before
them, and would not be troubled with the enclosures in front
of the village, which would have made a charge impossible
if Montrose's own force had kept nearer to his subordinate.[2]

---

[1] Shaw, *Hist. of the Province of Moray* (ed. 1882), ii. 260. The line
of the present village lies more east and west, old houses having been
pulled down, and new ones built along the modern high road.

[2] We have the two accounts of this battle from Wishart and Patrick
Gordon. Patrick Gordon's account of the ground in front of Macdonald
is elaborate and may be taken as accurate. Wishart says of Auldearn that

Admirable as were Montrose's arrangements, they were nearly foiled through the smallness of Macdonald's force. The Battle Macdonald, himself outnumbered by the enemy, of Auldearn. was, in spite of his vigorous charges, driven back amongst the walled gardens in his rear. In vain he dashed out

'oppidulum eminentiori loco situm convallem vicinam operiebat. Et colliculi a tergo supereminentes oculorum aspectum adimebant nisi quam propissimè astantium. In istam convallem copias suas educit, hostibus minime spectandas.' This is not very intelligible, and there is no valley answering to the description, but it may perhaps be taken as a way of putting the fact that, by placing his men behind the crest, Montrose would have them out of sight of an enemy approaching from Nairn. It is evident, however, that Wishart, who was not present, had no knowledge of the formation of the ground.

When we reach the descriptions of the battle itself, both writers are agreed about Macdonald's proceedings, but Gordon is vague where Wishart gives details. Gordon has the Royalists drawn up in the ordinary fashion with horse on both sides, the right wing under Lord Gordon and the left under Aboyne. The narrative which follows is too completely wanting in detail, as far as the fighting is concerned, to inspire confidence, though one or two anecdotes were evidently derived from some who were present. Wishart's narrative is much more in agreement with the probabilities of the case, and is in much greater detail. He does not mention Aboyne at all, and only speaks of the Gordon horse as a body on Montrose's left. It seems exceedingly improbable that Montrose should have put any horse on the right side. The hill is very steep there—too steep, I should imagine, for a charge down—and the rocky and boggy ground below was unfitted for cavalry. Again, the skeletons which are now under the modern plantation called Deadman's Wood were described to me as all brought together from the ground in front of Montrose's own position. Those killed in Macdonald's fight would lie in or about the enclosures, and would naturally be taken up after the fight by the villagers and buried probably in the churchyard, whilst, if there had been any killed in that part of the field after a successful cavalry charge, they would have been found much farther off from the village, and have been buried where they fell, like their comrades on Hurry's right. Though I have no other evidence than Wishart's bungling statement for placing the left wing of the Royalists behind the crest, my view is supported by the fact that Montrose was able to conceal Macdonald's defeat from Lord Gordon, as the place where Macdonald was fighting is visible from the western slope, and it may, therefore, be fairly argued that Montrose's men could not have been deceived if they had been on it. The thing too was so easy to do, and so advantageous, that Montrose can hardly have failed to do it.

again, only to be again pressed back. Performing prodigies of valour, the last man to retreat, he sliced off the heads of the pikes which were thrust into his target, keeping off the foemen with the swing of his broadsword. Yet, in spite of all his valour, he and his would have been doomed to slaughter if help had not been at hand. No sooner had Montrose heard of the recoil of his right wing than he turned to Lord Gordon, " Why," he cried, " are we lingering here? Macdonald is driving all before him. Is he to have all the glory of the day?"[1] The command was given, and the Gordon horse were launched over the crest and down the slope against the enemy. The Gordons were in no placable mood. James Gordon of Rynie had been left wounded in a cottage, and had been butchered by a party of Hurry's men. Not long before Donald Farquharson, one of Montrose's colonels, had been slaughtered at Aberdeen. With the words " Remember Donald Farquharson and James of Rynie," the Gordons dashed down the hill. They had skill as well as vengeance to direct them. For the first time in Scottish warfare the old practice of preluding a cavalry charge by the firing of pistols was abandoned, and Rupert's plan of rushing at the enemy with sword and horse was adopted.[2] Anything more different from the waiting tactics by which he had kept in hand the poor handful of mingled horse and foot at Aberdeen it is impossible to conceive. Montrose had at last got a sufficient force of cavalry, and he knew how to use it. The Gordon horse, finding Hurry's cavalry with their minds preoccupied with the fighting on their left, broke them and drove them off the field. Whilst some were following the pursuit, Aboyne remained behind to charge the now exposed flank,[3] Hurry's right wing of infantry,

---

[1] This is abbreviated from Wishart.

[2] " My Lord Gordon by this time charges the left wing, and that with a new form of fight, for he discharges all shooting of pistols and carbines only with their swords to charge quite through their enemies." Did Gordon think of this, or did Montrose, who had talked to Rupert's beaten men after Marston Moor, suggest it to him?

[3] This is not distinctly stated, but may be gathered from Patrick Gordon's ascription of all the success on this side to Aboyne.

already thrown into disorder by the flight of his horse.[1] Montrose himself led a body of foot against it, and after a short struggle drove it off the ground. The flight of the right wing of the Covenanting army determined the fate of the battle. Montrose turned fiercely on the centre and left wing of the enemy, which was entangled in the rough ground in front of Macdonald's position. Macdonald, feeling the weakening of the attack, again pressed forward. Hurry, at the head of the horse which remained to him, took to flight, whilst the greater part of his veteran infantry stood their ground and were slaughtered on the field [2]

Montrose had shown himself master of cavalry tactics, as he had shown himself elsewhere to be a master of the tactics of Highland war. In whatever form the enemy attacked him, whatever might be the varying components of his own army, he was always ready to take advantage of the weakness of the one and of the strength of the other. Yet, splendid as the victory was, it was not decisive. On May 3, when Montrose was on the Spey, Baillie had burst into Athol, and had since been ravaging it by fire and sword.[3] If the men of Athol were to be available for Lowland warfare, Montrose must show that he had the power to give them security at home.

Montrose's versatility.

May 3. Baillie ravages Athol.

Though the day when Montrose could descend into the Lowlands had not yet arrived, it is no wonder that the news from Auldearn startled Leven in Yorkshire, and drove him to that retreat into Westmoreland which had alarmed the English leaders.[4] To

Effect of Auldearn upon Leven's movements.

---

[1] The officer who commanded the horse which did the mischief was afterwards shot as a traitor at Inverness. (*Spalding*, ii. 473.) There is a long story printed in Mackenzie's *Hist. of the Mackenzies* (p. 187), taken from a document which the author calls the 'Ardintoul MS.,' according to which Hurry was himself a traitor, and shot the officer to prevent his telling tales. The story has no appearance of credibility in it. Hurry, it is said, wishing to spare Seaforth, placed him opposite to the weak centre o Montrose's position ; as if Hurry could have known at the time that Montrose had not men behind the houses.

[2] *Wishart*, ch. x. ; *Patrick Gordon*, 123.

[3] *Spalding*, ii. 471.

[4] See p. 214.

Leven the plain path of duty was to throw himself in the way
of any possible junction between Charles and his lieutenant.
Other reasons doubtless there were to make him sore at the
proceedings of the Government at Westminster. Whilst that
Unfair Government had thrown upon him the burden of
treatment the conflict with the King's army, it had kept its
of Leven's
army. own forces out of harm's way, 'tied by the leg' round
Oxford.[1]   Though the hard work thus devolved upon the
Scots, nothing had been done to pay or to supply them. An
assessment, indeed, had been made upon certain English
counties for the support of their army, but not a penny had
been raised, whilst Fairfax's troops received their pay fort-
nightly with the utmost regularity. Left to their own devices,
the Scottish soldiers had pressed hardly upon the districts in
which they were quartered, to the detriment of their own discipline as well as to the exasperation of the sufferers.

Accordingly, two days after the news of Leven's retreat
reached Westminster, the Scottish commissioners presented a
May 24. serious remonstrance to the English Parliament.
Remon- Not only did they complain bitterly of Leven's
strance of
the Scot- treatment, but they raised their voices clearly against
tish com-
missioners. the plan of campaign adopted by the Committee of
Both Kingdoms. The one thing needful, they rightly said,
was that Fairfax should be set free from control. Then the
two armies might crush the King between them, and the war
would be brought to an end.[2]

The efforts of the allied armies, if they could be brought
to co-operate with one another, would be the more formidable
as the King's chance of receiving help from Goring was grow-
May 17. ing less every day. On May 17 that boastful com-
Goring on mander mustered 11,000 men on Sedgemoor. With
Sedgemoor. these he hoped to prevent the troops which, under
Graves and Weldon, had relieved Taunton from leaving the
town, in the hope that, if the numbers within its walls were not
suffered to be diminished, a surrender would be inevitable in

[1] *The Moderate Intelligencer.* E. 286, 9.
[2] Remonstrance of the Scottish commissioners, May 24. *L.J.* vii.
390.

the case of a fresh blockade. On the other hand, he felt no doubt that, if the Parliamentary commanders succeeded in making their escape, he would be able, with his superior numbers, to crush them in the open country.[1] As soon as he was master of the field, he would—so at least he said—hasten to the succour of the King. "I am very fearful," he wrote on

May 19. *His intentions.* the 19th to Rupert, "lest Fairfax and Cromwell may disturb your Highness before we can despatch these

May 20. *He fails to defeat the enemy.* people to attend them."[2] On the very next day he had to acknowledge that he had failed completely either to keep Graves and Weldon at Taunton or to destroy them in the open country. "I shall beseech you," he characteristically wrote to Culpepper, "to inform the Prince that I am kept from destroying the greatest part of the rebels' army by the most fantastical accident hath happened since the war began." It is hardly necessary to repeat Goring's story, as it was flatly contradicted by a narrative which reached Culpepper from another source, and as in such a case it is safe to conclude that truth did not lie on the side of Goring.[3]

Great as had been the error of the Committee of Both Kingdoms in persisting in the siege of Oxford, they were fully alive to the necessity of keeping Goring employed in the West.

May 25. *Massey to command in the West.* On the 25th they appointed Massey to lead a force against him which would place Taunton beyond the reach of further accidents. Before he left the district in which he had accomplished so much, Massey rendered one last service to the Parliamentary cause in Gloucestershire

May 26. *Evesham stormed.* and its neighbourhood. On the 26th he stormed Evesham, thus interposing a barrier between Oxford and Worcester, and dislocating the King's line of defence in a region in which the Royalists had hitherto been supreme.[4]

[1] Sir John Digby to Digby, May 18. *S. P. Dom.* dvii. 70.

[2] *i.e.* 'Send on my soldiers to follow them up.' Goring to Rupert, May 19. *Add. MSS.* 18,982, fol. 61.

[3] Goring to Culpepper, May 20; Culpepper to Digby, May 22. *S. P. Dom.* dvii. 79.

[4] *L.J.* vii. 393; D'Ewes's Diary, *Harl. MSS.* 166, fol. 213b.

Weakened as he was in territory, and in the strength which territory brings, Charles was nevertheless in a position to march

May 22.
The King
at Drayton. whither he would in the Midlands. On the 22nd he heard, just after leaving Drayton, that Brereton had broken up from before Chester, and he had now to decide upon his next step. Though he could not as yet know that Leven had thrown himself in the way of a march

He resolves
to march
to the east. through Lancashire in search of Montrose, he resolved to avoid the rough and hilly roads by the western coast, and to aim at reaching Scotland by the easy route through the Vale of York.[1] He was the more readily induced to take this course as he did not feel confident in the power of Oxford to hold out, and the few marches to the east, which would place him on the track to the north which he had now selected would also enable him to defer turning his back on Oxford for some days longer. If, on the other hand, it appeared desirable to pursue his way towards Scotland, he would have no difficulty in obtaining considerable reinforcements as he passed through Yorkshire, where the population was deeply exasperated against Leven and his Scottish soldiers.

Charles was now at the head of a force of at least 11,000 men, and he calculated that before long he would be followed

He expects
to be joined
by Goring. by an army of overwhelming strength. He had summoned Goring from the West, and Gerard from South Wales. The appointed rendezvous was in Leicestershire. Should he resolve in the end to turn northwards, he might find time before he recommenced his march to do enormous damage in that region.[2]

When the news that the King was marching through

Excitement
at West-
minster. Staffordshire reached Westminster, the interpretation put upon his movement was that he intended to throw himself upon the Eastern Association. On the 26th Cromwell, although his term of command had now

---

[1] See the map at p. 209.

[2] *Walker*, 127; The King to the Queen, May 23, *Hist. MS. Com. Reports*, i. 9; Digby to Nicholas, May 26, *S.P. Dom.* dvii. 79; Symonds Diary, 166, 182.

expired, was sent to fortify the approaches to the Isle of Ely, and on the 31st, as no money was available for Leven's army,

May 26.
Cromwell
sent to Ely.

May 31.
Supplies for
Leven.

orders were despatched to the northern counties to supply his soldiers with provisions as soon as they had completed their circuitous march through Westmoreland, and had started in pursuit of the King. Yet of what avail was such tardy strategy if Charles was allowed to roam freely through England, choosing when and where his blows should fall?

Three or four days after Charles left Drayton he learned that he was no longer master of his own movements. A

May 22.
Oxford in
straits.

serious despatch from Nicholas warned him that Oxford was so short of provisions that it could not hold out long.[1] Whatever he had gained by the strategical superiority of his own commanders or by the blunders of his opponents was rendered useless by the want of material supplies, which made it impossible for him to rely on the continued resistance of Oxford during a few weeks' campaign.

With his usual versatility Digby threw himself into the situation thus created. He could not believe that in face of

May 26.
Digby's
appeal for
time.

the actual situation the Parliamentary army could remain fixed round Oxford. "If Cromwell and Fairfax advance," he wrote to Nicholas from Tutbury on the 22nd, "we shall endeavour to fight with them. I believe it will be about Leicester. I hope by this time Goring is about Oxford with his horse. If we can be so happy as that he comes in time, we shall infallibly crush them between us. For God's sake quicken his march all that's possible." Late at night a second letter, written by the orders of the King and Rupert, assured Nicholas that in case of necessity Oxford should be relieved, but at the same time urged him not to represent the wants of the garrison as more pressing than they were. If only it could hold out for a month or six weeks, or if Goring could relieve it without help from the King, all would yet be well. "I say," continued Digby, "if either of these can be, we never had more cause to thank God since

[1] Nicholas to the King, May 22. *Hist. MSS. Com. Reports*, i. 8.

this war began, than for putting it into their hearts to engage in that stop, there being nothing more probable than that within the time mentioned, the King having such an army as he hath, we shall be able to put His Majesty's affairs into such a condition as that the relieving of you then shall do both all and the whole work at once. For God's sake lay this to heart and give us all the time you can." [1]   In three days, he ended by saying, the army would be close to Leicester.

On the day on which this letter was written, fresh orders were despatched to Goring. He was to march, not, as had Fresh orders been previously arranged, to Harborough, but to to Goring. Newbury, from which point he was either to relieve Oxford, or, if that proved impracticable, so to embarrass the besiegers as to impede their operations. The King, Goring was informed, expected to be joined by Gerard in the neighbourhood of Leicester. After that his course would depend Digby's on information from Oxford. "If the Governor of hopes. Oxford," wrote Digby, "assure us that he is provided for six weeks or two months, we shall then, I make no question, relieve our northern garrisons, beat the Scots, or make them retreat, and march southwards with a gallant army indeed. Pontefract once succoured, we are assured of great things from Yorkshire." If, on the other hand, it appeared that Oxford was unable to hold out, the King would march southwards at once, join Goring between London and Oxford, and thus not only save the besieged city, but cut off the besiegers from their own basis of operations. [2]

If some days must pass before an answer could be received, they could be utilised by a sudden blow at Leicester. Such an Leicester to undertaking was fully after Rupert's heart. Imbe attacked. portant as the place was, its fortifications were incomplete and its garrison small. Between the soldiers and

---

[1] Digby to Nicholas, May 26. *S.P. Dom.* dvii. 92. The greater part of this letter is in cipher, but it is easy to read it with the help of the deciphered letters in *Add. MSS.* 18,982.

[2] Digby to Goring, May 26. *Clar. MSS.* 1889. The paper is torn at the word 'Pontefract,' only the initial remaining, but I have filled the blank without hesitation.

the committee which represented the civilian population there
was no good understanding.   On the 28th the first

May 28.
Approach of
the King's
army.
parties of the King's armies approached the place
and for three days citizens and soldiers were kept in

May 30.
Preparations
for a storm.
constant alarm.   On the evening of the 30th Rupert's
batteries played upon the walls and a breach was

effected.   Shortly before midnight the storming parties rushed
forward to the assault.   Before two in the morning

May 31.
Leicester
taken.
of the 31st all resistance was at an end.   About a
hundred of the defenders were slain either in fair

fight or in the heat of victory, and some women and children
were found amongst the dead.   There was, however, no general
massacre.   As a matter of course, the town was given over to
plunder.   The shops were stripped of their wares, and the
hovels of the poorest fared no better than the dwellings of the
richer townsmen.   In the course of the day a hundred and
forty carts laden with the spoil of Leicester rolled off to
Newark.[1]

[1] *Merc. Aulicus*, E. 288, 48 ; *A perfect relation of the taking of
Leicester*, E. 288, 4 ; *A narrative of the siege*, E. 288, 6 ; *An examination of a printed pamphlet*, E. 261, 18.   It is a Parliamentary newspaper
(*The Moderate Intelligencer*, E. 261, 18) from which we learn that 'some
women also were seen dead, which was casual rather than on purpose.'
For a refutation of the supposition that Bunyan was in the Royal army,
see Brown's *Life of Bunyan*, 50.

CHAPTER XXXI.

NASEBY.

NEVER to all outward appearance had Charles's prospects been brighter than when he was nearing his sudden and irreparable

May 31.
Charles's apparent prosperity.
overthrow. A concurrence of circumstances—the holding back of Leven's army by Montrose's victory at Auldearn, and the ill-judged retention of Fairfax and the New Model at the siege of Oxford—had given him for the moment a free hand, and the storm and sack of Leicester

Real weakness of his situation.
had been the result. Yet the very fact that Charles was at Leicester at all was fatal to his prospects. His march thither had been a compromise between Rupert's plan of rallying the ·Yorkshiremen for an attack on Leven and Digby's plan of rallying Goring and Gerard for an attack on Fairfax. The capture of Leicester was followed by a fierce conflict between the advocates of the rival schemes. It may reasonably be doubted whether either of the schemes was really feasible. Each of them left out of account one or other of the cardinal facts of the situation. Rupert's plan must have been ruined, if Oxford could not hold out for six weeks, whilst Digby's plan would just as certainly be ruined, if Gerard could not and Goring would not come to Charles's aid. The rashness with which the Committee of Both Kingdoms had pinned their best army round Oxford on the faith of such old intriguers as Savile and Newport, had been surpassed by the still greater rashness with which Charles and Rupert had undertaken a distant enterprise without previously ascertaining whether the city which was their base of operations was sufficiently provisioned to stand a siege.[1]

[1] The words of Nicholas, in the letter cited at p. 231, seem to establish the point that Oxford was poorly supplied, though it is true that

As usual the vacillation of the commander produced divisions in the army.   The Yorkshire horse under Langdale were

*The York-
shire horse
dissatisfied.*

touched by the same spirit of local patriotism which had proved fatal to Newcastle's success in 1643. They petitioned the King, probably whilst he was still at Leicester, for leave to betake themselves to the North, 'so far forth as' his 'occasions in these parts will give leave.'[1]

*June 4.
They
mutiny,*

On June 4 they received orders in common with the rest of the army to march in the direction of Oxford. They positively refused to stir, though Charles personally gave them his word that as soon as Oxford was relieved

*June 5.
but return to
their duty.*

he would lead them into their own country.   It is true that on the following day they consented to return to their duty, but the temper which they had manifested might have dangerous consequences yet.[2]

*June 7.
Charles at
Daventry.*

*Oxford
relieved.*

On June 7 the Royal army entered Daventry, where the news reached Charles that his immediate purpose was accomplished, and that the besiegers had of their own accord abandoned the siege of Oxford.   Yet in spite of the good news some time must elapse before Charles could again set forward on his northern march.   Oxford must not only be relieved from immediate danger, but it must be so supplied as to make it unnecessary to relieve it again for some time to come.   Droves of sheep must be collected and despatched to feed the garrison.   Some days must pass before the work could be accomplished, and the advantage of freedom of action which had hitherto been on the side of Charles would pass over to the side of the enemy.   Charles was now pinned at Daventry, as Fairfax had formerly been pinned round Oxford.

If Charles did not realise the change which had come over his prospects, it was because neither he nor any of his followers had any conception of the strength of the New Model army. It was the fashion at Oxford to ridicule it in every way.   "I

neither Southampton nor Dorset concurred with him.   The King to Nicholas, June 9.   *Evelyn's Memoirs,* ed. Bohn, iv. 149.

[1] Petition, undated.   *Warburton,* iii. 71.

[2] Symonds, *Diary,* 186 ; Slingsby, *Diary,* 149

believe," wrote Charles to his wife, "they are weaker than they
are thought to be, whether by their distractions,
which are very great—Fairfax and Browne having
been at cudgels, and his men and Cromwell's likewise at blows together where a captain was slain—or wasting
their men, I cannot say." [1]

June 8.
The King
despises the
New Model.

At Westminster the real qualities of the New Model were
perhaps hardly better known. Yet on June 2, after
the sad news from Leicester, the Committee of Both
Kingdoms, abandoning its blundering policy, had
advised the Houses to direct Fairfax to take the
field at once. On the following day, under the
impression that the Eastern Association was threatened, orders were sent to him to march to its defence.[2]

June 2.
Fairfax to
leave the
siege of
Oxford,

June 3.
and to defend
the Eastern
Association.

Outside the walls of Parliament even stronger measures
were demanded. On the 4th the Common Council forwarded
a petition to the House of Commons, requesting
among other things that a committee might accompany Fairfax to give him encouragement on the
spot, 'without attending commands and directions
from remote councils,' and asking that Cromwell might be
placed, at least for a time, at the head of new forces to be
raised in the Eastern Association, though forty days had
elapsed since the passing of the Self-Denying Ordinance. No
wonder there was a hot and long debate for nearly three hours,
when the daring request was thus lightly made.[3] Yet the
crisis was too imminent to allow any who were not wilfully
blind, to ignore the absolute necessity of postponing political
to military considerations. For the present the deputies of the
Common Council were thanked by the House. It would not
be long before their petition would be answered in the spirit in
which it was conceived.

June 4.
Petition
from the
Common
Council.

On the 5th Fairfax broke up from Oxford. After an un-

[1] The King to the Queen, June 8. *The King's Cabinet Opened*, p. 14,
E. 292, 27.

[2] *L.J.* vii. 403, 404.

[3] *C.J.* iv. 163; *L.J.* vii. 411; D'Ewes's Diary, *Harl. MSS.* 166, fol
216.

successful attack on Boarstall House, he marched in a north-

June 5.
Fairfax
marches
towards the
north-east.

easterly direction, in order to meet Vermuyden, who had been despatched to reinforce Leven, and had now returned from his ineffectual mission. On the 7th Vermuyden joined the main army at

June 7.
Is joined by
Vermuyden.

Sherington, in the close vicinity of Newport Pagnell. The combined forces numbered about 13,000 men.[1]

On the 8th Fairfax learnt that the King was still at Daventry. A council of war was called, and declared for the simple

June 8.
Fairfax
prepares
to fight.

plan of seeking out the enemy and fighting him wherever he could be found. Skippon was directed to draw up a plan of battle so that each regiment

might know the post to which it was assigned. Urgent letters were addressed to the commanders of all the scattered forces within call, to hasten to aid in the great struggle which was impending.

At such a moment the name of the man whose courage and conduct had scattered the army of Rupert and Newcastle

Cromwell's
appointment
as Lieut.-
General
asked for.

at Marston Moor could not fail to be on every lip. The London petition for Cromwell's employment must by this time have been known in the army, and the officers present at the council of war now unani-

mously signed a letter to the Houses asking that the first cavalry officer in England might be appointed, not to the command of the Eastern Association, but to the vacant Lieutenant-Generalship of their own army, an office which by prescription amongst the Parliamentary forces carried with it the command of the cavalry.[2]

When Colonel Hammond, who was the bearer of the letter, arrived at Westminster, he found the opinion of the Commons more favourable to any step recommended on purely military considerations than it had been a few days before. On the

---

[1] *The Scottish Dove*, E. 288, 11; *Sprigg*, 31. The next day Vermuyden resigned his command and went to the Netherlands.

[2] *L.J.* vii. 420; *Sprigg*, 32. Wogan in his narrative (Carte, *Orig. Letters*, i. 127) says that Cromwell had himself ridden over to take leave of the army; but Wogan's story was written long afterwards, and there is no hint of such a thing in any contemporary pamphlet or in Sprigg.

9th all former restrictions were taken off Fairfax's authority,

June 9.
All restrictions taken off Fairfax's authority.

and he was directed to march whither he would, so long as he had the advice, not of a committee of politicians, but of his own council of war. Military questions were at last to be decided by military men.[1]

Having taken such a resolution, it was hardly possible to pass over the request of the council of war. During the last

June 4.
Cromwell and the Association.

few days Cromwell had shown what marvels could be effected by his presence. Since his arrival in Cambridgeshire he had put the Isle of Ely in a state of defence, and had roused the committee of the Association to bestir itself to raise the necessary troops. He was soon able to announce that 3,000 foot and 1,000 horse would before long be available in support of Fairfax. Volunteers came pouring in, 'threescore men out of one poor petty village in Cambridgeshire, in which, to see it, none would have thought that there had been fifty fighting men in it.'[2]

The man who had done these things was, in reality, indispensable. The Commons at once agreed to appoint him

June 10.
The Commons consent to appoint Cromwell Lieutenant General.

Lieutenant-General as long as circumstances might require his presence in the army. It was true that there was nothing in the Self-Denying Ordinance to stand in the way of Cromwell's reappointment, as he had fulfilled its only condition by abandoning his post at the end of forty days after the passing of the Ordinance. For a formal reappointment, however, the consent of the Lords was necessary, and the Lords, though they did not positively reject the proposal, postponed the consideration of so unwelcome a subject to a more convenient season. Both Fairfax and Cromwell considered that, for all practical purposes, the vote of the Commons was sufficient.[3]

Among the Parliamentary officers the utmost harmony prevailed. It was far otherwise in the King's councils at

[1] Com. of B. K. to Fairfax, June 9. *Com. Letter Book.*

[2] *The Exchange Intelligencer*, E. 288, 3 ; *A Diary*, E. 288, 5 ; *Perfect Occurrences*, E. 288, 7.

[3] *C.J.* iv. 169.

Daventry. Rupert, urged on by the Yorkshire officers, and fretting at every hour's delay, pleaded for the resumption of the

Divisions in the Royal council. old plan of marching to the North with the least possible delay. Digby and the civilians did their best to retain the army in the South, and to prepare for a raid upon the Eastern Association, with a just appreciation of the advantages which would follow on the ruin of these hitherto undevastated lands, but with a rash contempt for the Parliamentary forces which might be brought to their defence. To carry his point, Digby even proposed that Charles should visit Oxford, where he would be in personal communication with the councillors who, having been left behind in that city, were naturally desirous of keeping in their own immediate neighbourhood the army on which they relied for their defence.[1] It was thus that Charles was becoming more subject than he had been before to other than military considerations, just at the moment when the interference of civilians with the movements of the Parliamentary army was being discredited at Westminster.

Though Charles refused to stir from Daventry, his councillors met at Oxford on the 10th. It is needless to say that they

June 10. The Council at Oxford recommends an attack on the Association. arrived at a conclusion in which Rupert's plan of campaign was utterly condemned, and the opposite proposal of an attack on the Association was warmly supported. Their letter to the King was supplemented by a private communication from Nicholas to Rupert, in which the Prince was adjured, if he hoped for future advancement in England, to take care how he set himself against the unanimous opinion of the Privy Council.[2] Rupert does not seem to have had much difficulty in rousing the King's displeasure against his officious advisers at Oxford.

June 11. A sharp Reply. "You know," replied Charles to Nicholas, "that the Council was never wont to debate upon any matter not propounded to them by me, and certainly it were a strange thing if my marching army—especially I being at the head of them—should be governed by my sitting Council at

[1] Rupert to Legge, June 8. *Warburton*, iii. 100.
[2] Nicholas to Rupert, June 10. *Add. MSS.* 18,982, fol. 64.

Oxford, when it is scarce fit for myself at such a distance [1] to give any positive order. . . . I desire you to take the best care you may that the like of this be not done hereafter." [2]

It was to little purpose to maintain the supremacy of the military element over the civilian in matters of war if the com-

June 12.
Over-confidence of Rupert.

manders of the army neglected even those ordinary precautions which in similar circumstances would be taken by a civilian of average common sense. That the King should be hunting in Fawsley Park on the evening of the 12th is a fact hardly worthy of the condemnation which it has received. It was not on his shoulders that the weight of ordering the movements of the army rested. It was Rupert, who, if he had not underestimated his opponents, would have acknowledged it to be his duty to seek information on every side as to the position and numbers of the enemy. So great, however, was his contempt for the New Model army, that he knew no more of Fairfax's movements than if he had been in another island. In fact, on the morning of the 12th Fairfax

Fairfax at Kislingbury.

had established himself at Kislingbury, a village about eight miles [3] from Daventry, on the Northampton road. In the evening the appearance of a party of Parliamentary horse gave the alarm. The King was summoned from the chase, and the scattered regiments recalled to their central post on Borough Hill, an eminence which in the days of old had been guarded by the Briton and the Roman. In the minds of the King's soldiers this sudden and unexpected danger could have but one explanation. Ironside, they said to one another, was now in the Parliamentary army. [4]

---

[1] *i.e.* 'if I were at such a distance.'

[2] The King to Nicholas, June 11. *Evelyn's Memoirs*, ed. Bohn, iv. 150.

[3] Sprigg incorrectly speaks of it as being five miles from Borough Hill, instead of seven. His geography, too, is in fault amongst the Northamptonshire villages. He calls Kislingbury, Gilsborough, and Guilsborough, Gilling.

[4] *A more exact and perfect relation of the great victory.* E. 288, 28. The word is Ironsides in the pamphlet, but I have kept the original form (see p. 1). It will be observed that the nickname is still used by Royalists only.

Natural as it was to imagine that every vigorous effort was a token of Cromwell's presence, the thought did less than justice to Fairfax. If he had not Cromwell's eye for the chances of a battle, he was not without considerable strategical ability, and he had the homely sense of duty which, combined with dashing courage and a practical acquaintance with the military art, goes far, except in the direst emergencies, to supply the place of genius. On his return to Newbury, after he had despatched Graves and Weldon to the relief of Taunton, he had given orders that the arduous work of forming a rearguard should be taken by each regiment in turn. When his own regiment was called on to fulfil the task it refused to obey orders, on the plea of its connection with the General. Other commanders might have picked out the ringleaders of the mutiny for punishment. Fairfax sprang from the saddle, placed himself at the head of the recalcitrant regiment, and marched with them through the mud in the rear. After this there was no further resistance. How well his men were inured to discipline was shown at Kislingbury. Riding out to view the outposts in the depth of the night, a sentry stopped him and demanded the word. Fairfax had forgotten it, and the soldier refused to allow him to pass till he had himself obtained the permission of his commanding officer. The commander-in-chief, well pleased under such conditions to be kept standing in the rain, rewarded the sentry for his obedience.[1]

Fairfax's merits as a commander.

Before Fairfax returned on the morning of the 13th from his midnight ride there were signs of movement on the top of Borough Hill. The huts were fired, and when the morning dawned the Royal army descended the hill, making its way westwards in the direction of Warwick. Soon, however, it swung round to the right, and by the evening had taken up its quarters in the villages about Harborough, the King himself sleeping at Lubenham.[2] The northern march, it seemed, was to be persisted in. Yet before leaving Daventry it was unanimously acknowledged by all

June 13. The King marches away.

[1] *Sprigg*, 22, 34.
[2] *Sprigg*, 35; *A true relation*, E. 288, 22.

present at a council of war held there that, if Fairfax followed
hard, a battle was unavoidable.[1]

That Fairfax would follow hard was beyond doubt, especially as he had on that morning received a reinforcement of
unspeakable value. Not tarrying, when a battle was
impending, for the 4,000 men whom he had hoped
to bring with him,[2] Cromwell hastened to Kislingbury at the head of only 600 horse.[3] Fairfax's troopers
welcomed him with 'a mighty shout.'[4] They knew now that
they would not want guidance in the day of battle. For that
day they were longing earnestly. All who had a heart to feel
were bitterly indignant at the spoils and outrages committed
by Charles's soldiers as they swept over the country, gathering
in the sheep and oxen which they needed for the support of
the Oxford garrison. Baser souls—and such were not altogether wanting in the New Model army—were encouraged
by the prospect of recovering some part at least of the spoil.
It was said that scarcely a prisoner was brought in who had
less than forty or fifty shillings in his pocket.[5]

The battle could not be much longer delayed. Harrison,
eager to smite the enemies of the Lord, was sent towards
Daventry to gather intelligence, and Ireton, thought-
ful as he was brave, was bidden to ride in advance,
to outmarch the enemy if possible, and to fall on his flank if it
seemed advisable. The bulk of the army pushed more slowly
northwards. On the evening of the 13th Fairfax's
headquarters were at Guilsborough. Ireton was three
miles in advance. Dashing into Naseby, he made
prisoners of some twenty of Rupert's horsemen who
were playing quoits at their ease, as well as of
another party which was sitting at supper in a neighbouring
house. Before the night was over Fairfax learnt that he was
freed from one danger which had of late been imminent.

Marginal notes: Cromwell joins Fairfax. / The pursuit. / Fairfax at Guilsborough. / Naseby occupied by Ireton.

[1] Digby to Legge, June 30. *Warburton*, iii. 125.
[2] See p. 238.
[3] *Sprigg*, 35.
[4] *A more exact and perfect relation.* E. 288, 28.
[5] *Perfect Diurnal.* E. 262, 8.

Scout-master Watson brought in an intercepted letter which

A letter
from Goring
intercepted.

proved to be a despatch from Goring to the King
announcing the impossibility of his leaving the West,
and begging Charles to postpone a battle till he was
able to join him.[1]

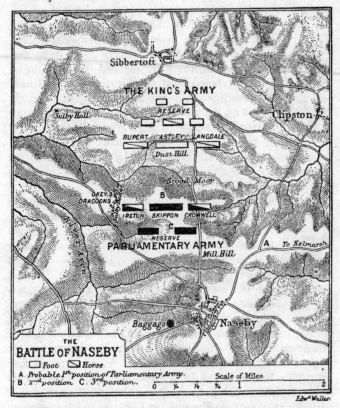

THE
BATTLE OF NASEBY

☐ *Foot*　☐ *Horse*

A *Probable 1st position of Parliamentary Army.*
B *2nd position* C *3rd position.*

Scale of Miles

0　¼　½　¾　1　　2

Edw Weller

Whilst all men's thoughts in the Parliamentary army were
bent to the coming battle, Charles had once more fallen a
prey to his accustomed vacillation. "I assure you," he wrote

---

[1] *God's Doings and Man's Duty*, by Hugh Peters, p. 19A, 114, e. 15.
Goring's letter is in *Perfect Occurrences*. E. 262, 10.

to Nicholas, after announcing his intention of pushing on to Belvoir, "that I shall look before I leap farther north." [1]   In

The King doubtful about his course. the depth of the night he was roused from his sleep at Lubenham to learn that the advanced guard of the Parliamentary army was too near to allow him even to make for Belvoir. Rising early, he rode to Harborough, where,

June 14. A council at Harborough. at a hasty council, it was resolved to await the enemy's attack on a long hill which rises about two miles south of the little town. [2]   It was here that Astley, who commanded the foot, intended the battle to be fought. If Fairfax chose to take the offensive, he would have

First position of the King's army. to mount the hill in the face of an enemy strongly posted on the top. There was the more reason for leaving the attack to the Parliamentarians, as the King's army was decidedly outnumbered. The Parliamentarians, now that they had been joined by Cromwell, numbered about 13,600 men, whilst on the highest calculation the King's troops can hardly have exceeded 7,500.

The King's army was early drawn up in array, and, as the morning hours sped by without any appearance of the enemy,

Rupert grows impatient, Rupert grew thoroughly tired of inaction. At eight he sent forward Ruce, the scout-master, to discover the position of the enemy. Ruce lazily returned with a tale that Fairfax was nowhere to be found. Rupert determined to seek for the enemy himself, and, taking a party

and rides forward. of horse and musketeers with him, rode forwards over the rolling ground on the road to Naseby, till, after passing through the village of Clipston, he mounted a rising ground from which he descried the Parliamentary army,

The Parliamentary rendezvous. as he fancied, in full retreat. As a matter of fact, Fairfax had ordered his army to rendezvous early in the morning on the brow of the hill north-east of Naseby at a spot on the road to Clipston and Harborough. From this point he had an excellent view of the enemy gather-

[1] The King to Nicholas, June 13. *Evelyn's Memoirs*, ed. Bohn, iv. 151.

[2] Walker says it was one mile only, but the hill stretching from East Farndon to Oxenden is evidently meant.

ing on the opposite ridge at some three miles distance, and he soon came to the conclusion that Charles had abandoned all notion of further retreat. In the meanwhile the Parliamentary regiments, with the instincts of pursuit strong upon them, had pushed on down the hill, and as soon as it was known that a battle was imminent, preparations were made to draw up the army in battle array on one of the lower ridges in advance of the line of the Naseby plateau. The chosen position may have been a strong one, but Cromwell saw at a glance that the plateau itself would afford one stronger still. The hill-top was higher there, and the hillside up which the enemy's horse would be forced to charge was steeper. He therefore begged Fairfax to draw back. Fairfax acknowledged the wisdom of his Lieutenant's advice, and directed that the army should retire to the higher ground.

Cromwell advises Fairfax to draw back.

Such was the true explanation of the movement in retreat which lured Rupert forwards. When, however, he arrived opposite the Parliamentary army, even Rupert could not but acknowledge the skill with which his adversaries had chosen their position. Not only if he persisted in attacking was he condemned to an uphill charge, but the valley which separated him from the Parliamentary army was wet and unsuitable for a charge of cavalry. Rupert therefore edged away to the right towards an eminence known as Dust Hill, and sent back orders to the whole army to advance with all speed to that position.

Rupert on Dust Hill.

On the appearance of the Royalists on the crest of Dust Hill, Fairfax, fearing to be outflanked, had no choice but to move to the left in a line parallel with the enemy's movement, especially as the wind blew from the west and would consequently be in favour of soldiers attacking from that quarter. Here Skippon, whose duty it was as Major-General to draw up the foot, began to place them in array on the northern slope of the hill in a fallow field, by the side of which a hedge, known as Sulby hedge, running at right angles to his front, offered protection to his left flank, whilst furze bushes and rough ground on the other side constituted a sufficient defence to the other wing. The

The Parliamentary army moves to the left.

position was a strong one, as the ground fell steeply away to Broadmoor at the bottom of the valley in front. Fairfax, however, we know not whether by Cromwell's advice or not, thought that it could be yet more improved. It is possible that he wished to conceal his superior numbers from the enemy, or that he feared that some confusion amongst the young soldiers in his own ranks might give encouragement to Rupert. The Parliamentary troops, therefore, much to the disgust of Skippon, who probably thought the movement risky when the enemy was so near, were drawn back and posted behind the brow of the hill, where their numbers and position would be unnoticed by the enemy. The marshalling of the foot was left to Skippon, whilst to Cromwell was assigned the marshalling of the horse. Skippon was himself to take charge of the foot; Cromwell, as Lieutenant-General, commanded the horse on the right. Ireton had, at Cromwell's request, been appointed Commissary-General on that very morning, an office which carried with it the command of the horse on the left wing. Okey, with a thousand dragoons, all of them picked men, was stationed behind Sulby hedge. It would serve admirably as a cover from behind which a galling fire could be directed on the flank of a body of cavalry charging across its front.

A retrograde movement.

The marshalling of the army.

The King's army was arranged in much the same fashion as that of his adversaries. The main body of infantry was in the centre under Astley, the King himself taking up his position at a little distance in the rear at the head of a reserve composed of horse and foot. The bulk of the cavalry was on the wings, Rupert and Maurice commanding on the right, Sir Marmaduke Langdale with the horse from Newark and the discontented Yorkshire horse on the left.

Array of the King's army.

Amongst the fierce Puritans of the Parliamentary cavalry there was stern joy at the arrival of the long-wished-for time when through their arms the cause of God was to be put to the test of battle. " I can say this of Naseby," wrote Cromwell afterwards, " that when I saw the enemy draw up and march in gallant order towards us,

Feeling of the Puritan soldiers.

and we a company of poor ignorant men to seek how to order
our battle, the General having commanded me to order all the
horse, I could not—riding alone about my business—but smile
out to God in praises in assurance of victory, because God
would, by things that are not, bring to naught things that are,
of which I had great assurance—and God did it." [1]

The company of poor ignorant men, amongst whom the
veterans of Marston Moor and Newbury were to fight side by
The opening of the battle. side with recruits who had never seen a battle, and
who had, for weeks past, been ridiculed by the
Cavaliers and only half trusted at Westminster, stepped forward as soon as their ranks were in order to the brow of the
hill. At the very opening of the battle, Rossiter, who had been
summoned from Lincolnshire, rode up to join Cromwell on the
right, and thus raised the Parliamentary army to a force numbering little short of 14,000 men, almost twice as many as the
7,500 who fought for Charles. Recollecting how little execution had been done by the large guns at Marston Moor, Fairfax
contented himself with giving but two or three cannon shots to
check the advance of the Royalists. On came the enemy,
horse and foot, pouring down into Broad Moor, at the bottom
of the valley which separated the two armies, and pushing up
the opposite height. A little below the top the armies crashed
together almost at the same time, though Rupert's wing, galled
as it was by Okey's fire from the hedge, struck first upon the
Parliamentary left. Either from something in the nature of the
ground or because Ireton was new to the command, there was
a want of cohesion in this wing of Fairfax's army which neutralised its superiority in numbers. Some of the regiments
dashed forward to meet Rupert as he approached. Others
hung back irresolutely to receive his charge. Ireton, who with
the troops immediately around him drove back the enemy, was
distracted from his proper work by seeing the infantry on his
right hand pressed by the Royalist foot, which was by this
time hotly engaged. Turning sharply to the right, he fell upon
the enemy's infantry. The attempt was premature, and Ireton

---

[1] Cromwell to ——, July. *Good news out of the West.* E, 293, 18.

himself was struck down with wounds in his thigh and face,
and fell for a time into the hands of the enemy.   Rupert, good

Royalist vic-
tory on the
Parliamen-
tary left.

horseman as he was, took instant advantage of the
distraction in the opposite ranks, and pushing the
charge home, drove the Parliamentary horse in wild
confusion before him.

Unfortunately for Charles, it was not in Rupert's nature to
draw rein to see how the battle went in other parts of the field.

Rupert
pushes his
success too
far.

Galloping on, he came upon the baggage train at the
outskirts of Naseby village.   On his summoning the
guard to surrender, he was answered by a stern refusal and a volley from the defenders.   Yet musket shots were
no permanent defence against cavalry, and if the defenders of
the baggage escaped destruction, they may have owed their
safety to unwonted caution on the part of Rupert.   He must
have perceived, if he looked round at all, that there were no
signs of a Royalist victory in any other part of the field.   It
is, at least, certain that he abandoned the prey before him, and
hastened back to take his part in the battle raging before him.

Like the cavalry on the left, the Parliamentary infantry in
the centre soon lost the services of its commander.   Early in

The fight in
the centre.

the day Skippon was struck down, and though he
refused to leave the field, he was helpless to exercise
authority.   In spite of their numerical superiority, having
7,000 foot to oppose to 4,000 of the enemy, the Parliamentary
infantry were discouraged by their loss, and their left flank
being exposed since the flight of Ireton's cavalry, the front
ranks fell back in disorder, whilst the officers of the broken
regiments, finding it impossible to induce them to make a
stand, threw themselves into the squares of the second line.
It was no light issue that was at stake.   Whichever leader could
bring a preponderant force of horse to bear upon the confused
struggle of footmen in the centre would have England at his
feet.

While Rupert was wasting time in his pursuit of the Parliamentary left and in his attack on the guardians of the baggage,
Cromwell was winning the victory.   Even before Rossiter's
appearance, he had outnumbered the cavalry opposed to

him, and it was now at the head of 3,600 sabres that he watched the 2,000 horsemen of the enemy toiling up the slope.

Cromwell on the right wing.

Then with all the advantage of numbers and the ground on his side, he gave the order to charge.

Though his extreme right was checked by furze bushes and a rabbit warren, the enemy took no advantage, as Rupert had taken advantage on the other side of the field, of the consequent dislocation of the Parliamentary line. Whalley,

Whalley defeats Langdale.

who had smooth ground before him, charged Langdale's own regiment and routed it after a sharp engagement. The Northern horse had long been sullen and discontented, and it may be that their arms were the weaker for the burden on their hearts. Thrown back upon their reserves, they left the flank of their infantry exposed.

With prompt decision Cromwell held back part of his force to employ it in mastering the Royalist foot. Three regiments

The advance against the reserve.

he could well spare out of his overwhelming numbers for another task, and he pushed them on in pursuit of the beaten enemy. Charles, it is true, did not quail before the rush of the horsemen bearing down upon him, and he bade the regiments which remained intact to charge and to retrieve the fortunes of the day. Though he had the strength of will to give this command, he had not the strength of will to meet friendly but positive resistance. As he rode forward to share in the peril, the Earl of Carnwath snatched at his bridle, crying out, "Will you go upon your

Charles hesitates.

death?" Charles hesitated, and almost at the same moment some one, perhaps gathering a hint from the King's movements, gave the order "March to the right." The

Retreat of the reserve.

whole of the cavalry of the reserve wheeled about at the word, carrying the King with them, and rode hurriedly to the rear. After a flight of about a quarter of a mile with broken ranks and dispirited hearts, they halted to see what further lot might be in store for them.

The stress of battle did not as yet fall upon this panic-stricken rout. Cromwell, with the main body of his horse, amongst whom Fairfax had now thrown himself, flew at the doomed infantry which was still struggling heroically for

victory in the centre. Rupert had not yet returned from his
ill timed pursuit, and Okey, finding the field in front of him
General empty, ordering his dragoons to mount, launched
attack on the them against the rear and flank of the Royalist
Royalist
foot. foot. Some too of the broken regiments of Ireton's
wing had by this time rallied and joined in the attack. Before
such a mass of horsemen sweeping down upon them no infantry
could in those days make a stand, and least of all a force which
had not yet succeeded in overpowering the resistance of the
enemy's foot in front. The King's foot—Welshmen for the
most part—were in no case to repeat, with such odds against
them, the marvels of the London trained bands at Newbury.[1]
Regiment after regiment flung down its arms and was admitted
to quarter. One regiment alone held out beyond expectation.
Complete Fairfax, whose helmet had been struck off in the
defeat of the fight, but who continued to expose himself bare-
Royalist
centre. headed to the chance of war, bade the colonel of
his guard to attack it in front whilst he himself fell upon it in
the rear. The double assault broke up the last resistance, and
with the overthrow of this gallant regiment Charles's infantry
ceased to exist. Fairfax had borne himself all through the
fight with the bravery which he shared in common with many
of his troopers. There is no sign that he in any way impressed
his mind upon the course of the battle as Rupert and Cromwell did after their respective fashion; but his modesty was all
his own. After he had slain with his own hand the ensign of
the last regiment which resisted, he left the colours on the
Modesty of ground. A soldier who picked them up boasted
Fairfax. that he had won them by killing the officer in
charge. "I have honour enough," said Fairfax when he heard
of the braggart's lying tale; "let him take that honour to
himself."

The whole battle was practically at an end when Rupert
came back from his too precipitate charge. Not venturing to
attack the victors, he rode off to rejoin his sovereign in the rear.
There were those in the Parliamentary ranks who wished to

[1] See vol. i. 214.

direct a cavalry charge on his disorganised horsemen as they passed across the field, but Fairfax refused to run the risk.

Rupert comes back too late.

He halted his cavalry till his foot had reformed, and then advanced to the line of hill from which the King's army had descended before the fight. Here he drew up his whole force in battle array. To attack a complete army with his scanty force, and that composed of cavalry alone, was a rashness from which even Rupert recoiled. Both

Flight of the King's cavalry.

he and Charles knew that the day was lost, and, wheeling round, the Royalist horse sought safety in retreat. The retreat soon quickened into flight, and for fourteen miles, till the walls of Leicester were reached, Fairfax's troopers, slaughtering as they rode, swept after them in pursuit.

Result of the battle.

The victorious foot meanwhile remained behind to guard the captives, and to strip them of the plunder which they had gathered since they had broken up from Leicester.

From a military point of view the blow had been decisive. The King's infantry was almost to a man destroyed or captured. Five thousand prisoners of both arms were in the hands of the victors. What was more disastrous still was that of this number nearly 500 were officers. Even if Charles succeeded in raising fresh regiments of infantry, he could hardly hope to find officers competent to train and command them. Further, his whole train of artillery, forty barrels of powder, and arms for 8,000 men passed into the enemy's hands. To win such a victory almost every element of success had combined. On the Parliamentary side was a better cavalry officer and a far more numerous army. Part, at least, of Fairfax's horse had been superior to anything which could be produced on the other side. Yet, after all, a victory in which 14,000 men defeated 7,500, and that too not without difficulty, cannot be reckoned amongst the great examples of military efficiency. The truth is that a great part of the Parliamentary army was composed of raw soldiers hardly as yet inured to discipline, or to the sight of an enemy in the field.

The slain were few in proportion to the prisoners, about

700 having been killed in the battle and 300 in the pursuit. The worst fate was reserved for the unhappy women who followed the camp. About a hundred, being of Irish birth, 'with cruel countenances,' were knocked on the head without mercy. The faces of the English harlots were gashed in order to render them for ever hideous, and it is not improbable that some officers' and soldiers' wives shared the fate of their frailer sisters. Puritanism was intolerant of vice, and it had no pity for the sex on which its hideous burden falls most heavily.[1]

Whatever else may have been the result of the victory at Naseby, it loosed Cromwell's tongue. Ever since the day

Cromwell pleads for liberty.

when he had discovered that the aid of the Scots was a necessity if the King was to be defeated he had kept silence on that subject of liberty of conscience which was so near to his heart. "Honest men," he now wrote to Lenthall before he sought rest after returning from the pursuit, "served you faithfully in this action. Sir, they are trusty; I beseech you, in the name of God, not to discourage them. . . . He that ventures his life for the liberty of his country, I wish he trust God for the liberty of his conscience, and you for the liberty he fights for."[2]

So little did the House of Commons share Cromwell's sentiments on this matter, that in sending his letter to the

His letter mutilated by the Commons.

press they omitted this paragraph. It was to no purpose that they exercised their censorship. The House of Lords, probably in mere thoughtlessness,

---

[1] *Walker,* 130; *Slingsby's Diary,* 151; *Sprigg,* 37; *Whitelocke,* 151; *Perfect Occurrences,* E. 262, 10; *A glorious victory,* E. 288, 21; *A true relation,* E. 288, 22; *Three Letters,* E. 288, 27; *A more exact and perfect relation,* E. 288, 28; *The weekly account,* E. 288, 33; *A more particular and exact relation,* E. 288, 38. The letter attached to *An Ordinance,* E. 288, 26, from a gentleman of public employment, is ascribed to Rushworth, in a note in Thomason's hand. For a discussion on the movements preliminary to the battle, and for an acknowledgment of my obligations to Colonel Ross, see the note at the end of this volume.

[2] *Carlyle,* Letter XXIX.

simultaneously ordered a complete copy of the letter to be sent forth to the world. Yet there were not wanting some, even amongst usually well-informed persons, who maintained that the mutilated copy was alone genuine.[1]

[1] The two forms are both amongst the Thomason Tracts (E. 288, 26 ; E. 288, 27). Thomason notes that the copy without the paragraph was as Cromwell wrote it, imagining the most characteristic portion of the letter to have been forged.

CHAPTER XXXII.

LANGPORT AND BRIDGWATER.

IF Cromwell's political advice was disregarded at Westminster, it was more than ever impossible to dispense with his services as a military commander. On June 16 the Lords agreed to confirm his Lieutenant-Generalship for three months,[1] and as the command was again confirmed from time to time as its term expired, it practically became permanent. The same favour was accorded to Sir William Brereton and Sir Thomas Middleton, who respectively commanded the Parliamentary forces in Cheshire and in so much of North Wales as was not under the dominion of the King.[2]

In none of these cases was there, properly speaking, an exemption from the operation of the Self-Denying Ordinance. That Ordinance did not take away from the Houses the power of appointing their members to offices after the expiration of the term fixed for their resignation.

Amongst the friends of the Parliament hope was at last high of bringing the long weary war to a close. On June 18 Leicester surrendered,[3] and Fairfax was set at liberty to pursue the beaten King. Every effort was made to press men to enable him to follow up his victory Yet, from both military and political reasons, there was in some quarters a strong disposition to bring the Scottish army southwards, either to supplement or to counterbalance the success of the New Model. Soldiers might remember that Fairfax could not at the same time

*1645.
June 16.
Cromwell continued in the Lieutenant-Generalship.*

Similar favours to Brereton and Middleton.

*June 18.
Surrender of Leicester.*

The Scots to advance.

---

[1] *L.J.* vii. 433.   [2] *Ibid.* vii. 367, 599.
[3] *A copy of a letter.* E. 289, 42.

follow the King and besiege his fortresses. The Presbyterians, on the other hand, had already begun to depreciate Naseby. " We hope," wrote Baillie, " the back of the malignant party

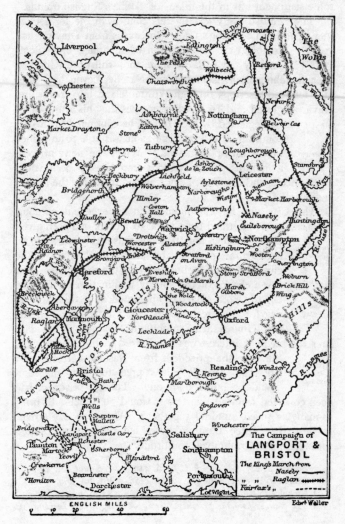

The Campaign of
LANGPORT &
BRISTOL
The King's March from
         Naseby ———
   "   " Raglan ✕✕✕✕✕✕
   "   " Fairfax's " ‑ ‑ ‑ ‑ ‑

ENGLISH MILES

Edwᵈ Weller

is broken. Some fear the insolence of others, to whom alone the Lord has given the victory of that day. It was never more necessary to haste up all possible recruits to our army." [1] The same sentiment was in the minds of Baillie's English friends.

The Scottish army was by this time available for service in England. The King's march eastwards from Drayton had removed all apprehension of an attack upon Scotland by way of Lancashire, and, whilst the King had been marching upon Leicester and Naseby, Leven had carefully retraced his steps through Westmoreland into Yorkshire. Having required and received assurances that his army would no longer be neglected by the Houses, he continued his march southwards, and on June 20 he was able to announce his arrival at Mansfield.[2] When the news arrived, a month's pay of 31,000*l.* had already been voted for the Scots, and the City at once agreed to supply the money in advance.[3]

Leven's movements.

June 20. He arrives at Mansfield.

The City was for the moment in an excellent humour. The free hand which had been given to Fairfax had been given at its bidding, and it might reasonably attribute to itself some part of the glory of Naseby.[4] The citizens felt no inclination to close their purses now that they saw a chance of the speedy termination of the war. On the 19th, the day appointed as a thanksgiving day for the great victory, the City entertained the two Houses at a sumptuous banquet. Two days later the scene of interest was transferred to the streets. On the 21st the prisoners from Naseby were to enter London. The Royalists predicted that the show would be but a poor one. Though prisoners had been collected from all quarters it would be difficult to bring as many as seven hundred together.[5] When the day arrived no less than three thousand were led through the streets thronged with a triumphant multitude.[6]

The City in a liberal mood.

June 19. The City banquet.

June 21. Entry of the prisoners.

---

[1] *Baillie*, ii. 287.   [2] *L.J.* vii. 449.   [3] *Ibid.* vii. 441.
[4] Sabran to Brienne, June 19. *Add. MSS.* 5,461, fol. 269.
[5] Nicholas to Rupert, June 23. *Add. MSS.* 18,982, fol. 65.
[6] *The manner how the prisoners are to be brought into London.* E.

Most of these unfortunate men were of Welsh origin. The Houses were by no means anxious to be burdened with their maintenance, and after an effort to bring home to them the misery of their condition, by forcing them to pass some nights in the open air in Tothill Fields, they sent Dr. Cradock, a Welsh clergyman, to preach to them two sermons in their own language, after which they were invited to take the Covenant in order to qualify themselves for employment in Ireland. About five hundred only accepted the offer at once, and two or three hundred more followed their example after the interval of a few months. The Spanish ambassador picked up some recruits for his master's service in the Netherlands, but the greater part remained in custody till the end of the war brought with it a general release of prisoners.[1]

Their treatment.

Welsh sermons.

Disposal of the prisoners.

That the war must be carried on with unflagging energy was now on the lips of all who were not Royalists. Yet the very greatness of the success could not fail to encourage in some minds the hope that the King would be at last sufficiently conscious of weakness to accept the proposals which he had rejected at Uxbridge.

The war to be vigorously prosecuted.

On the 20th the Lords took fresh propositions of peace into consideration, and on the following day they received the support of the Scottish commissioners, who added a request that the war might be vigorously prosecuted during the negotiations, and that there might be a 'speedy settling of religion and the House of God.' The rift between Presbyterians and Independents was still open.[2]

June 20. The Lords suggest a fresh negotiation.

288, 48. 4,000 had been taken, but some of the prisoners had escaped on the road, and others were for various reasons kept back. It is not easy to say what became of Irish prisoners. An order was given by Parliament that they should be put to death without mercy, and that too at Fairfax's special request. *L.J.* vii. 433; *C.J.* iv. 182; Nicholas to Rupert, July 11, *Add. MSS.* 18,982, fol. 68. On the other hand, there is a later order that the mere Irish were to be committed to prison. *C.J.* iv. 21.

[1] *The Moderate Intelligencer*, E. 292, 3; Sabran to Brienne, July $\frac{3}{13}$, Sept. $\frac{4}{14}$, *Add. MSS.* 5,461 fol. 284, 368b.   [2] *L.J.* vii. 441, 442.

However anxious the Lords might be for the resumption of negotiations, it was impossible for them to proceed further in the teeth of the excitement caused by the revelation of the

The King's cabinet. King's most secret intrigues. The King's cabinet had been captured at Naseby, and had been sent up to Westminster by Fairfax. The greater part of the letters contained in it were drafts or copies of those written by Charles

Revelations contained in the letters found in it. to his wife. From these and from other papers in the same collection it appeared beyond a shadow of doubt that Charles, whatever had been declared in his name at Uxbridge, had never really acknowledged the Houses at Westminster as a lawful Parliament. Worse still, in the eyes of contemporaries, was the King's negotiation for the landing of an Irish army in England, and his readiness to abolish the laws against the English Catholics. Nor was it easy to forgive his attempt to introduce upon English soil the wild soldiery of the Duke of Lorraine.[1]

The papers justifying these grave accusations were for the most part read first in the two Houses and then at a Common

July. Publication of the letters. Hall in the City. Shortly afterwards they were printed for the reading of all men. That no doubt of their genuineness might be entertained, any persons who wished to put it to the test were invited to examine the originals. The effect of their publication was enormous.[2]

It seemed hopeless to treat with a King who was at heart so

They render a present negotiation impossible. little of an Englishman, and whose professions were so little in accordance with his practice. "The key of the King's cabinet," wrote a London pamphleteer, "as it hath unlocked the mystery of former treaties, so I hope it will lock up our minds from thoughts of future."[3]

It was no mere record of a dead past which had been suddenly unveiled. One of the captured letters had been written as late as June 8. There was no reason to suppose that Charles's conduct in July would differ from his conduct in June.

The King's Cabinet Opened. E. 292, 27.

L.J. vii. 465; *C.J.* iv. 190. Thomason's date of publication is July 14. [3] *The City Alarum.* E. 292, 12.

Charles, in fact, was far from being discouraged by his overthrow at Naseby. His cavalry, though defeated, was almost intact, and he could not believe that there would be much difficulty in levying foot amongst those rugged Welsh hills which had supplied him so well before. On June 19 he reached Hereford. The news which met him there was disquieting. A large party of his supporters had been defeated at Stokesay on the 8th, and Sir William Crofts, the ablest of the Herefordshire Royalists, had been slain in the action.[1] Yet the county professed its willingness to support the King in his misfortune. Gerard too at last arrived with 2,000 men from Wales. Charles was thus able, with reinforcements which he had picked up on the way, to muster 3,000 foot and 4,000 horse, and might therefore hope soon to find himself at the head of a force not inferior, numerically at least, to that with which he had fought at Naseby. In the West, Goring could dispose of a considerable army, and if the siege of Taunton could be brought successfully to an end he would be able to advance—so at least it was fondly hoped at Hereford—with a force of 8,000 foot and 6,000 horse.[2] If the two armies could only be brought together, Charles would be far stronger in numbers than he had been at the beginning of the campaign.

June 19.
The King at Hereford.

He hopes to repair his losses.

It would not have been characteristic of Charles to depend on English troops alone. "The late misfortune," he wrote to Ormond the day before his arrival at Hereford, "makes the Irish assistance more necessary than before. For if within these two months you could send me a considerable assistance, I am confident that both my last loss would be soon forgotten, and likewise it may, by the grace of God, put such a turn to my affairs as to make me in a far better condition before winter than I have been at any time since this rebellion began."[3]

June 18.
He appeals to Ormond.

Charles, in fact, had persuaded himself that his last con-

[1] Intelligence from Shropshire. E. 290, 11. For the date of the action, see Webb's *Civil War in Herefordshire*, ii. 193–196.

[2] Digby to Ormond, June 19. Carte's *Ormond*, vi. 301.

[3] The King to Ormond, June 18. *Ibid.* v. 14.

ccssions to the Irish must by this time have brought about a

He feels sure that peace is concluded. conclusion of the long-desired peace. "We all," wrote Digby, "take it for granted that the peace of Ireland is concluded." [1]   Glamorgan had now finally

Glamorgan sets out. set out for Dublin to smooth away all remaining difficulties. [2]   Lest Glamorgan's intervention might prove insufficient, another emissary, Colonel Fitzwilliam, was

Mission of Colonel Fitz-william. almost at the same time despatched to Ireland. Like Glamorgan, he was ready to take the command of 10,000 Irish soldiers, and to transport them into England. He had recently arrived from France with a letter of recommendation from the Queen. His only stipulation was that the Irish were to have 'free use of their religion, a free Parliament, and the penal laws to be taken off.' Charles, who had already expressed his readiness to grant all these things, raised no objection. [3]   In expectation of a successful

June 26. Langdale sent to North Wales. result, Langdale was appointed Governor of North Wales, to be ready to receive the Irish when they landed, and was directed in the meanwhile to

June 27. Daniel O Neill sent to Cornwall. cross the sea to confer with Ormond on the most suitable way of shipping them. Almost at the same time Daniel O'Neill received instructions to repair to Cornwall to get transports ready for the purpose. [4]

[1] Digby to Ormond, June 19. Carte's *Ormond,* vi. 301.

[2] The King to Glamorgan, June 23. *Harl. MSS.* 6,988, fol. 114. I gather from this letter that Glamorgan started without any fresh directions, as the King merely writes, "I am glad to hear that you are gone to Ireland." The language of Byron supports this view. "Upon these considerations," he writes—*i.e.* upon the necessity of obtaining aid after Naseby—"my Lord of Glamorgan hath thought fit to hasten his journey into Ireland." Digby to Ormond. *Carte MSS.* xv. fol. 99.

[3] Propositions offered by Fitzwilliam, May $\frac{16}{26}$, *The King's Cabinet Opened,* p. 21, E. 292, 27; Fitzwilliam to Digby, July 16, *S.P. Dom.*; the King to Ormond, June 18, Digby to Ormond, June 19, Carte's *Ormond,* v. 14, vi. 304.

[4] Digby to Ormond, June 26, *Ibid.* vi. 302; Instructions to O'Neill, June 27, *Ludlow's Memoirs* (ed. 1751), iii. 305. The King was at this time confident that Ormond would do his best to send the Irish over. "As for my letter to Ormond," he had written to the Queen about a month before Naseby, "he understands it clearly enough, but he is some-

Sanguine as Charles was, he could not but have moments of despondency. In a letter written to his son on June 23, he

June 23.
The King's
instructions
to his son.

faced the possibility of his own capture. In such a case the Prince was never to yield to any conditions that were dishonourable, unsafe for his own person, or derogatory to regal authority, even to save his father's life.[1]

The outlook on Charles's side was indeed more gloomy than Charles, even in his most despondent moments, could

Effect of the
King's
appeal to the
Irish.

possibly imagine. His persistent efforts to master his rebellious subjects by Irish and foreign aid were converting the New Model into a national army.

It was all very well for mere soldiers like Byron and Langdale[2] to applaud any means which would bring recruits to their diminishing forces. To them an Irish soldier was as good as one of English birth, if only he knew how to handle a musket or a pike. To civilians who were Englishmen first and Royalists afterwards the difference was immense. Even in Royalist districts the hearty co-operation of the mass of the people was hardly to be expected after the revelation of Charles's secrets in the letters captured at Naseby.

In the meanwhile Fairfax was pressing on towards the

June 21.
Proposal to
subordinate
Fairfax to
the Commit-
tee of Both
Kingdoms.

West. On June 21 one more attempt was made in the House of Commons to subject him to civilian authority. The members who sat for eastern and southern constituencies wished to confer upon the Committee of Both Kingdoms authority to recall

him, if it thought fit to do so. Their proposal was couched

what fearful to take that burden upon him without the Council there; but I have now so cleared that doubt likewise to him that nothing but his disobedience—which I cannot expect—can hinder speedily the peace of Ireland." The King to the Queen, May 12. *Letters of Henrietta Maria*, 303.

[1] *Clarendon*, x. 4.

[2] "It is in your power," wrote Langdale to Ormond, "to make yourself famous to all ages for your loyalty to His Majesty, and for the deliverance of the English nation from the greatest rebellion and anarchical government that ever yet threatened the ruin thereof." Langdale to Ormond, July 3. *Carte MSS.* xv. fol. 190.

in the interests of their own districts, though the form in which it was made gave it the appearance of being inspired by a wider patriotism. Their motion was rejected, but the Committee was instructed 'to take care for the safety of the West, and with regard to the whole kingdom.' The Committee, wiser than the House, simply directed Fairfax to act according to his own judgment.[1]

June 25.
Fairfax to do what he thinks best.

Fairfax had not altogether an easy task before him. On the 26th he reached Lechlade on his way to Marlborough. His army was in much distress. Horses and arms were wanting, and desertions had been frequent. The associated counties, having been called on to supply the full tale of men which they were bound by the New Model Ordinance to furnish, were slack in complying with the demand, and when at last they pressed the recruits and sent them off, they took no pains to stop desertion, or to seize the runaways after their return to their homes. Fairfax now appealed to the Houses to remedy this mischief, and the Houses at once complied with his request as far as it was in their power to do so.

June 26.
Fairfax's difficulties.

Condition of his army.

Even after the efficiency of the Parliamentary army had been restored, the difficulties of the military position which Fairfax was called on to face were by no means slight. He had only one army to dispose of, whilst the enemy had two. He could not afford to divide his own force, and whether he turned upon Charles or Goring, he would leave the way open for plundering raids upon the Parliamentary districts by whichever army he left unopposed. He now announced to both Houses that he had made his choice. Of the two hostile armies he considered Goring's to be the more dangerous. Taunton was for the third time straitened, and Massey's force, previously ordered to keep the country open around the town,[2] had, since Goring's return to the West, been found quite inadequate to the task. Fairfax therefore resolved to make the relief of Taunton and the

The military position.

[1] *C.J.* iv. 182; D'Ewes's Diary, *Harl. MSS.* 166, fol. 220b; the Com. of B. K. to Fairfax, June 25, *Com. Letter Book.*

[2] See p. 229.

defeat of Goring his immediate care. It was for the Houses to devise a mode of keeping the King in check.[1]

Fortunately for the Houses, they had now the Scottish army to fall back upon. As long as Carlisle held out there would be difficulty in inducing Leven to move farther south. The governor, Sir Thomas Glemham, made a desperate resistance, and for some time the garrison had been reduced to the scantiest and most loathsome food. At last, on June 28, its power of defying starvation was at an end, and Glemham capitulated to David Leslie.[2] In spite of the objections of his English auxiliaries, Leslie placed Carlisle in the charge of a Scottish garrison. At Westminster this addition to the material pledges in the hands of the Scots was viewed with grave dissatisfaction, but it was not a moment when the Houses could afford to quarrel with their allies. They invited Leven to march forward and to lay siege to Hereford, thus performing the double task of assailing an important garrison and of opposing Charles in a district in which his influence was still great. Leven rested at Nottingham till he had ascertained that money was really being provided for the pay of his men. He then pushed forward, and on July 8 he established himself at Alcester. He had been joined by an English force under Sir John Gell, and after this reinforcement his army numbered somewhat more than 7,000 men.[3] It was hardly capable of rapidly manœuvring, if it is true that it was followed by no less than 4,000 women and children. Till the promised money arrived the army was compelled to live at free quarters, a system which was always accompanied by wastefulness and oppression out of all proportion to the gain of the soldiers.[4]

June 28.
Surrender of Carlisle.

The Scots to besiege Hereford.

July 8.
Leven at Alcester.

---

[1] Fairfax to the Houses of Parliament, June 26. *L.J.* vii. 463.

[2] *Rushw.* vi. 118.

[3] *C.J.* iv. 205.

[4] "They plunder notably in the country," writes Nicholas of the Scottish women, "nothing inferior to the Irish women slain at Naseby. I hear that the Earl of Leven is troubled that the rebels gave no quarter to the Irish at Naseby, and saith that he will not engage his Scots but at

Fairfax was already far advanced towards the West. On July 1, when not far from Salisbury, he found himself con-

July 1.
Fairfax near Salisbury.

fronted by an unexpected obstacle. The burdens of the war lay most heavily on the agricultural

May 25.
The Club-men in Wells and Dorset,

population. On May 25, 4,000 farmers and yeomen from the counties of Wilts and Dorset had met to appoint an organised body of watchmen to seize plunderers, and to carry them for punishment to the nearest garrison of the party to which the offenders belonged.[1] On

June 2.
and in Somerset.

June 2 a similar body in Somerset presented to the Prince of Wales a petition asking for redress of grievances.[2] Further experience showed that it was useless to expect the officers of the garrisons to do justice on

June 30.
Further proceedings.

their own men. On June 30 they resolved not only to inflict the punishment themselves, but to offer protection to pressed men who had deserted the service into which they had been driven.[3] The men of Wilts and Dorset took a still more daring step. They resolved to send messengers both to King and Parliament to request them to make peace, and they gave a testimony of their earnestness by subscribing a sum of money to enable the neighbouring garrisons to subsist without plunder till an answer had been received. The movement set on foot in three counties by the Clubmen—as the countrymen were called from their appearance without pikes or firearms at the county musters—had

June 29.
A conflict with Massey's troops.

already assumed a distinctly political aspect. On June 29 a quarrel broke out between some of them and a party of Massey's men at Sturminster Newton, and lives were lost on both sides.

---

good advantage, for he finds the country not well satisfied with their coming southward, and if the King's generals should give private order that no quarter be given to his Scots soldiers . . . which he confesses were but equal, the small number which he hath would be soon destroyed, and he should speedily be at the mercy of the English." Nicholas to Rupert, July 11. *Add. MSS.* 18,932, fol. 68.

[1] *The desires and resolutions of the Clubmen.* E. 292, 24.

[2] Answer of the Prince of Wales. *Clar. MSS.* 1,894.

[3] *Perfect Occurrences.* E. 262, 20.

No man living was better qualified than Fairfax to deal with such a movement. On July 2, when he was on his way to Blandford, he showed his determination to meet with fairness the only demand of the Clubmen of which it was possible to take account, by executing a soldier who was caught plundering. On the 3rd, when he reached Dorchester, he received a deputation from the Clubmen of Dorset. Their leader, Holles,[1] demanded a passport to enable him to present a petition to King and Parliament. In this petition the Clubmen asked that there should be a cessation of hostilities, that all soldiers who wished to return to their homes might be allowed to do so, and that they might themselves have the custody of all places in the county garrisoned by either party. In making these requests Holles spoke in a tone of menace. If they were rejected, he said, the Clubmen were strong enough to enforce obedience. Fairfax would soon be engaged with Goring. If he got the worst, every fugitive would be knocked on the head without mercy.

Fairfax answered with admirable temper. He desired peace, he said, as much as they did themselves. It appeared, however, from the King's letters taken at Naseby 'that contracts are already made for the bringing in of 10,000 French and 6,000 Irish.'[2] How could they ask him to agree to a cessation and to loose his hold on the port-towns at a time when a foreign invasion was expected? Good discipline was all that he could promise them, and with that they must be content. Fairfax's argument was enforced by the arrival of news that a body of Clubmen had been routed with some loss by the Governor of Lyme, and the Parliamentary army was allowed to continue its march without hindrance.[3]

The danger which Fairfax had apprehended from the western Royalists seemed less formidable as it was approached.

Marginal notes:
July 2. A soldier executed.
July 3. A deputation to Fairfax.
July 4. Fairfax replies.
A body of Clubmen routed.

---

[1] He was a brother of Thomas Holles, of Salisbury, who led the Wiltshire Clubmen.

[2] The numbers appear to be inverted.

[3] *Sprigg*, 61–66.

Their forces were without the coherence which discipline alone can give. The rapacity of the generals had alienated all but the King's most devoted partisans. In Devonshire the greedy and unscrupulous Grenvile, now recovered from his wound,[1] was placed in command of the troops blockading Plymouth. He used his authority to bring into his own hands the sequestered estates of the few Parliamentarian gentlemen of the county. The tenants soon learnt to regret the change. As a landlord he rack-rented them. As the King's officer he forced them to pay out of their own pockets every penny of the contribution to military purposes which had been laid on the estate. He insisted on keeping in his own hands the whole of the contribution of the county, though some of it might fairly have been spent in providing for the soldiers engaged in the siege of Taunton. Inoffensive Royalists who were rich enough to be fit subjects for his extortions were flung into gaol at Lidford, and one unlucky lawyer, whose only offence was that he had many years before taken part in a suit against the resentful tyrant, was hanged without mercy as a spy.

State of the King's army in the West.

Conduct of Sir Richard Grenvile.

At last, to the great joy of the whole neighbourhood, Grenvile was induced to leave the task of keeping watch over Plymouth to Sir John Berkeley, whose sterling qualities were in glaring contrast with the vices of the man whom he superseded. To Grenvile was assigned a post under Goring, which, however, gave him what was practically an independent command in East Devon. Yet it was impossible to satisfy him. Finding that his troops were less numerous than he wished them to be, he wrote to the Prince's secretary, demanding a court-martial on his conduct, or, as an alternative, permission to leave the country.[2]

June 29.

Goring's misconduct was no less glaring than Grenvile's. When he was not drinking or gambling, he spent his time in disputes with the Prince's council and with the commanders

---

[1] See p. 206.

[2] *Clarendon*, ix. 52, 59; Grenvile to Fanshaw, June 29; Grenvile to the Prince's council, July 3, *Clar. MSS.* 1,910, 1,911; Grenvile's Narrative, Carte's *Orig. Letters*, i. 96.

of the neighbouring garrisons. If he had any policy at all it was that of conciliating the Clubmen in order to induce them

and of
Goring to enrol themselves under him. He promised solemnly that if the contributions were duly paid he would allow no plundering, and in order to take hold of the popular imagination he requested that prayers might be offered in all the churches for the success of his undertakings. The simple peasants flocked to him with their contributions, only to find themselves plundered more cruelly than before. Yet he could not understand that he had alienated them past re-call. Abominably as he had behaved to the Clubmen, he again spoke fairly to them, and reproached Sir Francis Mack-worth, the Governor of Langport—who happened, it is true, to be one of his numerous personal enemies—with venturing to defend himself against their attack. At the same time he kept the garrison at Langport so straitened for provisions that it could only subsist by plunder, and was, even then, incapable of offering a prolonged resistance to the enemy.[1]

June 29.
He abandons all hope
of taking
Taunton.

July 4.
Fairfax
hears that
the siege is
raised. For some time, as his manner was, Goring had been boastfully confident of reducing Taunton. On June 29 he announced that, in consequence of the approach of the enemy, it would be necessary to retreat.[2] On July 4, on his arrival at Beaminster, Fairfax learned that the siege had, for the third and last time, been raised.[3]

Fairfax's march, like that of all the Parliamentary com-manders, had been deflected more to the south than any route

His line of
march.

July 5.
He comes
up with the
enemy.
Goring's
position. which a modern traveller would be likely to take, possibly in order to keep up his communications with the seaports of Weymouth and Lyme. He thus turned the defences on the line of the Yeo and Parret, the bridges over which rivers were entirely in Goring's hands. On the 5th, as he was pushing through Crewkerne, he first came in contact with the enemy,

[1] *Clarendon*, ix. 46.

[2] Goring to Culpepper, June 29. *Clar. MSS.* 1,909.

[3] *Sprigg*, 67. Sprigg calls this the raising of the siege for the second time, not counting the relief by Holborne.

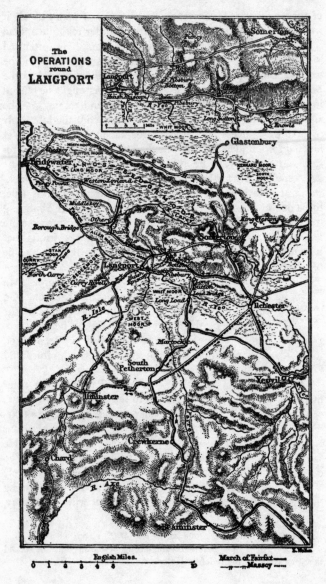

The
OPERATIONS
round
LANGPORT

English Miles.

March of Fairfax
Massey

and learnt that his opponent had taken up his position on the north bank of the two rivers. Goring would thus be in communication with the King, if Charles should by any possibility be able to advance to his succour ; whilst if he were compelled to retire by the road down the valley, guarded as it was by the fortifications of Langport and by a less important fort at Borough Bridge, he would have an easy way of retreat to the strongly guarded fortress of Bridgwater.

In the meanwhile the Royalist position was easily guarded against an attack from the south. The Yeo runs, during the greater part of its course, in a channel cut through the peat, which can only be crossed by bridges erected at the points where higher land projects towards the stream from either side. Such bridges were to be found at Ilchester and at Long Sutton, the one leading from the latter village being known as Load Bridge, while there was a third over the Parret at Langport below its junction with the Yeo. All three were held by Goring, the whole line from Ilchester to Langport being about seven miles in length.

Valley of the Yeo and the Parret.

Fairfax was hardly likely to succeed by a direct attack on an army nearly equal in numbers to his own, and so strongly posted. He resolved to outmanœuvre Goring rather than to storm his position. On the morning of the 7th, leaving a strong force near Ilchester and Load Bridge, as if he intended to force his way across the stream at one or other of these points, he despatched a strong body of foot to seize Yeovil, higher up the stream, where the enemy had contented himself with breaking down the bridge without occupying the town. In Goring there was no resourcefulness in danger, no grasp of a complicated situation as a connected whole. Making no attempt to throw himself upon any part of Fairfax's divided force, he at once gave up all hope of maintaining the line of the river. In the night of the 7th, as soon as he heard that Yeovil bridge had been repaired, he evacuated Long Sutton and Ilchester, thus leaving two more bridges over the Yeo free to Fairfax to cross at his pleasure. Yet he could not resolve upon the only practicable alternative policy of throwing himself into Bridgwater

July 7. Goring outmanœuvred.

His line forced.

to await relief.   Leaving a considerable part of his force at

July 8.
He attempts
to surprise
Taunton,

Langport, he galloped off on the morning of the 8th with a large body of cavalry towards Taunton, in the mere hope that he might be able to surprise the town, now that its garrison was thrown off its guard by the withdrawal of the besiegers.   Fairfax was too quick for him,

July 9.
but is sur-
prised by-
Massey.

and despatched Massey in pursuit.   Massey overtook him the next morning by the side of a stream near Ilminster where his men were bathing and disporting themselves, as if they had been out of the enemy's reach. They were soon scattered with heavy loss, and Goring, who had himself been wounded in the affair, fled back to Langport with such of his men as he could collect around him.

In the meanwhile Fairfax, having nothing now to gain by crossing the bridge at Yeovil, retraced his steps to Ilchester.

Fairfax
crosses the
Yeo.

Crossing the Yeo there, he pushed on to Long Sutton, on the north bank of the river, and found that Goring, who had by this time returned from his misadventure, had drawn up his army about a mile in advance of Langport, on a hill sloping down to Pisbury Bottom, a small marshy valley through which a little stream runs into the Yeo. There was some skirmishing in the evening, but it was not till the morning of the 10th that Fairfax advanced with his army to force the position.

The position was not ill chosen.   The lane along which Fairfax's horse would have to pass, to avoid the marshy ground

July 10.
The position
at Pisbury
Bottom.

on either side, led across the little stream by a deep but narrow ford, while the hedges on the slope of the hill beyond were lined by Goring's musketeers. Yet, strong as the ground was,[1] Fairfax had hardly any choice

---

[1] In the summer of 1887 I examined the ground in the company of the late Mr. F. H. Dickinson, of King Weston.   At present there are two bridges across the stream, one at the hamlet of Wagg, the other opposite Huish Episcopi lower down.   The slope of the hill is so slight at the latter place as to put out of the question the view that it was the scene of the battle, which I had adopted before examining the locality, having been misled by the dark shading of the Ordnance map.   The site of Wagg Bridge, to which Mr. Dickinson called my attention, answers every requirement. All the authorities except Baxter (*Reliquiæ Baxterianæ,* 54) describe a

but to fight. He did not know that the conditions were more favourable to him than they appeared to be. Goring had already sent off to Bridgwater his baggage and the whole of his artillery except two guns, and the Royalists would, therefore, enter upon the combat depressed by the knowledge that their commander had already determined upon a retreat, and that he now called on them to shed their blood for no visible object. His purpose could hardly have been merely to secure the passage of his stores, as, in that case, his obvious course would have been to send them with his whole force across the bridge at Langport, breaking it down after he had passed.

Whatever Goring might have done, Fairfax could not afford to decline the challenge. The battle commenced by a brisk

The Battle of Langport.

fire from the Parliamentary artillery, posted on the crest of the slope on the eastern side of the stream. Goring's two guns were soon silenced, and musketeers were then sent down to clear the hedges on either side of the ford. As soon as this had been accomplished it was possible for cavalry to charge. Yet even then a charge could only be executed at every possible disadvantage. The ford was deep and narrow, and the lane up the hill was scarcely less narrow. On the open ground at the top Goring's cavalry were collected in seemingly overwhelming numbers, ready to fall upon the thin stream of horsemen as they struggled up the lane before they had time to form.

Desperate as the enterprise appeared, the officers of the New Model army were never wanting in audacity. Major

ford and not a bridge, and as Baxter did not write till after the Restoration, his evidence on a point of this kind need not be taken into account. Whether there was a ford at Huish I have not been able to ascertain. Local tradition does not go very far back. It asserts, however, that the ground about the stream was once more boggy than it is now. The weather at the time of the battle had been hot and dry for some time, and the notion that the stream was swollen by rain is therefore a modern invention. The ford was probably across a deep hole with a natural or artificial hard bottom. The stream is now a very small one, and, as its course is short and it comes from comparatively high ground, it can hardly have had much more water in it in 1645 than it has at present.

Bethel, whose name stood high amongst the military saints, was ordered to make the perilous attempt at the head of a small force of 350 men, and Desborough, with another small force, was told off to second him.[1] Through the ford and up the narrow lane this handful of heroes charged. If an army equal in spirit and discipline to their own had been ranged on the heights, they could hardly have escaped destruction. As it was, they had to do with an enemy irresolute and fonder of plundering than of fighting. Bethel, when he arrived at the end of the lane, flew at a body of horse more than three times his number. He was checked at first, but Desborough soon arrived to his succour. Together they broke the regiments opposed to them, whilst at the same time the Parliamentary musketeers, stealing up amongst the hedges, poured a galling fire upon the enemy. The Royalists, horse and foot alike, turned and fled. A few troops of horse and a small force of musketeers had beaten the whole of Goring's army. No wonder that Cromwell, as from the opposite height he watched the dust-clouds rolling away, gave glory to God for this marvellous overthrow of His enemies, or that Harrison, the most enthusiastic of enthusiasts, broke 'forth into the praises of God with fluent expressions, as if he had been in a rapture.'

Then came the pursuit. Of the enemy's horse, some fled through Langport, setting fire to the town as they passed to cover their retreat. Cromwell was not to be stopped so easily. Charging through the burning street, he fell on them as they hurried across the bridge, where most of the fugitives were slain or captured. The larger part of the Royalists retreated by the northern bank of the Parret. Though they made a stand near Aller, they dared not await an attack from their pursuers. Goring's foot, entangled in the ditches of the moor, surrendered as the King's foot had sur-

The pursuit.

[1] Baxter complains that Bethel got the credit of the achievement because he was a sectary, and Evanson got no credit because he was not. But by Baxter's own showing Bethel was a major, and Evanson only a captain. Commanding officers usually, though sometimes unfairly, get more credit than their subordinates.

rendered at Naseby. His army, as an army capable of waging

July 11.
Goring
returns to
Barnstaple. war, ceased to exist. On the 11th, scantily attended, he retired to Barnstaple, leaving Bridgwater, as he hoped, in all points prepared to stand a siege.[1]

Unless Bridgwater could be taken the Battle of Langport had been fought in vain. The line of the Yeo and Parret Strength of
Bridgwater. could not be held without its possession. Yet the place was strong both by nature and art, and, as it might seem, beyond the reach even of Fairfax's victorious army. The first step to its capture was, however, taken on the 11th, The Club-
men satis-
fied. when Fairfax won over the Clubmen to his side by promises of that fair dealing and punctual payment which they could no longer expect from any Royalist commander. On the 13th the small fortress at Borough Bridge July 16.
Siege of
Bridgwater. surrendered to Okey, and on the 16th, every other suggestion having been rejected as impracticable, it July 21.
The eastern
suburb
taken was resolved to storm the fortifications. In the early morning of the 21st the attack was made on the quarter of the town lying on the east of the Parret. The ditch was speedily crossed on portable bridges, and the wall scaled in the teeth of a stout resistance. The assailants rushed for the drawbridge and let it down. The Parliamentary horse poured in, and the conquest of the eastern suburb was accomplished.

The defenders of the western and more important part of the town, on the other side of the Parret, still held out vigorously. They were resolved that, although Fairfax had gained and burnt
by the
Royalists. the suburb, he should hold no more than its fortifications. Grenades and red-hot shot poured upon the houses. By the morning of the 22nd the place was, July 22. with the exception of three or four houses, reduced to ashes. Always averse to bloodshed, Fairfax summoned the western town to surrender, and on the rejection of his offer

---

[1] *Sprigg*, 71 ; *An exact and perfect relation of the proceedings of the army*, E. 292, 28 ; *A true relation of a victory*, E. 292, 30 ; *A more full relation of the great battle*, E. 293, 3 ; Cromwell to ——? Carlyle's *Cromwell* (ed. 1866), iii. App. No. 8 ; *The Parliament's Post*, E. 293, 2 ; Fairfax to the Speaker of the House of Lords, July 12, *L.J.* vii. 496.

by the governor, Sir Hugh Wyndham, he suspended his attack till the women and children had been sent out beyond reach of danger. Then at length Fairfax's cannon began to play upon the town with grenades and hot shot, as the Royalists' artillery had played on the eastern suburb two days before. The frightened citizens allowed the governor no peace till he gave up a contest of which their property was to bear the burden, and on the morning of the 23rd Fairfax was in possession of a fortress which the Royalists had believed capable of prolonged resistance,[1] and to which they had looked to keep in check the New Model in the West till Charles had gathered sufficient strength to enable him to take the field once more in the Midlands with effect.

The western town summoned, and attacked.

July 23. Its surrender.

The material acquisitions of the victorious army were very great. Large stores of ordnance and ammunition, together with considerable stores of provisions, were captured in the town. It was of even greater importance that Fairfax was now in possession of a chain of fortresses from Lyme through Langport to Bridgwater, which, with the advanced post at Taunton, would enable him to hold in check the Royalist troops still in the field in the western peninsula. He would thus be free to devote himself to service elsewhere, and to make it impossible for the King again to hold up his head in England. He was not likely to repeat the blunder of Essex, and to march into Cornwall with an enemy unconquered in his rear.

Stores captured in Bridgwater.

Chain of fortresses held by Fairfax.

The capture of Bridgwater had indeed been a heavy blow to Charles. Whilst Fairfax had been fighting in Somerset, the King had been attempting to raise an army in South Wales which would redress the balance of the war on the Parret. On July 1 he reached Abergavenny. He had already received promises from the gentry of Herefordshire to levy troops for the new campaign, and the

July 1. Charles at Abergavenny.

---

[1] *Sprigg*, 26 ; *Sir T. Fairfax entering Bridgwater*, E. 293, 27 ; *Three great Victories*, E. 293, 32 ; *The continuation of the proceedings of the army*, E. 293, 33 ; *A fuller relation from Bridgwater*, E. 293, 34 ; *Goring to Digby, July* 12, *Warburton*, iii. 137.

gentry of South Wales now flocked in with similar promises.[1]

July 3.
He moves
to Raglan.
On the 3rd he betook himself to Raglan Castle to await the result. In that magnificent palace-fortress of the Herberts he was received with stately courtesy by the old Marquis of Worcester, whose son Glamorgan had constituted himself Charles's knight-errant, and was already on the way to do his bidding in Ireland. To those who judged by the outward appearance, Charles's stay at Raglan was but a waste of precious time. In reality his days were spent in active negotiation with the Welsh, and in eager preparation for the days of activity to which he looked. He could not understand how hard it is to rally men round a defeated cause, and

He hears
bad news
from
Langport.
when the bad news from Langport surprised him whilst the Welsh levies were still hanging back, he had to learn with difficulty that each additional disaster makes recovery harder than before. At a council of war held on the 13th it was resolved still to struggle on. Goring was to be encouraged to hold out in Devonshire. As long as Bristol and Bridgwater were held for the King, it would always be possible for Charles's army, when it was at last complete, to move to the succour of the West.[2]

Whilst Charles continued at Raglan disappointment followed disappointment. In Herefordshire, where an attempt had been made to press men for his service, the new levies

Desertion
of Charles's
levies.
deserted almost as soon as they were raised. In Wales things were little better. The gentry promised fairly, but ordinary Welshmen had little enthusiasm for a falling cause. Few offered themselves willingly, and though compulsion was not without effect, the pressed men took every opportunity of running away.[3] As time passed, Charles, rather than continue in inaction, was inclined to cross the Severn with what forces he was able to muster, and to attach himself to Goring.

Before taking a final resolution, Charles thought it well to

[1] *Clarendon*, ix. 67.

[2] Digby to Rupert, July 13. *Warburton*, iii. 141.

[3] *Clarendon*, ix. 67 ; Digby to Ormond, Aug. 2, Carte's *Ormond*, vi. 306.

confer with Rupert. The meeting took place at Blackrock, at the northern end of the New Passage. On the whole,

July 22.
Charles con-
fers with
Rupert.

Rupert approved of the design, though he refused to be answerable for its success.[1] In fact, Charles's position at Raglan, if the new levies failed him, would soon be untenable. Leven's army was now in the neighbourhood of Worcester, and it would shortly be reinforced by a body of 1,200 horse under David Leslie, which had been set free from service in the North by the surrender of Carlisle.[2] It is probable that Rupert's military judgment had already convinced him that victory was no longer attainable, and that in faintly recommending Charles to try what he could do in Somerset, he meant little more than to indicate his opinion that the final defeat might as well take place in one part of England as in another.

It was therefore arranged that Charles should in a few days betake himself to Bristol, and that from Bristol he should

The King
to go to the
West.

July 24.
He changes
his mind,
and hears
that Bridg-
water is
taken.

make his way to Bridgwater. On the 24th he returned to Blackrock to cross the ferry. The Welsh gentry, however, gathered round him, and urged him to rely on their help. His vacillating mind was already giving way, when tidings that Bridgwater had fallen the day before arrived to strengthen their arguments. On the edge of the water a council was held, and Charles, drawing back from what had now become an evidently hopeless enterprise, rode off to discover whether Welsh promises could be better trusted than before.[3] In a few days he would have to defend himself against Fairfax as well as against Leven.

---

[1] *Clarendon*, ix. 68 ; *Symonds*, 210.

[2] *The Kingdom's Weekly Intelligencer.* E. 293, I.

[3] *Clarendon*, ix. 68 ; *Symonds*, 211.

CHAPTER XXXIII.

ALFORD AND KILSYTH.

EACH successive failure only made Charles turn with fresh confidence to some new scheme as hopeless as the last. He

1645.
July.
An invita-
tion from
the North. now thought of taking up again the plan which had miscarried in May. The gentlemen of the North had long been pressing for aid. Pontefract and Scarborough—so at least it was believed in the King's quarters—occupied the forces of the enemy. Charles had cavalry enough to spare, and the gentry of Yorkshire assured him that, if only he would bring cavalry with him to give consistency to their levies, they would soon raise an army in his service.[1] Means would thus be found

Charles
thinks of
sending
Langdale, of opening communications with Montrose and of forcing a way into Scotland. At the time when Charles was bent upon a combination with Goring,

and of
going in
person. he had directed Langdale to carry out this suggestion.[2] Now, when this project was abandoned, he inclined to go in person. On the 28th the encouraging news reached him that Montrose had won yet another victory.

Even after his success at Auldearn, Montrose had to contend against forces numerically superior to his own. The

May.
Montrose
eludes
Baillie, cautious Baillie, leaving the plunder of Blair Athol, crossed the Dee with some 2,000 men, and was joined near Strathbogie by Hurry with a hundred horse, the poor remains of the host defeated at Auldearn.

---

[1] Digby to Ormond, Aug. 2, Carte's *Ormond*, vi. 306; Rupert to Lennox, July 28. *Warburton*, iii. 149.

[2] Note of the King's letter to Langdale, July 19, in Yonge's Diary, *Add. MSS.* 18,780, fol. 148.

Montrose's own force was, as usual after success, sadly diminished by the desertion of the Highlanders. He was therefore in little case to fight, especially as he knew that Lindsay, who, in consequence of the Parliamentary forfeiture of his kinsman's earldom of Crawford, now bore that title in addition to his own, was advancing from the southern Lowlands with a newly-raised force. He therefore determined to shift his quarters.

CAMPAICN of ALFORD

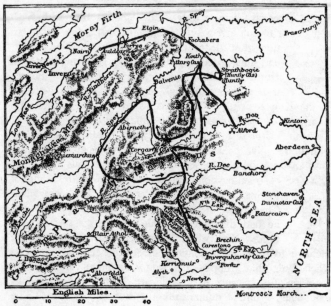

Outmarching and outmanœuvring Baillie, he mounted the valley of the Spey and took up a position so strong that Baillie did not venture to attack him. Before long the Covenanting general was driven by scarcity of food to betake himself first to Inverness and then to the country to the east of the Spey, where Hurry left him under the pretext of indisposition.

Having thus shaken himself free of Baillie, Montrose

dashed at Lindsay,[1] who was gathering another army in
Forfarshire. Lindsay, whose troops were still undisciplined,
but dashes had no mind to pit them against Montrose's vete-
at Lindsay. rans, and he therefore drew back to Newtyle.
Montrose was eager for the fray, but was unexpectedly
Desertion of deserted by the greater part of the Gordons.
the Gordons. Huntly, it was said, had taken this way of showing
his jealousy of Montrose. It is more probable that he was
alarmed at Baillie's approach. However this may have been,
Huntly's feelings were not shared by his heir. To the young
Lord Gordon Montrose was an ideal hero, whose every word
and glance he treasured and whose every command he obeyed
with unquestioning devotion. But for Montrose, Lord Gordon
would have dealt out summary vengeance on the deserters.
Montrose knew that it was better to endure all things rather
than to convert his own unintentional rivalry with the head of
the Gordons into a death-feud with those who bore that name.

Men from one source or another Montrose must have.
He sent Alaster Macdonald to the Highland glens to gather
together the runaways and to collect new levies.
June. Colonel Nathaniel Gordon was despatched to
Fresh forces
levied. Huntly's country on the same errand, and Lord
Gordon, as soon as his blood had cooled, was allowed to
follow him. Montrose, planting himself with his scanty force
in a secluded spot where the ruins of Corgarff Castle looked
upon the head waters of the Don, and where the mountains
offered a shelter near at hand, quietly awaited the reinforcements.

Few as were Montrose's followers for the time, he was at
least master in his own camp. The like could not be said of
Baillie. The Committee of Estates, of which Argyle
Baillie dis-
trusted by was the leading spirit, distrusted his slow and
the Estates. methodical method of warfare, and they were perhaps reasonably alarmed at Lindsay's inability to take the
field. They ordered Baillie to surrender more than 1,000

---

[1] As the new title was not acknowledged by the King, it is better to
keep to the old style, especially as it is necessary to distinguish him from
his relative the Royalist Earl of Crawford.

veterans to Lindsay, receiving merely 400 recruits from him in exchange.[1] If Lindsay, with his ranks thus stiffened, had co-operated with Baillie against Montrose, there would have been something to say for the proceeding. Lindsay, however, retreated southward and threw himself upon Athol, where he wasted and destroyed whatever had escaped Baillie's torches a month before.[2] Baillie was ordered to remain in the North to ravage Huntly's lands and, if possible, to reduce his castles.[3]

Separation of Baillie and Lindsay.

Montrose had by this time been rejoined by Lord Gordon, bringing back the deserters to their duty. With a weakened enemy before him, Montrose felt himself sure of victory, and though Macdonald was still absent, he marched in search of Baillie. Finding him strongly posted at Keith, he did his best to allure him out of his fastness by bidding him to come down to fight on the level ground. "I will not fight," was the reply, "to please the enemy." If Baillie could not be taunted into fighting, he could be manœuvred into it. Marching deliberately southwards, Montrose crossed the Don and established himself at Alford. Baillie could not but follow unless he wished to leave the road to the Lowlands open.

Montrose offers battle near Keith.

July 1. Montrose at Alford.

On the morning of July 2 Montrose drew up his army for battle. Wishing to lure Baillie on, he placed the greater part of his men, as he had himself done at Auldearn, and as Fairfax had done at Naseby, behind the crest of the hill. There was the more reason for the concealment now, as the river Don flowed between him and Baillie. If Baillie could be induced to cross it by the only practicable ford, he would be compelled to pass first over some rough ground, and then over a piece of boggy land,[4]

July 2. Disposition of the forces.

---

[1] According to Wishart 1,000 were given on each side, but Baillie says he had to give up three regiments, one of which was 1,200, and four or five companies besides 100 horse, and only received 400 foot in exchange. [2] See p. 227.

[3] *Wishart*, ch. xi. ; Baillie's Narrative, *Baillie*, ii. 419.

[4] "A tergo" (*i.e.* in Montrose's rear), writes Wishart, "erat locus palustris, fossis stagnisque impeditus, ne ab equitatu circumveniretur."

before he could reach the dry slope which led up to Montrose's position. After surmounting these difficulties, he would

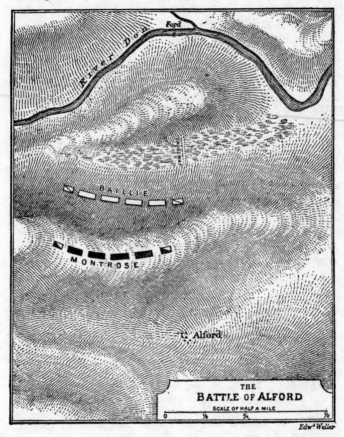

THE
BATTLE OF ALFORD
SCALE OF HALF A MILE
0   ⅛   ¼   ½

Edwᵈ Weller

have to charge up-hill, and, in the event of a defeat, his army,

Nothing of the kind exists or is likely to have existed. Mr. Farquharson, who conducted me over the battle-field, told me that the ground had been marshy at some distance to the south-east of Montrose's position, but this spot is too far off to have had the effect which Wishart ascribes to it. The real bog, which is even still wet in rainy weather and across which the old causeway is still discernible, is not mentioned by any authority.

with a bog and a river behind, could hardly escape annihilation.[1] It is impossible to speak of the numbers engaged on either side with even an approach to accuracy ; but it is on the whole probable that the foot of the two armies were nearly equal, whilst the superiority in horse was on the side of the Covenanters.

It has been said that Baillie, conscious of danger, hesitated to cross the river, but that Balcarres, confident in the superiority of the cavalry which was under his own command,[2] insisted on pushing forward. Montrose, being informed by a party which he had sent in advance of the enemy's approach and arrangements, drew up his infantry in the centre, and giving the horse on the left to Aboyne, placed Lord Gordon on the right. This time he repeated the tactics of Aberdeen, assigning to the horse on either wing an infantry force to support them if they found themselves in difficulties.[3] One part of the Irish infantry, under O'Cahan and Colonel Macdonald—Alaster being absent—was assigned to Aboyne ; whilst the other part, under Nathaniel Gordon, was directed to support Lord Gordon. The infantry in the centre was composed partly of Huntly's tenants from the Lowlands, partly

[1] " The Don . . . is fordable almost everywhere in its course when the river is in its ordinary state." Alexander Smith, *Hist. of Aberdeenshire*, i. 212. Mr. Farquharson, however, assured me that this is not the case, and that it was even less true in former times than it is now.

[2] These are Wishart's figures : 2,000 foot on both sides, with 600 horse under Baillie, and 250 under Montrose. Baillie, however, says that the Royalists 'were a little above our strength in horsemen, and twice as strong in foot.' This is, however, probably the exaggeration of a beaten man. He says that when he parted from Lindsay he was left with 'betwixt twelve and thirteen hundred foot and about two hundred and sixty horsemen.' It seems unlikely that after he marched further north he should not have been joined by the Covenanting gentry, who, after the devastation of their lands, were bitterly hostile to Montrose. Patrick Gordon makes Montrose's horse 200, and gives to Balcarres on the Royalist left 300, and an undescribed number on the other wing. Guthry speaks of the numbers being ' very unequal,' implying that they were greatest on Baillie's side.

[3] That Montrose should have done this is some evidence of his inferiority in cavalry.

of Farquharsons and of the Highlanders from Badenoch who acknowledged Huntly's sway.

For some time the battle raged with little apparent success on either side. Lord Gordon succeeded in breaking the enemy's horse at the first charge, but they were quickly rallied by Balcarres, who was personally in command of the horse on Baillie's left wing. At last Nathaniel Gordon called on his musketeers to throw down their guns, to draw their swords, and to stab or hough the enemy's horses. The movement was decisive, Balcarres' horse quailed and gave way, whilst the Covenanting horse on the other wing joined their comrades in flight. Baillie's foot, taken in flank by the victorious cavalry like the King's infantry at Naseby, were slaughtered as they stood. No quarter was given by the followers of O'Cahan and Macdonald. After the last charge the gallant heir of the Gordons was struck down mortally wounded by a shot from behind him. The joy of the victors was changed into mourning. His youth, his constancy of purpose, and his winning courtesy had endeared him to the whole army, and most of all to Montrose.[1]

The Battle of Alford.

The good news from Alford made no slight impression in Charles's quarters. "It is certain," wrote Digby, "that the King's enemies have not any man in the field now in Scotland."[2] As Charles's prospects grew darker Digby's influence increased. His adventurous activity dragged along with it Charles's passive resolution. With Digby every gleam of hope was as the rising of the day-star, every fresh disaster a mere unfortunate accident to be banished from the memory. He shared with Charles that trust in the success of incongruous projects which contributed so much to the destruction of the Royal cause.

July 28. Reception of the news in the King's quarters.

Digby's influence over Charles.

Sanguine as Charles and Digby were, they had need of all their courage in the face of misfortunes for which the

---

[1] *Wishart*, ch. ix. ; *Patrick Gordon*, 128–135 ; Baillie's Narrative in *Baillie's Letters and Journals*, ii. 409.

[2] Digby to Rupert, July 28. *Add. MSS.* 18,982, fol. 74.

distant success of Alford could hardly compensate. On the

July 21.
Surrender of
Pontefract,

21st Pontefract surrendered, and on the 25th Scarborough Castle was handed over to its besiegers.[1]

July 25.
and of Scarborough
Castle.

On the 30th Leven's army, passing round Worcester, sat down before Hereford, with every prospect of being able to reduce the city.[2] What was still worse

July 30.
Siege of
Hereford.

was that the hopes raised by the Welsh gentry at Blackrock had proved illusive. On the 25th, indeed,

July 25.
Offers in
Monmouth-
shire.

the gentlemen of Monmouthshire[3] met Charles at Usk, and offered the whole adult male population of the county for local defence and a select number of

July 30.
Application
to the gentry
of Glamor-
gan.

960 for general service.[4] When, however, Charles, pleased with his success at Usk, moved on to Cardiff and applied to the gentry of Glamorgan for 2,000

men, the answer which he received was less satisfactory than he had expected. The gentlemen appeared with a following of some three or four thousand countrymen, in whose name

The answer
of the men of
Glamorgan.

they replied that they were ready 'to defend the Protestant religion, the law of the land, his Majesty's just prerogative, the privilege of Parliament, and

property of the subject,' but that if they took arms it must be under officers of their own county, who would defend them against plunderers. Further, in the assessment of their contribution, regard must be had to their poverty, the payment of arrears must not be demanded, and the obligation to entertain soldiers at free quarter must be limited to a single night. The King might protest as much as he pleased against a resolution which gave him little money and a force which was hardly more than a local militia, but he could not obtain its modification.[5]

Depressing as was the discovery of the lukewarmness of Wales, the absence of any satisfactory intelligence from Ireland

[1] *Rushw.* vi. 118.

[2] *Ibid.* vi. 122.

[3] Practically Monmouthshire may be counted as Welsh.

[4] The King's propositions, July 25. *Harl. MSS.* 6,852, fol. 302.

[5] The King's demands with the answer of the inhabitants, July 30. *Harl. MSS.* 6,852, fol. 305–309. *Walker,* 117.

was no less depressing. Ormond had nothing to tell of any near chance of concluding peace, and Glamorgan, if he really

No good news from Ireland.

started for Dublin in June, had been delayed for some cause now unknown, and only reached his destination in August. On July 31, Charles, having

July 31. Charles sends for Ormond.

apparently abandoned the hope of obtaining an Irish army, wrote to Ormond directing him to come in person to England, bringing with him whatever troops he could muster, and to leave Ireland to its fate.[1]

Not long before, Charles had received an overture from an unexpected quarter. Between the English Parliament and the

Ill-feeling between Parliament and the Scottish army.

Scottish army there was an increasing feeling of mutual dissatisfaction. The Parliament complained that the army had accomplished little or nothing since the reduction of Newcastle, and that the in-

habitants of the districts in which it happened to be present suffered grievously from its exactions. The Scots complained that Parliament had broken its engagements, and that, whilst money could easily be found for Fairfax, it could scarcely ever be found for Leven. The aggrieved Scots were strengthened in their wish to come to terms with the King; whilst the fanaticism of those of them who were convinced Presbyterians, and the worldliness of those who had adopted the defence of the Covenant from merely political motives, combined to hinder any true perception of the real obstacle in the way of an understanding with Charles, his unbending and conscien-

July 21. Overtures from Scottish lords to the King.

tious devotion to episcopacy. On July 21 certain Scottish lords in Leven's army, Callander, Sinclair, Montgomery, and Lothian, attempted to open a communication with the King through Callander's

nephew, Sir William Fleming, who was at that time with Charles at Raglan. An attempt made by them to obtain from Leven permission for Fleming to visit the Scottish camp failed, probably in consequence of the general's reluctance to compromise himself. The lords nevertheless contrived on August 5 to hold a secret meeting with Fleming beyond the reach of Leven.

[1] The King to Ormond, July 31. Carte's *Ormond*, vi. 305.

As far as general promises were concerned, Fleming's words
were all that could be desired.   Charles, he told them, was

Aug. 5.
Fleming's
assurances
fail to secure
assent.

anxious 'to bring the matter to an honourable treaty
with the Scots.'   His instructions, however, were to
promise nothing definite,[1] and even if the nobles
could have been won over by an engagement so
vague, Leven was not to be gained.   When at a later time
Digby wrote to urge him to come to terms with the King, he
forwarded the letter to the English Parliament.[2]

In fact, the real obstacle to an understanding came from
the King.   The Scots insisted on the establishment of Presby-

Digby urges
the King to
give hopes
about Pres-
byterianism.

terian government in England.   Digby had tried
hard to induce Charles—not indeed to abandon
episcopacy—but to make the Scots believe that he
was ready to discuss its abandonment.   "Thus
much," he wrote to Jermyn, "I must necessarily tell you that,
unless we allow the Scots, without engagement, to hope that
the King may possibly be brought in time to harken unto such
a change of government at least by referring it to a synod,
there is no hope that ever they will be brought so much as to
a parley with us, wherein if once skilfully engaged by letting
them promise themselves what the King will never promise
them, we shall find means so to entangle them as that it shall
be impossible for them ever to get off again."   Unhappily, he
continued, the King's constancy to his religion was such 'as
none can possibly prevail with him so much as to act his part
in letting them swallow any hopes, though he give them not.'[3]

It was not likely that Charles would yield to Digby's
temptation, at all events for the present.   His whole mind is
disclosed in a correspondence which he was carrying on with

---

[1] The documents relating to this affair are printed in *L.J.* vii. 513.
In Yonge's Diary (*Add. MSS.* 18,780, fol. 157) there are notes of a letter
written on July 29 by the Scottish Lords to Fleming, and also of one from
Digby to Fleming on Aug. 5, from which latter the words quoted above
are taken.   We also learn from this source that Fleming's instructions
were to win over the Scots, but to promise nothing definite.

[2] *L.J.* vii. 638.

[3] Digby to Jermyn, Aug. 5.   *Bankes MSS.*

Rupert contemporaneously with this abortive negotiation. On July 28 Rupert wrote to Richmond begging him to dissuade the King from his project of marching to the North. If he were asked, he continued, what better proposal he had to make, his only advice would be to conclude peace. "His Majesty," he urged, "hath now no way left to preserve his posterity, kingdom, and nobility but by treaty. I believe it a more prudent way to retain something than to lose all." At all events let all further negotiation with the Irish be abandoned, now that they had shown themselves to be unreasonable.[1]

July 28. Rupert urges Charles to make peace.

Richmond, as Rupert expected, showed the letter to Charles, and Charles replied directly to his nephew. "As for your opinion of my business," he wrote, "and your counsel thereupon, if I had any other quarrel but the defence of my religion, crown and friends, you had full reason for your advice ; for I confess that, speaking as a mere soldier or statesman, I must say there is no probability but of my ruin : yet, as a Christian, I must tell you that God will not suffer rebels and traitors to prosper, nor this cause to be overthrown ; and whatever personal punishment it shall please Him to inflict upon me, must not make me repine, much less give over this quarrel ; and there is as little question that a composition with them at this time is nothing else but a submission, which, by the grace of God, I am resolved against, whatever it cost me ; for I know my obligation to be both in conscience and honour, neither to abandon God's cause, injure my successors, nor forsake my friends. Indeed I cannot flatter myself with expectation of good success more than this, to end my days with honour and a good conscience ; which obliges me to continue my endeavours, as not despairing that God may yet in due time avenge His own cause ; though I must aver to all my friends that he that will stay with me at this time, must expect and resolve either to die for a good cause, or—which is worse—to live as miserable in maintaining it as the violence of insulting rebels can make him." Low as he was, continued Charles, he would never go beyond the

Aug. 3. Charles rejects the proposal.

[1] Rupert to Richmond, July 28. *Warburton*, iii. 149.

terms offered by him at Uxbridge. "As for the Irish," he added, "I assure you they shall not cheat me ; but it is possible they may cozen themselves : for, be assured, what I have refused to the English I will not grant to the Irish rebels, never trusting to that kind of people—of what nation soever—more than I see by their actions ; and I am sending to Ormond such a despatch as I am sure will please you and all honest men." [1]

These words were the highest of which Charles was capable until he came to translate word into action on the scaffold.

Charles prepares for martyrdom.

He saw his own resolution in the light of a Divine will strengthening and comprehending it. His fixed determination to suffer all and to allow, as far as in him lay, the whole English world to fall into ruin rather than abandon his witness for God's cause would in the end be stronger than Rupert's military perception of the hopelessness of resistance. The Church, in spite of all that had happened, was more large-minded and more suited to the religious needs of a sober, unenthusiastic people than either the Presbyterian or the Independent system could possibly be. As long as Charles lived, its leaders, estimable and conscientious as they might be, could never hope to recover their lost ground. A nation after the storm of a civil war craves for something which has at least the appearance of stability, and Charles with his incapacity to understand the needs of his times, his fondness for intrigue, and his habit of explaining away his engagements, could offer no stability in Church or State. One service alone, a service beyond price, could Charles offer to the Church, and that was to die for it. The Church needed a martyr to replace the memories of Laud, and to appeal to that vein of enthusiasm which exists even in the most realistic natures. Nothing short of death would suffice. Captivity and suffering would leave Charles what he had been before. The impression which he would make on his contemporaries would be that of a prisoner who was always trying to outwit his gaolers, and always trying

---

[1] The King to Rupert, Aug. 3. *Rushw.* vi. 132. I have adopted one correction from the copy printed in *Clarendon*, ix. 70 ; but that given by Rushworth seems from internal evidence the more accurate of the two.

in vain. As long as he lived it was impossible to fix greatness upon him. If, in an evil hour for their own cause, those who held him down should deprive him of life, all these petty details of his vexed existence would be forgotten, and the one fact of his persistent refusal to buy back his crown and his life at the price of a surrender of his Church would alone be remembered.

Whatever the future might bring with it, South Wales no longer afforded a place of refuge to Charles. At the end of
Aug. 1.
Laugharne
defeats
Stradling, July the Parliamentary commander Laugharne inflicted a crushing defeat upon Sir Edward Stradling and the Royalists of Pembrokeshire. On the 5th he
Aug. 5.
and storms
the Castle
of Haver-
fordwest. stormed the castle of Haverfordwest.[1] The blow fell the heavier as all the country between Pembrokeshire and Raglan was honeycombed with disaffection. Sir Charles Gerard, who had been in command for the King, had made himself detested by the harshness of his con-
Complaints
against
Gerard. duct, and the men of Glamorgan followed up their refusal to give Charles the troops which he needed by thrusting themselves into his presence and compelling him to listen to a long tirade against his officer. Gerard replied by bitter taunts against the Welshmen, and Charles, whose interests were lost sight of in the quarrel, could but sit
Gerard
dismissed
and raised
to the
peerage. by in silence. In the end Gerard was removed from the command, and an attempt was made to console him by the grant of a peerage. A peerage, however, in the distressed condition of the monarchy, was but little consolation for the loss of active employment, and the new Lord Gerard continued to bear a grudge against the King
He is suc-
ceeded by
Astley. who had displaced him from his post. His successor was Astley, who had been created Lord Astley at the end of the preceding year. The new commander was likely to do his best to organise the country without giving offence to anyone ; but he could not undo the past, and he soon discovered that it was impossible again to raise the South Welsh to any enthusiasm for the King.[2]

[1] *A true relation of the late success.* E. 298, 6
[2] *Walker,* 117.

By this time Charles had made up his mind to march northwards in search of tidings from Montrose. On August 5

Aug. 5.
Charles
leaves
Cardiff. he set out from Cardiff. On the road he sent an order to the Prince of Wales to convey himself to France if in no other way he could avoid capture.[1] Taking a route amongst the Welsh mountains, he escaped observation, and turning to the right as soon as he was out of reach of the Parliamentary forces, at last reached Welbeck on

Aug. 15.
The King
at Wel-
beck. the 15th. Welbeck had lately been retaken by the Royalists, and after resting there and holding a conference with Sir Richard Willis, the governor of Newark, Charles continued his march, arriving on the 18th at

Aug 18.
He reaches
Doncaster. Doncaster. He had brought with him 2,200 horse and 400 foot.[2] His hopes were once more raised. The Yorkshire gentlemen flocked in to offer their services. He might expect soon to be again at the head of an army. His condition, he wrote to Nicholas, considering what it had been at the beginning of the month, was 'miraculously good.'[3]

Two days later all this hopefulness had passed away. Major General Poyntz, who had just reduced Scarborough Castle, had

Aug. 20.
His retreat. gathered the Parliamentary forces of the county to oppose the King's advance, and David Leslie had been despatched from Hereford with 4,000 horse, the whole of Leven's cavalry, with orders to follow his steps. Leslie had now reached Rotherham, and if Charles remained at Doncaster much longer he would be taken between the two forces. To await the gathering of the Royalist levies would therefore be to court destruction, and with a heavy heart he gave the order to retreat.[4]

In his desperation, Charles resolved to make a dash at the Associated Counties. He marched hurriedly forward, fearing

---

[1] The King to the Prince, Aug. 5, *Clarendon*, ix. 74.

[2] *Iter Carolinum*; *Symonds*, 225. See map at p. 255.

[3] The King to Nicholas, Aug. 18, *Evelyn's Memoirs* (ed. Bohn), iv. 159.

[4] *Walker*, 135; *Slingsby's Diary*, 158; *Baillie*, ii. 309; The Com. of B. K. to Leven, Aug. 15, *Com. Letter Book.*

to be overtaken by David Leslie, whom he believed to be
hastening after him. When he reached Huntingdon on the

He makes
for the
Associated
Counties.

24th, surprise was expressed in his court that nothing
had been heard of Leslie. Before long it was known
that the Scotchman had a more dangerous enemy

Aug. 24.
Charles
hears from
Montrose.

to cope with. Montrose had won a victory by the
side of which the glories of Auldearn and Alford
paled, and which to all appearance had finally decided
the fate of Scotland.[1]

On July 8, six days after the Battle of Alford, the Scottish
Parliament met at Stirling. With the exception of Lindsay's

July 8.
The Scottish
Parliament
at Stirling.

small army, there was no longer any force to oppose
to the victorious Montrose, the appearance of whose
host in the South would be the irruption of a horde
of plunderers without pay, without a commissariat, and without
even the lax system of military taxation by which the Royalist

A new army
to be levied.

armies in England were supported. The Parliament
therefore resolved to levy a force of 8,800 foot and
485 horse from the counties south of the Tay, and called upon
the noblemen and gentry of those counties to place themselves
at its head. Baillie, who had had some experience of the self-

Baillie's
resignation
not
accepted.

will of the Scottish nobility and gentry, tendered his
resignation. Parliament, after voting a formal approval of his past services, ordered him temporarily
to retain his command. The new army, raw and untrained,
was to rendezvous at Perth on July 24.[2] Its only chance of
safety lay in strict subordination to military command, whether
that command was left to Baillie or was given to some abler
general. If, as seemed but too probable, Baillie was to be
accompanied by a crowd of noblemen, each of them proud of
his military skill in proportion to his ignorance, the disaster of
Aberdeen would be repeated on a larger scale.

Some respite the Covenanting levies were to be allowed.

Montrose
after Alford.

Montrose's Highlanders had hurried back to their
glens with the plunder of Alford. Macdonald had
not yet returned from his recruiting expedition, and Aboyne,

---

[1] Digby to Jermyn, Sept. 4. *S.P. Dom.* dx. 90.
[2] *Acts of the Parl. of Scotl.* vi. 429-437.

now heir to the marquisate of Huntly, had been sent to his
father's estates to gather fresh recruits.　When Aboyne joined
Montrose he brought with him a band so scanty that
he was sent back to increase his numbers.　It is
probable, though there is no evidence to adduce,
that the Gordons shrank from advancing into the South of
Scotland, as they had shrunk at the time of the capture of
Dundee.　It was not only amongst the Highlanders that the
local spirit prevailed.

A scanty re-
inforcement
of Gordons.

On the other hand, the more untamed elements of Montrose's army received support by the coming in of Macdonald
with 1,400 Highlanders.　A few of these were from
Badenoch and Braemar, but the greater part were
from the wilder tribes of the West, the Macdonalds
of Glengarry and Clanranald, the Macleans, the Macgregors,
and the Macnabs.　At the same time Patrick Graham brought
in the men of Athol.　Montrose, who had for some time awaited
these reinforcements at Fordoun, was ready to start southwards
before the end of July.

A large
increase of
High-
landers.

Already on July 24 the Parliament had transferred itself to
Perth to watch over the arrival of the new levies.　Montrose's
object was to disturb them as far as it was possible
to do so.　Having but eighty of the Gordon horse
with him, he mounted a body of infantry on his own
baggage horses and on the cart-horses of the neighbourhood, so as to create the impression that he had
a considerable cavalry force at his disposal.　Though the
stratagem might serve as long as the armies were at some distance from one another, it would not avail in the stress of battle,
and Montrose was therefore obliged to content himself with
manœuvring round Perth without making any attempt to bring
on a general engagement.　In the skirmishes which followed
the advantage was always on his side, and when at last he retreated the soldiers of the Covenant consoled themselves by
butchering a bevy of women, wives or followers of Montrose's
men, whom they lit upon in Methven Wood, not far from
Perth.　As at Naseby, the notion of avenging injured morality

July 24.
The Parlia-
ment at
Perth.

Montrose
manœuvres
round Perth.

Campaign of
KILSYTH

Montrose's March

ENGLISH MILES

E. Weller.

probably covered from the eyes of the murderers the inherent brutality of their act.[1]

The ill-starred Baillie would gladly have thrown off the responsibility of coming failure. Not only were his troops for

Baillie's forebodings.

the most part mere raw levies, ill suited to cope with the hardy clansmen of Montrose, but he was himself subjected to a committee which hampered him at every turn, and the members of which frequently quarrelled

Aug. 5. Baillie compelled to remain as general.

with one another. On August 5 he again offered his resignation, and again reluctantly gave way on the assurance that the committee would content itself with the general direction of the war, and that he should be left to his own judgment in carrying out the orders which he received.[2]

Montrose was not long in reappearing. Aboyne had joined him at Dunkeld with a strong body of horse and foot,[3] and at

Aboyne joins Montrose.

the same time the old Earl of Airlie rode in with eighty horsemen, for the most part of the name and race of Ogilvy. Montrose knew that Lanark was raising against him the Hamilton tenants in Clydesdale, and

Montrose's plan.

he resolved to fight Baillie before so powerful a reinforcement reached him. Yet it did not suit him to give battle anywhere near Perth. He wished to drag the Fifeshire levies away from their homes, being well aware that they would either march with little heart or would refuse to march at all. Throwing himself upon Kinross, as if he were about to plunder Fife, he then turned sharply westwards,

Aug. 14. Montrose at Kilsyth.

crossing the Forth above Stirling, and reached Kilsyth, half way to Glasgow, by the evening of August 14. Baillie, unless he were prepared to give up Lanark to destruction, had no choice but to follow.

The Covenanting commander was, however, naturally anxious to avoid a battle, at least till he could effect a junction with Lanark. The Fifeshire levies proved as diffi-

---

[1] *Wishart*, ch. xii.; *Patrick Gordon*, 136.

[2] *Acts of Parl. of Scotl.* vi. 447, 448.

[3] Wishart reckons them at 200 horse and 120 musketeers; Patrick Gordon asserts that there were 800 foot and 400 horse.

cult to manage as Montrose had foreseen, and the noblemen of the committee were even more troublesome than the men

Condition of the Covenant- ing army. of Fife. The spirit of the committee descended upon the inferior officers, and Baillie, finding his orders slighted, disclaimed all further responsibility, though he still professed his readiness to carry out such orders as the committee might be pleased to give.

On the morning of the 15th the committee, thus strangely entrusted with the command, broke up from Hollinbush, a

Aug. 15. Its advance towards Kilsyth. hamlet on the road from Stirling about two and a half miles from the spot where Montrose had bivouacked. Contrary to Baillie's advice, they left the road and made straight for the enemy across the hills. The ground at last became so rough that progress in orderly ranks was impossible, and Baillie, assuming the authority which he had quitted, gave orders to halt in a position which he considered to be unassailable.

Whilst the Covenanters were toiling over the rugged ground, Montrose was preparing to receive them. He knew now that

Montrose prepares for battle. Lanaik with 1,000 foot and 500 horse from Clydes- dale was but twelve miles distant, and would be ready in a few hours to fall on his rear. The spot on which he had halted was a large open meadow surrounded by hills. To draw up an army in such a position, with an enemy posted anywhere on the heights, would have been to court destruction, had the enemy been supplied with modern weapons. As it was, with muskets which could only do execution at close quarters, the danger was of the slightest. Moreover the slope was not a gentle declivity like the slope above Marston Moor, down which an army could charge with advantage. If the Covenanters chose to march down the hill-side towards the level where Montrose was posted, they would arrive with their infantry in disorder, and with their cavalry in still greater disorder, through the steepness and ruggedness of the descent. If, on the other hand, they awaited the attack, they must do so on ground on which a single Highlander was worth at least three of the peasants from Fife or the Lothians.

In numbers alone was the superiority on the side of the

Covenanters. They had 6,000 foot and 800 horse, whilst Montrose disposed of only 4,400 foot and 500 horse. To raise the spirits of his men, the Royalist commander put the question to them whether they would fight or retreat. The answer could not be doubtful for an instant, and as soon as the cry for battle was heard, he bade his horsemen to throw their shirts over their clothes to distinguish them from the enemy, whilst the Highlanders knotted between their legs

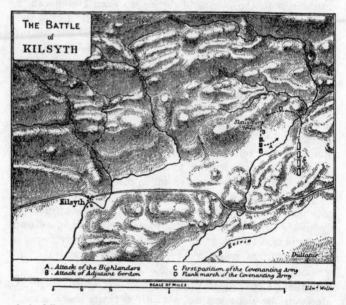

THE BATTLE of KILSYTH

A. Attack of the Highlanders
B. Attack of Adjutant Gordon
C. First position of the Covenanting Army
D. Flank march of the Covenanting Army

SCALE OF MILES

Edw⁴ Weller

their kilts, at that time worn longer than at present. The day was likely to be hot, and it was important that the foot-men at least, who would have to charge up a hillside, should be as unencumbered as possible.[1]

---

[1] There is a discrepancy between Wishart and the author of the Clan-ranald MS. According to the former, Montrose, 'suis insuper omnibus, equiti juxta ac pediti, imperat, ut positis molestioribus vestibus, et solis indusiis superne amicti, et in albis emicantibus, hostibus insultarent.' The latter says that 'the Royal army were . . . . barefooted, with their shirt-

It can hardly be doubted that Montrose was preparing for a struggle amongst the hills. He cannot possibly have expected that the enemy would commit a blunder so enormous as that of which they were guilty at the moment when he was drawing up his men. The sapient leaders of the committee, Argyle, Elcho, and Balfour of Burleigh, the captains who had respectively been crushed by Montrose at Inverlochy, at Tippermuir, and at Aberdeen, together with the Earls of Lindsay and Tullibardine, had made up their minds that the one thing to be guarded against was Montrose's flight, and they imagined that they saw a way of making his flight impossible. At right angles with their own position, and separated from it by a brook running through a glen, was a long hill, smoother and more fitted for military operations, which sloped down upon Montrose's left flank. They thought that if only their army could reach that hill, it would be as far west as he was, and would be able to hinder his escape. In vain Baillie protested. The loss of the day, he said, would be the loss of the kingdom. In the whole committee Balcarres alone, who had led the cavalry at Alford, took his part. The unfortunate soldier who bore the

The blunder of the Covenanting committee.

tails tied between their legs; the cavalry had white shirts above their garments.' The bard of the Macdonalds of Clanranald was present, and must have known what the Highlanders looked like. The late Mr. Burnett, Lion King-at-arms, pointed out to me the supporters granted in 1625 to Macpherson of Cluny, of which a copy is preserved in the Register House at Edinburgh. They are two Highlanders prepared for battle. The upper part of the body is clothed in a tartan jerkin. Below is a white kilt, longer than that at present in use, tied in a knot at the bottom, so as to leave the whole of the legs bare. This answers to the description of the bard of Clanranald, especially if this kilt was the lower part of a shirt, the upper part being covered by the jerkin. Its whiteness is probably accounted for by the Highlanders represented being supposed to be of superior rank. Mr. Skene (*The Highlanders of Scotland*, i. 233) comes to the conclusion that, 'among the common people the plaid was certainly not of tartan, but generally brown in colour, while the shirt worn by them was of tartan. Patrick Gordon says that Montrose ordered that 'for their cognizance every man should put on ane white shirt above his clothes,' but the evidence of the bard seems to show that this only affected the cavalry.

name of commander-in-chief was compelled much against his will to carry out the injunctions of his masters.

To move an army across the front of an enemy within striking distance is one of the most hazardous operations of
A flank march.
war. Baillie's only chance of escape from destruction lay in his being able to conceal his movements by keeping behind the brow of the hill. That chance was lost
The Battle of Kilsyth.
to him by the indiscipline of his men. A party of soldiers stole down into the meadow and attacked some cottages in which Montrose's advanced guard under Macdonald was posted. They were easily repulsed, but Macdonald could not endure to see an enemy retreat unpunished. Without orders from Montrose he pushed forward his own special followers in pursuit, together with the Macleans and the Macdonalds of Clanranald. Between these two clans there was fierce jealousy, and the bard of Clanranald recounted with triumph that though his clansmen were in the rear when they started, they were first at the place of slaughter.[1] No generalship could, as it happened, have directed the course of the assailants with better aim, as with targe and claymore the Highland warriors pushed up the hillside amongst the bushes of the glen which cut right across the enemy's line of march. If the charge thus undertaken at random proved successful the hostile army would be cut in two.

In the meanwhile Montrose, who had learned what was passing, despatched Adjutant Gordon with a body of foot to mount the hill on his left, and thus to anticipate the attempt of the Covenanters to seize upon the high ground.[2] At first

---

[1] Clanranald MS. in Nimmo's *Hist. of Stirlingshire*, i. 226.

[2] The topography of the battle rests on the determination of the locality of the hill to which the Covenanters were marching. For all geographical purposes Wishart may be thrown aside. His battle is a mere vague story told on the recollections of other people. Baillie and Patrick Gordon, though sadly wanting in precision, yet tell the story from opposite sides in such a way that it is possible to form a general impression of what went on. That the hill was the one on Montrose's left appears (1) from the name of 'Slaughter Howe' borne by a spot on it; (2) by Baillie's statement that after his advanced regiments had been routed he rode back to find the reserve, and that he found certain officers

Gordon was successful, but numbers were against him, and he was in danger of destruction. Aboyne, who had been placed by Montrose in the rear with a guard of twelve horsemen lest he should share the fate of his brother at Alford, unable to endure the sight, dashed to his kinsman's rescue. When he too was ingulfed in the tide of war, Montrose sent up Airlie and his Ogilvys, and commanded Nathaniel Gordon to second him with the whole remainder of the cavalry. By this time the battle was practically won. The Highlanders, with their heads down behind their targets, had taken in flank the thin line of the Covenanting advance in its very centre, whilst the Gordons, horse and foot, were wrecking the head of the column.

All thought of discipline or of any general plan of resistance was lost. Each colonel drew up his men as fancy or the immediate danger of the moment bade him. There was no longer the cohesion of an army, and in a few minutes there was no longer the cohesion of any single regiment. Baillie hurried back across the glen to bring up his reserves of the Fifeshire men. The Fifeshire men had already taken to flight.

Flight brought no safety to that doomed host. Highlanders were not accustomed to give quarter after battle, and The pursuit. the soldiers whose wives had been slaughtered in Methven Wood were not likely to spare the murderers. Of the 6,000 footmen who reached the field of battle in the morning, scarcely more than one hundred escaped. The horsemen were in better case for flight; yet even of them there were some who fell beneath the swords of the pursuers,

(*Baillie*, ii. 422†) 'at the brook that not long before we had crossed,' and it seems impossible to suppose that this brook can be other than that which flowed through the glen; (3) by Patrick Gordon's statement that Adjutant Gordon was sent to gain the high ground to which the Covenanters were advancing, and that when he reached it the Highlanders (who, as we know, had gone up the glen) 'stood at so large a distance as they could give no aid, to the adjutant thus engaged.' If the Covenanting army had simply pushed on towards the glen without crossing it, Gordon's attack on their van would have brought him close to the Highlanders' attack up the glen.

whilst others were swallowed up in an attempt to cross the bog of Dullatur.[1]

The noblemen who had been the principal cause of the disaster were better horsed than their followers, and had therefore less difficulty in escaping. Some of them made their way to Stirling; others, with Argyle amongst them, took refuge on board the shipping in the Firth of Forth, and did not hold themselves safe till they were under the protection of the Scottish garrison at Berwick. Others again fled to Carlisle, or even to Ireland. Montrose was now, what he had believed himself to be after Inverlochy, the master of all Scotland.

The escape of the noblemen.

[1] *Wishart,* ch. xiii. ; *Patrick Gordon,* 139 ; *Baillie,* 420.

CHAPTER XXXIV.

SHERBORNE, HEREFORD, AND BRISTOL.

THE news from Kilsyth reached Charles on August 24, shortly after his arrival at Huntingdon.[1]   Yet in spite of the brilliant

Aug. 24.
Charles
hears from
Kilsyth.

prospect opened to him in Scotland, his own position in England was so desperate, that Montrose's success afforded him but little pleasure.   A letter which he addressed to Nicholas on the day after he received the intelligence showed no signs of his usual hopefulness.

Aug. 24.
He declares
his resolu-
tion to
support the
Church and
the Crown.

"Let my condition," he wrote, "be never so low, my successes never so ill, I resolve, by the grace of God, never to yield up this Church to the government of Papists, Presbyterians, or Independents, nor to injure my successors by lessening the Crown of that military power which my predecessors left me, nor forsake my friends ; much less to let them suffer, when I do not, for their faithfulness to me ; resolving sooner to live as miserable as the violent insulting rebels can make me—which I esteem far worse than death —rather than not to be exactly constant to these grounds; from which whosoever, upon whatsoever occasion, shall persuade me to recede in the least tittle, I shall esteem him either a fool or a knave." [2]

After such a declaration there was nothing for Charles to do but to possess his soul in patience, leaving the floods of the world to go over his head without resistance.   It was the one thing which, without compulsion, he was unable to do.   He

[1] See p. 291.
[2] The King to Nicholas, Aug. 25.   *Evelyn's Diary* (ed. 1852), iv. 159.

must fight on, even if defeat were certain. Yet, whatever plans he might entertain for the future, he could not now tarry

Charles is unable to remain at Hunting-don.
at Huntingdon.[1] Poyntz was on his track with a superior force, which had indeed been mutinous in consequence of want of pay, but which was now expecting treasure from London, and would fight well enough when it arrived. The King's soldiers had no treasure

Royalist plunderings.
to expect. They plundered Huntingdon, and when Charles, who was cut off from the North by Poyntz, set out on his return to Oxford, roving parties of his cavalry stripped the country round of everything valuable on which they could lay their hands. It was all one to them whether the men whom they despoiled were Royalists or Parliamentarians. " To say the truth," confessed one of the King's warmest supporters, " our horse made all men delinquents where they quartered thereabouts." [2] Charles probably could not stop the

Aug. 27. A soldier hanged.
mischief if he would, but it is characteristic of him that the only case in which he exercised severity was that of a soldier who had stolen a chalice from a church. He ordered the man to be hanged on the nearest signpost.[3]

Even when Charles's sanguine disposition gave way in the flood of calamity which had come upon him, Digby was still

Digby's hopefulness.
ready to encourage him with hopes of assistance from the most distant quarters. In addition to the one solid fact of Montrose's victory at Kilsyth, there were shadowy expectations enough, which Digby was almost able to persuade himself to regard as foundations upon which a solid policy could be built up. With him the Irish auxiliaries were

French successes on the Continent.
always just about to start, and there was always cause for fresh hope in the ever-increasing preponderance of the French arms on the Continent. Though the fortunes of the campaign of 1645 were more chequered than those of the campaign of 1644, the French had on the whole been gaining ground. On their southern frontier they had

---

[1] See map at p. 255.   [2] Walker, 136.
[3] Slingsby's Diary, 161.

defeated the Spaniards in Catalonia. In Germany the skill
of Turenne and the valour of Enghien had won another blood-stained victory at Nördlingen. In the
meanwhile the diplomacy of Mazarin had not been
idle. Ever since the spring of 1644 a congress sitting
at Münster had been languidly attempting to restore
peace to Europe. Mazarin was more anxious that
the peace when it came should be favourable to France than
that it should be soon concluded, and he had thrown his energy
into the work of reconciling Denmark and Sweden, in order
that Denmark might be useful to France. By the
treaty of Brömsebro, the war between the northern
Powers was brought to an end—a treaty of which
the chief effect in England was to afford Digby a gleam of hope
that Charles might yet receive assistance from his
uncle, the King of Denmark. The Queen too, he
thought, would be able to collect money in France.
Desperate as the King's prospects appeared, if only he could
hold out to the winter—and of that Digby entertained little
doubt—all might be well when the spring arrived.

July 24.
Aug. 3.
Battle of
Nördlingen.

The Con-
gress of
Münster.

Aug. 3.
13
The peace of
Brömsebro.

Digby ex-
pects to tide
over the
winter.

Even Digby, full of trust in the future as he was, could not
deny that his hopes were shared by few. " Alas, my lord," he
complained to Jermyn, " there is such an universal
weariness of the war, despair of a possibility for the
King to recover, and so much of private interest grown from
these upon everybody, that I protest to God I do not know
four persons living besides myself and you that have not already given clear demonstrations that they will purchase their
own and—as they flatter themselves—the kingdom's quiet at
any price to the King, to the Church, to the faithfullest of his
party ; and to deal freely with you, I do not think it will be in
the King's power to hinder himself from being forced to accept
such conditions as the rebels will give him." Digby then proceeded to name three persons as the leaders of the party which
intended to force the King to make peace. Though their
names are carefully blotted out, it is still possible to read two
of them. They are the names of Rupert and Legge.[1]

General de-
spondency.

[1] Digby to Jermyn, Aug. 27. *Warburton*, iii. 157. In the copy

The mass of the Royalists, in short, were not inclined either to ruin themselves with Charles for the sake of an unattainable

Aug. 28.
Charles
arrives at
Oxford, ideal, or to trust to Digby's foreign combinations to revive the cause for which their own swords had been drawn in vain. Charles reached Oxford on

Aug. 30.
and marches
to the West. August 28. He left it again on the 30th. The faithful Richmond and a large number of noblemen and gentlemen who had hitherto clung to his fortunes remained behind, and refused to accompany him farther in pursuit of adventures.[1] He directed his course towards the West, where, during his absence in the North, events had been occurring which threatened to deprive him of his hold on all that still remained to him in England.

After the capture of Bridgwater in July Fairfax had turned back eastwards,[2] to make himself thoroughly master of the

Fairfax
turns
eastwards. country in his rear before attempting the reduction of the districts west of the Parret. He directed his march upon Sherborne, where the castle was held by a strong garrison under Sir Lewis Dyves, the stepson of its owner, the Earl of Bristol. Bristol himself, in order to avoid

The Earl of
Bristol at
Exeter. the obloquy which had marked him out as the fiercest opponent of all peaceful measures, had retired from Oxford to Exeter in the spring of 1644, and had thus withdrawn from consultations in which he had had, in reality, but little influence.[3]

On his way to Sherborne Fairfax heard that the garrison of Bath was weak and in disaccord with the citizens. Taking with him a mere detachment of cavalry he secured its surrender, and then continued his march.[4] On August 2 he

from which Warburton printed the names are omitted. They occur in the way described in the text in a copy which was kept by Digby, and having been afterwards captured at Sherburn, in Yorkshire, is now amongst the *Domestic State Papers.* I am rather inclined to read the third name as Culpepper's.

[1] *Iter Carolinum ; Walker,* 136.

[2] See map at p. 255.

[3] Bristol to Grey of Wark, May 22, 1646. *L.J.* viii. 342.

[4] *A full relation of the taking of Bath,* E. 294, 21 ; *A fuller relation of the taking of Bath,* E. 294, 30.

opened the siege of Sherborne Castle. Difficult as was the task of mastering its strong defences, Fairfax found it no less

July 30.
Surrender of
Bath. difficult to keep open his communications. In Somerset he had easily won over the Clubmen to

Aug. 2.
Sherborne
Castle
besieged. his side, because it was impossible for the most ignorant peasant to imagine that he could attain to peace and order by giving his support to Goring.

The Club-
men of
Dorset. In Dorset there was no Royalist army to plunder the homesteads of the people, and the garrisons, being commanded by the gentry of the county or by persons acting in their name, were not likely to commit outrages as long as the contributions for their support were duly paid. The Clubmen consequently here fell under the influence of the Royalist gentry and clergy, and looked upon a Parliamentarian invasion as the only source of trouble. As soon as Fairfax crossed the border of the county the Clubmen swarmed around him, cutting off his supplies and threatening to starve him out.

It was impossible for any commander to tolerate proceedings of this kind. On August 3 Fleetwood, who had been

Aug. 3.
Seizure of
the leaders
at Shaftes-
bury. despatched by Fairfax to stamp out the fire, seized about forty of their leaders at Shaftesbury. The word was passed through the district to rise in force to rescue the prisoners. On the 4th Cromwell himself was sent to put a stop to the agitation. On his way to Shaftesbury he fell in with a large party of the Clubmen, but these he persuaded to disperse peaceably, partly by a display of force, but still more by giving assurances that any of his soldiers found plundering would be severely punished. A

The Club-
men on
Hambledon
Hill. more formidable body, some 2,000 strong, was posted within the earthworks on the top of Hambledon Hill, whither, in all probability before even the Celt had set foot on the soil of Britain, the inhabitants of the rich valley of the Stour had been accustomed to climb for refuge. Cromwell's soldiers were, indeed, armed in a very different fashion from the foes of those ancient tribes, but the hillside was as steep as it had been in prehistoric times, and it was still crowned with fold upon fold of mound and trench.

Cromwell, it is true, had other than military reasons for wishing to be spared the necessity of an assault. He had pity for the peasants who took him for an enemy, when he came as a friend. Three times he sent messages of peace up the hill, and three times the messengers were repulsed. There were clergymen amongst the defenders, animating them to resistance. At last Cromwell ordered an attack ; but the only opening in the earthworks was narrow and strongly guarded,

Capture of Hambledon Hill. and it was not till Desborough, who had climbed the hill with a body of horse on the other side, charged the peasants in the rear, and about a dozen of them had been slain, that they threw down their arms and either submitted or fled. Three hundred prisoners were taken, most of whom, as Cromwell informed Fairfax, were 'poor silly creatures, whom if you please to let me send home, they promise to be very dutiful for time to come, and will be hanged before they come out again.'

With as little expense of life as possible a dangerous move-

Suppression of the Clubmen. ment had been arrested. The Clubmen of Dorset, indeed, professed to come out merely in defence of their properties. The doggerel upon one of their flags which was captured—

> " If you offer to plunder or take our cattle,
> Be assured we will give you battle,"

did not indicate any political feeling whatever. Yet, for all

They are practically Royalists. that, they were virtually Royalists. Some of them had been heard to boast that Hopton was on his way from the West to command them ; that multitudes were about to join them from Wiltshire ; and that, with their combined forces, they would raise the siege of Sherborne. There was no room for a third party in England, and even the Clubmen had ceased to claim to be anything of the sort.[1]

Whilst Fleetwood and Cromwell were clearing the line of communication, Fairfax was vigorously pushing on the attack

---

[1] *Sprigg*, 86 ; *Carlyle*, Letter XXX. ; *Two great Victories*, E. 296, 6 ; *Two Letters*, E. 296, 7 ; *The proceedings of the army*, E. 296, 14.

upon Sherborne Castle. On the 11th money arrived to pay his soldiers, and a train of siege-guns to batter the walls. On

Aug. 11.
Arrival of a
siege-train
at Sher-
borne. the 14th a serious breach was effected and a mine was ready for explosion. Early on the following morning, before the mine was fired, the soldiers drove the defenders from their works, leaping over the

Aug. 15.
The castle
taken. walls and rendering further resistance hopeless. Dyves hung out the white flag, too late to save the castle from plunder, though quarter was given to all within. Evidence was discovered which placed it beyond doubt that the Royalists had used the Clubmen for their own purposes.[1]

The capture of Sherborne Castle gave to Fairfax the command of a shorter road to the West than that through

A council of
war resolves
to attack
Bristol. Blandford and Dorchester. A council of war was at once assembled to decide on the next step to be taken. There were some who urged the importance of returning to the West before Goring could recover strength, but the majority were of opinion that Bristol must first be taken. The position of Bristol, near the head of the channel which divides the western counties from Wales and the English borderlands of Wales, was of the very greatest importance, and, guarded as it was by more than 2,000 men with Rupert at their head, it might easily, if the King saw fit to join his troops to those of his nephew, become a basis of operations which would be very dangerous to an army advancing into Devon and Cornwall. It was true that the defences of the city were understood to be formidable, and that, as the plague was raging within it, the danger to the army even in the case of success would be to the full as great as whilst it was still exposed to the fire of the artillery of the garrison. All these objections were, however, overruled. " Seeing," said Fairfax, as soon as the vote had been taken, " our judgments lead us to make Bristol our next design, as the greatest service we can do for the public ; as for the sickness, let us trust God with the army, who will be as ready to protect us in the siege from infection as in the field from the bullet." There was a simplicity of piety in Fairfax which

[1] *Sprigg,* 90-96.

bound the soldiers to him as much as his conspicuous bravery
in action. On August 18, the day on which the
King turned back from Doncaster, the Parliamentary
army set out on its march to Bristol.[1] On the 23rd
Fairfax fixed his headquarters at Stapleton, and the
investment of the city was completed. The capture of a fort at Portishead on the 28th closed the
mouth of the Avon against all relief by sea. It was of quite
as much importance that Fairfax's habit of paying in ready
money for all that his army consumed won over the population,
not only to supply the besiegers with provisions, but even to
render armed assistance.[2] Fairfax was the more
anxious to reduce Bristol as speedily as possible, as
Hereford was as yet untaken, and if Leven were
detained before it, the King might easily slip past him and
bring his available forces to the assistance of his nephew.

Aug. 18.
The army leaves Sherborne.

Aug. 23.
The siege of Bristol opened.

Danger lest the King may relieve it.

The siege of Hereford had, indeed, lasted longer than had
been expected at Westminster. The governor, Sir Barnabas
Scudamore, defended himself with vigour and ability,
and the Scottish attack was proportionately weak.
Leven complained with justice that, although everything was
done to supply the wants of the English army, the
very pay which had been solemnly promised to the
Scottish soldiers had been kept back, and that he was therefore reduced to provide himself by force with provisions—a
course which both exhausted his own soldiers and exasperated
their victims. The departure of David Leslie with the whole
of the cavalry in pursuit of the King brought matters to a
crisis, it being impossible that Leven's infantry could take their
part effectively in the siege and scour the country for supplies
at the same time. As no payment was to be expected, the
peasants of the neighbourhood refused to bring in their provisions to his camp, and those of his soldiers who were kept to
serve the batteries were therefore compelled to keep themselves
alive by eating the apples, the peas, and the wheat which were
still growing in the fields round the city.[3] Parliament, when

The siege of Hereford.

Leven's complaints.

---

[1] *Sprigg*, 97.   [2] *Ibid.* 98–103.
[3] *L.J.* vii. 538; *The Kingdom's Weekly Intelligencer*, E. 297, 2.

these facts were brought to its notice, might regret that its engagements were unfulfilled, but having no power to provide constant pay for more than one army, it gave Leven good words, but nothing more.[1]

The result of the continued detention of the soldiers' pay was quickly seen. Herefordshire was systematically plundered

Hereford-
shire
plundered.

by roving bands. Against the Scottish soldier, indeed, no attacks upon life or upon female honour are recorded, but the soberest men quickly learn to rob rather than to starve. The cattle and horses of the farmer, and the loaves out of the oven of the housewife, were mercilessly swept into the Scottish camp, and as a natural consequence the men of Herefordshire, never friendly to Puritanism, now became bitterly hostile to its supporters from the North.[2]

The necessity of subsisting upon plunder rapidly deteriorates an army, and in this instance bad weather came to render

The siege-
works
flooded.

Prepara-
tions for an
attack.

Sept. 1.
The King at
Worcester.

David
Leslie
resolves to
go to
Scotland.

more desperate an already difficult situation, the siege-works being flooded by heavy rains.[3] Yet, in spite of all obstacles, Leven did not lose heart, and he made preparations for a storm. On September 1, however, news arrived that the King, who was on his way from Oxford[4] to raise the siege, had reached Worcester with 3,000 horse. Since David Leslie's departure Leven had had scarcely a single horseman left, nor had he any hope of making good his loss. David Leslie had recently written from Nottingham, telling him that, on receiving the bad news from Kilsyth, he had resolved to march with only half his force into Scotland. He had, however, found it impossible to carry out his intention. Now that Scotland was in peril, not a single man under his orders would remain behind in England, and he had therefore been compelled to take them all.[5]

To await a strong cavalry force with infantry embarrassed

[1] *The Parliament Post*, E. 300, 9.

[2] Webb's *Civil War in Herefordshire*, ii. 391.

[3] *The Parliament Post*, E. 300, 9.

[4] See p. 304.

[5] David Leslie to Leven, Aug. 26. *A Declaration.* E. 301, 8.

by the investment of Hereford would be simple madness,
Sept. 1.
Raising of
the siege of
Hereford. and Leven had no choice but to abandon his enterprise. On September 1 he directed the raising of
the siege, and on the following morning his whole
army was on the march for Gloucester. His Majesty, as the
Governor of Hereford expressed himself, drawing near 'like
the sun to the meridian, this Scottish mist began to disperse,
and the next morning vanished out of sight.'[1] In sober
earnest, Leven's failure at Hereford was but a distant result
of Montrose's achievement at Kilsyth.

On the 4th Charles entered the city amidst the joyful
acclamations of a delivered people. He had indeed accom-
Sept. 4.
The King
enters the
city. plished something, but his task was less than half
done unless Bristol could be rescued as well as
Hereford. For that purpose his force was miserably
inadequate. The horse which he had brought with him was
exhausted by long marches, and even if it had been in the best
condition it could not have ventured to cope with the more
numerous and better disciplined horse of Fairfax's army, the
movements of which were directed by Cromwell himself.

With Digby, indeed, the difficulties in the way counted for
little. The Scots, he wrote on the 4th, were in full retreat
Sept. 4.
Digby
hopeful of
the future. for their own country, where Montrose would complete God's judgment on them. Fairfax's whole army
was likely to be ruined before Bristol.[2] Even more
triumphant was the tone of a letter which Digby despatched
on the 7th to the Prince of Wales. "These things,
Sept. 7. sir," he wrote in ecstasy, after recounting Montrose's
successes, "are things rather like dreams than truths, but all
most certain. God is pleased to point out the way by which
He will bring upon the rebellion of both kingdoms the judgments that are due upon it, having already brought so heavy a
vengeance upon that which hath been the original of all our
misery. You see from what a low condition it hath pleased
God to bring his Majesty's affairs into so hopeful a one again,
as that if, while Fairfax's army is entertained before Bristol,

---

[1] Scudamore to Digby. *Webb*, ii. 385.
[2] Digby to Jermyn, Sept. 4. *S.P. Dom.* dx. 90.

your Highness can but frame a considerable body, such as
may give his Majesty leave, with the forces he hath together,
to play the fairest of his game in these countries, and northward for the assistance of Montrose with horse, or, at least,
for the withholding Leslie's [1] army of foot from him, I see no
cause to doubt but that, upon the whole matter, his Majesty
may conclude the campagna more prosperously than any, and
with fairer foundations for a mastering power the next year
than ever." [2]

The very day after these exulting lines were penned Charles
learnt that his old recruiting ground in South Wales was closed

Sept. 8.
Charles
fails to
recruit his
army in
South
Wales. against him. Astley had, indeed, succeeded in keeping the Welshmen from openly siding with the
enemy, but they hung back from making further
exertions on the King's behalf.[3] In order to convert disaster into success, it was necessary to inspire
others besides Digby with the belief that success was attainable.

In Oxford incredulity as to the possibility of converting
defeat into victory was as strong in Charles's absence as it had

Eagerness
for peace. been in his presence. Hitherto no one had been
more cheery than Nicholas, or more inclined to
exaggerate the weaknesses of the Parliamentary army. On

Aug. 31.
Nicholas
grows de-
spondent. August 31 he told his master plainly that he was
lost, unless he could induce his Continental allies to
declare in his favour and to bring the rebels to reason
by placing an embargo on their shipping. Actually to invite
foreign forces into England, he added, would be hazardous.

Sept. 4.
A lawyer
refuses
promotion. On September 4 the trusty Secretary had a still more
ominous communication to make. A lawyer had
actually refused to take promotion from the King.
Lord Keeper Lyttelton had lately died, and Charles, when
he last visited Oxford, had appointed the Chief Baron, Sir
Richard Lane, to the office thus vacated. Lane's post was
now offered to Sir Edward Herbert, the Attorney-General.

[1] *i.e.* Leven's.

[2] Digby to the Prince of Wales, Sept. 7. *S.P. Dom.* dx. 99.

[3] Desires of the gentlemen of Carmarthenshire, Sept. 8. *Ibid.* dx.
101.

Herbert, however, explained to Nicholas that he was disqualified for a place on the bench by a vote of the Parliament
at Westminster, and that, as matters stood, he was not prepared to face the consequences of insulting even a rebel

A peerage
not taken
up.

Parliament. It was no less significant, in another
way, of the decline of Charles's fortunes that the
Earldom of Lichfield having been conferred on the
brother of the Duke of Richmond, Lord Bernard Stuart, that
gallant soldier was unable to take advantage of the honour,
because he had not sufficient money to pay the necessary fees.[1]

Digby's sanguine expectations were, however, not to be
measured by the standard of other men. On the 9th he was

Sept. 9.
Digby
continues
sanguine.

to the full as elated as he had been on the 4th. " I
must confess," he wrote with a fervour which would
almost have gained him acceptance amongst the
zealots at Westminster, "that these miracles, besides the
worldly joy, have made me a better Christian, by begetting
in me a stronger faith and reliance upon God Almighty than
before, having manifested that it is wholly His work, and that
He will bring about His intended blessing upon this just cause,
by ways the most impossible to human understanding, and
consequently teach us to cast off all reliance upon our own
strength." Gerard, added Digby, was collecting troops in
Shropshire, and the Welsh difficulty would soon be settled.
Goring too was reported to be advancing to the relief of
Bristol with a considerable force. Rupert was wearing Fairfax
out with frequent sallies, and Poyntz and Rossiter, who had
arrived at Tewkesbury in pursuit of the King, would, in
consequence of the distress to which the besieging army was
reduced, be compelled to turn aside towards Bristol to supply
its deficiencies.[2]

At the very moment at which Digby was writing, this house
of cards was falling to the ground. On August 31 Fairfax
had intercepted a letter from Goring, from which he learned
that three weeks would elapse before the western Royalist
army could arrive to raise the siege. As it was known that

[1] Nicholas to the King, Aug. 31, Sept. 4. *S.P. Dom.* dx. 79, 89.
[2] Digby to Byron, Sept. 9. *Id.* dx. 102.

the King had already left Oxford, and would therefore, after
liberating Hereford, be ready to co-operate with
Goring when he at last appeared, it was resolved
not to trust to the slow effects of a blockade, but to
storm the works whilst yet there was no enemy to
take the besiegers in the rear.

Aug. 31.
Fairfax intercepts a letter from Goring.

On September 4, as a preparatory step, Fairfax summoned
Rupert to surrender his trust. The wording of the missive
was unusual. The Parliamentary general had eagerly
seized the opportunity of urging the soundness of
the principles on which he had taken up arms.
"Sir," he declared, "the crown of England is, and will be,
where it ought to be. We fight to maintain it there;
but the King, misled by evil counsellors, or through
a seduced heart, hath left his Parliament, under God
the best assurance of his crown and family. The maintaining
of this schism is the ground of this unhappy war on your part;
and what sad effects it hath produced in the three kingdoms is
visible to all men. To maintain the rights of the crown and
kingdom jointly, a principal part whereof is that the King in
supreme acts is not to be advised by men of whom the law
takes no notice, but by his Parliament, the Great Council of
the Kingdom, in whom—as much as man is capable of—he
hears all his people, as it were, at once advising him, and in
which multitude of counsellors is his safety and his people's
interest ; and to see him right in this, hath been the constant
and faithful endeavour of the Parliament, and to bring these
wicked instruments to justice that have misled him is a
principal ground of our fighting."

Sept. 4.
Fairfax summons Rupert.

He declares his principles,

Fairfax ended with a personal appeal to Rupert himself.
"Let all England judge," he wrote, "whether the
burning of its towns, ruining its cities, and destroying
its people, be a good requital from a person of your
family, which had the prayers, tears, purses, and blood of its
Parliament and people." On the day on which this
appeal was despatched, two thousand countrymen
flocked in to the Parliamentary camp, offering to
share with the soldiers the dangers of the siege. Their presence

and appeals to the Prince.

The country people support Fairfax.

must have served to justify to Fairfax his assertion that the heart of the country was with him and not with Rupert.[1]

Men of action rarely succeed in grasping the whole of the issues of the conflict in which they are engaged, and Fairfax

*Imperfec-
tion of
Fairfax's
reasoning.* was no exception to the rule. It is not likely, however, that, if his argument had been more perfect than it was, it would have made any impression upon one who, like Rupert, had little comprehension of English political or religious controversies. Yet if Rupert cared little for the argument, he was in a mood to take into consideration

*Difficulties
of Rupert's
position.* the practical conclusion to which it led. His own position was one of exceeding difficulty. Bristol lay in a hollow, and Fiennes, by whom the greater part of the existing fortifications on the north of the Avon had been raised, had, in order to take advantage of the high ground to the west, placed them at a considerable distance from the city. The whole circuit of the fortress thus created was about four miles, and though attempts had been made to strengthen the works, they were in many places slight and defective. For the defence of such a place Rupert's forces were entirely inadequate. He had reckoned on having 2,300 men under his orders, but only 1,500 appeared to man the walls at the beginning of the siege, and every day this force, insufficient as it was, was thinned by desertion.

Material weakness was accompanied by moral discouragement. In the immediate future all was dark. There were no

*Weakness of
the garrison.* tidings from Charles, or promise of relief from any quarter whatever. A considerable number of the citizens were disaffected. The superior officers were as despondent as the soldiers, and at a council of war gave their opinion that, though they might resist a first assault, they must inevitably succumb to a second.

That Rupert shared in the belief of his officers there can

*Sept. 5.
Rupert asks
leave to send
to the King.* be no reasonable doubt. Even if it had not been so, he was hardly the man, dashing cavalry officer as he was, to conduct a stubborn defence in a cause which he knew to be lost. On the 5th he replied to Fairfax by a

[1] *Sprigg,* 108.

request for permission to communicate with the King. When this request was necessarily refused, he opened negotiations for

A negotiation opened.

a surrender, spinning out the time by haggling for the most favourable terms, in the hope that before any-

Sept. 10. Bristol stormed.

thing was concluded he might hear of approaching relief. At last Fairfax lost patience. In the dark hours of the morning of September 10 the besieging

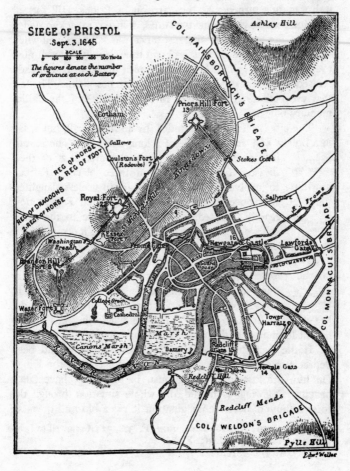

SIEGE OF BRISTOL
Sept. 3. 1645.
SCALE
0   100 200 300 400 500 Yards
The figures denote the number of ordnance at each Battery

army was let loose for an assault upon the southern and eastern defences. On the south the storming parties were repulsed, but the whole of the eastern line, in some parts of which the wall was no more than five feet high, was carried without difficulty. The horse broke in, and routed a body of cavalry sent by Rupert to drive back such of the enemy as might succeed in effecting an entrance. The western line of wall was thus turned, but the garrison of Prior's Hill fort, at the northern angle of the two lines, refused to acknowledge defeat. For two hours the resistance was kept up, and when at last the Parliamentarians broke in they slaughtered well-nigh every one of the gallant band, on the plea that they had already refused to accept quarter when summoned to yield. The few that escaped owed their lives to the entreaties of the Parliamentary officers.

The city itself was surrounded by an inner wall, but it lay in a hollow and was incapable of a long defence. The Royalists, as soon as they knew the greatness of their disaster, fired the town in three places. Fairfax, unwilling to involve citizens and soldiers in useless slaughter, sent once more to offer terms, which Rupert now readily accepted. Articles honourable to the garrison were soon agreed on, and on the morning of the 11th the Prince passed out of the gate on his way to Oxford.[1]

Rupert surrenders,

Sept. 11. and evacuates Bristol.

The news of the surrender of Bristol reached Westminster on the 12th. The Commons, smitten with compunction, at once voted that Nathaniel Fiennes should return to the seat which he had occupied before his surrender of Bristol in 1643.[2] The general feeling was that he had at least acquitted himself better than Rupert.

Sept. 12. Fiennes restored to his seat.

If the first thought of the House of Commons had been depreciatory of Rupert, what was to be expected of the King? On him the loss of the city must, in any case, have fallen heavily. Viewing, as he did, the whole situation through the rosy medium of delusive imagination, it was a blow all the more

---

[1] *Sprigg*, 110; *Rupert's Declaration*, E. 308, 32; Cromwell to Lenthall, Sept. 14; *Carlyle*, Letter XXXI.

[2] *C.J.* iv. 272. See vol. i. 179.

crushing because it was so absolutely unexpected. The surrender, in fact, had taken place only one day after Digby had
Sept. 14. Effect of the surrender upon Charles. written the triumphant letter in which he had chanted the song of victory to come.[1] Only one explanation—the explanation of gross dereliction of duty—seemed possible to Charles. Without stopping to inquire into the hard facts of the case he dismissed Rupert from all his offices, and bade him seek his fortune beyond the sea.

Rupert dismissed.

Violent as Charles's action was, there was more of wounded affection than of anger in the letter in which he announced his
The King's letter to Rupert. resolution. "Nephew!" he wrote, "though the loss of Bristol be a great blow to me, yet your surrendering it as you did is of so much affliction to me, that it makes me not only forget the consideration of that place, but is likewise the greatest trial of my constancy that hath yet befallen me; for what is to be done, after one that is so near me as you are, both in blood and friendship, submits himself to so mean an action?"[2]

The King's letter was sent to Oxford to await Rupert's arrival, and was accompanied by another instructing Nicholas
Legge's arrest. to put Legge under arrest, and informing him that Glemham was appointed to succeed Legge as governor of Oxford. That Legge had done nothing to deserve this treatment was subsequently admitted by all, but he was known to be a confidant of Rupert's, and, like Rupert, to be favourably disposed to peace. At such a moment Charles was likely to call up again before his mind the knowledge which he

---

[1] See p. 312.

[2] The King to Rupert, Sept. 14, *Clarendon*, ix. 90; Passport for Rupert, *Warburton*, iii. 186. Compare Digby to Nicholas, Sept. 15, *Nicholas Papers*, i. 64. The testimony of Colonel Butler, who commanded the convoy assigned by Fairfax to protect Rupert on the way to Oxford, is interesting. "I am confident," he writes, "we are much mistaken in our intelligence concerning him. I find him a man much inclined to a happy peace, and will certainly imploy his interest with his Majesty for the accomplishing of it. . . . On my word, he could not have held it "— *i.e.* Bristol—"unless it had been better manned." Butler to Sir W. Waller, *ibid.* i. 65.

possessed that Legge lay under suspicion of having earlier in the year intrigued with Savile for the delivery of Oxford,[1] though at the time he had treated the suspicion lightly. His own heart was very sore. " Tell my son,"[2] he added in a postscript to these instructions, "that I shall less grieve to hear that he is knocked on[3] the head than that he should do so mean an action as is the rendering of Bristol castle and fort upon the terms it was."[4]

[1] See p. 212.
[2] *i.e.* the Duke of York.
[3] "in the head" as printed.
[4] The King to Nicholas, Sept. 14. *Evelyn's Diary* (ed. 1859), iv. 163.

CHAPTER XXXV.

CURRENTS OF OPINION.

On the day on which Charles signified his displeasure to Rupert, Cromwell, by Fairfax's orders, was giving to Lenthall a long account of the siege of Bristol. To him the success achieved was but a step to the higher object which he had continually before him. If there was nothing in his letter of the conciliatory feeling which had led Fairfax, in summoning the garrison of Bristol, to dream of Rupert, and even of Charles himself, as rallying to the great principle of Parliamentary counsel and control, Cromwell grasped more fully than Fairfax had done the higher spiritual issues of the war. " All this," he wrote, as Fairfax might have written, " is none other than the work of God : he must be a very atheist that doth not acknowledge it." The remainder was all his own. " It may be thought," he continued, "that some praises are due to those gallant men, of whose valour so much mention is made :—their humble suit to you and all that have an interest in this blessing is that in the remembrance of God's praises they may [1] be forgotten. It's their joy that they are instruments of God's glory and their country's good. It's their honour that God vouchsafes to use them. . . . . Our desires are that God may be glorified by the same spirit of faith by which we ask all our sufficiency, and have received it. It is meet that He have all the praise. Presbyterians, Independents, all had here the same spirit of faith and prayer; the same presence and answer ; they agree here, know no names of difference ; pity it is it should be otherwise any-

1645.
Sept. 14.
Cromwell's
despatch.

---

[1] This word is omitted by Carlyle.

where ! All that believe have the real unity, which is most glorious because inward and spiritual, in the Body and to the Head. As for being united in forms, commonly called uniformity, every Christian will, for peace' sake, study and do as far as conscience will permit. And from brethren, in things of the mind we look for no compulsion but that of light and reason. In other things, God hath put the sword in the Parliament's hands, for the terror of evildoers and the praise of them that do well. If any plead exemption from that, he knows not the Gospel ; if any would wring that out of your hands, or steal it from you, under what pretence soever, I hope they shall do it without effect." [1]

Of Cromwell's warnings the Commons took little heed. They indeed ordered that his despatch should be printed, but

Sept. 17.
Cromwell's
despatch
mutilated.

they took care to mutilate it as they had mutilated his despatch from Naseby.[2] No word of his referring to the difference between Presbyterians and Independents was for the time suffered to meet the public eye.[3]

Out of the heart of the present, Cromwell had already grasped the promise of the future, not indeed in all its breadth

Contrast
between
Cromwell
and Fairfax.

and fulness, but as far as it was given to a human soul to grasp it. Fairfax had spoken in his message to Rupert of a Parliamentary foundation for a constitutional monarchy. Cromwell traced the limits outside which Parliamentary control is merely noxious. For a while the two men could heartily co-operate with one another. Yet in one is already to be discerned the future Lord Protector ; in the other the man who more than any single person, except Monk, brought about the Restoration.

That Cromwell could work so long, not only under Fairfax, but under the Parliament, is in no way wonderful. He loved

---

[1] Cromwell to Lenthall, Sept. 14. *Carlyle*, Letter XXXI. The text has been corrected from the original letter in the Portland MSS. *Hist. MSS. Com. Rep.* xiii. part 1, 271.

[2] See p. 252.

[3] *Lieut.-General Cromwell's Letter.* E. 301, 18. The omitted paragraph was afterwards printed in a pamphlet entitled *Strong Motives.* E. 304, 15. Thomason's date of the publication of this later tract is Oct. 8.

to be, as he said when he strode into Ely Cathedral, a man under authority. He had used no empty phraseology when he declared his belief that God had put the sword in the Parliament's hands. These words represented at this time his constant and unfeigned conviction. As in the long years of unparliamentary government he had waited silent and reserved, without taking part in such resistance against the King as was then possible, till the moment of crisis brought it home to his mind that God's ordinance was not in the King, so it would be now. Duty retained him in fidelity to Parliament till the moment came when duty bade, or appeared to bid, otherwise, and he would then be convinced, as by a flash of divine inspiration, that God's ordinance was not in the Parliament. For the present he would fight on, and watch for the time when Parliament might clear away the mist which obscured its vision.

Cromwell a man under authority.

Cromwell's temper of obedience to authority was the temper of the New Model army. From Fairfax to the meanest pikeman there was no thought of resistance to the will of Parliament, no breath of that contempt for the interference of civilians which is so rarely altogether absent where soldiers meet. The New Model was in very truth a Parliamentary army, as the armies of Essex and Manchester had never been.

The New Model a Parliamentary army.

Yet if the New Model was Cromwellian in its reverence for authority, it was Cromwellian also in its large-heartedness. "Presbyterians, Independents, all," as Cromwell said, " . . . agree here, know no names of difference." Even those—and they were not a few—who had no special religious bent were accepted without contempt as fellow soldiers.

A man after Cromwell's own heart was Hugh Peters,[1] the

---

[1] The reputation of Hugh Peters has perhaps suffered more than that of any other man from the neglect of Mr. Spedding's dictum that, if you wish to know whether a statement is true, you should ask who said it first, and what opportunity the sayer had of knowing the truth. The personal charges brought against him accused him of being a mountebank and a loose liver. With respect to the former charge, there can be no doubt that he was fond of jesting, though it may be seen by the MS. notes appended to an edition of his tales and jests in the British Museum

chaplain to the train—that is to say, to the regiments in charge

Hugh
Peters. of the baggage-waggons and the artillery. Hugh Peters, who was born at Fowey in 1598, was descended from a family which had emigrated from the Nether-

(12,316, p. 5) that many of those ascribed to him were certainly, and many more probably, in circulation before he was born. The other charge is more serious. Against the tales told after the Restoration we have to set his own statement made to his daughter just before his death : "By my zeal, it seems, I have exposed myself to all manner of reproach ; but wish you to know that—besides your mother—I have had no fellowship —that way—with any woman since first I knew her, having a godly wife before also, I bless God " (*A dying Father's last legacy*, 106). The denial is not explicit concerning the writer's earlier years, but on the other hand it may be merely awkwardly expressed, Peters intending to refer to his first marriage, or it may be held to imply the acknowledgment of sins of his youth committed before conversion. Even if we take them in their best sense, there still remains the question whether Peters was speaking the truth. It is certain that the scribblers of the Restoration had no means of knowing whether Peters was guilty of committing adultery about thirty or forty years before they wrote, unless indeed it had become matter of public fame. Dr. Yonge indeed only insinuates instead of directly stating this (*England's Shame*, 19), but he puts himself out of court by the assertion that Peters continued a lecturer at St. Sepulchre's for near twenty years, *i.e.* from some date not much later than 1620 to nearly 1640 —a statement notoriously untrue. On the other hand it may safely be said that a man who was treated as a friend by Thomas Hooker, Ames, Winthrop, and Cromwell cannot have been known as an evil liver. Even those who believe Cromwell to have been a hypocrite have never suggested that he was a fool, and what could be more foolish than for him to risk his reputation by giving his confidence to Peters if his character had been no better than the Royalist pamphleteers afterwards represented it ?

If the evidence of *Noscitur a sociis* is favourable to Peters, another line of evidence is also in his favour. A man may give a false account of his own life, but he cannot lie in those unconscious revelations of himself which spring to the surface when he is neither writing nor talking of himself. For this indirect knowledge of Peters's character there are three sources : (1) a series of letters written in America and published in the collections of *The Massachusetts Historical Society*, series iv. vol. vi. p. 91 ; (2) a sermon entitled *God's doings and Man's duty*, preached on April 2, 1646 (E. 330, 11); and (3) *Mr. Peters' Last Report of the English Wars* (E. 351, 12). Unless I am mistaken, any candid reader of these will find that there is little difficulty in understanding the character of the writer, especially as the character here unconsciously drawn

lands in consequence of religious persecution.[1] He entered
His early life. Trinity College, Cambridge, in 1613, at the age of
fifteen.[2] About 1620 he visited ·London, and was
there convinced of sin by a sermon which he heard at St.
Paul's. Retiring to Essex, he fell under the influence of
Thomas Hooker, and it was there that he married a widow,
whose daughter by her first husband was afterwards the wife
of the younger Winthrop. Upon his return to London he
entered the ministry, and was licensed to preach by Bishop
Montaigne. He became a lecturer at St. Sepulchre's, where
according to his own statement he preached to an overflowing
congregation, and where ' above an hundred every week were
persuaded from sin to Christ.'

The days of Laud's influence were approaching, and shortly
after Laud's translation to the see of London Peters found it
Peters in Holland. expedient to remove to Rotterdam, where he became
the minister of a Separatist congregation, and was
not long in showing how little bigotry was in him. Both

is just the one to give rise to the libellous attacks which have been made
upon it. It is on these self-revelations that I have based my account of
the man. In spelling the name I have adhered to the form Peters, which
was usually adopted at the time, though in his own signature his name
appears as Peter. The omission of the final 's' seems to have been a
mere matter of habit, as in the cases of Bate for Bates, and Dyve for
Dyves. I may add that Peters's last production, *A dying Father's last
legacy*, appears to me a pious, sensible, and veracious work.

[1] He was baptized June 11, 1598. His father's name was Thomas
Dyckwood, *alias* Peters. *Parochial Hist. of Cornwall*, ii. 31.

[2] He took his degree of B.A. from Trinity in 1617–18, and his M.A.
in 1622. (Felt's *Memoir* and information supplied by Professor Mayor.)
The date of his birth contradicts the assertion of the Royalist pamphleteers, that he was a Fool in Shakspere's company. His entry at
Trinity is not given in the college registers, which do not notice the entry
of pensioners so early, but his graduation from that college may be set
against the statement of Dr. Yonge in *England's Shame* that he was ' sent
from school to the University of Cambridge, and there was admitted into
Jesus College,' and that being ' obdurate and irrefragable to the civil
government of that collegiate society' he was ' expulsed the University.'
If writers blunder about matters concerning which the truth was ascer-
tainable without difficulty, no credit is due to them when they tell us what
passed in the bedroom of the first Mrs. Peters before her marriage.

Ames, the English Separatist, and John Forbes, the Scottish Presbyterian, found in him a friend with whom they could converse on things which stand above the divisions of the churches.[1] Laud's arm was, however, long enough to reach Peters even in Rotterdam, and in 1635 the same ship which bore the younger Vane carried Peters to New England.

With Peters, who was soon engaged as a preacher at Salem, there was no impassable gulf between divine things and the ordinary ways of human life. Never had any minister less of the professional clergyman than Peters. His letters show him as he really was— fond of a jest, much concerned in the price of corn and butter, and taking the opportunity of a sermon to recommend the settlers to raise a stock for fishing,[2] but anxious withal for the righteousness as well as for the material prosperity of the colony. This idea of righteousness was not, indeed, altogether in advance of his age. There had been a war with the Pequod Indians, and Peters had learned that captives had been taken. "We have heard," he wrote to Winthrop, "of a dividence of women and children in the Bay, and would be glad of a share, viz. a young woman or girl and a boy if you think good." Probably the children, if, as was very likely the case, their parents had been slain, would be better off in Peters's family than if they had been left to the chances of the woods. On another point at least he was altogether for self-sacrifice. "We are bold," he continued, "to impart our thoughts about the corn at Pequoit, which we wish were all cut down or left for the Naragansicks rather than for us to take it ; for we fear it will prove a snare thus to hunt after their goods whilst we come forth pretending only the doing of justice, and we believe it would strike more terror into the Indians so to do. It will

margin note: 1635. Peters in New England.

---

[1] "I lived about six years near that famous Scotchman, Mr. John Forbes, with whom I travelled into Germany, and enjoyed him in much love and sweetness constantly, from whom I never had but encouragement though we differed in the way of our churches. Learned Amesius breathed his last breath in my bosom." *Mr. Peters' Last Report of the English Wars.* E. 351, 12.

[2] Winthrop's *Life of Winthrop*, ii. 132.

never quit cost for us to keep it." [1]   It is characteristic of the
man that, although he was at one with Vane on the great
question of religious liberty, he was shocked by the intolerant
spirit of the party of toleration to which the young Governor
had attached himself. [2]   He told Vane plainly that ' before he
came the churches were at peace.' [3]

    Peters's love of liberty was not a high intellectual persuasion
like that of Vane or Milton, nor did it arise, like that of Roger

*Peters's
views on
liberty of
conscience.*
Williams, from Biblical study undertaken under the
stress of persecution.   It sprang from the kindliness
of a man of genial temper to whom minute theological study was repulsive, and who, without disguising his own
opinions, preferred goodness of heart to rigidity of doctrine.
Peters could not handle a religious subject without attempting
to apply it in some way to the benefit of men in the world.
Three things, he declared in his last apology for his life, he had
ever sought after : ' First, that goodness, which is really so,
and such religion might be highly advanced ; secondly, that
good learning might have all countenance ; thirdly, that there
may not be a beggar in Israel—in England.' [4]   With Peters
the difficulty was not to avoid quarrels, but to understand why
men should quarrel.   " Truly it wounds my soul," he wrote at
a time when, though the civil war was at an end, ecclesiastical
bitterness was at its height, "when I think Ireland would
perish and England continue her misery through the disagree-
ment of ten or twenty learned men. . . . Could we but conquer each other's spirit, we should soon befool the devil and
his instruments ; to which end I could wish we that are
ministers might pray together, eat and drink together, because,
if I mistake not, estrangement hath boiled us up to jealousy
and hatred." [5]   There must have been an absolute hostility to
cant in a Puritan divine of the seventeenth century who could
recommend dining together as a remedy for the disputatious-

[1] Peters to Winthrop.   *Mass. Soc. Hist. Collections,* series iv. C. p. 95.
[2] See *Hist. of Engl.* 1603–1642, viii. 175.
[3] Winthrop's *Hist. of New England,* 209.
[4] *A dying Father's last legacy,* 112.
[5] *Mr. Peters' Last Report.*   E. 351, 12.

ness of the clergy. His own evident enjoyment of a good dinner when it came in his way led, in the natural course of things, to the charges which were brought against him by his enemies of being a glutton, if not something worse.[1]

Such was the man who, at the opening of the civil troubles, returned to England, and after an expedition to the Irish coast in the company of Lord Forbes,[2] ultimately drifted into the

Hugh Peters as an army chaplain. position of an army chaplain in the New Model. It was a post for which he was eminently fitted. It is easy to imagine how he could chat and jest with the soldiers, and yet could seize an opportunity to slip in a word on higher matters. His influence must have been such as Cromwell loved—an influence which in every word and action made for concord. The wildest vagaries, the most rigid orthodoxy, were equally secure of a mild and tolerant judgment from Peters. On the other hand Peters was not the man to slacken the arms of the soldiers. For Royalism and the religion of Royalism he had a hearty detestation, and whenever there was a battle to be fought or a fortress to be stormed, he was always ready with a rousing appeal to the warriors of God's army to quit themselves like men in the struggle against wickedness in high places. It was one of the saddest results of Laud's despotism that it had taught one who seemed born for the widest practical sympathy to regard the piety of the Church of England as absolutely outside the bounds of charity.

Whatever judgment may be passed on Peters, there can be no doubt that he was in high favour with both Fairfax

Peters employed by Fairfax and Cromwell. and Cromwell. It was Peters who had been selected to unfold at Westminster the tale of the surrender of Bridgwater; and he was now again employed to explain to Parliament, as an eye-witness only could explain, the full details of the surrender of Bristol.

Hugh Peters was in his place as a chaplain of the New

---

[1] See a satire entitled *Hosanna.* E. 559, 11.

[2] Under the date of 1649 Whitelocke states that letters from Ireland affirmed of Peters that at the beginning of the troubles in Ireland he led a brigade against the rebels, and came off with honour and victory. The

Model.   Richard Baxter would have been in his place as the minister of a large town congregation.   Some little time after the war broke out he had been compelled to retire from Kid-

Baxter at Coventry.   derminster by the attack of a Royalist mob, and had shortly afterwards removed to Coventry, where he preached to the townsmen and the soldiers of the garrison. His strong sense of the reality of the spiritual world and his tenderness in dealing with individual cases endeared him to

His mental position.   his congregation.   Yet Baxter was above all things a controversialist, one who loved to set forth the gospel as addressed indeed to the hearts of men, but as guarded by all the minute distinctions of Puritan theology.   For forms of church government he did not care much.   He did not altogether approve of the system which Parliament and Assembly were attempting to set up, and he would probably at any time of his life have been content with a compromise, if such could be found, between Presbyterianism and Episcopacy. His mind, in fact, was essentially unpolitical.   He could comprehend ideas, but he could not comprehend men, and even in 1645 the common-place about fighting for King and Parliament was still for him a stern reality, which every man in England was bound to do his best to carry into effect.

A visit to some old friends in the army two days after the fight at Naseby opened Baxter's eyes to the temper which pre-

Baxter visits the army.   vailed there.   All manner of opinions made themselves heard amongst the soldiers.   Arminians and Anabaptists, Independents and Antinomians discoursed freely in favour of their special views.   It was perhaps against these men less as sectarians than as heretics that Baxter was disposed to wage war.   He regarded them, doubtless not without reason, as men who, being uneducated in theological lore, threw themselves into the exposition of the most delicate mysteries without adequate preparation, and who added to their rash ignorance a no less rash contempt for the authorised clerical exponents of truth.   Rough military jokes

evidence is not very good, but the thing is likely enough if it means that he suddenly urged on a brigade to fight.   He had certainly been in Ireland with Lord Forbes.

about the Priest-biters, the Dry-vines, and the Dissembly men filled him with horror. He resolved to be the St. George who should slay this dragon with the sword of the Spirit, and he fancied his work would be the easier because he discovered that there were plenty of orthodox Christians in the army, and still more who were, in his sense, hardly Christians at all. The sectaries, he thought, were not one in twenty in each regiment.[1]

Without difficulty Baxter obtained an appointment as chaplain to Whalley's regiment, and for some months he

Baxter as chaplain to Whalley's regiment.

accompanied the army on its marches. His whole time was spent in fruitless disputations with men who were as resolute as they appeared to him to be unintelligent. Each one had his own petty theory of the relations between God and man to maintain, and what was worse was that 'their most frequent and vehement disputes were for

Liberty of conscience in the army.

liberty of conscience, as they called it ; that is, that the civil magistrate had nothing to do to determine of anything in matters of religion, by constraint or restraint, but every man might not only hold but preach and do in matters of religion what he pleased ; that the civil magistrate hath nothing to do with but civil things, to keep the peace and protect the Church's liberties, &c.'

No wonder that Cromwell, as Baxter, much to his astonishment, discovered, looked askance on a man who controverted

Cromwell is cool towards Baxter.

the doctrine which alone enabled the army to hold together. Already, when Baxter had announced at Coventry his intention of setting forth to reform the army, Colonel Purefoy had warned him to abstain from the rash enterprise : "Let me hear no more of that," he said. "If Noll Cromwell should hear any soldier speak but such a word, he would cleave his crown. You do them wrong : it is not so." As often happens, the subordinate had exaggerated

---

[1] "For the greatest part of the common soldiers, especially of the foot, were ignorant men of little religion, abundance of them such as had been taken prisoners, or turned out of garrisons under the King, and had been soldiers in his army ; and these would do anything to please their officers." *Rel. Baxterianæ*, 53. This passage ought to have been sufficient to put an end to the popular notion about the New Model.

the intentions of his superior, and Cromwell contented himself with leaving the new chaplain without the notice which Baxter conceived to be his due.

Nor was it only the religious opinions of the soldiers which struck Baxter with horror. Those who had strange views about religion had also strange views about the State. "I perceived," declares Baxter, "they took the King for a tyrant and an enemy, and really intended to master him or to ruin him, and they thought if they might fight against him they might kill or conquer him, and if they might conquer, they were never more to trust him further than he was in their power; and that they thought it folly to irritate him either by wars or contradictions in Parliament, if so be they must needs take him for their King, and trust him with their lives when they had thus displeased him." These audacious reasoners, too, had more to say on another head. "What," they argued, "were the Lords of England but William the Conqueror's Colonels, or the Barons but his Majors, or the Knights but his Captains?" "They plainly showed me," continued the bewildered chaplain, "that they thought God's providence would cast the trust of religion and the kingdom upon them as conquerors; they made nothing of all the most wise and godly in the armies and garrisons that were not of their way. *Per fas aut nefas*, by law or without it, they were resolved to take down, not only bishops, and liturgy, and ceremonies, but all that did withstand their way. They . . . most honoured the Separatists, Anabaptists, and Antinomians; but Cromwell and his council took on them to join themselves to no party, but to be for the liberty of all." [1]

The military view of Royalty,

and of Nobility.

Cromwell for the liberty of all.

To be for the liberty of all was so truly the highest wisdom that there is some difficulty in turning the attention to the weakness which underlay the aspirations of these military sectaries. There was in them much vigour and moral earnestness, but there was also much ignorance and fanaticism. It was not merely that they could not satisfy the theological niceties of Baxter. They were too

Danger of revolutionary changes.

[1] *Rel. Baxterianæ*, 51.

sternly moral to commend themselves to a nation content with laxer habits, and too deficient in broad culture to satisfy its intelligence. To liberty they had a claim, but they had no claim to rule. Yet it was upon ruling that their hearts were set. They wanted to cut across the old lines of progress without the power of establishing new ones. They wished to cast down king and nobility, with no nation inspired by the spirit of democracy behind their backs. It could hardly be other-

Cromwell's moderating influence.

wise, but the fact that it was so goes far to explain the long patience with which Cromwell pleaded with Parliament to grant liberty of conscience, but to keep the control of the army in its own hands.[1]

It is possible that the House of Commons was the more unwilling to comply with Cromwell's request because it had recently been irritated by Lilburne, who had forfeited his position in the army through his refusal to take the Covenant,

The revolutionary spirit of the army.

but who, nevertheless, embodied more than anyone else the revolutionary spirit by which the army was pervaded. Prynne had not forgotten Lilburne's attack upon him in the winter, and Prynne, like Laud, was by no means indisposed to call in the arm of the flesh to rid

May 16. Lilburne arrested.

him of his adversaries. On May 16 Lilburne was arrested and carried before the Committee of Examinations to give account of the letter in which he had declared against the payment of tithes.[2] His reply was a

May 17. He justifies himself.

scathing denunciation of the treatment to which good Christians and sturdy defenders of the Parliamentary cause were frequently subjected, if they refused to comply with the prevailing system of religion. Some had been thrust into prison, others set in the stocks, or driven from their homes, by order of magistrates or of military commanders. Private violence was sometimes as dangerous as the abuse of authority. A man with a crossbow had lately shot bullets at the noted leader of the Baptists, Hanserd Knollys, though in this case Lilburne honestly acknowledged that the offender had been apprehended.[3] Upon this the

[1] See p. 319.   [2] See p. 111.
[3] *The reasons of* . . . . *Lilburne's sending his letter to Mr. Prynne.*
E. 288, 12.

committee declared that the arrest of Lilburne had been a mistake, and declined to trouble him further.

Here the matter might have ended if Lilburne had been content with a merely dialectical victory. Lilburne was, how-
ever, inspired with all Cromwell's devotion to the service of the public, without Cromwell's reticence or sense of the limit which divides the practicable from the impracticable. Silence was impossible for him as long as there were grievances to be redressed and oppression to be assailed. On June 13, when all London was in suspense on the eve of Naseby fight, he printed, without submitting his pamphlet to the licenser, the arguments in favour of the oppressed which he had urged before the committee. In so doing he had committed an offence in comparison of which the unlicensed publication of Milton's *Areopagitica* was as nothing. His was no philosophical argument in behalf of liberty of speech and writing. He had used the unlicensed press to stir up public feeling in favour of men whom he alleged to be ill-treated, instead of contenting himself with appealing to Parliament as a court of final resort.

Accordingly, on June 18, Lilburne was again arrested and brought before the committee, though even on this occasion there was no attempt to press the charge home, and his imprisonment does not seem to have lasted more than a single night. Besides public grievances Lilburne had a private grievance of his own. The money which had been voted to him by Parliament in compensation for his sufferings at the hands of the Star Chamber had never been paid, and his arrears of pay as an officer were still unsatisfied. He accordingly rode down to the Western army to obtain a good word from Cromwell. On July 14 he witnessed the Battle of Langport, and brought back the news of the victory to Westminster, as well as a letter from Cromwell urging the House of Commons to take up the cause of a brave and honest man who was asking no more than his due.[1]

Almost as soon as Lilburne was back in London, he was

[1] *Innocency and truth justified.* E. 314, 21.

Margin notes:
June 13. Lilburne prints his reasons.

June 18. He is again arrested.

Lilburne's claims on Parliament.

July 14. Cromwell supports him.

again in trouble. Before Naseby had been fought, whilst
anxiety as to the issue of the strife prevailed at
Westminster, there was enough combustible matter
in Parliament to produce a conflagration. The
Independents threw the blame for all that went wrong upon
the Presbyterians, whilst the Presbyterians cast it back upon
the Independents. After the great victory the wrath of the
rival parties cooled down, and there was, for the time, a common desire to extinguish the embers of strife. Of
this change of feeling Savile was the first victim.
He charged Holles with having been in correspondence with Digby, but the only evidence which it was in his
power to adduce was that of a correspondent at Oxford, whose
name he declined, from motives of honour, to betray. Many
months later he alleged that his correspondent was the Duchess
of Buckingham, and, though Savile's character for truthfulness
did not stand high, it is likely enough that the
charge was well founded. At all events, Savile had
no friends at Westminster, and the Lords sent him
to the Tower for refusing to name his informant.[1]

State of Parliamentary feeling.

Savile's charge against Holles.

June 20. Savile sent to the Tower.

The imprisonment of Savile could not stop men's mouths,
and when Lilburne returned from Langport he not only found
that Holles's alleged negotiation with Digby was the
subject of common talk, but that it was also noised
abroad that the Speaker and his brother, Sir John
Lenthall, in the dark days of the plots at the opening of 1644, had had a hand in forwarding 60,000*l.* from Sir
Basil Brooke in London to the King at Oxford. Though
there was nothing intrinsically improbable in the
charge,[2] Lilburne had no means of testing its truth.
Nevertheless he blurted out the story without compunction. The Speaker of the House of Commons was a

Lilburne hears rumours affecting Holles and Lenthall.

July 19. Lilburne again taken into custody.

[1] *L.J.* vii. 440; viii. 302. There was also a charge brought by Savile against Holles and Whitelocke.

[2] We know from the Verney MSS. that in 1647 Sir John's wife took a bribe of 50*l.* from Lady Verney for favouring her case before a committee, which she could hardly do except by using the influence of her brother-in-law.

dangerous man to provoke, and Lilburne was at once taken into custody by order of the House.[1]

Once more from his captivity Lilburne appealed to the people through the press. In a *Letter to a Friend* he justified

His *Letter to a Friend.* his conduct in every respect. In his advocacy for liberty of speech in its extremest form, Lilburne

His view on the authority of Parliaments, rejected the despotism of Parliament as he had rejected the despotism of the King. "For my part," he wrote, "I look upon the House of Commons as the supreme power of England, who have residing in them that power that is inherent in the people—who yet are not to act according to their own wills and pleasure, but according to the fundamental constitutions and customs of the land, which, I conceive, provide for the safety and preservation of the people—unto whom I judge I am bound in conscience to yield either active or passive obedience; that is to say, either to do what they command, or to submit my body to their pleasure for not yielding active obedience to what I conceive is unjust. And truly I should much desire to know

and on the Committee of Examinations. of you what you conceive of the Committee of Examinations : for either it is a court of justice or no court of justice, and either it is tied unto rules or not tied ; but if it be a court of justice and tied unto rules when it sits upon criminal causes betwixt man and man concerning life, liberty, or estate . . . . methinks they should observe the method of other courts of justice, and that which they themselves did in all or most of their committees at the beginning of this Parliament, that the doors might be open to all the free people of England that have a desire to be present to see what they say or do, not kept close to keep out men's friends and suffer their enemies to be in ; and that men should have the liberty of *Magna Carta* and the Petition of Right— for which I have fought[2] all this while—and not to be examined upon interrogatories concerning themselves as we used to be in the Star Chamber and High Commission, and for refusing to answer to be committed."[3]

---

[1] *C.J.* iv. 213.　　　　　[2] Printed 'fought for.'
[3] *The Copy of a Letter to a friend*, p. 41.　E. 296, 5.

New Parliament, in short, was but old King writ large. Revolutions raise fresh questions every day, and Lilburne was but the first to ask what would soon be in many mouths. Yet it was a question which could receive no adequate answer as yet. In 1645 Lilburne's was a cry raised out of due time. As Cromwell well knew, so long as there was war in the land, no responsible politician could venture to narrow the sphere within which Parliamentary authority was exercised. For all that, a later generation, to whom Lilburne's dreams have become self-evident truths, does well in honouring the man who, wrong-headed and impracticable as he was, took his stand in advance with the framers of the Kentish Petition in the days of Anne, with the supporters of Wilkes's election and of the publicity of Parliamentary debate in the days of George III.

Lilburne's constitutional position.

The remainder of the story of Lilburne's present struggle is soon told. Suiting his action to his words, he refused to answer before the Committee of Examinations unless the cause of his committal were shown, in accordance with the Petition of Right. The House of Commons at once ordered his prosecution at quarter sessions on the ground of notorious scandals contained in his *Letter to a Friend*, but it either soon forgot its indignation in the multiplicity of its affairs, or discovered the folly of making a martyr of its critic. When the sessions were opened no charge was preferred against Lilburne, and the prisoner at once asked to be liberated on the ground of the silence of his accusers. Though the magistrates refused to interfere, the House of Commons itself on October 14 directed his discharge.[1]

Aug. 9. Lilburne refuses to answer.

Aug. 11. His prosecution ordered,

and dropped.

Oct. 14. His liberation.

Lilburne's case was not the only one which, though threatening at one time to breed a political storm, was allowed quietly to sink into oblivion. The circumstances under which

---

[1] *C.J.* iv. 235, 236, 239, 253, 307; *A just defence of J. Bastwick,* E. 265, 2; *The Liar Confounded,* by Prynne, E. 267, 1. Bastwick's pamphlet is as amusing as one of Lilburne's. He explains how he had taken the trouble to teach Lilburne manners in his youth.

the Independent leaders had attempted to negotiate for the surrender of Oxford[1] had been such as easily to give fair

July 19.
Cranford committed to the Tower.

ground for a suspicion that they had betrayed their trust. In July a Scotch minister named Cranford, having been detected in asserting that Say and his friends had carried on unauthorised negotiations with persons at Oxford, was promptly sent to the Tower. It soon, however, appeared that Cranford was a harmless retailer of gossip, and without any long delay he recovered his liberty.[2] It was plain that the Commons had no wish to proceed to extremity against offenders on either side.

No such conciliatory feeling manifested itself in Parliament so far as the King was concerned. Before the end of July, indeed, the Scottish commissioners had again urged

July 29.
The Scots ask that negotiations may be opened.

the importance of reopening negotiations for peace. It was difficult for the Houses to refuse the request abruptly, but on August 18 they resolved that the negotiation should take the form of definite propo-

Aug. 18.
Bills to be prepared for presentation to the King.

sitions contained in Bills to which Charles should be requested to signify his assent without discussion. As, however, the preparation of these Bills would of necessity occupy considerable time, the proposed negotiation would have to stand aside for the present.[3] The mistake was perhaps made of thinking that a few more victories might induce Charles to accept Bills which he would at present be certain to reject.

There was one way in which the House of Commons might strengthen its position in dealing with the King on the one hand and with the Scots on the other. It had long been reproached with being no more than a mere fragment of the national representation. On August 21 it was re-

Aug. 21.
New writs to be issued.

solved, though only by the narrow majority of three, that a new writ should be issued for the borough of Southwark. During the following week a large number of constituencies received favourable answers to their petitions for permission to hold fresh elections. It is noticeable that,

---

[1] See p. 212. [2] *C.J.* iv. 212, 213; *Baillie,* ii. 311.
[3] *L.J.* vii. 515, 530; *C.J.* iv. 232, 245.

in the course of debate, the issue of the new writs was opposed by the Peace-party and supported by the War-party. The discussion turned on points too technical to bring to light the real motives of the speakers. It can, however, hardly be doubted that those who wished to see the benches filled with new members were actuated by the belief that in the existing state of affairs the constituencies would send to Parliament members favourable to a vigorous prosecution of the war as the shortest road to peace, whilst their opponents feared lest members elected in the temper engendered by the recent victories would re-echo the revolutionary feelings prevailing in the army.

Significant as was the step thus taken, it must not be imagined that the House of Commons had adopted the modern doctrine of the supremacy of the majority in the constituencies, on whichever side its vote might be thrown. Special care was taken to exclude the Royalist element. Not only was a resolution passed that none who had borne arms for the King should have a seat, but a writ was refused to Beverley, where the Yorkshire Royalists seemed likely to influence the election.[1] The business of Parliament was still to carry on war, and so long as war was waged there must be no admission of enemies into the camp.

Safeguard against Royalist elections.

[1] *C.J.* iv. 249; Whitacre's Diary, *Add. MSS.* 31,116, fol. 227. Yonge's Diary, *Add. MSS.* 18,780, fol. 104.

CHAPTER XXXVI.

ROWTON HEATH AND PHILIPHAUGH.

THE confidence with which the House of Commons was appealing to the constituencies was in marked contrast with the increasing despondency of the other side. The great majority of the Royalists were evidently anxious to submit to necessity. In the West especially the oppressions of the King's army were intolerable. Early in August Goring boasted of the victories he was to win as loudly as if he had never been beaten at Langport. Before many days he was throwing all the blame of his inaction upon his fellow-officers, and declaring that nothing would be done unless he were appointed Lieutenant-General to the Prince, with full power over the whole of the Western armies. If Goring had been fit to command even a regiment his request would have been reasonable. As it was, it is difficult to decide whether the King's service would have suffered most by complying with his wishes or by disappointing them. He remained at Exeter for some weeks carousing at his ease, and replying with flippant jests to all who complained of the outrages committed by his soldiers.[1] It is not unlikely that he considered the King's cause to be lost, and that he had no other object in view except to enjoy himself, in his own peculiar fashion, as long as possible.

The Prince's councillors who, with their young master, had retreated to Launceston after the Battle of Langport, but who, so long as Bristol held out, imagined that there were still some chances in their favour, were almost brought to despair by Goring's misconduct. As a last resource they recommended young Charles to go in person

1645. August.
The Royalists anxious for peace.

Goring after Langport.

Aug. 29. The Prince at Exeter.

[1] *Clarendon*, ix. 76.

to Exeter to bring his authority to bear on the unruly general. His exhortations had little effect on Goring,[1] but his appearance at Exeter brought him face to face with an unexpected difficulty. The secret of a letter in which his father had commanded him to leave the country if he was exposed to danger[2] had oozed out, and was taken by all who heard of it as implying a confession that further resistance was hopeless.

The gentry ask him to open negotiations for peace.

The gentry assembled at Exeter openly talked of asking the Prince to make overtures to Parliament without consulting his father. To avert the necessity of engaging himself in so unseemly a course, he was recommended, as soon as the loss of Bristol was known, to ask Fairfax for permission to send Hopton and Culpepper to the King to urge him to entertain proposals for peace. Fairfax replied with courtesy, and forwarded the letter to Westminster, where, as might be expected, no action was taken upon it. At Exeter its sole object had been obtained in quieting for a time the minds of the gentry of Devon.[3]

Sept. 15. The Prince writes to Fairfax.

To Englishmen the best course open to Charles seemed to be that he should come to terms with Parliament, and should thus restore the national unity on the most advantageous terms procurable. The able minister who was himself the Government of France took a very different view. Mazarin had no wish to see a monarchy, such as he was accustomed to deal with, succeeded in England by a vigorous and military republic, and as the embodiment of the authority of the Crown of France he had doubtless some sympathy with the sorrows of a Court. His main object, however, in his relations with England was undoubtedly to keep England weak and divided, in order that it might be unable to interfere in Continental affairs to the detriment of France. To strengthen the power of the Scots, with whom France had, for more than three centuries, been on excellent terms, and to induce the King to throw himself upon their support and upon

Mazarin's relations with England.

[1] *Clarendon*, ix. 81.   [2] *Ibid.* ix. 74.

[3] *L.J.* vii. 600; Fairfax to the Prince, Sept. 19, *Clar. St. P.* ii. 192; *Clarendon*, ix. 82.

that of their Presbyterian allies, seemed to him the shortest road to the end at which he aimed. It would at least serve to keep in check the New Model army and its supporters in Parliament. Reasonably distrusting the qualifications of the resident ambassador, Sabran, for so delicate a task, he despatched, at the end of July, a young diplomatist, Montreuil, to England, nominally as an agent to the Scottish Government and its commissioners in London, but in reality to negotiate a settlement of the English troubles which might be satisfactory to France.

Whether an alliance between the King and the Scots was reached by Charles's abandoning Episcopacy, or by the Scots' ceasing to insist upon imposing Presbyterianism upon England, was a matter of absolute indifference to Montreuil or his employer. The new diplomatist first tried his powers upon the Scots. Finding that they were impervious to his arguments, he hoped to find Charles more yielding. "The King," he wrote, "ought to prefer the preservation of his crown to that of all the mitres in the country." In this anticipation he was supported by the Earl of Holland, who, vexed at his long seclusion from political power and its material advantages, was glad enough to renew his old friendly relations with the French embassy.[1]

Aug.
Montreuil
in London.

His nego-
tiations
with the
Scots.

In the middle of September the time seemed to have arrived when a forward step might be taken. The Scottish commissioners supposed that, after the surrender of Bristol, the King would be ready to concede what he had refused before, whilst the knowledge that their own country had fallen under the sway of Montrose made them desirous of obtaining such a position in England as would enable them to turn their attention to their struggle with the victor of Kilsyth. At the same time the ill-feeling between themselves and the English Parliament was on the increase. On September 13 Loudoun not only informed the Houses

Sept.
The Scots
anxious for
peace.

---

[1] Montreuil to Mazarin, Aug. $\frac{14}{24}$, $\frac{21}{31}$, *Arch. des Aff. Etrangères*, ii. fol. 539, 546 : Montreuil to Brienne, Aug. $\frac{21}{31}$, *Carte MSS.* lxxxiii. fol. 94.

that Leven must follow David Leslie across the Tweed, but summoned them to send assistance to Scotland in virtue of their obligations under the Covenant, as Scotland had formerly assisted England. The House of Commons was in no hurry to comply with the demands of their brethren in the North. It retaliated by asking whether the whole of the Scottish army was to leave England, and whether in that case the Scots intended to withdraw their garrisons from Newcastle, Berwick, and Carlisle, and to make over those strongholds to English troops.[1]

Sept. 13.
They ask the English to aid them against Montrose.
A counter-demand.

As might have been expected, in his conversation with Montreuil Loudoun launched forth into unmeasured denunciation of the English leaders. The Scots, he said, were anxious for peace, and he believed that all parties in England were of the same mind. Under these circumstances Holland offered himself as an intermediary between the commissioners and the Presbyterian party in the English Parliament, and it was finally agreed that terms should be drawn up to be despatched to Henrietta Maria. If she agreed to them, and was also able to obtain for them her husband's approval, France would compel their acceptance by the English Parliament. Balmerino, who was one of the Scottish commissioners, reminded Montreuil that it was to the interest of Mazarin to support Scotland in order to be sure of her assistance if ever the time came when he needed aid against England.[2]

Such was the project on which, with blinded eyes, men like Holles and Stapleton were ready to embark. Though able to command a majority in the Commons whenever there was any question of imposing fetters on sectarian preaching, they were so hopelessly in a minority whenever they wished to impede the energetic prosecution of the war, that they did not

[1] Paper of the Scottish commissioners, in *Divers papers presented*, p. 11, E. 307, 4 ; Whitacre's Diary, *Add. MSS.* 31,116, fol. 232 ; *C.J.* iv. 273.

[2] Montreuil to Mazarin, Sept. $\frac{13}{23}$, *Arch. des Aff. Etrangères*, ii. fol. 568 ; Montreuil to Brienne, Sept. $\frac{18}{28}$, *Carte MSS.* lxxxiii. fol. 100.

at this time venture to divide the House in favour of any open overture to the King.[1] They preferred to take refuge in a secret intrigue with the Scots and the French. They did not perceive what strength they were adding to their opponents, the Independents, by enabling them to stand forth more evidently than before as the guardians of the national interest and the national honour.

For the present, however, in spite of the loss of Bristol, Charles was not brought so low as to despair of success.

The King's projects. Under the guidance of the restless Digby, he was aiming for the third time at a junction with the victorious Montrose. In a letter written on September 18

Sept. 18. Culpepper's plan. from Barnstaple, Culpepper, who had lately visited Digby at Cardiff, and had drunk in with pleasure some of the notions of that sanguine schemer, laid down a complete plan of action. If Bristol had been lost, why should they not endeavour to get London instead of it? Goring undoubtedly could not long hold out where he was. Let him, therefore, join the King at Oxford or Newark. Let Montrose come south and add his strength to the united armies. One battle gained would place London in the King's hands. French or Irish soldiers might be brought in to occupy the West after Goring had deserted it. One piece of advice Culpepper added. "The next ingredient," he wrote, "must be a severe and most strict reformation in the discipline and the manners of the army. Our courage is . . . enerved by lazy licentiousness, and good men are so scandalised at the horrid impiety of our armies that they will not believe that God can bless any cause in such hands."[2] Whatever may have been the value of Culpepper's strategical disquisitions, a plan requiring the endowment of Goring and Grenvile with all

---

[1] At first sight the reader is puzzled to find Montreuil writing as if the Independents were in a constant majority in the House, till he remembers that a Frenchman cared nothing for their attitude towards the sects, and a great deal for their attitude towards the war. There was a cross division of parties, as there had been in the earlier days of the Parliament.

[2] Culpepper to Digby, Sept. 18. *Clarendon St. P.* ii. 188.

the virtues of the New Model was ruined before it was attempted.

In part, at least, Digby had already anticipated this advice.

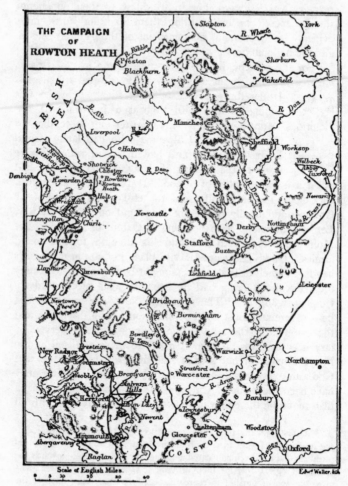

He had written to the Prince's Council in the West directing them to send Goring to join the King with a picked body of horse. On the 19th Goring was directed to carry out these orders.[1] But it was one thing to give instructions to that self-willed officer and another thing to induce him to execute them. Whilst Bristol was besieged he had spent weeks in haggling with the Council over the terms on which he was to march to its relief, and in this supreme hour of the King's necessity he could think of nothing except his own position in the army.[2]

Sept. 19.
Goring
ordered to
join the
King.

Charles's position at Raglan, whither he had retired after the relief of Hereford, was rapidly becoming untenable. To the east was Poyntz; to the west were the Welsh levies, which, since the loss of Bristol, threatened at any moment to exchange their smouldering discontent for open hostility.[3] There was nothing for it but to set out once more in search of Montrose. It was probably before the King started that Digby made an appeal to Leven and the other Scottish commanders to join their forces with his own and with those of Montrose, on the understanding that, whatever might be done in England, the Scottish Church and State should be unassailed.[4] It seems that the letter never reached Leven,[5] and, though we have no information on the subject, it is possible that it was delivered to the friendly Callander,[6] and was suppressed by him as likely to render the prospects of accommodation more hopeless than they were already.

Charles at
Raglan.

Temper of
the Welsh.

On September 18, after some days of hesitating movements, Charles set out once more on his quest in the North. Eluding Poyntz, he reached Presteign that evening, and after long and weary marches over the Welsh hills, rested at Chirk Castle on the night of the 22nd.[7]

Sept. 18.
Charles
marches to
the North,

Sept. 22,
and reaches
Chirk Castle.

---

[1] Berkshire to Goring, Sept. 19. *Clar. MSS.* 1,965.

[2] Goring to Culpepper, Sept. 28. *Ibid.* 1,974.

[3] *Symonds,* 239.

[4] Digby to Leven, Callander, &c., in *Clarendon St. P.* ii. 189.

[5] Leven to the commander of the King's forces, Oct. 9. *L.J.* vii. 638.

[6] See p. 285.

[7] Digby was as usual buoyant with hopefulness. "The Scots army here in England," he wrote on the 21st, "is drawn into the North, but

At Chirk Castle Charles learnt that his presence was sadly needed at Chester. Though the city had not been completely invested, a local besieging force under Colonel Michael Jones had carried the eastern suburbs on the 20th, but had been repulsed in an attempt to storm the city itself on the night of the 22nd. The approach of the King filled the garrison with fresh hopes. On the 23rd Charles with his life-guard, some 340 strong, rode into the city, whilst Sir Marmaduke Langdale with a party of horse was despatched over Holt Bridge to take up a position on Rowton Heath, about two miles from the south-eastern side of the fortifications. In this way it was hoped that Jones would be caught and ruined by simultaneous blows from Langdale and the reinforced garrison.

State of Chester.

Sept. 23. Plan for the overthrow of the besiegers.

Well laid as the King's scheme was, he had omitted Poyntz from his calculations. That active commander had started in pursuit as soon as he learnt that Charles had given him the slip, and had reached Whitchurch on the 23rd, the day on which the King entered Chester. Here he was met by a messenger from Jones, and, on hearing from him of Charles's arrival, he pushed on all night, arriving on the morning of the 24th at an open space known as Hatton Heath. Langdale had already posted himself on Rowton Heath, about two miles nearer Chester,[1] and being already warned of his danger, had faced round to meet the advancing enemy.

Poyntz's movements.

A night march.

Sept. 24. Battle of Rowton Heath.

Both the opposing forces were almost entirely composed of

doubtless dares not look into Scotland unless to submit to Montrose. . . . My dear Lord, are not these miracles of Providence able to make an atheist superstitious? For my part I profess to you I never did look upon our business with that assurance that I do now, of God's carrying us through with His own immediate hand, for all this work of Montrose is above what can be attributed to mankind." Digby to Jermyn, Sept. 21. *Bankes MSS.*

[1] The south-east end of Rowton Heath, which is the one towards Poyntz's advance, was known as Miller's Heath, and is so called in some of the narratives of the battle, but the whole was also known as Rowton Heath, and I have therefore, for convenience sake, dropped the name of Miller's Heath.

cavalry, and Poyntz would therefore gladly have remained on the defensive, as a narrow lane with hedges on either side separated him from Langdale. As, however, the Royalists, having no mind to place themselves at a disadvantage, refrained from making an attack, Poyntz at last gave the word to advance. With one vigorous charge he drove the enemy before him, but Langdale soon rallied his men, and after repeated efforts Poyntz was compelled to draw back. Repulsed as he was, the Parliamentary commander did not abandon hope. Keeping the enemy in constant alarm by a series of feints, he despatched a courier to Jones to beg for assistance. Jones sent him a few horsemen and, what was far more welcome, a small body of musketeers. Poyntz had now the advantage of the enemy. His musketeers occupied the defensible ground on either side of the road, stealing forward from hedge to hedge. Having thus secured command over the passage between the two heaths, he ordered the horse to make one more attempt to charge down the road. As the horsemen emerged on Rowton Heath, they again engaged in a desperate struggle, but this time they were supported by foot, and a well-directed volley of musketry from behind the hedges scattered Langdale's reserve and decided the fortune of the day. The Northern horse, whose misconduct at Naseby had brought disaster upon their master's cause, turned round and fled, and the remainder of the cavalry imitated their example, with Poyntz's victorious troopers in hot pursuit behind. Whilst Langdale had still been holding his own on Rowton Heath, Lord Lichfield, the gallant soldier who

Sally from Chester.

had found it impossible to pay the fees of his new peerage, headed a sally from the city.[1] For a time he was successful, but in the end his men were driven back and he himself was slain. A tablet in the city wall still marks the spot from which Charles looked down to watch the attack upon the besiegers.[2]

The blow was a crushing one. Not only was Chester, the

---

[1] See p. 312.

[2] *Walker*, 139; *The King's forces totally routed*, E. 303, 18; *A letter from Poyntz*, E. 303, 24; Digby to Ormond, Sept. 26, Carte's *Orig. Letters*, i. 90; *Slingsby's Diary*, 169; *Iter Carolinum*.

one port of importance through which supplies could arrive from Ireland, endangered, but, girt about with enemies as he was, Charles could no longer entertain the hope of reaching Scotland by a march through Lancashire. It was not without surprise that his bewildered followers scrutinised the cold unimpassioned features which showed no signs of grief or depression. It was difficult for them to realise the thoughts which moved in a sphere untroubled by the reverses or the successes which counted for so much with other men.[1] Yet even Charles did not live wholly in the spiritual world. In the worst of times he never lost confidence in mundane resources, and as long as he had Digby at his side he was never likely to give himself completely up to blank despair. On the 25th he rode out of Chester, and, with the 2,400 horse which remained to him, established himself at Denbigh.

Result of
Charles's
defeat.

Sept. 25.
Charles at
Denbigh.

Digby, at least, was in high spirits. In writing to Ormond on the 26th, he almost succeeded in representing the conflict on Rowton Heath as a victory. Five hundred Welshmen, he informed his correspondent, had now been added to the garrison of Chester, and with the fortified ports on the western side of the Dee in their hands, it would be easy for the Royalists to hinder the enemy from blocking up the city. Nor was there any reason to despair of success elsewhere. According to report, Montrose had sent a large force under the Earl of Crawford and Lord Ogilvy into Westmorland, and David Leslie, who had met them there, had been deserted by his own soldiers and miserably routed. Whatever might be the truth of this rumour, it was essential that Charles should join Montrose. "If," wrote the enthusiastic Secretary, "his Majesty can once see his person secure from being thus daily hazarded and chased about, I see no reason why we should be at all dismayed with our many late misfortunes here, since no man can think England divided— though the major part against the King—able to resist Scotland and Ireland entire for him with any considerable party here." All this was followed by a postscript containing the latest news.

Sept. 26.
Digby's
sanguine
reports.

[1] *Slingsby's Diary*, 169.

It was quite true, according to Digby, 'that the rebels were much more broken' than the King's troops. They had 're-treated northwards.' Crawford had 'advanced as far as Kendal with a brave army.'[1] On the same day, in writing to Nicholas, Digby revealed Charles's plan of action.

Charles's
plan of
action.

Reports were being spread abroad that he was about to take refuge in Anglesea or to take ship for some port in Scotland. His real intention was 'to steal or break through to Newark, from whence, by God's blessing,' they would without doubt be able to join Montrose.[2] The project which had failed in August[3] was to be again attempted in September.

On the very next day the edifice of fancy so lightly reared was roughly shattered. A letter from Byron, the governor of Chester, informed Digby that Poyntz was preparing to follow the King across the Dee, and that, unless Charles were able to cut off the enemy's supplies, the Parliamentarian army would have little difficulty in establishing a complete blockade of the city. If this were accomplished a speedy surrender was inevitable. To this doleful intimation Byron added intelligence still more doleful. A deserter who had come in had told him that there had been great rejoicings in Poyntz's army for a victory over Montrose.[4] The news, as Digby subsequently learnt, was true, whilst his own news of Crawford's victory over David Leslie was a pure fabrication.

Sept. 27.
Chester in
danger.

In point of fact, never had Montrose's difficulties been greater than when the victory of Kilsyth appeared to have placed him at the height of power. He was well aware that with his loosely compacted following he could not even hold the Lowlands; much less reconquer England for the King. Before his sanguine mind indeed

Aug. 15.
Montrose's
difficulties.

[1] Digby to Ormond, Sept. 26. Carte's *Orig. Letters,* i. 90.

[2] Digby to Nicholas, Sept. 26. *S.P. Dom.* dx. 153. This copy so dated was the one preserved by the writer. In *The Nicholas Papers,* p. 66, the letter is printed with the date of Sept. 28. In the original (*Egerton MSS.* 2,533, fol. 401) the 26 is altered to 28. I suppose therefore that the letter was written on the 26th, before the news from Philiphaugh had arrived, but not sent off. A postscript is dated Sept. 29.

[3] See p. 290.

[4] Byron to Digby, Sept. 27. *S.P. Dom.* dx. 157.

there arose the vision of a mighty host of Lowlanders weary of the tyranny of Argyle and the Kirk, hastening to take service under the King's Lieutenant. Yet it was hard to see how any hearty co-operation was to be expected between the hard-working peasants and farmers of the South and the untamed clansmen of the North, who boasted that in the course of twelve months no less than 15,000 Lowland Scots had fallen beneath their swords.

Montrose's first difficulty was with his Highlanders. At some time—it would seem before the Battle of Kilsyth had

Aug. 16. Montrose at Glasgow. been fought [1]—he had promised them the plunder of Glasgow in the belief that the town was unalterably devoted to the interests of his enemies. As he approached the town he was met by a deputation of citizens, who assured him of their submission, and offered him a sum equivalent to 500*l.* of English money to be divided amongst

He finds it difficult to maintain discipline. his followers. [2] Though Montrose in return offered them his protection, he found, when he entered Glasgow, that he had enough to do to maintain discipline. The untold wealth, as it appeared to the simple mountaineers, which was displayed in the stalls and in the streets was too tempting to be forgone. Yet, unless the good-will, not only of Glasgow, but of every town in the Lowlands, was to be forfeited, plundering must be suppressed with a heavy hand. Montrose did what he could, and some of the worst

Aug. 18. and goes out to Bothwell. offenders he hanged upon the spot. After two days, however, finding it impossible to maintain order as long as his rude soldiery remained in the town, he led them out to Bothwell, where they would be out of the reach of temptation.

For a few days all seemed to go well. Alaster Macdonald

---

[1] See his letter to the town of Glasgow, in which he promises protection, written just after the battle. Napier's *Memorials of Montrose,* ii. 222.

[2] "A thousand double pieces." *Patrick Gordon,* 153. Mr. Oman, of All Souls College, informs me that the double piece was probably the 'double crown' of James VI. and the 'half-unit' of Charles I., and was a gold piece value 6*l.* Scots, *i.e.* ten shillings in the English coinage.

scattered some bands which Cassilis and Eglinton had raised in the West. On the 20th Montrose summoned a Parliament to meet at Glasgow in October. Within a few days Edinburgh and all the South had acknowledged the authority of the King's Lieutenant. Edinburgh was grievously visited by the plague, and could not, therefore, invite him within her walls, but the prison-gates were thrown open, and Lord Napier, Lord Crawford, Lord Ogilvy, Stirling of Keir, with many more of Montrose's friends, stepped forth into liberty. Montrose despatched a messenger to the King to assure him that he would soon cross the Border at the head of 20,000 men.[1]

Aug. 20.
Montrose summons a Parliament.

Liberation of prisoners.

The determination to summon a Parliament brought matters to a crisis. To gain the support of a Parliament it was necessary for Montrose to have the good-will of the towns and of the middle class in the country, and this was not easily to be had on terms which would satisfy the Highlanders. The Glasgow citizens reminded him that the holding of a Parliament within their walls would compel them to incur a considerable expenditure, and begged for the remission of the 500*l.* which they had promised to raise. Montrose could not but comply with their request, and, assembling the Highlanders, begged them to forgo the money for the present, assuring them that before long they should be even better rewarded for their toils.

Montrose disappoints the Highlanders.

Montrose's address was received with murmurs of discontent. Each Highland clan discovered pressing reasons which necessitated its return to the mountains. The Macleans had to rebuild their ruined habitations. The Macdonalds, with the redoubtable Alaster at their head, had yet to fill up the measure of vengeance due to the tyrannical Campbells. The necessity of storing up the plunder which they had acquired in a place of safety could always be pleaded as soon as there was no hope of acquiring more ; and after three or four days not a Highlander was to be seen in Montrose's camp. It is true that all, or most of them, loudly professed their intention to return, and that on former occasions professions of

Their desertion.

---

[1] Digby to Jermyn, Sept. 21. *Bankes MSS.*

this kind had been fulfilled. Never before, however, had the deserters taken offence at their leader, and a Highlander who had taken offence was not likely to be lured back, especially if he had reason to believe that the service of the commander at whose conduct he had taken umbrage would be profitable no longer.

Aboyne was as capricious as the Highlanders. In response to Montrose's call the lords and gentlemen of the Lowlands

The Gordons return home. who were dissatisfied with Argyle's government flocked in to Bothwell. Aboyne complained that neither the new-comers nor Montrose himself treated him with sufficient respect. The Earl of Crawford, just released from prison, was to command the cavalry, a post which Aboyne regarded as due to himself. Sir William Rollock had written a narrative of Montrose's campaigns, in which the exploits of the Gordons were passed over with insufficient mention, and Montrose, when appealed to on the subject, had refused to recall the book. Aboyne, therefore, rode off at the head of 400 horse and a not inconsiderable number of foot. Of the whole army which had fought at Kilsyth there remained but three or four score horsemen, under the old Earl of Airlie, and about 500 foot, the remains of the 1,600 who had crossed from Ireland twelve months before, and who still clung to Montrose, though their own leader had deserted him.[1]

It was no accidental mishap that had befallen Montrose. With the means at his disposal no genius short of his own

Causes of Montrose's failure. could have gained victory in the field. It was impossible for any man to use them effectively in the organisation of a government. Montrose, therefore, had to change the basis of his operations in more than a military sense. He had to appear as a liberator and a statesman where he had hitherto been known only as a destroyer.

The principles on which Montrose wished to act were set down in a Remonstrance, which he probably intended to lay before the new Parliament at its meeting, but which did not see the light till after the lapse of two centuries. In this

[1] *Wishart,* ch. xiv. ; *Patrick Gordon.* 153; *A more perfect. . . . relation,* E. 303, 4.

Remonstrance he announced himself as a foe to Episcopacy and a true Presbyterian, but at the same time declared himself as being still the resolute champion of the royal authority against usurping churchmen as much as against their allies, the usurping nobles.[1]

Montrose's Remonstrance.

Such a remonstrance was the work of an idealist, not of a statesman. On the battle-field Montrose had all Cromwell's promptness of seizing the chances of the strife, together with a versatility in varying his tactics according to the varying resources of the enemy, to which Cromwell could lay no claim, whilst his skill as a strategist was certainly superior to that of his English contemporary. His mind, however, in its intellectual working, was the very antithesis to that of Cromwell. Whilst Cromwell always based his action upon existing facts, and contented himself with striving to change them for the better with due regard for the possibilities of the case, Montrose fixed his eye upon an organisation in Church and State which had not only no real existence, but which was very far removed from anything that, in his day at least, could possibly come into existence. There was, as he fancied, to be a king in Scotland—and that king Charles—who would rule in righteousness and support an unpolitical Presbytery. There was to be a clergy content with the fulfilment of its spiritual duties, and a nobility forgetful of its own interests and eager only to support the authority of the king. All loyal Scotsmen were to be as generous, as unselfish as himself.

Montrose and Cromwell.

The absence of all grasp on the concrete facts of politics is the more astonishing because it was coincident in Montrose with the most intense realisation of the concrete facts of war. He seems, indeed, to have had no conception of the temper in which Scotland, after the

Character of Montrose's followers.

[1] Montrose's Remonstrance. Napier, *Memoirs of Montrose*, i. App. xliv. It is there printed from the original in Lord Napier's hand. There is, as has often been said, no external evidence that Montrose ever saw it, but there is a Montrosian ring about it, and I accept it as his, though possibly with some element of Napier in it. Those who object to the difference of the view here taken of Presbyterianism and that taken in Montrose's advice to Charles II. in 1649, forget that different circumstances beget different shades of opinion.

slaughter of her sons in the battles in the North, regarded the leader of those who had done them to death. It was no Puritan or Covenanter who passed the strongest condemnation upon the licence of Montrose's followers. "This, indeed," wrote Patrick Gordon, it may be hoped with considerable exaggeration, after ascribing Montrose's victories to the miraculous intervention of God, "from mortal men to the immortal God deserveth a great deal of thankfulness . . . which, it seems, they were not careful enough to perform, ascribing too much to their own merits, as if a man were able to lift up his arm against an enemy if God work not with him. This also could not but offend the Holy of Holies that, when God had given their enemies into their hands, the Irishes in particular were too cruel; for it was everywhere observed they did ordinarily kill all they could be master of, without any motion of pity or any consideration of humanity; nay, it seemed to them there was no distinction between a man and a beast; for they killed men ordinarily with no more feeling of compassion and with the same careless neglect that they kill a hen or capon for their supper; and they were also without all shame, most brutishly given to uncleanness and filthy lust. As for excessive drinking, when they came where it might be had, there was no limits to their beastly appetites. As for godless avarice and merciless oppression and plundering the poor labourer, of these two crying sins [1] the Scots were also guilty as they."

[1] In the records of the Presbytery of Turriff, shown me by Dr. Milne of Fyvie, is an entry which shows how Montrose's presence interfered with clerical work. With the exception of a single entry about the death of a minister, there is nothing in the book from August 14, 1644, to May 13, 1646. At its recommencement the record begins as follows: "The next day convened the brethren of the Presbytery of Turriff, and praised God from their hearts for granting them liberty in health and peace to meet for promoving of the Lord's work; from the which benefit they have been restrained by reason of the enemy lying and tyrannising within the precincts [?] of the Presbytery for the space almost of ane year and ane half, except some three or four diets they had met together in great fear and hazard, both of their lives and fortunes. The rolls of which meetings was left with Mr. Thomas Mitchell, and rent and destroyed by the enemy when his books, papers, and goods were plundered and destroyed."

If Montrose knew little of the loathing with which his connection with these men was regarded, he knew as little of the hold which the Kirk had gained upon the Southern population by its popular organisation and its services in the cause of national independence. The only strong feeling to which he could possibly appeal was the jealousy entertained by many of the gentry and nobility of clerical interference with the freedom of their lives, and it was this jealousy which had in all probability brought so large a number trooping into Bothwell. Yet so many of the more powerful nobles had found that their interest was better served by leading the Kirk than by opposing it, that, even as an aristocratic party, Montrose's new supporters were singularly weak, and even those who willingly proffered loyal service to him joined him in a half-hearted fashion as men well aware of the real strength of the government which to all outward appearance he had utterly destroyed.

Montrose and the Kirk.

Montrose's new supporters.

Conspicuous in their offers of assistance were the Border lords, the Earls of Roxburgh, Home, and Traquair. Their past history was sufficient testimony that they would have preferred a government by the King to a government by Argyle and the Kirk. Though they were hardly the men to expose themselves to ruin for the sake of any cause, they now urged Montrose to come amongst them to give his countenance to the levies which they were making. Home and Roxburgh played a double game from the first. Whilst Montrose believed them to be raising levies for himself, his opponents imagined that they were raising them for the Covenant. David Leslie, however, by September 6 had crossed the Border, and Middleton, who was despatched by him in advance, came, as he gave out, upon evidence of their treason. He arrested them both, and on the 9th they were lodged as prisoners in Berwick. Amongst Montrose's supporters it was afterwards believed that they had themselves asked Leslie to take them prisoners.[1]

The Border lords.

Sept. 6. David Leslie in Scotland.

Sept. 9. Imprisonment of Home and Roxburgh,

---

[1] *Wishart*, ch. xv. Wharton in his letter of Sept. 10 (*L.J.* vii. 581) simply mentions that they were brought prisoners 'upon suspicion, or

Traquair, for the present at least, maintained an apparent fidelity, and directed his son, Lord Linton, to join Montrose. The Marquis of Douglas, who, without any afterthought, had declared for Montrose, had actually levied the force which he had promised to raise; but great as was still the influence of a Scottish lord over his tenants, he was unable to keep them from deserting in masses a cause which they detested. When, shortly after the arrest of the two earls, Montrose appeared at Kelso, he found himself at the head of his 500 Irish foot and of a body of cavalry 1,200 strong, which was entirely composed of noble-men and gentlemen.[1] Not a man of the lower or middle classes would serve under him. No wonder that Traquair saw that Montrose's cause was lost. He recalled his son from the Royalist army, and, unless common fame is to be distrusted, sought to purchase immunity by betraying Montrose's weakness to the enemy. Ignorant though the Royalist commander was of Traquair's treachery, he found so little encouragement in the Eastern Borders that he resolved to transfer himself to the West in hope that he might there meet with better success.

Traquair and Douglas.

Quality of Montrose's army.

David Leslie had almost missed his prey. Having been reinforced as he passed through Newcastle, he was now at the head of some infantry in addition to the 4,000 horse which he had brought with him from Hereford. Marching along the sea coast towards Midlothian, where Montrose had been a few days before, he determined, after due consultation with his officers, to pursue his course up the Forth, and to lie in wait for Montrose's inevitable retreat to the Highlands. The letter from Traquair, if Traquair was indeed the sender of it, changed his purpose, and marching rapidly southwards along the course of the Gala Water, he reached the little village of Sunderland on the

David Leslie's march.

some discovery of their holding intelligence with Montrose.' A fuller account is given out of a letter from Scotland in *The Weekly Account*, E. 301, 17. It is here that Middleton's part in the matter is stated.

[1] *Wishart*, ch. xv. ; *Patrick Gordon* states that Montrose had at Philiphaugh 1,200 horse, 'all gentlemen, barons, and noblemen.'

night of September 12. Montrose with his scanty force was at Selkirk, not four miles distant.

Montrose had ordered his army to rendezvous the next morning on the long level meadow which lies along the Ettrick Water below the hillside on which Selkirk stands, and which bears the name of Philiphaugh. His men were still in disorder when David Leslie burst upon them with 4,000 horse out of the mist which lay heavily on the flat.

Sept. 13.
Battle of
Philip-
haugh.

The 500 veterans who had once followed Alaster Macdonald were faithful to the last. For them in a foreign land there was no safety but in the grave. Of the 1,200 mounted gentry who should have given them the support of cavalry, only 150 under the old Earl of Airlie and Nathaniel Gordon rallied round their leader. The others, bewildered and confused, without confidence in themselves or in their cause, gathered in knots far in the rear without making an attempt to take part in what, to them at least, seemed to be a hopeless struggle. In spite of their defection, Montrose, with Crawford and Ogilvy at his side, did his best to guide the unequal battle. Twice he drove back with his scanty numbers the rush of Leslie's horsemen, but at a terrible cost. Soon, out of the 150 who followed him in the first charge but forty or fifty were left. Further resistance was useless, and the hitherto unvanquished captain fled for his life. Crawford and Airlie also escaped, as well as the Marquis of Douglas, the only one of the Southern nobility who drew sword on that field of destruction. The remainder of the combatants were slain or taken. Those who had stood aloof at the beginning of the engagement had already dispersed, and were in full flight towards their homes.

The victors, having thus disposed of Montrose's scanty cavalry, turned upon his foot. Three hundred were still standing in the ranks. After 250 of them had been slain, Stuart, the adjutant, asked for quarter, and quarter was granted to the remaining fifty.[1]

---

[1] *Wishart,* vi. ; *Patrick Gordon,* 156.

Then ensued a butchery more horrible than any that had followed upon any of Montrose's victories. The wild clansmen of the North had contented themselves with taking vengeance upon men. The trained and disciplined soldiers of the Covenant slaughtered with hideous barbarity not only the male camp followers but 300 Irish women, the wives of their slain or captured enemies, together with their infant children.[1] To the Scotchman every Irish man or woman was but a noxious beast. It soon repented the conquerors that they had spared the lives of fifty soldiers. The churchmen and the noblemen of the Covenant remonstrated warmly against the act of clemency. Quarter, it was said, by a vile equivocation, had been granted to Stuart alone, not to his men. As the triumphant army passed through Linlithgow, Leslie weakly gave way, and stained his honour by abandoning his prisoners. The soldiers were bidden to fall on, and they did as they were bidden.[2]

Butchery of Irish women.

According to a later tradition, fourscore women and children, who had perhaps escaped from the general massacre, were thrown from a bridge near Linlithgow, to be drowned as English Protestants had been drowned at Portadown.[3]

[1] "Three hundred women that, being natives of Ireland, were the married wives of the Irishes." *Patrick Gordon,* 160. The quotation at p. 352 shows that Gordon was not likely to be too lenient in his judgment of the Irish.

[2] Guthry, *Memoirs,* 162; *Patrick Gordon,* 160.

[3] Wishart (ch. xvii.) states the fact, but does not give the place. According to a statement quoted by Napier (ii. 587) from a speech of Sir G. Mackenzie, the place was Linlithgow.

CHAPTER XXXVII.

BASING HOUSE AND SHERBURN.

THE news from Philiphaugh failed to convince Charles and Digby of the hopelessness of further resistance. Their idea of making their way to Newark was not abandoned, though, as far as their plan for reaching Scotland was concerned, there was no longer any reason why they should be at Newark rather than anywhere else. The march, however, it was thought, might be converted into a means of saving Chester. Charles calculated that Poyntz would be sure to follow him with the bulk of his cavalry, and would leave the forces engaged in the siege weakened by his absence. If, therefore, as soon as the King was safe in Newark, Sir William Vaughan were sent back towards Chester with a strong detachment he would be able to make short work of the besiegers.[1] Charles felt the more hopeful when on September 28 Prince Maurice brought him a reinforcement from Worcester of six or seven hundred horse.[2]

1645
Sept. 28.
Effect of the news from Scotland upon Charles.

Plan for baffling Poyntz and saving Chester.

Maurice brings reinforcements.

Charles, however, if he resembled Digby in hoping for the best, differed from him in being also prepared for the worst. On the 29th he wrote to Culpepper peremptorily ordering him to send the Prince of Wales to France, and to despatch Goring with his horse to join the Royal army at Newark or wherever else it might be.[3]

Sept. 29.
Fresh orders to Culpepper.

[1] Digby to Byron, Oct. 5. *S.P. Dom.* dxi. 2.
[2] *Symonds*, 244.
[3] The King to Culpepper, Sept. 29. *Clarendon*, ix. 96.

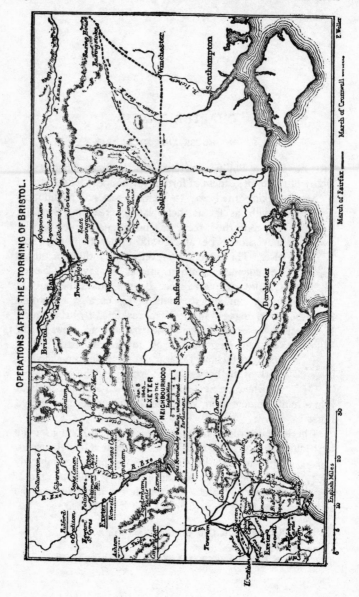

To abandon the West and to concentrate all the remaining forces at his disposal for a final blow was thus the course decided on by Charles. At Bridgnorth on October 1 [1] he received news which ought to have convinced him that the obstacles in the way of the realisation of his scheme were well-nigh insuperable. Fairfax had occupied his time since the surrender of Bristol in clearing the country round of the enemy's garrisons. On September 23 the strong castle of Devizes surrendered to Cromwell after a faint shadow of resistance. On the following day Laycock House made its submission, and on the 26th Sir Charles Lucas abandoned all further attempt to prolong the defence of Berkeley Castle. [2]

The King's plan.

Sept. 23. Surrender of Devizes,

Sept. 24. of Laycock House,

Sept. 26. and of Berkeley Castle.

In the face of such news, Charles had much ado to drag his little army after him in pursuit of further adventures. To still the murmurs in his camp he issued a declaration that he had formally abandoned his intention of marching in search of Montrose. [3] He now looked to his projected combination with Goring as his anchor of safety; forgetting that, as Fairfax's army had been set at liberty by the successful termination of the siege of Bristol, it would be almost impossible for the western Royalists, even if they had been better disciplined and better commanded than they were, to make their way through a country occupied by their victorious enemies.

Oct. 1. Charles declares that he will not go to Montrose.

He expects help from Goring.

On October 4 Charles reached Newark. In a letter written to Nicholas on the day of his arrival, he took it for granted that Goring would soon pass through Oxford on his march towards the Midlands, and directed the Secretary to take advantage of the convoy to send him the young Duke of York. "Since," he added bitterly, "it is the fashion to yield towns basely, none can blame me to venture my children in an army, rather than to be besieged." [4]

Oct. 4. He reaches Newark.

[1] *Symonds*, 244.   [2] *Sprigg*, 132.
[3] *Walker*, 143 (misprinted 135).
[4] The King to Nicholas, Oct. 1. *Evelyn's Diary* (ed. 1859), iv. 162.

Even if Fairfax had been less formidable than he was, it was unlikely either that Goring would sacrifice the glory of his independent command, or that the men of Devon and Cornwall would subordinate their own welfare to the common interests of the nation. For the present, however, Charles was not ready to despair. On the day after the King's arrival at Newark Digby assured Byron that all was well. "I have received now," he wrote, "an express from Montrose, who was betrayed, and lost two or three hundred men at most; and since that he hath given David Leslie a great blow. General Goring hath had a victory against Massey, and Fairfax is marched back into the West in great haste to encounter him." [1]

Charles's miscalculation.

Oct. 5.
Digby thinks that all is well.

Except that Fairfax had marched into the West, every word of these exultant sentences was without foundation. [2] Fairfax indeed had thought so little of serious danger from Goring's disorganised troopers, that he felt himself strong enough to despatch Cromwell to reduce the Royalist garrisons in Hampshire, whilst he conducted the remainder of his army to complete the work which he had left unfinished after the surrender of Bridgwater. There was no longer any danger of an interruption of his communications whilst he was engaged in the western peninsula.

Sept. 28.
Separation of Fairfax and Cromwell.

Fairfax's progress was indeed delayed from an unexpected cause. The taxes levied for the support of his soldiers had come in but slowly, and for some time there had been no money to send into the West. The discipline of the army depended on constant pay, and on the first day's march many of the men were seen to look over their

The army without pay.

---

[1] Digby to Byron, Oct. 5. *S.P. Dom.* dxi. 2.

[2] The 'express from Montrose' may have been some fugitive who picked up reports on the way. It is not to be imagined that any despatch of Montrose can have contained such falsehoods. It is just possible that, when he wrote of Goring's victory over Massey, Digby may have heard of an attack on Bampton and Minehead by some of Goring's men, in consequence of which, after the defeat of the half-armed inhabitants of those places, the houses were plundered. The affair made some noise in the newspapers. See *Merc. Civicus*, E. 304, 8.

shoulders to espy the treasure carts from London. A few days later they were ready to mutiny. If the money, they said, did not arrive soon, they would go back to London to fetch it. On October 6, when they reached Chard, it was found necessary to halt. It was not till the 11th that the long-expected convoy arrived. At that time the army had been without pay for nearly a month.[1]

Danger of a mutiny.

Oct. 11. Arrival of the money.

On the 14th Fairfax, having paid his soldiers, was ready to advance. Goring, who of late had been boasting of his own readiness to fight,[2] made no serious attempt to impede his progress. The Parliamentary army made for Tiverton, and on the 19th the siege of the castle was opened. In the course of the afternoon the chain of the drawbridge was cut in two by a shot. The bridge fell down, and a party of the besiegers rushed across it, and carried the place without difficulty. Goring, abandoning all thought of meeting Fairfax in the field, hurriedly retreated westwards. If he had ever entertained the thought of breaking through the enemy to join the King, that thought was now definitely abandoned.

Oct. 14. Advance of the army.

Oct. 19. Tiverton Castle taken.

On the 20th Fairfax summoned a council of war at Silverton. Winter was approaching,[3] and it was the general opinion that it would be unwise to engage the army in the deep and miry Devonshire lanes in bad weather. The soldiers were, therefore, directed to take up their quarters in the villages round Exeter, where they would be usefully employed in straitening the garrison of the capital of the West till a siege could be undertaken with some prospect of success.[4]

Oct. 20. Fairfax resolves to remain near Exeter.

In the meanwhile Cromwell had been accomplishing the task assigned to him in Hampshire. As usual he did not tarry. On the morning of the 28th of September, two days after

---

[1] *Sprigg,* 145 ; *The Moderate Intelligencer,* E. 304, 11.

[2] Goring to Culpepper, Oct. 13. *Clarendon MSS.* 1,990.

[3] It must be remembered that the day was Oct. 30 according to the rectified calendar.

[4] *Sprigg,* 145, 157 ; *Clarendon,* ix. 102, 105.

parting from Fairfax at Devizes, he entered Winchester without opposition. Almost his first act was to offer to Bishop

Sept. 28.
Cromwell at
Winchester.

Oct. 5.
The Castle
surrenders.

Curl a convoy to conduct him to a place of safety. The Bishop, however, preferred to take refuge in the Castle.[1] He was not likely long to remain in peace. By October 5 Cromwell's batteries opened fire, and a practicable breach being soon effected, the governor gave up hope and surrendered. "You see," wrote Cromwell to the Speaker, "God is not weary of doing you good. I confess, sir, His favour to you is as visible when He comes by His power upon the hearts of His enemies, making them quit places of strength to you, as when he gives courage to your soldiers to attempt hard things."[2] In the cause of the doomed King all but the very staunchest slackened their effort, whilst the least vigorous of his enemies knew now that failure was impossible.

Cromwell was as prompt in the execution of discipline as he was in the attack upon a fortress. Six of his men were

Oct. 6.
Punishment
of plun-
derers.

caught plundering the disarmed soldiers of the garrison as they marched out. He hanged one of them on the spot, and sent the others to Oxford, that the new governor, Sir Thomas Glemham, might deal with them as he pleased. Glemham, however, thanking Cromwell for his courtesy, set the rogues at liberty.[3]

From Winchester Cromwell marched to Basing House, to which Dulbier—an old German officer who had served under

Oct. 8.
Cromwell
before
Basing
House.

Buckingham, and had been equally ready to drill the Parliamentary troops—had for some weeks been laying siege. Cromwell arrived on the 8th,[4] bringing with him a complete train of artillery. It was through the possession of siege-guns that he hoped to win his way where so many of his predecessors in command had failed.

[1] *A Diary.* E. 304, 13.

[2] Cromwell to Lenthall, Oct. 6. *Carlyle*, Letter XXXII. Carlyle follows Rushworth in calling this a letter to Fairfax; but see *C.J.* iv. 249; and *Perfect Diurnal*, E. 264, 26.

[3] *Sprigg*, 144.

[4] *The Weekly Account.* E. 304, 27.

On the 11th, when he was ready to open fire, he summoned the garrison to surrender. The defenders of the noble mansion

Oct. 11.
A peremptory summons.

of the Catholic Marquis of Winchester—Loyalty House, as its owner loved to call it—were not the professional soldiers to whom Cromwell was always ready to give honourable quarter. They had, so at least ran his accusation, been evil neighbours to the country people. Their house was 'a nest of Romanists,' who, of all men, could least make good their claim to wage war against the Parliament. If they refused quarter now it would not be offered to them again.[1]

There were no signs of yielding on the side of the garrison, but those who treated Cromwell's summons thus lightly had

Oct. 13.
Breaches effected.

Oct. 14.
Cromwell's preparations.

miscalculated the power of his heavy guns. By the evening of the 13th two wide breaches had been effected, and at two in the morning it was resolved to storm the place at six, when the sky would be growing clear before the rising of the sun. The weary soldiers were directed to snatch a brief rest, but Cromwell spent part at least of the remainder of the night in meditation and prayer. He was verily persuaded that he was God's champion in the war against the strongholds of darkness, and as he figured to himself the idolaters and the idols behind the broken wall in front of him, the words, "They that make them are like unto them, so is every one that trusteth in them," rose instinctively to his lips.

At the appointed hour the storming parties were let loose upon the doomed house, rising for the last time in its splendour

Basing House stormed.

over field and meadow. It had been said that the old house and the new were alike fit to make 'an emperor's court.' The defenders were all too few to make head against the surging tide of war. Quarter was neither asked nor given till the whole of the buildings were in the hands of the assailants. Women, as they saw their husbands, their fathers, or their brothers slaughtered before their faces, rushed forward with the intrepidity of their sex to cling to the arms and bodies of the slayers. One, a maiden of no

[1] *The Moderate Intelligencer.* E. 305, 3.

ordinary beauty, a daughter of Dr. Griffiths, an expelled City clergyman, hearing her father abused and maltreated, gave back angry words to his reviler. The incensed soldier, maddened with the excitement of the hour, struck her on the head, and laid her dead at her father's feet. Six of the ten priests in the house were slain, and the four others reserved for the

The sack.

gallows and the knife. After a while the rage of the soldiers turned to thoughts of booty. Plate and jewels, stored gold and cunningly wrought tapestry, fell a prey to the victors. The men who were spared were stripped of their outer garments, and old Inigo Jones was carried out of the house wrapped in a blanket, because the spoilers had left him absolutely naked. One hundred rich petticoats and gowns which were discovered in the wardrobes were swept away amongst the common plunder, whilst the dresses were stripped from the backs of the ladies. On the whole, however, the women were, as a contemporary narrative expressed it, 'coarsely but not uncivilly used.' No one of them in the very heat of the soldiers' fury had to fear those worst outrages to which their sisters have too often been subjected when fortresses have been stormed by armies in every military sense as disciplined as that which was under the command of Cromwell.

It is impossible to count with accuracy the number of the sufferers. The most probable estimate asserts that 100 were

Destruction of the house.

slain and 300 taken prisoners. In the midst of the riot the house was discovered to be on fire. The flames spread rapidly, and of the stately pile there soon remained no more than the gaunt and blackened walls. Before it was too late the booty had been dragged out upon the sward, and the country people flocked in crowds to buy the cheese, the bacon, and the wheat which had been stored within. Prizes of greater value were reserved for more appreciative chapmen.[1]

---

[1] Cromwell's letter and Peters's relation are printed in *Sprigg*, 149; Peters's relation is more fully given in *The full and last relation*, E. 305, 8. See also *The Moderate Intelligencer*, E. 305, 3; *The Scottish Dove*, E. 305, 6; *Merc. Veridicus*, E. 305, 10.

The Marquis himself owed his life to the courtesy with which he had formerly treated Colonel Hammond, who had been his prisoner for a few days. Hammond now in turn protected his former captor, though he could not prevent the soldiers from stripping the old man of his costly attire. After this the lord of the devastated mansion was safe from all but one form of insult. Consideration for fallen greatness never entered into the thoughts of a Puritan controversialist, even when that controversialist was of as kindly a disposition as was Hugh Peters. A Catholic, too, was beyond all bounds of religious courtesy, and Peters thought it well, as Cheynell had thought it well in the presence of the dying Chillingworth, to enter into argument with the fallen Marquis. Did he not now see, he asked him, the hopelessness of the cause which he had maintained? "If the King," was the proud reply, "had no more ground in England but Basing House, I would adventure as I did, and so maintain it to the uttermost. Basing House is called Loyalty." On the larger merits of the Royal cause he refused to enter. "I hope," he simply said, "that the King may have a day again." [1]

"I thank God," wrote Cromwell to the Commons, "I can give you a good account of Basing." For slaughter after a summons had been rejected he did not, as the laws of war then stood, consider himself bound to give account at all. He went on to recommend that what remained of the fortifications should be destroyed, and that a garrison should be established at Newbury to keep Donnington Castle in check.[2] Having given this advice he moved rapidly west-

The Marquis and Hugh Peters.

Cromwell's advice.

---

[1] *A full and last relation.* E. 305, 8.

[2] Cromwell to Lenthall, Oct. 14. *Carlyle*, Letter XXXIII. The feeling of the day about the slaughter is well brought out in a contemporary newspaper. "The enemy, for aught I can learn, desired no quarter, and I believe that they had but little offered them. You must remember what they were: they were most of them Papists; therefore our muskets and our swords did show but little compassion, and this house being at length subdued, did satisfy for her treason and rebellion by the blood of the offenders." *The Kingdom's Weekly Post.* E. 304, 28.

wards to rejoin Fairfax. On the 17th Langford House surrendered without the formality of a siege.[1] On the
24th he reached Crediton, where Fairfax was for the
present quartered.[2]

Oct. 17.
Langford
House
surrenders.

Whilst Cromwell and Fairfax were beating down resistance
in the South, Charles had a little breathing-time allowed him
in the refuge which he had sought at Newark. Yet
even here he was driven almost to despair by the
demoralisation which always follows in the train of
hopeless disaster. Commissioners had been appointed to bring in the contributions of the surrounding
districts and to pay them over to the officers of the garrison
for the support of their men, and these commissioners now
complained that the officers detained the money for their own
use, and that the soldiers had consequently been forced to
supply their wants by plundering the neighbourhood. It was
with the greatest difficulty that Charles succeeded in bringing
this system of rapine to an end.[3]

Oct. 4.
Condition
of the
garrison of
Newark.

To pacify the farmers of Nottinghamshire was, however, of
little avail, unless some means could be discovered of defeating
the apparently invincible enemy. In this crisis of
Charles's fortunes Sir Richard Willis, the governor
of Newark, proposed a scheme which, desperate as
it was, had at least the merit of soldierly directness. Let the
King, he urged, destroy every fortification which he possessed
in the Midlands—Newark, Ashby, Tutbury, Lichfield, Belvoir
Castle, Weston, Bridgnorth, and Denbigh. Let him collect
together the whole strength of their garrisons, and thus reinforced let him march into the West to join Goring. His
own and Goring's forces combined ought then to be able to
dispose of Fairfax.

Willis's
plan of
campaign.

Charles at first accepted the plan thus indicated. Even
Digby professed to like it. Then came the usual
delays and questionings. The gentry of the neighbourhood who acted as commissioners were naturally dissatisfied

Objections
raised.

[1] *The Weekly Account.* E. 305, 19.
[2] *Sprigg*, 159.
[3] *Walker*, 143 (misprinted 135).

with a scheme which by depriving them of armed support would

Digby still
hankers after
a junction
with Mont-
rose.

expose them to the vengeance of the enemy.[1] Digby too still hankered after his old plan of a junction with Montrose. One more rumour of a victory of the Scottish Royalists had lately reached Newark,

and it was even added that Montrose had reached the Borders

Oct. 12.
Charles
marches
northwards.

with a victorious army. On October 12, Charles, listening to Digby rather than to Willis, turned his steps northwards with no fixed intentions, but in the

hope of falling in with a courier who might bring him confirmation of the favourable news. It was believed by some that Digby's eagerness to leave Newark was caused by his unwillingness to meet Rupert, who having been at last relieved from arrest was on his way from Oxford to lay his case in person before the King.[2]

However this may have been, it is certain that the rumour of Montrose's victory was absolutely without foundation.

Sept.
Montrose's
movements
after his
defeat
at Philip-
haugh.

After his defeat at Philiphaugh he had swiftly made his way back to Athol, hoping to be able to rouse the Highlanders to renewed efforts. Then, turning north, he summoned Aboyne to forget his imaginary wrongs and to bring with him the Gordon chivalry.

Aboyne answered the summons, and joined him with 1,500 foot and 300 horse. Aboyne's brother, Lord Lewis, who was even more fickle than himself, followed with additional re-

Favourable
prospects.

inforcements. For a moment Montrose had every prospect of seeing himself again at the head of an

army as numerous as that with which he had held the field at Kilsyth, and of being able once more to press southwards to the succour of the King.

This hopeful enterprise was brought to nought by the

---

[1] *Symonds*, 270. Symonds seems to have had his information from Willis in 1659. It is true that Willis is made to speak of Bristol as still untaken, but this may be fairly set down as a slip of memory. It is possible also that he threw more blame than necessary on the commissioners.

[2] The King to Nicholas, Oct. 10, *Evelyn's Memoirs* (ed. 1859), iv. 167; *Walker*, 143 (misprinted 135).

desertion of the Gordons. Huntly bade his followers to

Oct.
The
desertion
of the
Gordons.

return, and they obeyed the orders of their chief. By Montrose's champions Huntly has been described as actuated by no other motive than jealousy of a man greater than himself. Yet it must not be forgotten that the local feeling, powerful even in England, was far

Huntly's
view of the
case.

more powerful in Scotland. Huntly's own districts were in grave peril. David Leslie had despatched Middleton with 800 horse to attack the country of the Gordons, and Middleton was now at Turriff. To Huntly it must have seemed all-important to dissipate this threatening cloud before a forward movement was attempted. His drawing back was probably neither more nor less traitorous than Newcastle's drawing back in 1643 ; but whatever the motives of either leader may have been, they were attended with the same disastrous results.

To Montrose, on the other hand, local interests were as nothing. He could not bear to be delayed an instant in

Montrose's
view of the
case.

carrying out his great undertaking, and he believed that the decisive blow must be struck at Glasgow and not at Turriff. Other motives urged him in the same direction too ; pity for the brave and unfortunate youths who had been captured at Philiphaugh, and who were now awaiting trial and execution, summoned him to Glasgow.

Montrose's
mistake.

Yet, strong as the inducement was, Montrose had everything to gain by turning upon Middleton and winning Huntly to his cause. A few days would have disposed of a petty force cooped up in a remote angle of the North. On the other hand, Montrose was powerless without the Gordons, and though, in spite of their desertion, he pushed on towards the south, his following was too scanty to give hope of any satisfactory achievement.[1]

It was to meet this phantom host that Charles had set out

Oct. 13.
A council of
war at
Welbeck.

from Newark. On October 13, at the end of his second day's march, a council of war was held at Welbeck. Alone amongst the councillors, Digby and Langdale urged that there should be no drawing back, and

[1] *Wishart,* ch. xvii. ; *Patrick Gordon,* 162.

their advice was warmly supported by the King. Charles, finding himself outvoted, declared that he had not asked the opinion of the council whether he was to go or not, but by what route he was to proceed. In the extremity in which he was, he must either make the adventure or be 'brought to a worse condition.' All mouths were stopped by this declaration, and the proposal to advance was reluctantly accepted.

The next morning—the morning on which Basing House was stormed—all was changed. News arrived that Montrose was still in the Highlands, whilst David Leslie was still in the Lothians, and Leven was quartered with the bulk of the Scottish army on the Tees. The King's northward march was of necessity abandoned. Yet, at the risk of diminishing still more his already weakened force, he resolved to despatch Langdale with the Northern horse to make his way if possible to Montrose, unburdened with the responsibility of watching over the King's person. Langdale, who had never been at his ease south of the Humber, cheerfully consented, but he asked that Digby might have the chief command. His request was at once complied with, and the energetic but unwise Secretary of State found himself suddenly in command of 1,500 horse, bound on a service of perilous adventure. Charles returned to Newark with one rash counsellor the less by his side.[1]

Oct. 14.
The King's advance stopped.

Digby and Langdale to go north.

On the morning after he left the King Digby learnt that the indefatigable Poyntz was marching across his line of advance to block his way to the north. Poyntz, however, was in complete ignorance that any enemy was in his neighbourhood, and did not keep his force well together. He posted his foot on the northern road at Sherburn, while his horse was still some distance in the rear. Digby knew well that on open ground mere infantry could not withstand an attack of cavalry. In the morning of the 15th he surprised Poyntz's isolated foot in a field outside Sherburn, and succeeded in capturing the whole of it.

Oct. 15.
Digby defeats Poyntz's infantry at Sherburn.

After this feat Digby found himself in advance of the

[1] *Walker*, 143 (misprinted 135).

enemy's horse, which would before long appear from the south.
He at once made his preparations to surprise them as they
passed through Sherburn.   Placing his own men out of sight
beyond the town at its northern end, he hoped to
be able to fall upon them as they came out of the
narrow street, before they had time to draw up in array
of battle.   In the meanwhile he despatched Langdale to the
southern end of the place with a small force to gain intelligence
of the enemy's approach.   Langdale sent out scouts, but, unluckily for him, his scouts were deceived by the irregularities
of the ground, and reported that the advancing force, which
was in reality composed of 2,000 horse under Colonel Copley, was a small party numbering only a quarter of that
number.

Prepares a surprise for the horse.

Digby's skilful plan was at once thrown to the winds.
Langdale, instead of falling back through the town, ordered
up a strong party of his own men, and dashed at
the enemy.   The vigour of the assault, unexpected
as it must have been, told upon the Parliamentarians,
and one body of horse after another took to flight before it.
For a time it seemed as if Langdale's troopers were about to
wipe out the sad memories of Naseby and Rowton Heath.
Victory was, however, snatched out of their hands almost by
accident.   A group of the enemy's horsemen, after it had been
routed, fled northwards into the town, instead of following
their comrades in a southerly direction, and dashed headlong
through the street with Langdale's men after them in hard
pursuit.   Strange to say, the flight of these beaten horsemen
changed the whole current of fortune.   Digby's cavalry posted
in the fields beyond the northern end of the street, never
dreaming that Parliamentarians would fly in that direction,
imagined the fugitives to be Langdale's troopers, and, seeing
every sign of defeat, turned round and galloped off the field.
The flying Parliamentarians were not slow in availing themselves of so unexpected a stroke of fortune.   They became
pursuers instead of fugitives, and gathered prisoners at every
stride.   Their companions at the other end of the town
quickly rallied.   Langdale, deserted by Digby, could no longer

Cavalry fight at Sherburn.

hold his own. The Royalist horse, did not draw rein, till it reached the friendly defences of Skipton Castle.[1]

Digby was incapable of despair. Gathering his beaten horsemen round him, and obtaining a small reinforcement

Oct. 21.
Digby makes for Scotland.

from the Skipton garrison, he made for Scotland. Still, as he marched, the country was full of rumours that Montrose had defeated Leslie somewhere in the Highlands, and had advanced to Glasgow. As he passed round Carlisle, which was now in the hands of a Scottish garrison, though the horse which had followed him from Skipton was routed by Sir John Brown, the Scottish officer in

He reaches Dumfries.

command, Digby himself pushed on for Dumfries. The Scottish peasants seemed unable to think of Montrose in any other character than in that of a conqueror, and they now averred that he had defeated not Leslie, but Middleton, and that all the forces of Scotland were drawn up to offer him battle as he issued from the hills. Even if the rumoured victory had had any basis in fact, it would be hopeless for a small and discouraged party of horsemen to dash itself against this intervening army. Retreat itself seemed now impossible for Digby. As he drew back into England the levies of the northern counties closed around him. His

Oct. 24.
Digby's escape to the Isle of Man.

men deserted and sought refuge in the hills of Cumberland. He and his officers found a vessel at Ravenglass, whence they shipped themselves for the Isle of Man. On the 27th he assured Charles that he intended to cross to Ireland, where he expected to be able to organise such troops as were ready to come to England to serve his Majesty.[2]

Would Charles be much longer in a condition to accept

---

[1] Digby to the King, Oct. 17 ; *Clarendon MSS.* 1,992. Digby's account of Langdale's success may have been overdrawn, but it is in the main corroborated by the silence of Poyntz on the details of the fight. See *A Great Victory*, E. 305, 14. Slingsby (*Diary*, 171) says that the Royalist cavalry 'at the first charge beats Copley, but being received by Col. Lilburne and not seconded by ours, they were put to the worst, and so quite routed.'

[2] Digby to the King, Oct. 27. *Clarendon MSS.* 2,003.

such help? On October 13 he turned back from Welbeck,

Oct. 13.
Charles
turns back
from
Welbeck.
and on the 15th, the day after his arrival at Newark, he learnt that Rupert, who had now become the rallying-point of all who longed for peace, had cut his way through the squadrons of the enemy, and,

.Oct. 15.
He hears at
Newark that
Rupert is at
Belvoir.
bringing his brother Maurice with him, had reached Belvoir with the intention of pleading his own cause before his uncle. Charles at once wrote to warn

Charles
interrogates
him by
letter.
him against coming further until he had stated whether he intended to justify his surrender of Bristol or to beg for merciful consideration. "Least of all," added the King, in allusion to his nephew's declaration in favour of peace, "I cannot forget what opinion you were of when I was at Cardiff, and therefore must remember you of the letter I wrote to you from thence in the Duke of Richmond's cipher,[1] warning you that if you be not resolved to carry yourself according to my resolution therein mentioned, you are no fit company for me."[2]

Braving Charles's resentment, Rupert on the 16th rode on towards Newark. By the military party there his arrival was
Oct. 16.
Rupert's
reception at
Newark.
awaited with impatience. Willis and Gerard were sore at the attention which had been paid by the King to the complaints of the civilian commissioners, and still more sore at his preference of Digby's advice to their own, even in matters relating to the conduct of the war. They now determined to welcome the Prince with unusual demonstrations of respect. Charles himself, on his arrival, two days before, had been received by Willis, the governor, at the gate of the fortress. The same Willis now rode out two miles with an escort of a hundred horse to do honour to Rupert.

Almost immediately after entering Newark, Rupert sought

---

[1] See p. 287.

[2] The King to Rupert, Oct. 15. *Add. MSS.* 31,022, fol. 68. The letter is written in lemon juice, and is in parts almost illegible. After I had failed to make it out, I submitted it to the practised eyes of Mr. E. M. Thompson, with the result as given above. The modern copy appended is not to be relied on.

out the King and demanded to be judged by a council of war.

Oct. 18.
A council of war,

His request was granted, and on the 21st Charles, after hearing the evidence, announced himself satis-fied that the Prince was 'not guilty of any the least want of courage or fidelity in the surrender of Bristol,' and the council, as might have been ex-pected, came to the same conclusion.[1]

Oct. 21.
absolves
Rupert.

If the charge against Rupert had been withdrawn, the deeper causes of ill-feeling between the uncle and the nephew

Continued
ill-feeling
between
Charles and
Rupert.

were beyond removal. The disaster which had befallen Digby at Sherburn must have gone far to confirm Rupert in his contempt for the infatuation which had placed an army under the control of a civilian. The resentment thus fostered was soon brought to

Movements
of Poyntz
and
Rossiter.

a head. Poyntz, leaving Digby to his fate, had turned south to watch the movements of the King, and had now reached Nottingham, and together with Rossiter, who was stationed at Grantham, threatened to

Oct. 26.
Charles to
leave
Newark.

cut off Charles's retreat from Newark towards the south. It was therefore resolved that Charles should make his escape to Oxford while yet there was time, and the night of the 26th was fixed for the attempt.[2]

It would have been plainly unwise to leave Willis in com-mand at Newark in hostile relations with the commissioners,

Willis to
accompany
him.

and Charles, with strained courtesy of language, announced to him that he was to change posts with Lord Bellasys, who had commanded the horse-guards since Lichfield's death before Chester. To Willis the promotion, if promotion it was, was most distasteful, and there were not wanting those who did their best to aggravate the wrong which he believed to have been done to him. Rupert and Gerard saw in his removal a fresh concession to the absent Digby.

As the King was finishing his dinner on the day which had been named for his journey, Rupert, followed by Willis and

[1] Proceedings of the council of war, Oct. 21. *Warburton*, iii. 201.

[2] *Walker*, 146. Clarendon follows Walker in naming the 20th, but see *Symonds*, 268.

Gerard, walked sullenly up to the table at which he was seated.[1]
The King, seeing in what mood his nephew was, rose and
drew him into a corner of the room. Willis began
by respectfully asking to know his accusers, and
to be dismissed only upon trial. Here Rupert broke in.
"By God," he said, "this is done in malice to me because
Sir Richard hath been always my faithful friend." The discussion threatened to grow warm, but Willis again brought it
back within the limits of loyalty and reverence. Gerard had
no such self-restraint. Beginning with a defence of Willis, he
was soon hurried away by passion into an unseemly altercation
with the King on the subject of his own dismissal from his
Welsh command. Once more Rupert intervened. "By God,"
he said plainly, "the cause of all this is Digby." Hot words
were launched backwards and forwards. "Why do not you
obey," pleaded Charles, "but come to expostulate with me?"
"Because," said Gerard, "your Majesty is ill informed."
Gerard had struck home. It was but what the Westminster
Parliament had been saying for so many years. "Pardon
me," answered Charles with plaintive indignation. "I am but
a child; Digby can lead me where he list. What can the

A noisy scene.

---

[1] This scene has hitherto only been known from the mutilated copy in
Symonds's Diary, p. 268. Symonds tore part of the pages out of his
book. "Such stuff was printed," he says, "as I have torn out, for, being
many times since in Sir Richard Willis's company, 'tis all a feigned formed
lie, for he said not one word to the King all that while, and Lord Gerard
said most, and that was concerning Lord Digby. This Sir Richard told
me Oct. 28, 1659." This word 'formed,' from the original *Harl. MSS.*
944, fol. 66, is omitted in the printed book, but was read for me by
Mr. Kensington, of the British Museum Library. The stuff which 'was
printed' was copied by Symonds from *The Bloody Treaty.* E. 211, 27.
We are therefore now able to read the whole report unmutilated. Is it,
however, all 'a feigned formed lie'? On Oct. 28, 1659, Willis, who
had been acting as a spy for Cromwell, had every reason to clear himself
from any part in a scene in which the King was treated with disrespect,
and his denial must not therefore be held to be of much weight. It is not
to be supposed that the report was taken down in the room, but it is
so characteristic of the speakers that it may fairly be held to be sub-
stantially accurate. The pamphleteer at least was too dull a man to
invent it.

most desperate rebels say more?" Fresh attempts to change his resolution proved fruitless. "I beseech your Majesty," said Rupert at last, "to grant me your gracious leave and pass to go beyond seas." "Oh, nephew," replied Charles, "it is of great concernment, and requires consideration." Something was then said by Rupert about Bristol. "Oh, nephew——" Charles began. He could not finish the sentence. Rupert had no such hesitation. "Digby," he reiterated, "is the man that hath caused all this distraction betwixt us." Charles was nettled. "They are all rogues and rascals that say so," he sternly replied, "and in effect traitors that seek to dishonour my best subjects." After this there was no more to be said. Gerard bowed and left the room. Rupert departed without any sign of reverence. Willis remained to utter a contemptuous remark on the Newark commissioners, the only intemperate remark to which he had given utterance during the whole of the proceedings.

In the evening a petition signed by the two princes, Rupert and Maurice, and twenty other officers, was handed in to the King, asking that no commission might be taken from anyone who had not been heard in his own defence by a council of war, or that, if this were refused, passes to leave Newark might be granted to the petitioners.

A petition to the King.

After this there was no setting out to be thought of for Charles on that night. He would not, he replied to the petitioners, make a council of war the judge of his actions. On the following day Rupert followed by 200 horsemen rode off in the direction of Belvoir Castle, whence he sent Colonel Osborne to Westminster to ask for passports to enable the whole company to leave the country.[1]

Charles's departure postponed.

Oct. 27. Rupert leaves the King, and requests Parliament to allow him to leave the country.

If the meeting at Newark reflected no credit on any of those who took part in it, this was but the natural outcome of Charles's incapacity for the direction of armies. Unable to form any consistent scheme of

[1] *Symonds,* 270; *Walker,* 147; Rupert to the Houses of Parliament, Oct. 29, *Warburton,* iii. 207.

operations, he had thrown himself into the hands of an adviser who was not only no soldier, but who, with some of Buckingham's brilliancy, reproduced only too faithfully Buckingham's extravagances. The revolt of the officers was the result of the natural dislike of military men to be subjected to the control of an incompetent civilian. Yet, true as this explanation is, it is not the whole truth. If Charles found himself isolated, it was not merely because soldiers looked askance upon him. It mattered indeed but little except to the officers concerned whether Gerard or Willis retained their commands or not, but it mattered a great deal to all Charles's followers whether a hopeless war was to be any longer persisted in. In opposing Digby as the fountain of promotion Rupert spoke on behalf of the officers. In opposing him as the advocate of the prolongation of the war, he spoke on behalf of well-nigh the whole of the Royalist party. Soldier and civilian were of one mind in demanding peace.

It was not long before Charles was made to feel how truly he was alone. At last, on the night of November 3, he left Newark, leaving Bellasys behind him as governor of the fortress. With some difficulty he made his way across a country infested by the enemy, and entered Oxford on the 5th. It was almost a year since he had returned to that city after the modified success of the campaign of Lostwithiel and Newbury, when he had been able to persuade himself, not without some show of reason, that he had the promise of victory in his hands. He was under no such delusion now. Fresh disasters were of weekly, almost of daily, occurrence. Before the end of October Morgan, Massey's successor as governor of Gloucester, had captured Chepstow and Monmouth, and Laugharne, having entered Carmarthen, had persuaded not only Carmarthenshire, but Cardigan, Glamorgan, and Brecknock, to submit to the obedience of Parliament. In all South Wales and Monmouthshire—the country from which Charles had drawn the infantry which had surrendered at Naseby—Raglan Castle alone preserved its allegiance to the

*Nov. 3.
The King leaves Newark,*

Nov. 5, and enters Oxford.

South Wales lost to the King.

King.[1] Sandal Castle and Bolton Castle in Yorkshire had

Nov. 1.
Vaughan's
defeat. also fallen. On November 1 Sir William Vaughan, having been despatched to the relief of Chester, had

Nov. 3.
Shelford
House
stormed. been defeated near Denbigh.[2] On the 3rd, the very day on which the King left Newark, Shelford House, an outlying garrison between Newark and Nottingham, was stormed, and of the 200 men who composed its garrison, all except forty were put to the sword.[3]

Yet, when Charles arrived at Oxford, his soul was wrung by sorrows even more bitter than those which were aroused by

Nov. 5.
Charles's
reception
in Oxford. the crash of his military strength. He could well detect the lip-service of those who bowed before him in outward sign of welcome, but whose hearts in their longing for peace were turned against him. To Dorset,

His reply
to Dorset. who congratulated him with effusion, he replied sharply, "Your voice is the voice of Jacob, but your hands are the hands of Esau." [4] He knew full well what was

Desire for
peace at
Oxford. passing in Dorset's mind. There was scarcely a Royalist in Oxford who did not wish overtures for peace to be openly made, and, as far as can be judged from existing indications, they would rather have made overtures to the Independents and the army than to the Presbyterians and the Scots.

Another policy there was, far more attractive to Charles. "Sir," Glemham is reported to have said to him about a month

Glemham's
suggestion. before, as he was leaving him to take up his command at Oxford, "although you be too weak for your enemies, yet they are strong enough to fight one with another, the Independents against the Presbyterians, and doubt not but

---

[1] *Two letters from Col. Morgan*, Oct. 23, 24, E. 307, 14 ; *Laugharne's letter*, Oct. 12, E. 307, 15 ; *The Kingdom's Weekly Intelligencer*, E. 307, 16 ; *C.J.* iv. 320 ; Whitacre's Diary, *Add. MSS.* 31,116, fol. 239.

[2] Whitacre's Diary, *Add. MSS.* 31,116, fol. 240b ; *Symonds's Diary*, 258.

[3] *L.J.* vii. 678 ; *Hutchinson's Memoirs* (ed. Firth), ii. 81. It is here stated that 140 prisoners were taken ; Poyntz, writing at the time, gives only forty, which is far more likely to be accurate.

[4] Montreuil to Brienne, Nov. $\frac{13}{23}$. *Carte MSS.* lxxiii. fol. 109b.

that will be a means for your recovery." [1]   Charles had neither the freedom from scruples of conscience nor the flexibility of intellect requisite to enable him to play the game thus indicated by Glemham.

[1] Letter printed in *Merc. Civicus.* E. 305, 5. "This discourse," says the writer, "I had from one that heard it."

NOTE.

ON THE STRENGTH AND PRELIMINARY MOVEMENTS OF THE ARMIES AT NASEBY.

MY account of the Battle of Naseby was already in proof before I saw Colonel Ross's calculation of the numbers on both sides contained in an article in *The English Historical Review* for October 1888, p. 668. He estimates the Parliamentarians at 13,600 after Cromwell's arrival on June 13, and the Royalists at ' no more than 8,000 men in horse and foot,' and probably, ' as stated by the Royalist authorities,' as 'actually only 7,500 in all.'

As far as the Parliamentary army is concerned, I have had little to change, as I originally gave it as about 13,000 men. On reviewing this opinion I am inclined to take the calculation of *The Scottish Dove* as a basis, and to accept 13,000 as the number after Fairfax's junction with Vermuyden. In that case the subsequent arrival of Cromwell and Rossiter would bring up the whole force to at least 14,000.

June 5, Fairfax and Vermuyden	13,000
June 13, Cromwell, at least	600
June 14, Rossiter, at least	400
	14,000

With respect to the King's army I had written in a note that 'the King had only 7,500 with him when he left Leicester, of which 3,500 were horse,' basing this on a letter of June 4 from the King to Nicholas, printed in *Evelyn's Memoirs*, iv. 146. This letter escaped Colonel Ross's notice, and it is so far satisfactory to find an independent corroboration of the evidence which led him to think it most probable that the King had 4,000 horse and 3,500 foot.

Having got so far, I am sorry to say that I ran away from my guns. The consensus of contemporary authorities was so strong in favour of the virtual equality of the two armies in numbers, that I fancied myself driven at least to approximate to their statement, and on the ground that stragglers and reinforcements may have come in during the ten days which elapsed after the writing of the King's letter of the 4th, I allowed myself to put in the text that ' on the highest calculation the King's troops did not exceed ten or eleven thousand.' Having read the authorities carefully again, I can find no trace of any such reinforcements or of any augmentation of the army, and I am convinced that Colonel Ross's calculations are beyond dispute. My own attempt to find a middle course was as useless as it was baseless. The difference between the numbers as I conceived them was not great enough to enable me to draw any practical conclusion, whereas the knowledge that there was a difference between 7,500, or even 8,000, on the one side and 13,500 or 14,000 on the other, changes our whole conception of the battle. Wherever, therefore, in my account of the fighting, attention is drawn to the result of the inequality of numbers, it will be understood that the passages in which this occurs are entirely due to Colonel Ross, and not in any way to myself.

I now come to examine the movements of the armies on the morning of the 14th, before they stood opposite to one another on their respective sides of Broadmoor. I have here had the advantage of a long and friendly correspondence with Colonel Ross. The subject is not one on which conclusion can be drawn with absolute confidence, but, after rejecting in consequence of his arguments several ideas which I had previously formed, and after a personal examination of the road along which the Royal army advanced, the proceedings on both sides can, I think, be made out with more than mere probability.

The first movements of the Royal army are beyond doubt. It marched out early in the morning to what Slingsby calls a 'hill whereon a chapel stood,' evidently the ridge between East Farndon and Oxendon, the chapel being East Farndon Church, the tower of which is a conspicuous object to anyone approaching from the Harborough side. Here it was drawn up in expectation of being attacked, and there it remained without further action on the part of its commander till 8 A.M. (*Walker*, 129). Slingsby (*Diary*, 150) tells us that on their first arrival—that is to say, some time earlier in the morning—'we could discern the enemy's horse upon another hill about a mile or two before us, which was the same on which Naseby stood.' The two parts of his description are irreconcilable, the ridge on which Naseby is being about three miles distant. To anyone standing on the hill at a spot a little south of East Farndon there can be no difficulty in deciding which part of the statement is accurate. Between him and the Naseby ridge is a large extent of undulating ground with nothing so conspicuous as to deserve the name of 'the hill,' whereas the Naseby ridge stands out like a wall behind, catching the eye at once and dominating the whole landscape. In point of fact, whilst the Farndon-Oxendon ridge rises at its highest (as appears from the six-inch ordnance map) to 519 feet, the Naseby ridge ridge reaches 603 feet at Mill Hill, where the Parliamentary army was ultimately drawn up, and rises to 648 feet in front of the obelisk, from which point it slopes gradually away to 581 feet about a mile from Naseby, where the ground falls sharply away towards the north. For purposes of defending a position or getting a view of an enemy advancing from the north, it is this point of 581 feet which would be selected, or at least one not very far behind it. The highest point of the ground between this and the Farndon Hill reaches 477 feet.

Taking Slingsby, therefore, to mean that the Parliamentary forces were to be seen at some time in the early morning on the Naseby ridge, let us ask at what part of the ridge they appeared. In the first place, the likely place to look for them is on the road to Clipston and Market Harborough. Fairfax had passed the night at Guilsborough, and his advanced guard had entered Naseby late in the previous evening. He would, therefore, naturally push on along the road leading to Harborough, where the Royal army was, and would halt on the brow of the hill in front of the spot on which the obelisk now stands, in order to look over the lower ground for signs of the enemy.

This is just what we should gather from Sprigg and Okey. "By five in the morning," writes Sprigg (p. 37), the army was at a rendezvous near Naseby, where his Excellency received intelligence by our spies that the enemy was at Harborough; with this further, that it was still doubtful whether he meant to march away or to stand us, but immediately the doubt was resolved; great bodies of the enemy's horse were discerned on the top of the hill on this side Harborough, which, increasing more and more in our view, begat a confidence in the general and the residue of the officers that he meant not to draw away, as some imagined, but that he was putting his army in order, either then to receive us, or to come to us to engage us upon the ground we stood." This must have happened before 8 A.M., and probably a good deal earlier, and is in favour of assigning the position of the rendezvous to that marked A in my map at p. 207, as no good view could be obtained of the Farndon ridge from any lower post farther north.

This view is, on the whole, corroborated by Okey. After stating that he had had the 'forlorn guard every night,' he adds that 'we drew near Naseby unto Clypsome (*i.e.* Clipston) Field, a mile and a half from our quarters where we had the guard the night before.' If, as I suppose there can be little doubt, the advance guard with Okey was quartered at Naseby, then a mile and a half beyond that place on the Harborough road brings us about half a mile beyond the spot marked A on the top of the hill, and to a point well within the boundary of Clipston parish.

The only difficulty in Okey's story arises from the fact that both his mileage and the mention of Clipston Field place him beyond the ridge, the Harborough road cutting the boundary a very short distance farther on at the foot of the steep fall to the lower ground.[1] It is, of course, possible that Okey, who was not likely to be familiar with the parish boundaries, merely talked of the spot as being open ground near Clipston, but another solution may perhaps be accepted. An army of 13,000 men cannot stand on the point of pin, and must spread out in one direction or another. This army came with the expectation of pushing on in pursuit, and it therefore was more than probable that some of the regiments would forge ahead in the direction of Clipston, and thus find themselves, probably with Okey's dragoons in advance, in the real Clipston Field.

At 8 A.M., therefore, we have the two armies facing one another on two ridges about three miles apart. Then Rupert (*Walker*, 130) sends out Ruce, the scoutmaster, to see what was going on, 'who in a short time returned with a lie in his mouth, that he had been two or three miles forward, and could neither discover or hear of the rebels.' Ruce probably advanced to Clipston, or a little beyond, and, if he could hear nothing of the enemy in the village, he was not likely to see anything of them if he rode forward, as the view on the road in front is extremely circumscribed, and he may therefore have felt justified in riding back to say that the rebels were not in pursuit, which was what Rupert really wanted to know. Upon his return Rupert grew impatient and rode off, followed by horse and musketeers, to see for himself. 'But he had not marched above a mile before he had certain intelligence of their advance, and saw their van.' Slingsby says that Rupert advanced towards the enemy, 'where he sees their horse

---

[1] From information supplied by the Rev. C. F. Blyth, late rector of Clipston.

marching up on the side of the hill to that place whereafter they embattled their whole army. It is impossible to draw any absolute conclusion from this, but it looks as if the Parliamentarians had in the interval between Ruce's and Rupert's reconnaissances pushed on somewhat in advance, and that they afterwards drew back. If this were so, we can fit in here a story which reaches us from a certain W. G., in *A just apology for an abused army* (1647), p. 5, E. 372, 22.

"I must never forget," he writes, "the behaviour of Lieutenant-General Cromwell, who, as though he had received direction from God Himself where to pitch his battle, did advise that the battalion might stand upon such a ground, though it was begun to be drawn up upon another place, saying, 'Let us, I beseech you, draw back to yonder hill, which will encourage the enemy to charge us, which they cannot do in that place without absolute ruin.' This he spake with so much cheerful resolution and confidence, as though he had foreseen the victory, and was therefore condescended unto, and within an hour and a half after the effect fell out accordingly. This action of his . . . I was an eye and ear witness of."

What took place, I suspect, was this. Somewhere about half-past eight—an hour and a half before the battle began—the Parliamentary army had got some little way off the main ridge in advance, and Fairfax directed it to be drawn up for battle on a smaller parallel ridge in the direction of Clipston. Such a ridge would be defensible, though not as strong a position as he main ridge behind. Then Cromwell advised that it should be drawn further back to the height on which the rendezvous had been in the morning. I do not think that the army can have got anywhere near Clipston, though, of course, a body of horse may have pushed on in advance. Ruce would have found the enemy out if they had gone far, and Cromwell's words, 'yonder hill,' indicate a hill in sight. The main hill, however, is soon hidden by intervening lesser heights as one advances towards Clipston.

It does not, however, follow that Cromwell's chosen ground was exactly on the scene of the rendezvous of the morning. It would be enough for him to cover the road with the horse of the right wing whilst the bulk of the army was drawn up to the left, its extreme left being thus at some distance to the west of the Harborough road, and not far from the point afterwards occupied by its right in the actual battle. This would account for the omission of most of the authorities to speak of two positions after the army was actually placed in order of battle. The subsequent drawing

off to the left was in their eyes not a removal from one position to
another, but a mere manœuvring to gain the advantage of the hill
and the wind. How this took place we learn from Slingsby and
Sprigg. Rupert, when he arrived opposite Fairfax, found Cromwell's position too hard to be attacked. "Being hindered," writes
Slingsby (p. 151), "of any near approach, by reason the place
between us and them was full of burts [1] (? bushes) and water, we
wheeled about, and by our guides were brought upon a fair piece
of ground, partly corn and partly heath, under Naseby, about half
a mile distant from the place."

Sprigg's account agrees pretty well with this. "And while
these things"—*i.e.* the drawing up of the army—"were in consultation and in action, the enemy's army, which before was the
greatest part of it out of view, by reason of the hill that interposed,
we saw plainly advancing in order towards us; and the wind
blowing somewhat westwardly, by the enemy's advance so much
on their right hand, it was evident that he designed to get the
wind of us, which occasioned the general to draw down into a
large fallow field on the north-west side of Naseby." What
Slingsby calls wheeling, in consequence of the nature of the
ground over which the Royalists would have to attack, Sprigg
speaks of as a deliberate movement to gain the wind, followed by
an equally deliberate movement to the fallow field marked B on
the map.

The Parliamentary army, however, was not allowed to rest
here. "Considering," says Sprigg, "it might be of advantage to
us to draw up our army out of sight of the enemy . . . we
retreated about a hundred paces from the ledge of the hill, that
so the enemy might not perceive in what form our battle was
drawn, nor see any confusion therein, and yet we to see the form
of their battle."

It is plainly this last movement which is referred to in the
passage from Orrery's *Art of War* (p. 154), quoted by Colonel
Ross in *The English Historical Review* : "I had often been told,
but could scarcely credit it, that at the fatal battle of Naseby, after
my Lord Fairfax's army was drawn up in view of his Majesty's, it
having been judged that the ground a little behind was better than
that they stood upon, they removed thither. I had the opportunity

[1] Mr. Henry Bradley informs me that this word was rejected from
the *New English Dictionary*, as not being found anywhere else. He
thought that it had the ring of a local word, but that on the other hand
it might be a mere blunder of the copyist or printer.

some time after to discourse on the subject with Major-General Skippon (who had the chief ordering of the Lord Fairfax his army that day), and having asked him if this were true, he could not deny it; but he obeyed the orders for doing it only because he could not get them altered."

At first I ascribed W. G.'s story to this movement, but gave way before Colonel Ross's arguments. The movement was too slight to give rise to Cromwell's entreaty to 'draw back to yonder hill,' especially as the fallow field in which Skippon had already drawn up his men was on the slope of the hill and therefore there can have been no talk of drawing back to it. Moreover, the retreat here was only a temporary one, made not for the purpose of fighting on a new position, but merely to conceal the army for a time till it was ready to step forward to the brow of the hill.

One word I should like to say on behalf of the raisers of that unfortunate obelisk which has been mocked at by successive visitors and writers as commemorating the battle on a spot on which the battle was not fought. What they did in their ignorance was not, after all, done so very much amiss. The obelisk stands where the Parliamentarian soldiers first learnt that the enemy meant to fight and not to retreat, and it rises on the 'yonder hill' to which Cromwell pointed as the true place of battle. If it has nothing round it to remind us of the conflict itself, it may serve as a monument to the genius of the man by whom the victory was decided.

Wishing to submit these conclusions to the judgment of a qualified military critic, I have asked Colonel Ross to express an opinion on them, and I am happy to be able to append his reply to my request.

ADDITIONAL NOTE BY LIEUTENANT-COLONEL ROSS.

MR. GARDINER, with whom I have had a correspondence, to me instructive as well as interesting, regarding the events which immediately preceded the Battle of Naseby, has honoured me by requiring from me an expression of opinion on the matters discussed in his supplementary note on that action. I have carefully studied that note, with the result that I believe the theories therein advanced, based, as they evidently are, on a very exhaustive analysis of all the contemporary evidence at present available, are, if not indisputable, at least probable in the highest degree.

To state my reasons for this belief would merely amount to a repetition of the arguments advanced by Mr. Gardiner. As it may, however, be some satisfaction to Mr. Gardiner, that I, as a soldier, should be found to be of the same opinion as himself on matters which are essentially military, and to some extent technical, in character, I gladly not only record my general acceptance of his conclusions, but even venture to illustrate one or two of them by offering a few additional remarks.

Although the successive stages of the action taken by both armies on the morning of the 14th of June, as mentioned by Mr. Gardiner, appear to me to be highly probable, there is among them one to which exception might be taken, as being not so near a certainty as are the rest. I allude to the circumstance of what may be called the first position of the Parliamentary army, after their rendezvous somewhat to the north-east of Naseby on the long ridge, the western half of which is called by Sprigg and Rushworth Mill Hill.

There is little room to doubt that before 8 A.M.—probably considerably earlier—the two armies stood opposite to each other, the Royalists on the Farndon-Oxendon ridge, and the army of the Parliament on the Naseby ridge. The former appear, by the accounts of their own party, to have been at this hour in battle formation, and in expectation of being attacked ; while the latter, certainly in some formation, would probably not be as yet in the battle order which, Sprigg tells us, had been definitely settled some days previously, but would, it is more likely, be ranged in a marching order suitable for an early advance in pursuit of the retiring enemy. Both armies, as Mr. Gardiner supposes, would almost certainly be placed across the Naseby-Harborough road. Even in modern times such a line of communication would be important, if not actually necessary, for the transport of the artillery; and in the seventeenth century, when the mobility of this arm left much to be desired, the advantages of such a highway, however bad a road it may then have been, could not be ignored by either army.

The Royalist army in battle line would, consequently, occupy a position, the frontal extent of which, in comparison with the depth, would be considerable, and its cavalry would be placed, we may naturally suppose, in line with and on the flanks of its infantry.

With the other army it would be otherwise. The whole formation would be more closely massed, and the depth of it probably greater than its frontal extension; at least one half of the cavalry of the army, as being about to cover an advance, would be found in the van, towards Clipston, and therefore on the northern spurs of the Naseby ridge, on the summit of which probably the rendezvous of the infantry would be fixed.

To put these suppositions in military phraseology: By 8 A.M. the Royalists were in line of battle, the Parliamentarians in column of route, both armies astride the Harborough-Naseby road, and some three miles apart; the former expecting and hoping to be attacked in a chosen position, and the latter in a marching formation, as yet uncertain whether to attack or to await the attack of the enemy, but both armies equally resolved to bring on a general engagement.

If the probability of these suppositions be admitted, many of the minor difficulties which arise in the interpretation of the statements of our various authorities disappear. For example, the statement of the Royal scoutmaster, that during his reconnaissance he saw no signs of the enemy, might be explained by the suggestion that the accidents of the ground between Naseby and Clipston may have concealed the more advanced bodies of Fairfax's army; that, assuming him to have reached Clipston, he saw on his way no vedettes or patrols of the enemy—a sufficiently curious circumstance—may be further explained by the probable fact, that in anticipation of a general rendezvous, those scouts—or "spies," as Sprigg calls them—which had been pushed forward during the night had been recalled, and that others, pending the decision as to the further movements of the army, had not as yet been thrown out. Okey's "Clipston Field" might also very well be an accurate description of the site of the rendezvous, considered as a general term for the position of the army, and certainly of the special point at which he and his dragoons, or part of them, were likely to have been placed. Again, the idea which appears to have possessed Rupert, that his enemy was retreating—an idea which was of the most fatal consequence to the Royalist army, not only as leading to an ill-judged and hasty advance, but also as ultimately determining Rupert to deliver an ill-prepared and premature attack on Broadmoor itself—may very well have arisen from the fact that he also saw, during his reconnaissance towards Clipston, no signs of the enemy, and found, when he first sighted his advanced horsemen, that they were falling back, and apparently in full retreat, although they were really doing nothing of the kind, but merely taking up their allotted positions in a line of battle which, just as he arrived in sight, was being discussed, and possibly being actually formed. Finding the ground unfavourable for the delivery of an immediate attack upon what he imagined to be a retreating foe, he began to edge off to the westward in search of a better line of advance, and meanwhile sent back for and hurried up the whole of his army, with the result that the men must have come up blown and disorganised, and the guns, already at the first or Farndon position distributed over an extended front, for the most part must have been left behind or brought up too late to be of service in the fight.

Meanwhile, at the rendezvous on the Naseby ridge, when it first became evident that the retiring enemy had turned to bay and intended to fight, it would be necessary for Fairfax to reconsider his plans, and to decide whether he should attack the Royalists in their position on the Farndon ridge, or should take measures to receive their onset in a position selected by himself. It is at this point that it becomes difficult to account with certainty for the tactical disposal of the Parliamentary army, and that two possible lines of action suggest themselves, either of which may have been adopted by Fairfax.

(*a*) One is that presented by Mr. Gardiner, which I am inclined to support. It is that Fairfax, as soon as he had decided to await the attack of the enemy, proceeded to commence drawing up his own forces in battle order across the Naseby-Harborough road, not, perhaps, on the actual summit of the Naseby ridge, but more in advance towards Clipston, and on the northern spurs of that ridge. In addition to the indications afforded by the statements of Sprigg and W. G. that some such position was possibly, at least partially, taken up, may be added certain tactical considerations which might be supposed to have influence with Fairfax in determining this position for his line of battle. Such an advanced position, as compared with one on the Naseby ridge, would have the advantage of the closer protection of the watercourse and broken ground which exists between Clipston and the Naseby ridge, and at the same time this obstacle to the advance of the enemy—an obstacle which was sufficient to deter, a little later on in the morning, the impetuous Rupert from attacking what he believed to be a retreating enemy—would be within better striking distance, for the delivery of a favourable counter-attack, should the enemy attempt its passage. Assuming that Fairfax resolved to take up such a position, the time at which the necessary evolutions for its occupation were being carried out by the Parliamentary army would be, I think, at some period between 8 and 8.30 A.M., and would, therefore, probably correspond with the interval of time which must have elapsed between the reconnaissances of Ruce and Rupert. The manœuvres may, indeed, have been going on while Ruce was at Clipston, or thereabouts, making inquiries from individuals who were possibly hostile to the King's party, and therefore not inclined to give him any information; and they might also not have been evident to him personally owing, as before said, to the nature of the intervening ground. By the time Rupert appeared on the scene, possibly the intention to occupy this position may have been reconsidered by Fairfax, after consultation with his chief officers, and the move to the westward towards the ultimate fighting position above Broadmoor already commenced. Such a supposition would explain how it was that Rupert came to entertain the idea that Fairfax was retiring. Or, again, it may be suggested that the movement of troops which deceived Rupert was only part of the manœuvres necessary for the occupation of the ground first selected in proper line of battle, the cavalry in advance of or at the head of the column of route, having necessarily to fall back to take up their positions on the wings or flanks of the infantry. In either case Fairfax's army would be, when Rupert arrived at Clipston, still too close to the watercourse and broken ground between the supposed position and Clipston for the latter to hazard an attack with the view of delaying the supposed retirement of his enemy, and so he proceeded, according to Slingsby, to look for a better line of advance by executing a flank movement to the westward. His doing so would naturally induce Fairfax to suppose that a turning movement was about to be attempted by the Royalists. Hastily calling a council of war, he resolved, on the suggestion of Cromwell, as recorded by W. G., to remove also his own force westwards, and somewhat backwards, to that western part of the Naseby ridge which is called Mill Hill, and there took up the ultimate Broadmoor position ·in a large fallow field below the crest of and to the north of Mill Hill.

The only objection that can be raised, it appears to me, against this theory of a first position of Fairfax's army is that which has been noticed by Mr. Gardiner, to the effect that none of the contemporary Parliamentary authorities take notice of the circumstance that such a position was actually taken up. But that objection may, I think, be fairly met by the plea that the statements of W. G. and Sprigg appear to indicate that something was done towards the formation of a line of battle before the army was ultimately drawn up on Broadmoor; but since this preliminary line was never completely formed, the partial occupation of ground which was contiguous to that on which the ultimate fighting position was formed was probably by them considered as not being really different and separable from the ultimate formation above Broadmoor.

(*b*) If this supposition be considered by some to be insufficient to nullify the objection, there remains the second theory on which we may fall back, and which is as follows. From the rendezvous Fairfax's army extended in a column of route placed along the Naseby-Clipston-Harborough road, and occupying perhaps nearly a mile in length of that road, with the crest of the Naseby ridge as its central point; it may have thence removed itself bodily, by means of a flank movement westwards, to the fighting position on Broadmoor without adopting any intermediate battle formation. And this movement may be supposed to have been ordered at the time when Fairfax and his principal officers began to imagine that Rupert contemplated a turning movement towards their left flank. But how, if this be supposed, can Cromwell's suggestion to move 'back' to 'yonder hill' be considered applicable to a movement which, regarded as having taken place from the crest of the Naseby ridge, is rather forward and on to ground of a generally lower level? To this objection it may be replied that Cromwell's words recorded by W. G., on the assumption of the distribution of the army in the column of route formation, would almost certainly have been uttered at some point towards the head of the column where he, as commanding the vanguard of horse, would certainly be and where Fairfax himself would also be found when the column, in anticipation of an immediate advance, was being formed along the road leading from Naseby to Harborough. From the head of the column, extending, as has been explained, for perhaps nearly a mile along the road, Cromwell's 'back' and 'yonder hill' would be perfectly appropriate expressions for a movement to be undertaken to the westward by the whole army; for the speaker would naturally allude to the proposed movement in terms adapted to the inter-relation that would exist between the selected position and the spot on which he himself stood. In carrying out the movement itself, the main body of infantry and train, which probably, in the column of route, occupied the crest of the Naseby ridge, would march along the ridge itself, the 'yonder hill,' till it was in a suitable position to be drawn 'down' into the 'fallow field' above Broadmoor; the cavalry of the vanguard, W. G. being amongst them, would march westwards along the lower northern spurs of the Naseby ridge in sight of Rupert and Slingsby, "marching up," says the latter, "on the side of the hill to that place where after they imbattled their whole army"; the rearguard horse, during the rendezvous drawn up probably between Naseby 'town' and Naseby ridge, would march by the fields between Naseby and Mill Hill proper—across those fields in one of which Okey tells us he was engaged in issuing ammunition to his dragoons, a meadow "halfe a mile behinde" (the main body of infantry), when Cromwell rode up to him "presently and caused me with all speed to mount my men and flanck our left wing"—to their allotted position on the left of the battle line; and the whole army, about 9.30, would be in position above Broadmoor ready to receive the attack of the enemy, and about to justify the wisdom of Cromwell's selection of the ground on which the combat was to take place.

Although, as I have said, of the two theories I am inclined to favour the first that has been here discussed, I am willing to admit that there is something to be said in favour of the second, while neither is contrary to such indications as may be gathered from a close study of the statements of eyewitnesses. The choice between the two must be left to the individual judgment of each student of the circumstances immediately preceding the Battle of Naseby.

Mr. Gardiner's suggestion that the Naseby obelisk—misplaced, unfortunately, if its intention was to point out the battlefield—should serve to remind us of the great part played by Cromwell, not only in suggesting the true place for the engagement, but towards obtaining a victory so important and well-timed, will commend itself to all who admire the military abilities of that great leader.

W. G. R.

END OF THE SECOND VOLUME.